**Systems of Care for
Children's Mental Health**

Series Editors:
Beth A. Stroud, M.Ed.
Robert M. Friedman, Ph.D.

Improving Emotional
and Behavioral
Outcomes for LGBT Youth

Other Volumes in This Series

The Leadership Equation: Strategies for Individuals Who Are Champions for Children, Youth, and Families, edited by Gary M. Blau, Ph.D., and Phyllis R. Magrab, Ph.D.

The System of Care Handbook: Transforming Mental Health Services for Children, Youth, and Families, edited by Beth A. Stroul, M.Ed., and Gary M. Blau, Ph.D.

Work, Life, and the Mental Health System of Care: A Guide for Professionals Supporting Families of Children with Emotional or Behavioral Disorders, by Julie M. Rosenzweig, Ph.D., and Eileen M. Brennan, Ph.D.

Social and Emotional Health in Early Childhood: Building Bridges Between Services and Systems, edited by Deborah F. Perry, Ph.D., Roxane F. Kaufmann, M.A., and Jane Knitzer, Ed.D.

Improving Emotional and Behavioral Outcomes for LGBT Youth

A Guide for Professionals

edited by

Sylvia K. Fisher, Ph.D.
Office of Research and Evaluation
Office of Planning, Analysis and Evaluation
Office of the Administrator
Health Resources and Services Administration
Rockville, Maryland

Jeffrey M. Poirier, M.A., PMP
American Institutes for Research
Washington, D.C.

and

Gary M. Blau, Ph.D.
Child, Adolescent and Family Branch
Center for Mental Health Services
Substance Abuse and Mental Health Services Administration
Rockville, Maryland

·P·A·U·L·H·
BROOKES
PUBLISHING CO.®

Baltimore • London • Sydney

Paul H. Brookes Publishing Co.
Post Office Box 10624
Baltimore, Maryland 21285-0624
USA

www.brookespublishing.com

Typeset by Integrated Publishing Solutions, Grand Rapids, Michigan.
Manufactured in the United States of America by
Versa Press, Inc., East Peoria, Illinois.

The individuals described in this book are composites or real people whose situations are masked and are based on the authors' actual experiences. Real names and identifying details are used by permission.

The content of this publication does not necessarily reflect the views, opinions, or policies of the Substance Abuse and Mental Health Services Administration, the Health Resources and Services Administration, the U.S. Department of Health and Human Services, or the American Institutes for Research.

Library of Congress Cataloging-in-Publication Data

Fisher, Sylvia K.
   Improving emotional and behavioral outcomes for LGBT youth : a guide for professionals / by Sylvia K. Fisher, Jeffrey M. Poirier, and Gary M. Blau.
     p.   cm.   — (Systems of care for children's mental health)
   Includes bibliographical references and index.
   ISBN-13: 978-1-59857-082-3
   ISBN-10: 1-59857-082-X
   1. Adjustment disorders in children. 2. Gay youth—Mental health. 3. Transgender youth—Mental health. 4. Bisexual youth—Mental health. I. Poirier, Jeffrey M. II. Blau, Gary M. III. Title.
   RJ506.A33F57   2012
   616.85'200835—dc23   2012008817

British Library Cataloguing in Publication data are available from the British Library.

2016   2015   2014   2013   2012

10   9   8   7   6   5   4   3   2   1

Contents

Series Preface vii
Editorial Advisory Board ix
About the Editors xi
About the Contributors xv
Acknowledgments xxv

1   Addressing the Needs of LGBT Youth and Their Families:
A Public Health Perspective 1
*Phillip Earl Jordan, Okori T. Christopher, Christopher Bellonci,
Sylvia K. Fisher, and Gary M. Blau*

2   Providing Culturally and Linguistically Competent
Services and Supports to Address the Needs of LGBT
Youth and Their Families 9
*Jeffrey M. Poirier, Kenneth J. Martinez, Karen B. Francis,
Timothy Denney, Sharon L. Roepke, and Nadia A. Cayce-Gibson*

3   Conducting Cultural and Linguistic Competence
Self-Assessment 25
Tawara D. Goode and Sylvia K. Fisher

4   Sexual Identity Development and Expression in LGB Youth 33
Coretta Jacqueline Mallery and Jeffrey M. Poirier

5   Transgender and Gender Nonconforming Children and
Youth: Developing Culturally Competent Systems of Care 43
Arlene Istar Lev and Laura Alie

6   Disorders or Differences of Sex Development 67
Matthew A. Malouf and Arlene Baratz

7   Becoming Who We Are Meant to Be: Native Americans
with Two-Spirit, LGBT, and/or Related Tribal Identities 87
Miriam L. Bearse

8   The Resilience U-Turn: Understanding Risks and
Strengths to Effectively Support LGBT Youth and Families
in Systems of Care 111
Katherine J. Lazear and Peter Gamache

9   Building Systems of Care to Support Effective Therapeutic
    and Programmatic Interventions and Resources for LGBT
    Youth and Their Families 127
    Katherine J. Lazear, Sheila A. Pires, Stephen L. Forssell,
    and Coretta Jacqueline Mallery

10 Standards of Care for LGBT Youth 141
    Kim Pawley Helfgott and Simon G. Gonsoulin

11 Fostering Welcoming, Safe, and Supportive Schools for
    LGBT Youth 159
    Jeffrey M. Poirier

12 Improving Outcomes for LGBT Youth in Out-of-Home
    Care Settings: Implications and Recommendations for
    Systems of Care 173
    Marlene Matarese

13 Addressing Suicide and Self-Harming Behaviors Among
    LGBT Youth in Systems of Care 189
    Keith J. Horvath, Gary Remafedi, Sylvia K. Fisher, and
    Christine Walrath

14 Addressing the Needs of LGBT Youth Who Are Homeless 207
    Rachael R. Kenney, Sylvia K. Fisher, Megan Edson Grandin,
    Justine B. Hanson, and Laura Pannella Winn

15 Social Marketing Efforts to Promote Social Inclusion and
    Help-Seeking Behavior 223
    Lisa Rubenstein, Mojdeh Motamedi, Ryan C. LaLonde,
    and Cody Mooneyhan

16 Internet-Based Information and Resources for Supporting
    LGBT Youth and Providing Culturally Competent Services. 251
    Stephen L. Forssell, Jeffrey M. Poirier, and Rachael R. Kenney

17 Where Do We Go From Here? Next Steps for Research,
    Practice, and Policy 267
    Sylvia K. Fisher, Gary M. Blau, and Jeffrey M. Poirier

References 273

Index 306

Series Preface

In 1995, at the request of Paul H. Brookes Publishing Co., we undertook the responsibility of editing a book series titled *Systems of Care for Children's Mental Health*. We are very pleased to report that there have now been 11 books published in this book series.

In the preface to the first books in this series, we indicated that our goals were to

- Increase the awareness of the system of care concept and philosophy among current and future mental health professionals who will be providing services to children and adolescents and their families
- Broaden the mental health field's understanding of treatment and service delivery beyond traditional approaches to include innovative, state-of-the-art approaches and evidence-based practices
- Provide practical information that will assist the mental health field to implement and apply the philosophy, services, and approaches embodied in the system of care concept

At the beginning of the series, the concept of a *system of care* was still relatively new, having been introduced to the children's mental health field only about 10 years earlier. Familiarity with the concept and knowledge about how to implement effective systems of care has clearly grown enormously since the book series was initiated. It is gratifying to see the progress that has been made through the leadership of the Substance Abuse and Mental Health Services Administration of the U.S. Department of Health and Human Services and the efforts of many parents, youth, and professionals around the country.

We have gained much knowledge through the years about the concept and vision of a system of care, and, perhaps most important, about how to bring about the type of change that is needed to implement systems of care effectively. Through the series, we have always sought to capture the complexity and challenge involved in bringing about system change and the importance of flexibility in implementation while retaining the strong value base that is the foundation of systems of care.

The challenge now is not just to continue to learn how to implement the system of care approach effectively in individual communities, but how, in the context of major changes in the health and human services fields, to continue to expand the implementation of the approach so that all children, youth, and families in need have access to effective services and supports. We sincerely hope that the information contained in this book series, including important contributions from parents, youth, providers, and policy makers, continues to assist in meeting this challenge.

We want to thank Paul H. Brookes Publishing Co. for the support it has provided for this series and all of the editors and authors who have made contributions, as well as the members of our editorial board. We look forward to the continued growth of the system of care field and to helping to chronicle the growth and share the new knowledge.

Beth A. Stroul   Robert M. Friedman

Editorial Advisory Board

About the Editors

Sylvia K. Fisher, Ph.D., Director, Office of Research and Evaluation, Office of Planning, Analysis and Evaluation, Health Resources and Services Administration, Parklawn Building, 5600 Fishers Lane, Room 10-49, Rockville, Maryland 20857

Dr. Fisher has consistently served the American public throughout more than 15 years of federal service. As Director of the Office of Research and Evaluation in the Health Resources and Services Administration (HRSA), Dr. Fisher manages evaluations to assess the effectiveness of federal health programs throughout the nation. Previously, as a research psychologist at the Bureau of Labor Statistics, Office of Survey Methods Research, she specialized in the application of cognitive methods to improve the quality of large government surveys. Dr. Fisher was the director of evaluation in the Child, Adolescent and Family Branch at SAMHSA from 2004 to 2010, and was project officer for the national evaluation of the systems of care program. She also coordinated program activities in the areas of suicide prevention, improving conditions for youth in residential care, and addressing the needs of LGBT children and youth.

Dr. Fisher has worked extensively throughout her career to improve the health and well-being of children and youth and LGBT populations. Among other activities, she has launched and served as chair of a national workgroup to address the needs of youth in systems of care who are LGBT and their families and is currently a member of both the Healthy People 2020 Committee on LGBT populations and the National Action Alliance on Suicide Prevention LGBT Task Force. She has served on organizational boards devoted to child abuse prevention and health services for LGBT populations and received the Leadership Award for Outstanding Volunteer Service from the Lesbian Services Program of the Whitman-Walker Clinic in Washington, D.C. The Commission of the White Helmets of Argentina honored her with the Volunteer in Solidarity award for coordinating an Argentine team of humanitarian assistance experts to deliver mental health services in New Orleans after Hurricane Katrina.

Dr. Fisher was formerly a counselor and psychological evaluator with children and adults with diverse clinical needs; has taught graduate and undergraduate courses in measurement, evaluation, systems change, and psychological assessment at several higher education institutions; and has presented and published in numerous academic and professional venues. Dr. Fisher and her spouse of almost 30 years, Susan, are the greatly blessed parents of an amazing daughter, Elise.

Jeffrey M. Poirier, M.A., PMP, Ph.D. Candidate, Senior Researcher, American Institutes for Research, 1000 Thomas Jefferson Street, NW, Washington, D.C. 20007

Mr. Poirier openly identified as gay at the age of 15, but personally acknowledged this orientation at the age of 5. He is very grateful for his accepting, loving family, who fostered a positive coming-out experience. He received his bachelor's degree from the University of Pennsylvania and his master's degree in education policy from The George Washington University, where he is currently a doctoral candidate in the Trachtenberg School of Public Policy and Public Administration. His dissertation is on conditions for learning for LGBT high school students, including case studies of gay–straight alliances and analyses of district and school policies and practices that enhance LGBT students' experiences. He is also a certified Project Management Professional (PMP). Mr. Poirier is motivated by a deep passion for ensuring all children/youth experience safe, supportive communities and improving the well-being and outcomes of LGBT youth.

Mr. Poirier is a senior researcher at the American Institutes for Research (AIR, www.air.org), where since 2000 he has studied and written about equity-related education and social issues, evaluated policy/program implementation, and provided technical assistance and consultation. He has carried out these activities for communities and various clients such as school districts; state and federal agencies; foundations; and the United Nations Education, Scientific and Cultural Organization. Among his roles at AIR, Mr. Poirier is a member of the Technical Assistance Partnership for Child and Family Mental Health (www .tapartnership.org), for which he leads the LGBTQI2-S Learning Community and provides related technical assistance and learning opportunities to communities. He has served as coordinator of the Substance Abuse and Mental Health Services Administration's National Workgroup to Address the Needs of Children and Youth Who Are LGBTQI2-S and Their Families since its inception in 2008. Mr. Poirier was also the lead author of a practice brief for providing more culturally and linguistically competent services and supports for LGBTQI2-S youth. At AIR, he is collaborating with colleagues and external partners to expand AIR's efforts, through its newly created Human and Social Development (HSD) Program, to develop the assets and promote the well-being of LGBT children/youth in schools and other youth-serving systems. HSD promotes the well-being and improves outcomes for children, youth, families, and communities.

Gary M. Blau, Ph.D., Chief, Child, Adolescent and Family Branch, Center for Mental Health Services, Substance Abuse and Mental Health Services Administration, 1 Choke Cherry Road, Room 6-1045, Rockville, Maryland 20857

Dr. Blau is a clinical psychologist and is currently the chief of the Child, Adolescent and Family Branch of the Center for Mental Health Services. In this role he provides national leadership for children's mental health and for creating systems of care across the country. Prior to this, Dr. Blau was the bureau chief of quality management and the director of mental health at the Connecticut Department of Children and Families (DCF), and the director of clinical services at the Child and Family Agency of Southeastern Connecticut.

Dr. Blau has been selected and appointed to numerous positions, including chairperson of the National Association of State Mental Health Program Director's Division of Children, Youth and Families and clinical faculty at the Yale Child Study Center, along with significant involvement in national level grant and contract reviews.

Dr. Blau has received many awards, including the prestigious Pro Humanitate Literary Award for literary works that best exemplify the intellectual integrity and moral courage required to transcend political and social barriers to promote recommended practice in the field of child welfare, the Governor's Service Award, the Phoebe Bennet Award for outstanding contribution to children's mental health in Connecticut, the Making a Difference Award presented by Connecticut's Federation of Families for Children's Mental Health, and the Outstanding Achievement Award presented by the National Association of Children's Behavioral Health. He was also the recipient of the 2009 HHS Secretary's Award for Meritorious Service for his national leadership in children's mental health. In 2011, he was the first recipient of the Rock Star Award, presented by Youth M.O.V.E. National for "being a true champion for the youth movement and advocate for youth voice," and after being nominated by his staff and colleagues, he was selected for commendation as a 2011 SAMHSA Outstanding Manager.

Dr. Blau has numerous journal publications and has been the editor of five books, including a book that he coedited with Dr. Phyllis Magrab, titled *The Leadership Equation: Strategies for Individuals who are Champions for Children, Youth and Families;* a book coedited with Beth Stroul, titled *The System of Care Handbook: Transforming Mental Health Services for Children, Youth and Families;* and a book coedited with Thomas Gullotta, titled *The Handbook of Childhood Behavioral Issues: Evidence Based Approaches to Prevention and Treatment.* Dr. Blau received his Ph.D. from Auburn University (Auburn, Alabama) in 1988. He is happily married for 29 years to Gwenn Blau, and they have two wonderful adult children, Jennifer and Andrew.

About the Contributors

Laura Alie, M.A., Psy.D. Candidate, John F. Kennedy University, 100 Ellinwood Way, Pleasant Hill, California 94523

Ms. Alie is a doctoral candidate in clinical psychology at John F. Kennedy University. She is currently completing a predoctoral internship at the University of California, Davis, where she serves on the Consult Team for Transgender Care. Ms. Alie is a member of the American Psychological Association's Division 44 Executive Committee, and she served on the revision team for the APA's *Guidelines for Psychological Practice with Lesbian, Gay, and Bisexual Clients*. Her research explores parental acceptance of transgender and gender nonconforming children.

Arlene Baratz, M.D., Family and Medical Adviser, AISDSD Parents Group, 1355 Oak Ledge Court, Pittsburgh, Pennsylvania 15241

Dr. Baratz is a mother of two adult daughters living with complete androgen insensitivity syndrome (CAIS). CAIS is one of the disorders of sex development, conditions in which there are unusual chromosomes, gonads (ovaries/testes), or genitalia. Through various advocacy and support organizations, Dr. Baratz has worked extensively with families and adults affected by various differences of sex development.

Miriam L. Bearse, M.A., M.Phil., M.A.C.P., Tribal Home Visitation Specialist, Tribal Law & Policy Institute, 8235 Santa Monica Boulevard, Suite 211, West Hollywood, California 90046

Ms. Bearse provides training and technical assistance to tribes and other jurisdictions on child welfare and mental health systems improvements. She has extensive experience in providing child welfare and mental health services to youth and families, and has taught and lectured in women's studies and sociology. She previously worked for the Department of Social and Health Services Office of the Secretary in Washington State as a policy analyst, enabling cross-system collaboration, and for the National Indian Child Welfare Association in community development and as a technical assistance provider to tribal grantees in the Substance Abuse and Mental Health Services Administration Systems of Care and Circles of Care initiatives. She lives near Seattle with her partner and daughter. Her tribal heritage is Wampanoag.

Christopher Bellonci, M.D., Assistant Professor, Department of Psychiatry, Tufts University School of Medicine, 800 Washington Street, #1007, Boston, Massachusetts 02111

Dr. Bellonci is a board-certified child/adolescent and adult psychiatrist and assistant professor at Tufts University School of Medicine. He has served on the Mental Health Advisory Board of the Child Welfare League for more than a decade and is the president-elect of the American Association of Children's Residential Centers. Dr. Bellonci coauthored the *Practice Parameter on the Prevention and Management of Aggressive Behavior in Child and Adolescent Psychiatric Institutions with Special Reference to Seclusion and Restraint* for the American Academy of Child and Adolescent Psychiatry.

Nadia A. Cayce-Gibson, M.P.A., Ph.D. Candidate, Technical Assistance Coordinator, Technical Assistance Partnership, National Federation of Families for Children's Mental Health, 9605 Medical Center Drive, Rockville, Maryland 20850

Ms. Cayce-Gibson is nationally known for her ability to lead systematic change based on her personal experience as a parent involved in various public systems. As a woman of color and caregiver of an LGBT youth, Ms. Cayce-Gibson has a personal commitment to the physical and mental health of youth and families, particularly those from culturally and linguistically diverse backgrounds.

Okori T. Christopher, M.S., Research Associate, American Institutes for Research, 1000 Thomas Jefferson Street, NW, Washington D.C. 20007

Mr. Christopher was born on the island of St. Croix, and moved to the United States in 1997. In 2011, he graduated with a master's of science in criminal justice from the University of Baltimore. Mr. Christopher has served on the Eliminating Mental Health Disparities planning committee and is currently on the International Initiative for Mental Health Leadership and the Family Engagement Symposium workgroup.

Timothy Denney, M.S., C.R.C., Training and Evaluation Director, Northwestern Mental Health Center, 603 Bruce Street, Crookston, Minnesota 56716

Mr. Denney provides real-world solutions to the difficulties faced by people with disabilities throughout Northwestern Minnesota. Working to empower consumers and increase the level of appropriate services available to them is the essence of that work. This is being accomplished primarily through training that leads to greater vision, knowledge, and skills for both consumers and the professionals who serve them.

Stephen L. Forssell, Ph.D., M.A., Adjunct Professor of Psychology, George Washington University, Department of Psychology, 2125 G Street, NW, Washington, D.C. 20052

Dr. Forssell has been a professor in the Psychology Department at The George Washington University in Washington, D.C., since 2002. Dr. Forssell's expertise is in sexual orientation issues, same-sex romantic relationships and parenting, HIV/AIDS risk behaviors, high-risk sexual behavior interventions, adolescent and young adult romantic and sexual relationships, and health psychology. His research activities continue to involve same-sex couples' romantic relationships and sexual behaviors, attachment, and child development. His most recent work was a collaboration with Dr. Charlotte Patterson at the University of Virginia in which they investigated parenting capabilities, partner relationship quality, and child outcomes in adoptive gay, lesbian, and bisexual parented families.

Karen B. Francis, Ph.D., M.A., Senior Researcher, American Institutes for Research, 1000 Thomas Jefferson Street, NW, Washington, D.C. 20007

Dr. Francis is a senior researcher at the American Institutes for Research focusing on cultural and linguistic competence, rural behavioral health, lesbian, gay, bisexual, transgender, questioning, intersex, and two-spirit (LGBTQI2-S) program and service delivery, and children's behavioral health programming. Dr. Francis also serves as an on-site consultant on cultural and linguistic competency to the Child Adolescent and Family Branch, Center for Mental Health Services, Substance Abuse and Mental Health Services Administration, U.S. Department of Health and Human Services.

Peter Gamache, Ph.D., M.B.A., M.L.A., M.P.H., President, Turnaround Achievement Network, 11322 Stratton Park Drive, Temple Terrace, Florida 33617

Dr. Gamache is a research and development specialist who serves as a member of the Substance Abuse and Mental Health Services Administration National Workgroup to Address the Needs of Children and Youth who are LGBTQI2-S and Their Families, a panelist of the National Network to Eliminate Disparities—Transition to Independence Learning Cluster, and a member of the American Institutes for Research LGBTQQA Advisory Board.

Simon G. Gonsoulin, M.Ed., Principal Research Analyst, American Institutes for Research, 1000 Thomas Jefferson Street, NW, Washington, D.C. 20007

Mr. Gonsoulin is a principal research analyst for Education, Human Development and Workforce Program for the American Institutes for Research (AIR), where he serves as the director for the National Evaluation and Technical Assistance Center for the Education of Children and Youth Who Are Neglected, Delinquent, or At-Risk. Additionally, Mr. Gonsoulin acts as the juvenile justice resource specialist for the Technical Assistance Partnership. Prior to joining AIR, Mr. Gonsoulin was appointed to the Governor's Cabinet in Louisiana as the deputy secretary of the Office of Youth Development where he led the state's juvenile justice reform efforts for 4 years.

Tawara D. Goode, M.A., Assistant Professor and Director, National Center for Cultural Competence, Center for Child and Human Development, Georgetown University, 3300 Whitehaven Street, NW, Suite 3300, Washington, D.C. 20007

Ms. Goode is recognized as a thought leader in the area of cultural and linguistic competency and has been actively involved in the development and implementation of programs and initiatives at local, national, and international levels. Ms. Goode leads efforts to increase the capacity of health care and mental health care programs to design, implement, and evaluate culturally and linguistically competent service delivery systems to address growing diversity and persistent disparities, and to promote health and mental health equity. These efforts address the needs of diverse audiences including health care, mental health, developmental and other disabilities, social services, early childhood/special education, community/advocacy organizations, professional societies/organizations, and institution of higher education.

Megan Edson Grandin, M.P.H., Senior Analyst, Center for Social Innovation, 200 Reservoir Street, Suite 202, Needham, Massachusetts 02494

Ms. Grandin specializes in project management, training, technical assistance, product development, communications, and marketing. As a senior analyst at the Center for Social Innovation, Ms. Grandin has led several projects and has overseen the production of many technical assistance projects including literature reviews, issue briefs, web-based curricula, and direct training. Ms. Grandin received her bachelor's degree in English from Stony Brook University, and her master's degree from the Boston University School of Public Health.

Justine B. Hanson, Ph.D., Associate, Center for Social Innovation, 200 Reservoir Street, Suite 202, Needham, Massachusetts 02494

Dr. Hanson is an associate at the Center for Social Innovation. She has provided leadership for a national Substance Abuse and Mental Health Services Administration–funded project dedicated to identifying recommended practices for serving lesbian, gay, bisexual, transgender, questioning, intersex, and two-spirit (LGBTQI2-S) youth experiencing homelessness. As part of this project, she has overseen an expert panel, a national listening tour, and the development of *Larkin Street Stories,* a three-part video series designed to engage and train homeless service providers on serving LGBTQI2-S youth.

Kim Pawley Helfgott, M.A., Senior Child Welfare Advisor, American Institutes for Research, 1000 Thomas Jefferson Street, NW, Washington, D.C. 20007

Ms. Helfgott is the associate director for the Western and Pacific Child Welfare Implementation Center which provides technical assistance to improve service delivery in public child welfare systems. She also served as senior child welfare advisor for the Technical Assistance Partnership for Child and Family Mental Health. In that role, she consulted with currently funded system of care grantees to address the mental health needs of children, youth, and families at risk or involved in the child welfare system.

Keith J. Horvath, Ph.D., Assistant Professor, Division of Epidemiology and Community Health, University of Minnesota, 1300 South 2nd Street, Suite 300, Minneapolis, Minnesota 55454

Dr. Horvath is an assistant professor in the Division of Epidemiology and Community Health at the University of Minnesota. His primary research focus is the use of technology in public health research and intervention, with a particular interest in HIV prevention and care. Dr. Horvath has served as principal investigator on several federally funded research grants and is on the scientific advisory committee for the Foundation for AIDS Research.

Phillip Earl Jordan, M.A., Research Analyst, ICF International (ICF Macro), 9300 Lee Highway, Fairfax, Virginia 22031

Mr. Jordan is a research analyst as a part of ICF Macro and services the Child, Adolescent, and Family Branch at the Center for Mental Health Services, Substance Abuse and Mental Health Services Administration. Mr. Jordan completed his graduate degree in developmental psychology from Columbia University in 2010. Notably, Mr. Jordan is a Gates Millennium and McNair Scholar and plans to pursue doctoral studies in the imminent future.

Rachael R. Kenney, M.A., Associate, Center for Social Innovation, 200 Reservoir Street, Suite 202, Needham, Massachusetts 02494

Ms. Kenney is a sociologist at the Center for Social Innovation, focusing on evaluation of training for human service providers. In addition to her training evaluation

efforts, she focuses on youth homelessness through developing trainings and technical assistance products. Ms. Kenney is a certified Mental Health First Aid instructor
and holds a bachelor's degree in sociology from the University of Massachusetts and
a master's degree in sociology from Boston College.

Ryan C. LaLonde, B.F.A., Creative Strategist, Libertyville, Illinois

Mr. LaLonde has been speaking, writing, and advocating about the rights of youth
with LGBT parents and their families for more than 15 years. As a child of a lesbian
parent, he has used his experience to support other youth growing up in LGBT
families. Mr. LaLonde was previously the art director for the Caring for Every
Child's Mental Health Campaign and continues to provide culturally competent
design support to this contract. He has been a board member and chapter leader for
COLAGE–Children of LGBT Parents United, has conducted trainings on LGBT
inclusion, and is the author and illustrator of a children's book about family diversity
and LGBT inclusion.

Katherine J. Lazear, M.A., Social and Behavioral Researcher, University of
South Florida and Human Service Collaborative, College of Behavioral and Com-
munity Sciences, Louis de la Parte Florida Mental Health Institute, 13301 Bruce B.
Downs Boulevard, Tampa, Florida 33612

Ms. Lazear is a social and behavioral researcher at the College of Behavioral and
Community Sciences, Department of Child and Family Studies, University of
South Florida, and a partner with the Human Service Collaborative in Washington, D.C. Ms. Lazear has more than 20 years of experience working with system
of care communities and on related state and national initiatives, including youth
suicide prevention and addressing the needs of children and youth who are LGBT
and their families. Some of her most exciting work has been in culturally and ethnically diverse communities, strengthening community-based systems of care
through partnerships between the communities' natural helpers and formal service
providers.

Arlene Istar Lev, LCSW-R, CASAC, Clinical Director, Choices Counseling and
Consulting, Lecturer, State University New York at Albany, 523 Western Avenue,
#2A, Albany, New York 12203

Ms. Lev is a social worker, family therapist, educator, and writer whose work addresses the unique therapeutic needs of LGBTQ people. She is the founder and
clinical director of Choices Counseling and Consulting and TIGRIS—The Institute for Gender, Relationships, Identity, and Sexuality, and a part-time lecturer at

the State University New York at Albany, School of Social Welfare and Empire College. Ms. Lev has authored two books: *The Complete Lesbian and Gay Parenting Guide* and *Transgender Emergence,* winner of the APA/Division 44 Distinguished Book Award, 2006.

Coretta Jacqueline Mallery, Ph.D., Researcher, American Institutes for Research, 1000 Thomas Jefferson Street, NW, Washington, D.C. 20007

Dr. Mallery is a mental health counselor with a focus on working with children/youth and their families. Dr. Mallery has also served as an adjunct faculty member for The George Washington University Department of Counseling and Human Development and previously worked on a project for the Substance Abuse and Mental Health Services Administration's Children's Mental Health Initiative. Currently, she conducts research to determine the best ways to engage the public (including consumers and caregivers) in health care research and is committed to integrating the patient/consumer/caregiver voice into health care.

Matthew A. Malouf, M.Ed., Ph.D. Candidate, Lehigh University, Counseling Psychology, 111 Research Drive, Iacocca Hall, Bethlehem, Pennsylvania 18015

Mr. Malouf is completing his doctorate in counseling psychology at Lehigh University, where his research and clinical experiences include multicultural competencies in counseling and supervision, qualitative methodologies, social justice, sexuality, and intersecting identities. Mr. Malouf has conducted multiple studies pertinent to his chapter in this book and has presented at local, regional, and national conferences. He also has lectured and conducted trainings on multiculturalism, served on numerous diversity and advocacy committees, and strives to promote the inclusion of a broad range of stakeholder voices in clinical practice, research, and policy.

Kenneth J. Martinez, Psy.D., Senior Research Analyst, American Institutes for Research, Post Office Box 2291, Corrales, New Mexico 87048

Dr. Martinez is a senior research analyst at the American Institutes for Research, based in Corrales, New Mexico. He is author and/or coauthor of several cultural and linguistic competence–related articles and chapters. Dr. Martinez was the State Children's Behavioral Health Director in New Mexico and is also a clinical assistant professor of psychiatry at the University of New Mexico Health Sciences Center. In addition, he is Vice President of the National Latino Behavioral Health Association, is Guest Lecturer in the Department of Child and Family Studies at the University of South Florida, and serves on other national boards.

Marlene Matarese, M.S.W., Director of Training and Technical Assistance, Institute for Innovation and Implementation, University of Maryland, 525 West Redwood Street, Baltimore, Maryland 21201

Ms. Matarese is the training and technical assistance director with the Institute for Innovation and Implementation at the University of Maryland School of Social Work. In her role, she manages the technical assistance and workforce development components of the Institute. Ms. Matarese is also responsible for the development of curricula and research efforts related to lesbian, gay, bisexual, transgender, questioning, intersex, and two-spirit (LGBTQI2-S) youth within systems of care.

Cody Mooneyhan, Editorial Associate, Vanguard Communications, 2121 K Street, NW, Suite 650, Washington, D.C. 20037

Mr. Mooneyhan has served for 10 years as a senior writer for the Caring for Every Child's Mental Health Campaign, a major federal effort to support the adoption of systems of care for children's mental health at state and local levels. He also has written white papers and promotional materials for numerous nonprofit and federal organizations and agencies.

Mojdeh Motamedi, B.S., Mental Health Social Marketing Specialist, American Institutes for Research, 1000 Thomas Jefferson Street, NW, Washington, D.C. 20007

Ms. Motamedi is a mental health social marketing specialist for the Substance Abuse and Mental Health Services Administration, U.S. Department of Health and Human Services, where she assisted with National Children's Mental Health Awareness Day, a part of a national social marketing campaign. She was also a member of the National Workgroup to Address the Needs of Children and Youth Who Are LGBTQI2-S and Their Families. She is now pursuing a Ph.D. in clinical child psychology at The Pennsylvania State University.

Sheila A. Pires, M.P.A., Partner, Human Service Collaborative, 1728 Wisconsin Avenue, NW, #224, Washington, D.C. 20007

Ms. Pires is a consultant to states on system design and financing of children's services. She is a former deputy commissioner of social services and child mental health director for the District of Columbia, and she cochaired the Clinton Health Reform Task Force subcommittee on children's behavioral health. She coauthored children's issue briefs for President Bush's New Freedom Mental Health Commission and serves on the boards of the National Wraparound Initiative Advisory Committee and National Federation of Families for Children's Mental Health. Ms. Pires is also the author of *Building Systems of Care: A Primer* (1st and 2nd editions).

Gary Remafedi, M.D., M.P.H., Professor, Department of Pediatrics, University of Minnesota Youth and AIDS Projects, 2929 4th Avenue South, Suite 203, Minneapolis, Minnesota 55408

Dr. Remafedi completed his undergraduate studies at Yale University and received his medical degree from the University of Illinois. He completed his pediatric residency in Chicago and his subspecialty training and master's degree in public health at the University of Minnesota. Dr. Remafedi pioneered research on adolescent homosexuality that brought about a sea change in understanding of the population. Once thought to be an adult phenomenon rooted in adverse childhood experiences, homosexuality was found to unfold during adolescence, with the passage of time and increasing sexual experience. Growing up gay came to be seen as a transformative experience that alters the course of life. While studying their sexual behavior, Dr. Remafedi found that LGBT individuals contribute importantly to leading causes of adolescent mortality. From their self-reported sexual behavior and drug use, Dr. Remafedi presaged the epidemic of HIV/AIDS in adolescents in the mid-1980s before testing was readily available. He established the Youth and AIDS Projects in 1989 as one of world's first AIDS service organization for youth.

Sharon L. Roepke, M.A./LLP, Regional Cultural and Linguistic Competency Manager, Kalamazoo Community Mental Health and Substance Abuse Services and Kalamazoo Wraps, 3299 Gull Road, Post Office Box 63, Nazareth, Michigan, 49074

Ms. Roepke is the regional cultural and linguistic competency manager of Kalamazoo Community Mental Health and Substance Abuse Services and the Southwest Michigan Affiliation. Ms. Roepke also is the cultural and linguistic competency coordinator for the Kalamazoo Wraps system of care initiative, coordinator of the Family Acceptance of Children and Teens Collaboration, former executive director of the Kalamazoo Gay/Lesbian Resource Center, and past director of the Family Resource Center for sexually abused children. Ms. Roepke serves on the Cultural Competency committee of the Michigan Mental Health Board Association and served as trainer and consultant with KinErgy, a private consulting practice on LGBT workplace issues.

Lisa Rubenstein, M.H.A., Public Health Advisor, Substance Abuse and Mental Health Services Administration, Center for Mental Health Services, 1 Choke Cherry Road, Room 6-1046, Rockville, Maryland 20857

Ms. Rubenstein has more than 25 years of experience in developing and implementing national social marketing campaigns. She is currently serving as the public health advisor at the Substance Abuse and Mental Health Services Administration, overseeing funded system of care communities and directing the children's social marketing campaign.

Christine Walrath, Ph.D., M.H.S., Vice President, ICF International, 40 Wall Street, 34th Floor, New York, New York 10005

Dr. Walrath is an expert in the areas of behavioral and emotional health and well-being with more 18 years of experience in related research and evaluation. Her experience includes the design, implementation, instrument development, and analysis of multimodal, multilevel, and multisite approaches to data collection.

Laura Pannella Winn, M.A., Senior Analyst, Center for Social Innovation, 200 Reservoir Street, Suite 202, Needham, Massachusetts 02494

Ms. Winn is an applied social scientist with broad experience leading and supporting projects to improve services at the provider and state level in addictions, mental health, and homelessness. In 2009 and 2010 she conducted a tour of programs across the country serving LGBT youth experiencing homelessness to gather information about recommended practices in care. She is currently a senior analyst at the Center for Social Innovation, a small business working to improve service delivery to vulnerable populations through online and alternate curricula and training to service providers and research on the effectiveness of technical assistance and skills development tools.

Acknowledgments

We would like to acknowledge and extend our appreciation to so many people for participating in the development of this book. First and foremost, we want to acknowledge LBGT youth and their families who must so often demonstrate courage and resilience in the face of the barriers and challenges that our society has created. We truly hope that this volume honors your experiences and provides information that will help move services and systems in the right direction.

We also appreciate the contribution and deep commitment of our authors. Their passion and expertise is the reason this book has come to fruition, and each chapter provides an important contribution to the collective literature. Many thanks are also extended to Series Editors Beth Stroul and Bob Friedman, and to our team at Paul H. Brookes Publishing Co. for supporting the idea of producing an entire book devoted to LGBT youth and families. Thank you for your courage and commitment.

In addition, we acknowledge the important work of professionals and other community members across the country to make their communities safer, more supportive, and more inclusive for LGBT youth and their families. We hope this book will be a valuable resource on your journeys.

We would also like to thank our families. Sylvia extends her gratitude and appreciation to many loving and supportive family members and friends, most especially her parents, Ronnie and Barbara Fisher, who have instilled the values of compassion and commitment to the well-being of others. Their legacy lives on in their granddaughter, Elise, whose kindness, sensitivity, sense of humor, and overall loveliness is a blessing to her parents and all who know her. During their shared 29-year journey through life, Sylvia and her spouse Susan have encountered the challenges and rewards shared by many LGBT individuals, including coming out together, marrying (albeit with limited legal recognition), becoming parents (and setting legal precedent as the first same-sex couple in their county of residence to be granted a two-parent adoption), and working to achieve equity and equality. Every day brings new promise and a renewed commitment to sharing their lives together.

Jeff acknowledges his parents, Carol and Mike Poirier, whose acceptance, strength, and love have been an inspiration in his life and work. He also acknowledges his deeply supportive colleagues at the American Institutes for Research, especially Cheryl Vince Whitman, and including David Osher, Debra

Grabill, Joyce Burrell, Karen Francis, Ken Martinez, Marketa Walters, Mary Thorngren, Regenia Hicks, Sandy Keenan, and Sharon Hunt. Their leadership and various efforts demonstrate a deep commitment to improving the services and outcomes of LGBT youth in youth-serving systems and communities through technical assistance, training, research, and evaluation. Jeff dedicates his work on this book to all LGBT youth and those questioning their sexual or gender identity, in particular those experiencing harassment, exclusion, and other challenges or struggles in their lives.

Gary feels incredibly fortunate to have the support of his wonderful wife, Gwenn. For nearly 30 years they have been in love and have been "partners in life." They have two amazing children, Jennifer and Andrew, and they are so proud of both of them.

1

Addressing the Needs of LGBT Youth and Their Families

A Public Health Perspective

PHILLIP EARL JORDAN, OKORI T. CHRISTOPHER,
CHRISTOPHER BELLONCI, SYLVIA K. FISHER, AND GARY M. BLAU

L esbian, gay, bisexual, and transgender (LGBT) and questioning individuals have historically been either ignored by the mainstream medical community or worse—pathologized by their medical practitioners. Until the publication of the *Diagnostic and Statistical Manual of Mental Disorders* (3rd ed.; *DSM-III;* American Psychiatric Association, 1980), homosexuality was considered pathology in need of treatment. In truth, public health researchers have not recognized LGBT individuals as a population with distinct health issues (Boehmer, 2002). Little was known about the health needs and experiences of LGBT individuals beyond the realm of HIV prevention and treatment for gay and bisexual men (Brotman, Ryan, Jalbert, & Rowe, 2002b). Despite their need for culturally and linguistically competent services and supports, distrust of the medical and behavioral health community has been a barrier impeding LGBT youth from seeking needed medical and behavioral health treatment (Anderson et al., 2002).

The Institute of Medicine (IOM; 2011) has identified specific risk factors associated with LGBT youth that would benefit from a public health approach, including harassment, victimization, violence, substance use, and homelessness. Substantive evidence also indicates that LGBT youth are at increased risk for elevated suicide attempt rates relative to their representation in the larger population of youth (Gamache & Lazear, 2009; see also Chapter 13). Social stigma and systematic discrimination on the basis of sexual orientation and gender identity and expression, however, have led to decades of obstructed access to adequate LGBT affirmative and culturally competent health care (National Coalition for LGBT Health, 2011). Furthermore, there is anecdotal evidence indicating that the public health community has not documented the extent of, or been responsive to, the public health needs of LGBT youth and their families.

Despite the benign neglect of the medical community toward the health needs of LGBT youth, there is increasingly a shift within the public health work force toward addressing the needs of LGBT and questioning (LGBTQ) youth and their families. This encouraging trend encapsulates the rich tradition of the public health system in embracing a holistic view of health in America. The central focus of the public health system is to ensure that societal conditions allow individuals to be healthy (Corliss, Shankle, & Moyer, 2007; Walker, 1989). Given this mandate, health services and programs must be inclusive of LGBT youth and work toward addressing the health disparities that exist within their communities. This book is dedicated to helping to address the behavioral health needs of LGBT youth and their families with the mission of reducing and, ultimately, eliminating the behavioral health disparities that exist for LGBT youth and their families, as well as families headed by LGBT adults.

Researchers encounter a number of challenges in understanding the health needs of the LGBT population, mainly stemming from a lack of data regarding LGBT individuals (IOM, 2011). The IOM recommends collecting research data about the LGBT population, primarily focusing on demographic research, social influences, health care inequities, intervention research, and transgender-specific health needs. A more solid knowledge base about LGBT health concerns must be developed and grounded in evidence to benefit LGBT individuals and ensure that vital health information is known about members of this community.

RISKS AND PROTECTIVE FACTORS

LGBT individuals are at risk for experiencing mental health challenges akin to those experienced by other oppressed minorities in American society. Increased rates of substance use, depression, and suicide attempts have all been reported in the literature and are hypothesized to be a secondary consequence associated with the burden of coming out with an identity that is still viewed with hostility in many parts of the country (Corliss et al., 2007).

A central task for adolescents is the formation of a positive and healthy identity, and a critical part of a healthy identity is developing a positive and consolidated understanding of one's sexual identity (Ryan, 2003). LGBT adults frequently report an awareness of being different at a very young age. As LGBT youth age into puberty, this general awareness of being different develops into an awareness of being attracted to someone of the same gender (Ryan, 2003). Transgender youth, sometimes even as young children, do not identify with their birth-assigned sex. Transgender youth and other youth who may not conform to the societally expected roles associated with the birth-assigned gender are often perceived to be "gender nonconforming" and may be ostracized as a result (Ryan, 2003).

LGBT youth, whose identity differs from that of the majority of youth with respect to sexual orientation or gender identity, face social stigmatization and higher risks of abuse and traumatic experiences compared with heterosexual and cisgender (i.e., youth who identify with their birth assigned sex) youth; in addition, LGBT youth of color must confront the challenges of identifying with multiple minority status and minority stress (Isaacs, Jackson, Hicks, & Wang, 2008). Culturally and linguistically diverse LGBT youth frequently toil with forming a sense of self through identity formation processes hindered by a hostile social environment. Depending on the youth's social, familial, racial, and religious community, the awareness of same-sex attraction or nonconforming gender identity may be greeted as an unwelcome and unacceptable sexual identity. This often leaves the sexual minority adolescent with a sense of suffering the stigma of being LGBT "in silence" and without needed supports (Isaacs et al., 2008).

Research findings have repeatedly demonstrated that higher rates of family rejection lead to poorer health results during adolescence (Ryan, Huebner, Diaz, & Sanchez, 2009). According to survey results, lesbian, gay, and bisexual young adults who reported higher levels of family rejection during adolescence were 8.4 times more likely to report attempted suicide, 5.9 times more likely to report depression, 3.4 times more likely to report use of illegal drugs, and 3.4 times more likely to report having engaged in unprotected sexual intercourse in comparison with peers from families that reported no or low levels of family rejection. Latino men were found to report the highest number of negative family reactions in regard to their sexual orientation in adolescence (Ryan et al., 2009).

Despite the perception of increasing societal acceptance of LGBT youth, recent findings suggest that LGBT youth displayed higher rates of emotional stress in comparison with heterosexual youth, specifically in the areas of suicidal ideation and self-harm (Almeida, Johnson, Corliss, Molnar, & Azrael, 2009). An alarmingly high rate of male LGBT youth (42%) reported that they had engaged in self-harming behavior, and more LGBT youth males (50%) experienced discrimination than females (25%). Findings also indicated that LGBT youth had significantly higher depressive symptomatology scores than heterosexual youth (Almeida et al., 2009).

Concerns also revolve around lifestyle behavioral choices in regard to LGBT youth. The sexual behaviors of men who have sex with men result in a higher risk for HIV and other sexually transmitted infections (STIs). Research has shown that young gay men are more likely to engage in high-risk sexual behavior and are particularly at risk for HIV. In 2006, a Centers for Disease Control and Prevention (CDC) study reported that 56,300 people became infected with HIV; of these, 34% were adolescents and young adults (13–29 years of age). Black and Hispanic men who have sex with men are more likely to become infected at the ages of 13–29 (Hall et al., 2008).

In a survey conducted with more than 7,200 middle and high school students, findings demonstrated that nearly 9 of 10 LGBT students had experienced harassment at school in the past year, and nearly two thirds felt unsafe because of their sexual orientation (Gay, Lesbian & Straight Education Network [GLSEN],

2010). One third of LGBT students skipped at least 1 day of school in the month before completing the survey because of safety concerns (GLSEN, 2010). The report also found that nearly 85% of LGBT students reported being verbally harassed, 40% reported being physically harassed, and almost 19% reported being physically assaulted at school in the past year because of their sexual orientation (GLSEN, 2010). In addition, almost 64% of LGBT students reported being verbally harassed, 27% reported being physically harassed, and nearly 13% reported being physically assaulted at school in the past year because of their gender expression (GLSEN, 2010).

Stress factors have also been examined to assess the experiences of lesbian, gay, and bisexual youth, and social isolation and vulnerability have been identified as principal concerns in this population (American Psychiatric Association, 2000a). Stressors have also been reported to be associated with high-risk sexual behaviors in this population (Rotheram-Borus, Rosario, Van Rossem, Reid, & Gillis, 1995). Major depression and conduct disorder were reported as four times more likely to occur among 28 lesbian, gay, and bisexual youths when compared with 979 heterosexual youths (Fergusson, Horwood, & Beautrais, 1999; Mustanski, Garofalo, & Emerson, 2010). Lesbian, gay, and bisexual youth must master highly complex challenges and tasks, such as learning how to identify and manage stigma and compartmentalize their identity depending on their surroundings (Block & Matthews, 2006).

Although lesbian, gay, and bisexual youth experience many challenges, it is important to identify supports that aim to increase their well-being. Studies have found that having supportive individuals, school policies, and the cultivation and embeddedness of a host of protective factors are vital in helping youth overcome discrimination and institutionalized heterosexism (Kosciw & Diaz, 2006). Lesbian, gay, and bisexual youth who establish relationships with adult role models seem to have more positive self-esteem and successfully acclimate to their lesbian, gay, and bisexual identity (Lemoire & Chen, 2005). The presence of supportive school personnel is instrumental in contributing to students feeling safer at school, increases students' attendance, increases students' sense of belonging, and heavily influences students' chances of planning to attend college (Kosciw & Diaz, 2006).

School policies that support lesbian, gay, and bisexual youth have been found to be a significant factor that protects youth against victimization and suicidality (Goodenow, Szalacha, & Westheimer, 2006). Sexual risk taking has also reportedly decreased in youth when gay-sensitive HIV prevention programs are offered in the school (Blake et al., 2001). The role of support groups and social support from other lesbian, gay, and bisexual youth play an integral role in the support, socialization, information exchange, and education of lesbian, gay, and bisexual youth and contribute to heightened self-esteem (Anderson, 1998; Crisp & McCave, 2007). In addition, the growth of LGBT youth support groups and gay–straight alliances (GSAs) to advocate and support LGBT youth has empowered LGBT youth to challenge health, mental, educational, and family providers to employ suitable services and care in serving these communities (Ryan, 2003).

GSAs offer an example of a population-based intervention that addresses the developmental conundrum that LGBT youth face. GSAs are school-based clubs with a focus on advancing LGBT causes and acceptance within the school community. They offer one solution to the dilemma of how at-risk youth who have not been identified can find support from a school-based "community." Youth benefit from this resource that supports healthy adaptation to one's sexual identity without actually having to declare that identity. No one knows whether the youth are attending the GSA because they themselves are LGBT or whether they are "straight allies" (GLSEN, 2010; Ryan, 2009).

LGBT YOUTH AND FAMILIES: COMING OUT, FAMILY REJECTION, AND FAMILY ACCEPTANCE

The threat of violence increases anxiety among youth who are questioning their sexual orientation and among lesbian and gay youth who have not yet disclosed their sexual identity. In the past, only a few adolescents revealed their sexual identities to their families and friends; most lesbian, gay, and bisexual individuals waited until they were adults to talk about their sexual identity with others (Ryan, 2009). The sexual orientation of LGBT youth may have an impact on their relationships with family members as a result of ingrained, familial, ethnic, or cultural norms; religious beliefs; or negative stereotypes (Chan, 1995; Greene, 1994; Matteson, 1996). Parents might even feel ashamed or embarrassed by their children's gender nonconforming behavior and often fear that these children will be hurt by others (Ryan, 2009).

The possible implications of disclosing one's sexuality may lead to an individual being ostracized or rejected by family members, parental guilt or self-recrimination, or conflict within the parents' relationship (Griffin, Wirth, & Wirth, 1996; Savin-Williams & Dube, 1998; Strommen, 1993). Many lesbian and gay youth are socially isolated and may feel unsure of their support within their families (Perrin, 2002). According to Perrin, this threat reinforces their sense of vulnerability and isolation and discourages them from "coming out." Previous findings have demonstrated that families who are conflicted about their child's LGBT identity believe that the best way to help their child survive is to help him or her assimilate with heterosexual peers (Ryan, 2009).

When these families block access to their child's gay or gender nonconforming friends or LGBT resources, they are often acting out of care and concern for their child's well-being; adolescents, however, may internalize this behavior as an indication that their parents hate them or do not love them (Ryan, 2009). The consequences of this perceived rejection can have a negative impact on the youth's self-esteem and exacerbate multiple risks for the youth's well-being. A lack of communication and misunderstanding between parents and their LGBT children can increase family conflict, potentially leading to fighting and family disruption that can result in an LGBT youth being removed from or forced out of the home. Because of family conflicts, LGBT youth are placed in foster care, or end up in juvenile detention or on the streets. These factors increase their risk for abuse and serious health and mental health problems (Ryan, 2009).

Research has linked family rejection to LGBT youth's health and mental health (Ryan, 2009). LGBT youth who were rejected by their families because of their identity have much lower self-esteem and have fewer people they can turn to for help (Ryan, 2009). They are also more isolated and have less support than those who are accepted by their families. LGBT adolescents have more problems with drug use; they feel more hopeless and are much less likely to protect themselves from HIV or STIs (Ryan, 2009). Research has found that highly rejected LGBT youth were more than eight times as likely to have attempted suicide, nearly six times as likely to report high levels of depression, more than three times as likely to use illegal drugs, and more than three times as likely to be at high risk for HIV and STIs (Ryan, 2009).

Many LGBT youth and those who question their identity feel they must hide who they are to avoid being rejected; these youth are afraid that parent(s)/caregiver(s) and other family members who believe that being gay is wrong or sinful will not accept them (Ryan, 2009). This results in LGBT youth hiding their identities, which undermines their self-esteem and sense of self-worth (Ryan, 2009). Reactions to the discovery of a lesbian, gay, or bisexual youth's identity by family members may not always be deemed as negative; however, it might take time to adjust and develop an understanding of the lesbian, gay, or bisexual family member (Laird, 1996). Some families are motivated to learn how to support their gay or transgender children when they realize that their words and actions have a powerful impact on their LGBT children's survival and well-being (Ryan, 2009). Families ultimately must face and acclimate to the loss of hopes, perceptions, or expectations connected with presumed heterosexuality (Ryan, 2009).

The coming out process has been linked with positive self-esteem and mental health among lesbian, gay, and bisexual youth (Boxer, Cook, & Herdt, 1999). Findings have shown that being out to one's mother and maintaining positive views about homosexuality are correlated with positive self-esteem for gay males (Savin-Williams, 1989). Being competent and possessing average/above average cognitive abilities is also a protective factor in lesbian, gay, and bisexual youth (Crisp & McCave, 2007). Other individual factors that promote resilience in gay youth include intimate friendships and close relationships with parents (Anderson, 1998; Savin-Williams, 1989). Lastly, family acceptance and the presence of a gay role model during childhood have been identified as among the most important resiliency factors, and family acceptance is the most protective factor against HIV infection (Diaz & Ayala, 2001; Ryan, 2003). Supporting families in their efforts to support their LGBT family member is a goal for system of care communities, and there is increasing adoption of resources and practices to assist LGBT youth and their families throughout this process nationally.

Race, gender, sexual orientation, and disability interact and reinforce the reality of oppression and the unpleasantness of personal biases (Carter, 1995; Sue & Torino, 2005). To expand the lenses of multicultural understanding and sensitivity, the existence of other group identities related to culture, ethnicity, social class, gender, and sexual orientation must be acknowledged (Sue, Bingham, Porche-Burke, & Vasquez, 1999). Systemic racism in mainstream and LGBT communities and homophobia in mainstream and ethnic communities leads to difficulties in finding support and generally requires an individual to choose one identity over another as opposed to integrating multiple identities (Ryan, 2003).

Culturally and linguistically competent policies and practices can help alleviate individual, community, institutional, and discriminatory health disparities while advancing means for LGBT youth to communicate and disclose who they are (McWayne et al., 2010). Regardless of sexual orientation or gender identity, all youth need the love and respect of parents, and need to make sense of their relationships as they mature into adulthood, face the influence of peers, desire love and sex, and have questions about their future (Savin-Williams, 2001). Proper policies and training are immediately needed to advance the care of LGBT youth; in turn, this will further prevent the discrimination and victimization of LGBT youth in school and community settings (Ryan, 2003).

LGBT YOUTH AND SERVICE NEEDS

LGBT youth may feel powerless and might need to consult with a mental health provider who can help them explore their varying issues and concerns (Isaacs et al., 2008). LGBT youth have different experiences relative to their peers and, accordingly, different service needs that necessitate a focused and tailored array of culturally and linguistically appropriate services and supports to promote positive outcomes (Block & Matthews, 2006).

System of care communities have made a commitment to improving the well-being of LGBT youth and their families through the provision of culturally and linguistically competent services and supports in a comprehensive, community-based service array. This book identifies a vast array of policies, practices, and interventions that can and should be implemented within system of care communities to effectively and successfully address the behavioral health needs of LGBT youth and their families. A desirable and significant result of appropriate interventions with LGBT youth and their families will be the reduction of health care disparities among these youth and a host of positive outcomes, including decreases in substance use, suicide attempts, and homelessness and increased well-being and integration and full inclusion within the larger community.

2

Providing Culturally and Linguistically Competent Services and Supports to Address the Needs of LGBT Youth and Their Families

Jeffrey M. Poirier, Kenneth J. Martinez, Karen B. Francis, Timothy Denney, Sharon L. Roepke, and Nadia A. Cayce-Gibson

Cultural and linguistic competence (CLC) is a core principle for enhancing policy and practice within mental health services organizations and communities. CLC provides a conceptual framework for systems, agencies, and practitioners to develop their capacity to effectively respond to the preferences,[1] needs, and identities of youth from diverse cultures. For lesbian, gay, bisexual, and transgender (LGBT) youth, CLC provides a rationale and framework for examining and improving organizational policies, structures, procedures, practices, behaviors, and attitudes toward LGBT youth in youth-serving systems.

This chapter applies CLC to LGBT cultures in a manner similar to other recent literature (e.g., Planned Parenthood Mid-Hudson Valley, Inc., et al., 2007; Poirier et al., 2008) to help ensure that LGBT youth receive culturally and linguistically appropriate services and supports in systems of care. Services and supports that are *not* culturally and linguistically competent are apt to be less responsive, not fully inclusive, and perhaps less efficacious than services and supports that are. Throughout this book a CLC lens is used to discuss and integrate strategies that can help ensure that youth-serving systems become more responsive to the multifaceted cultural identities of LGBT youth. Furthermore, CLC should be one basis for continuous quality improvement (CQI) and research efforts related to this population in systems of care.

---

[1] *Preferences* here does not refer to sexual orientation and identity in any way.

This chapter briefly reviews the evolution of CLC, including emphasis on cultural responsiveness, and related key literature and its growing application to mental health services and supports. The chapter discusses the implications of CLC for providing effective, appropriate services and supports, and presents recommended strategies and practices. It also shares community examples, including two in-depth descriptions of how systems of care in Michigan and Minnesota have worked to enhance CLC and improve supports and services for LGBT youth in their communities.

WHAT IS CULTURAL AND LINGUISTIC COMPETENCE?

Culture has many definitions, which reflects the diversity of culture itself. It can be defined as learned and shared knowledge, as well as patterns of human behavior such as communication styles, customs, and values (Cross, Bazron, Dennis, & Isaacs, 1989). Culture is complex, dynamic, and shapes our views of the world and our communities. Culture includes our beliefs and how these influence our behaviors, as well as how we interpret our experiences and interact with others and our social environments. Furthermore, cultures can and do evolve (as is true with LGBT cultures). Culture has multiple influences: the various contexts within which we live (ecology), important people and communities in our lives and in society, and what we learn. Together, these shape our values, beliefs, traditions, roles, and rituals, as well as our biases and prejudices, which are part of each person's cultural roots. Culture deeply affects our perspectives, interpretations, and experiences. Although some systems of care may use the term *culture* interchangeably with *race/ethnicity* (Goode & Jackson, 2005), it is important to acknowledge the broader scope of culture, including LGBT cultural identities, among others.

Competence pertains to individual, organizational, and system capacity to effectively address individual preferences and needs. Specific knowledge, skills, behaviors, and experience are needed to build this capacity and implement effective policies, procedures, practices, and CQI efforts (National Association of Social Workers [NASW], 2001). To be competent, individuals need sufficient proficiency of a particular topic. Many professions (e.g., social workers) require certifications to demonstrate competence, but competence is a minimum standard. Developing competence is a lifelong learning process that requires a unique path for each individual, a personal commitment to growth, and openness to diversity. CLC self-assessments can facilitate personal reflection about one's level of competence related to particular groups or topics. They are short surveys that ask an individual to respond honestly to a series of questions about self-perceived prejudice, discrimination, stereotypes, and other related biases (see Chapter 3).

Historically, *culture* and *competence* were not usually linked. During the last 20 years, however, the health and behavioral health care fields, in particular, have linked these concepts, including in a landmark monograph (i.e., Cross et al.,

1989). Cultural competence involves valuing the worth of individuals, families, and communities and is a process through which individuals, organizations, and systems effectively and respectfully interact with and support others from all cultural backgrounds (NASW, 2001). NASW (2001), for example, issued 10 standards for cultural competence in social work, including self-awareness of one's values and beliefs, as well as development and application of cross-cultural knowledge and skills.

In addition, cultural competence has evolved over time to include concerns related to language and communication. Linguistic competence has been defined as follows:

> The capacity of an organization and its personnel to communicate effectively, and convey information in a manner that is easily understood by diverse audiences including persons of limited English proficiency, those who have low literacy skills or are not literate, individuals with disabilities, and those who are deaf or hard of hearing. (Goode & Jones, 2009, p. 1)

In addition, linguistic competence involves a commitment to using appropriate language for describing and interacting with LGBT youth (e.g., preferred first names and identity-related terms, including gender pronouns) and acknowledging the importance of using these terms.

CLC integrates culture, language, and competence into a cohesive principle and has become one of three fundamental values defining systems of care (Stroul, Blau, & Sondheimer, 2008). Although CLC emerged to provide responsive systems of care for individual children and youth with emotional and behavioral challenges and their families, it has influenced a much broader population in many more systems beyond the behavioral health field (Wheeler, 2011). CLC theory and practice is applied ever increasingly in the health care industry because of greater concern about the quality of care and related liability issues.

Evidence of the benefits of CLC is emerging. This suggests that culturally and linguistically competent health care is associated with a number of positive outcomes, such as more effective patient–provider communication and increased patient satisfaction with care (Goode, Dunne, & Bronheim, 2006; Robert Wood Johnson Foundation, 2009). Legislation at the federal and state levels has influenced development of policies that emphasize culturally and linguistically competent practices. In particular, in 2001, The Office of Minority Health, within the U.S. Department of Health and Human Services, issued the National Standards for Culturally and Linguistically Appropriate Services in Health Care to correct inequities in the provision of health services and to be more responsive to the individualized needs of clients (U.S. Department of Health and Human Services, The Office of Minority Health, 2001). These standards include mandates, guidelines, and recommendations. For all recipients of federal funds, standards 4–7 are mandated practices related to language access services, such as the provision of bilingual staff or interpreter services for consumers; also, the provision of verbal offers as well as written notices in the preferred language of consumers informing them of their right to receive language assistance services. These standards are meant to be integrated throughout organizations in partnership with communities.

The behavioral health field applies *cultural and linguistic competence* in its system of care work. There is now debate about the word *competence,* which connotes a destination versus a process of ongoing learning, growing, and progressing. Individuals can never really be competent in another person's cultural experiences and perspectives. Even on many of the various iterations of *continuum of cultural competence,* the idea of the highest level, *cultural mastery,* can be misleading. Because this chapter and book do not focus on redefining CLC, but rather on describing its role in improving services and supports, the authors of this chapter use CLC but acknowledge that the underlying goal is to move systems of care toward being more responsive to the cultural and linguistic needs of LGBT youth and their families.

WHY A CULTURAL AND LINGUISTIC COMPETENCE STRATEGY FOR LGBT YOUTH AND THEIR FAMILIES?

Systems of care initially focused on children and families of color who were "un-served, underserved or inappropriately served" by most behavioral health delivery systems (Isaacs, 1998, p. 9). Resonating throughout this book, though, are the many challenges that LGBT youth may experience, often at disproportionately greater rates compared with non–LGBT youth (e.g., depression/anxiety, suicidal ideation, homelessness, harassment/assault). To address these behavioral health disparities and challenges, professionals in youth-serving systems should work to enhance their CLC efforts for LGBT youth and their families. This requires a cohesive strategy for providing more culturally and linguistically responsive services and supports through organizational change and work force development.

A CLC strategy can help to address barriers to accessing and appropriately utilizing care, including inadequate provider knowledge and stigma. Inadequate knowledge of providers, regardless of their attitudes, and insufficient training contribute to structural barriers to culturally responsive services and supports at institutional levels (Institute of Medicine [IOM], 2011). Another serious concern is *stigma,* which can be defined as the "inferior status, negative regard, and relative powerlessness that society collectively assigns to individuals and groups that are associated with various conditions, statuses, and attributes" (IOM, 2011, p. 61). In systems of care, stigma can be enacted (e.g., by biased behaviors), felt (e.g., by avoiding the experience of stigma because of fear of it, such as by not disclosing one's LGBT identity), and internalized (e.g., LGBT individuals feeling unworthy of the same access to health care as non-LGBT individuals [IOM,

2011]). Addressing these concerns should be the foundation of a community's CLC strategy.

LGBT YOUTH CULTURE

Although individuals may have a personal definition of self, others, including the systems and professionals with which they interact, also have preconceived notions about groups of individuals that may be quite divergent. Discrepancy and divergence between self and others may lead to stereotyping, bias, prejudice, and discrimination. Youth may identify with any of a host of cultural identities, including youth culture or their own ethnic, racial, religious/spiritual, or LGBT culture. These multiple overlapping identities that many youth experience can both enrich and sometimes complicate youth development, depending on the presence or absence of supportive families, peers, or other allies. The "jagged edges" around these overlapping identities can present challenges to youth as they attempt to reconcile aspects of their identities that do not complement each other as a result of nonacceptance by significant others or an inability to successfully integrate these identities in a way that benefits youth as they achieve developmental competencies. Historical or current trauma may also affect the development and health of youth navigating their LGBT identity. Progressing through this delicate and formative period in youths' lives can be challenging, but effective efforts to foster CLC for these youth and their families can provide opportunities for successful integration or, at least, a satisfactory conjunction of these identities that can support and strengthen youth and their families.

LGBT youth are especially vulnerable to societal and dominant culture biases that may judge, discount, and stigmatize them, but CLC can play a central role in helping youth successfully integrate the strengths of their multifaceted identities into a stronger and integrated whole. A challenge for system of care communities is that LGBT youth may be "invisible," experiencing their struggles quietly, secretly, or in fear of potential ramifications if others find out. They may fear their parents knowing they are LGBT, being "outed" by peers, being teased or bullied, having their sexual orientation or gender identity affect their future opportunities for education or employment, or being judged and ostracized in general by their peer groups. To foster trust so that LGBT youth access services and supports, as with any marginalized group, requires professionals in systems of care to create an atmosphere of openness and acceptance that allows for culturally and linguistically appropriate outreach.

INCREASING CULTURAL AND
LINGUISTIC COMPETENCE WITHIN ORGANIZATIONS

Because of the stigma related to LGBT identity and marginalization of youth with mental, behavioral, and emotional health needs, communities should carry

out specific CLC strategies to support LGBT youth. For organizations to develop their CLC capacity, they should 1) value diversity; 2) engage in cultural
and linguistic self-assessment; 3) address dynamics of difference (e.g., by acknowledging the effects of historical experiences among different populations
due to trauma or discrimination); 4) institutionalize cultural knowledge; and
5) adapt to diversity by making the appropriate policy, hiring, program, training,
coaching, evaluation, and other infrastructure changes (Cross et al., 1989). Organizations should sustain their CLC efforts so that they become a part of daily
operations and organizational culture. These efforts should also involve CQI activities to inform improvements of CLC efforts.

Organizational infrastructure "describes the basic components of an agency
including its leadership, legal documentation, staff policies and procedures, financial accounts and procedures" (U.S. Department of Health and Human Services,
The Office of Minority Health, 2008, para. 1). An organization's infrastructure
determines how it functions, how services are provided, and how responsive it
is to established goals and objectives. Developing a functional infrastructure
takes planning and time and involves a clear understanding of the population(s)
to be served, including their specific needs and cultural identities. To build organizational capacity and responsiveness to effectively meet the needs of LGBT
youth, diversity needs to be valued throughout organizations. Although inclusion
is important, it is insufficient to just state that a service delivery system wel-
comes all who come for services. Rather, service delivery needs to be established at several levels, including policies, procedures, practices, and supports,
so that LGBT populations are represented and cultural information is infused
within an organization's values, beliefs, and capacity.

Organizational infrastructure strategies include self-assessment and planning; creating a safe and supportive environment; work force hiring, retention,
and training; developing and providing culturally appropriate services and supports; and advocacy and education. Organizations should examine both structural and operational capacity for addressing the needs of LGBT youth. Operational capacity includes the development and implementation of a CLC plan
that identifies action steps and details specific tasks and responsibilities related to
developing culturally and linguistically competent programs and services. Administrative leadership is critical to cultivate and sustain culturally competent
practices at an organizational level and contribute to their success (Davis & Travis, 2010; The Workgroup on Adapting Latino Services, 2008).

STRATEGIES TO MOVE CULTURAL AND
LINGUISTIC COMPETENCE FORWARD IN YOUR COMMUNITY

CLC activities can be challenging, and related results have tended to be disap-
pointing in systems of care (Isaacs, Jackson, Hicks, & Wang, 2008). Strategies presented throughout this book and the following key recommendations, however,

can help advance the effective implementation of CLC approaches within systems of care. In particular, although LGBT culture is as heterogeneous as other diverse cultures, it is important to be as knowledgeable as possible about LGBT cultures through training, technical assistance, and culturally appropriate inquiry of those who have knowledge and experience. Professionals supporting LGBT youth do not need to be LGBT themselves (although it may help), but they need to be open to learning, engage in an authentic self-assessment process, and be able to speak as an authentic ally of LGBT youth.

Insensitive, biased systems can frustrate LGBT youth trying to access mental health services and affect the quality of these supports (U.C. Davis Center for Reducing Health Disparities, 2009). As system of care professionals improve their CLC for LGBT youth and their families, they will actively address heterosexism and transgender bias. Communities can frame bias and stigma as conditions to be ameliorated through active interventions. Conditions can improve over time as system of care staff and constituencies develop more culturally and linguistically competent attitudes, enhance their knowledge base, and expand their experience with LGBT youth and their families. Communities can then identify constructive steps to address these needs and improve individual and organizational competence. Linguistic competence is also central to organizational cultural competence (Goode & Jones, 2009). To help engage LGBT youth and families, communities should prohibit biased comments and behavior, refrain from making assumptions by using language that communicates respect for the terms youth use to describe themselves (e.g., queer, nongender), and avoid using gender-specific pronouns, when appropriate.

Assess Strengths and Needs

Individual and organizational assessments are another important strategy for moving CLC forward in systems of care. The information gathered from these assessments can inform strategic planning (e.g., development of CLC plans), decision making (e.g., service delivery), and, among individuals, a deeper awareness of their personal commitment and ability to meet the needs of LGBT youth and their families. Various resources to assess organizational and individual CLC are available, including an assessment adapted for this book (see Chapter 3). Understanding your community's strengths and needs provides a valuable starting place to develop a strategic plan and engage in activities that will build on strengths and address challenges.

Develop, Support, and Implement an Inclusive Cultural and Linguistic Competence Plan

Some system of care communities have struggled to establish responsibility and accountability among much-needed stakeholder groups, particularly for LGBT populations. A community's CLC plan, which should include LGBT youth as a priority population, is an important tool for communities to guide CLC development and implementation (Martinez et al., 2010). For those engaged in the process, the CLC plan can help raise awareness, create a sense of urgency for action, and manage progress. For example, most state child-serving systems, such as juvenile justice, are mandated to address disparities that exist in their systems, and these efforts should include disparities encountered by LGBT youth and their families.

It is important to develop a CLC plan, supported by a CLC committee that provides meaningful infrastructure and serves as a community leadership group, while clearly documenting a community's vision, mission, and goals (Martinez et al., 2010). A focus on LGBT, questioning, intersex, and two-spirit youth should be part of the broader organizational CLC plan (Martinez et al., 2010). Systems of care should identify and adequately support the key staff who will lead efforts focused on LGBT youth (e.g., inclusion of budget line items for CLC activities and services) so that these efforts are truly valued and sustainable. Although CLC is a shared responsibility, it is important to identify a leader who serves as the coordinator or "point person." For example, a CLC coordinator should help move LGBT CLC efforts forward by ensuring effective and efficient utilization of community resources, leading related CLC planning efforts, and providing support to community partners.

All partners in the system of care community should be involved in creating a shared vision that specifically includes youth, families, and culturally diverse community members. It is also important that stakeholders publicly embrace values and activities and provide in-kind and financial resources for LGBT CLC activities. Partners should include both formal and informal leaders to grow and ultimately sustain CLC values.

Provide Safe, Welcoming Environments

It is critical to foster and sustain a safe, welcoming environment for LGBT youth and their families. This recommendation cannot be overstated—the implementation of nondiscrimination policies, procedures, and practices is just one approach to fostering a safe, supportive environment. Maintaining a physical environment that promotes safety and security for these youth and families is also important. Organizations can create welcoming environments by displaying in visible locations LGBT-related materials (e.g., brochures and announcements from local LGBT organizations, LGBT-affirming literature, information on appropriate LGBT-related web sites) and symbols (e.g., rainbow flags, signage) that LGBT youth may embrace. For example, in 2009, the Substance Abuse and Mental Health Services Administration (SAMHSA) Child, Adolescent and Family Branch's Lesbian, Gay, Bisexual, Transgender, Questioning, Intersex, or

Two-Spirit (LGBTQI2-S) National Workgroup recommended adapting the systems of care logo to help communities identify safe spaces for LGBT youth and their families. Subsequently, the logo was modified to display a rainbow-themed background because rainbow symbols are frequently embraced within LGBT culture. You can view this logo online at www.tapartnership.org/COP/CLC/lgbtqi2s.php.

Enhance Work Force Capacity and Provide Community Learning Opportunities

Communities can also promote CLC through the hiring, retention, and training of a work force and staff who are equipped to address the unique needs of LGBT youth and their families. Not only do staff need to be committed to CLC, but they also need the skills and expertise to work appropriately with LGBT youth. Staff training and ongoing professional development opportunities are necessary to ensure that staff and volunteers possess the necessary knowledge and attitudes to provide effective and appropriate services and supports for LGBT youth. Professionals can easily access free CLC training materials on LGBT youth.[2]

Learning opportunities should be important components of a community's or organization's larger CLC strategy. For example, in September 2011, the Technical Assistance Partnership for Child and Family Mental Health's (TA Partnership) LGBTQI2-S Learning Community (http://tapartnership.org/COP/CLC/lgbtqi2s.php) provided LGBT "cultural and linguistic competence in focus" learning events in seven system of care communities (including three statewide, two urban county, and two rural regional systems of care) to build knowledge, share strategies and recommended practices, and disseminate resources to enhance cultural and linguistic competence and support LGBT youth and their families (SAMHSA, 2011). Participants included system of care community partners from child welfare, education, juvenile justice, mental health, and other youth-serving systems; administrators; clinicians and other front-line professionals; family members; and youth. The learning events included presentations, large and small group discussions, videos, and exercises. Between 40 and 130 participants attended each event. Completed feedback forms from more than

---

[2]For example, see the Child Welfare League of America and Lambda Legal's (2010) *Getting Down to Basics: Tools to Support LGBTQ Youth in Care*; the National Association of Social Workers' *Moving the Margins: Training Curriculum for Child Welfare Services with Lesbian, Gay, Bisexual, Transgender, and Questioning Youth in Out-of-Home Care* (Elze & McHaelen, 2009); the National Center for Lesbian Rights and Sylvia Rivera Law Project's *A Place of Respect: A Guide for Group Care Facilities Serving Transgender and Gender Non-Conforming Youth* (Marksamer, 2011); and the National Center on Cultural Competence's *Practice Brief 1: Providing Services and Supports for Youth Who Are Lesbian, Gay, Bisexual, Transgender, Questioning, Intersex or Two-Spirit.* (Poirier et al., 2008). In addition, see the recently published *A Sexuality & Gender Diversity Training Program: Increasing the Competency of Mental Health Professionals* (Jackson, McCloskey, & McHaelen, 2011).

320 participants indicated that almost all felt that the learning events increased their understanding of LGBT cultures, expanded their understanding of challenges LGBT youth may experience, and provided information they could use to enhance the cultural and linguistic competence of their community's services and supports for LGBT youth and their families (Technical Assistance Partnership for Child and Family Mental Health, personal communication, October 17, 2011).

Meaningfully Engage the Community

Community engagement involves processes and strategies for collaboration with groups of individuals affiliated by similar situations to address issues affecting their well-being (Centers for Disease Control and Prevention, 1997). To effectively provide services for LGBT youth, it is important to identify and mobilize community members, including allies, family members, community- and faith-based organizations, and service professionals involved in addressing the needs of these youth. Community engagement, which can help address the health and well-being of LGBT youth, provides opportunities to address challenges regarding availability, access, and appropriateness of services while building on existing strengths and resources. Community engagement can also enhance the availability of supports and should provide information about how LGBT youth are perceived within the community (Poirier et al., 2008). In addition, systems of care should implement CQI processes that include LGBT youth so all data-driven system of care decisions are credible in their efforts to improve these youths' experiences and outcomes. Related strategies should include gathering community input to learn about societal barriers and community needs of LGBT youth and their families, as well as creating safe, honest dialogues of diverse stakeholders, including youth, family, and leaders of LGBT organizations in the community and other allies.

Challenges to effective community engagement (e.g., mistrust, bias) require strategies that foster meaningful relationships, respectful and open engagement, inclusion, and partnerships with the LGBT community. Examples include 1) providing a safe and supportive environment for LGBT youth; 2) facilitating building a supportive community between LGBT youth and allies; 3) encouraging healthy community engagement; 4) empowering LGBT youth and allies through leadership building, recreation, and education; and 5) promoting outreach to local youth and youth groups (San Francisco Lesbian Gay Bisexual Transgender Community Center, 2011). It is important to capitalize on your community's assets, such as LGBT "cultural brokers" who can bridge different cultural groups and facilitate change because of their knowledge and credibility (Jezewski & Sotnik, 2001), by building mutual trust and fostering meaningful collaboration within the community on behalf of LGBT youth and their families.

Implement Other Strategies

It is important to also protect LGBT youth (and staff), enhance practice and service delivery, and support families. For example, LGBT youth and professionals should be included in nondiscrimination policies of all agencies and organizations partnering with a system of care. To improve services, it is important to discuss sexual orientation and gender identity/expression with youth in a supportive manner, avoid biased language and behavior (e.g., assuming that youth are heterosexual), avoid assuming that youth are distressed or troubled because of their LGBT identity, and demonstrate an open and positive attitude about LGBT youth, which can promote a positive therapeutic relationship (Poirier et al., 2008). Moreover, it is important to engage all family members of LGBT youth, who may be struggling with understanding or accepting the LGBT family member's sexual orientation or gender identity and may also need resources or supports (Ryan, 2009).

COMMUNITY EXAMPLES

System of care communities have incorporated CLC approaches for LGBT youth in core areas such as work force development, youth support and leadership, and collaboration and antistigma campaigning. For example, the Partnership for Children of Burlington County, New Jersey (funded in 1999 to implement wraparound care for children and youth ages 5–18 years), collaborated with its local youth-led organization and the Burlington County Family Support Organization to create an LGBT youth support group and identify safe zones in the community.

Across the country, grassroots LGBT organizations and groups already exist that could facilitate efforts to support LGBT youth. Unfortunately, these valuable community resources often go unnoticed and unfunded. Two system of care communities identified LGBT organizations challenging stigma by creating a public partnership and providing resources. Attempting to meet the needs of LGBT youth in Rhode Island, The Way Out began as a weekly support group at the YMCA in 1993. As the group expanded and members led various community activities, including HIV/AIDS awareness, the YMCA empowered the group to become its own 501(c)(3) organization. Youth leaders created the name Youth Pride. Funded in 2005, Rhode Island Positive Educational Partnership in conjunction with Parent Support Network of Rhode Island partnered with Youth Pride, Inc., to develop its system of care, including its youth movement. The system of care consulted with Youth Pride, Inc., to modify its approach and further integrate education, early childhood, and behavioral health systems.

Another system of care funded in 2005, Sarasota Partnership for Children's Mental Health of Sarasota, Florida, created a unique partnership with ALSO

Out Youth (ALSO), which provides peer support, educational and social activities, information/referral, and training for LGBT youth. One of its most successful programs includes the drop-in center, where youth can participate in peer activities in a safe and welcoming environment. All of these system of care programs were guided by LGBT youth who responded to their unique cultural and linguistic needs. The following two sections provide more detailed examples of system of care communities that have strategically implemented CLC activities.

Kalamazoo Wraps

Kalamazoo Wraps, Kalamazoo, Michigan, is a local partnership among Kalamazoo Community Mental Health and Substance Abuse Services, Advocacy Services for Kids, Kalamazoo Public Schools, and several area youth-serving organizations that seek to improve the lives of youth with mental health needs. In 2008, it initiated a collaborative effort to reduce the mental health challenges that LGBT youth experience.

Kalamazoo, Michigan, a city of 74,262 in a county of 250,331 residents (U.S. Census Bureau, 2011), lies midway between Detroit, Michigan, and Chicago, Illinois, and is surrounded by several small farming communities. Although Kalamazoo is in a conservative rural area, the city itself has a moderate to progressive electorate, and current political efforts have provided local forums for intense discussion about LGBT individuals. The Kalamazoo Gay & Lesbian Resource Center, a small nonprofit organization that serves gay and transgender individuals, conducted a Youth Health and Safety survey of area adolescents who attended community or school-based youth programs; approximately half of the 107 youth respondents self-identified as LGBT (Kalamazoo Gay & Lesbian Resource Center, 2005).

Survey findings were released to youth-serving organizations by a panel of young people who shared their coming-out stories, observations, and the elevated suicide attempt rate among LGBT youth (eight times higher than that of heterosexual youth). The Resource Center's results also revealed higher rates of drug and alcohol use and higher levels of harassment of LGBT youth (Kalamazoo Gay & Lesbian Resource Center, 2005). These study findings were used to receive a SAMHSA grant, and the Gay & Lesbian Resource Center director was invited to serve on the new Kalamazoo Wraps advisory board. Two years later, the Resource Center director was hired as the CLC manager for the system of care.

In 2008, the Kalamazoo Wraps project director and advisory group encouraged the CLC manager to connect with youth-serving organizations that worked with gay and transgender youth and invite them to submit a proposal for a mini grant. The CLC manager met with the board president of the Resource Center and the president of the local Parents, Families and Friends of

Lesbians and Gays (PFLAG) chapter to share information acquired from a conference presentation by Dr. Caitlin Ryan from the Family Acceptance Project. The Family Acceptance Project research demonstrates a clear relationship between LGBT health risks and the level of family acceptance or rejection. Furthermore, the results indicate that even a small improvement in acceptance by a gay youth's family results in significantly reduced levels of depression, suicidal gestures, HIV risk behavior, and illegal drug use (Ryan, 2009). The CLC manager's proposal for Dr. Ryan to train youth providers on recommended practices for working with LGBT youth was accepted, and Kalamazoo Wraps provided funding for four community education forums. These forums were designed to increase awareness of effective ways to help LGBT youth and their families and give families and professionals simple tools to support at-risk LGBT youth. The committee decided to plan a workshop specifically for faith-based leaders, and a fourth workshop was added for leaders of LGBT organizations. The collaboration partners invited various system of care partners and stakeholders, including community leaders, LGBT ally organizations, and mental health and substance abuse service providers, to attract diverse participation.

One of the challenges facing the Kalamazoo planning committee was how to provide the infrastructure necessary to successfully publicize, promote, and orchestrate bringing this training opportunity to Kalamazoo. Partnering with Kalamazoo Wraps increased the visibility of PFLAG and the greater Resource Center and strengthened their networking capability with larger institutions serving young people. Kalamazoo Wraps provided coordination and public education/marketing support to publicize the workshops.

Sixteen LGBT community leaders; more than 100 system of care leaders, parents, adults, and youth; 43 faith-based leaders; and 90 helping professionals attended the three workshops and community forum. The next day's *Kalamazoo Gazette* reported, "Talk on LGBT Tolerance, Family Support Draws Rapt Attention in Kalamazoo" (Barr, 2009). Ten weeks later, the Kalamazoo Family Acceptance collaborative held a brainstorming session at a local Episcopal church; 25 workshop participants, including parents of LGBT youth, attended the brainstorming session and developed action steps to engage the community in helping LGBT youth and their families. Participants shared what most affected them from the research, how they had used the information, and what they felt the community should do to help LGBT youth in the future.

Members of the planning committee gathered recommendations from the brainstorming sessions and developed plans for a Family Acceptance of Children and Teens (FACT) partnership. FACT's initial plan was to educate the public, families, and helping professionals about behaviors that reduce an LGBT child's risk for physical and mental health problems and behaviors that increase risk. FACT received permission from the Family Acceptance Project to cite its research in a two-sided flyer. In its first year, FACT flyers and examples were distributed to approximately 2,500 people. Future plans for FACT include an adaptation of a National Youth Suicide Prevention program for presentation to area mental health and youth-serving professionals, expanding collaboration with faith-based leaders, reaching out to ethnic communities, developing a media campaign, and ensuring that families of LGBT youth have access to research-based information and mentoring to help them promote resiliency in their children.

Our Children Succeed Initiative

Northwest Minnesota's Our Children Succeed Initiative (OCSI), a system of care community grantee funded in 2005, prioritized LGBT youth as a strategy to enhancing the CLC of its services. The organization that sought the cooperative agreement is a collaboration of more than 40 child-serving agencies in a six-county area of northwest Minnesota. The region served is rural with an agricultural-based economy and 68,708 residents (U.S. Census Bureau, 2011) across an area of approximately 6,500 square miles. More than half of the population lives away from communities on farms, and isolation is a common factor for many children and families. Although reputed to be a mostly Caucasian Scandinavian region, there is a culturally diverse population in the region (e.g., Norwegian, Hispanic, and Latino families; two Amish communities; Somali refugee families). Overlaying these cultural variations are factors such as significant religious and socioeconomic diversity, severe weather conditions for 5 months of the year, and a sense of individualism and isolation associated with diverse cultural backgrounds and the rural, frontier, farmland orientation of the region.

When OCSI activities began, there was little or no discussion of services for LGBT youth, and no agencies had formalized plans to identify needs or improve services for this population. Before the system of care grant, there was little history of working together at the service provision level on system improvement. Many youth with mental health difficulties were limited in seeking services as a result of distance and difficult weather conditions, as well as limited availability of services in small communities with small schools.

Few support organizations are formed in the region around any topic area, and local residents typically do not join organizations other than churches and organizations such as the American Legion. Within this setting, local service providers have not been successful in starting support groups for LGBT youth, and few youth have been willing to self-disclose, except in the two or three largest schools. Service providers have reported reluctance among youth to express their sexual orientation or gender nonconforming identity, as well as among school and human services providers to be accepting or supportive should any youth self-disclose.

OCSI leadership pursued a multidisciplinary effort to produce the improvements needed in the work force and service environments to provide appropriate services to LGBT youth. The OCSI leadership wanted to 1) move the discussion forward in a variety of ongoing training and discussion frameworks related to OCSI work force development efforts, 2) create new training materials relevant to local needs, 3) engage existing partners in work force development activities, and 4) develop new partnerships to promote this discussion. OCSI envisioned a social marketing strategy to reinforce systems of care values and principles relating to appropriate services for LGBT youth. Work force development and public training efforts, the starting point and main thrust of efforts, were scheduled and promoted throughout the region. Work force efforts focused on existing OCSI partner agencies (e.g., social services, public health, schools, mental health, juvenile justice) and were expanded to other organizations not affiliated with the system of care (e.g., faith-based organizations, law enforcement agencies, local postsecondary institutions).

LGBT service challenges were framed as professional service issues in work force development efforts and focused on recommended practices, identifying needs and threats to this population, and acknowledging that all youth deserve best professional practices. Training emphasized social factors that lead to isolation, exclusion, and rejection in the community, school, church, and family. Training also emphasized practical skills; creating an atmosphere of acceptance; genuineness and empathy for all youth in helping relationships; bullying and victimization; suicide interventions; identification of anxiety and mood difficulties; and appropriate services and supports in schools, juvenile detention, and faith-based organizations. Family support and training were covered with appropriate audiences. Law enforcement and corrections professionals were presented with a needs-based approach to training and the obligations of professionals to meet those needs without judgment or bias.

Parents and caregivers have discussed appropriate services and responses to the population of focus from the perspective of the needs of both youth and family. The system of care has implemented strategies to increase cultural responsiveness, including training for 1) all social services agencies, with most staff completing training; 2) approximately 475 of the estimated 650 school teachers, school social workers, and paraprofessionals in the region; 3) mental health professionals; 4) law enforcement and corrections professionals; and 5) faith-based organizations. Training topics have been well received by the more than 135 attendees at these faith-based events in the region. In addition, LGBT-related news, professional articles, and training events outside the region are regularly promoted, and LGBT youth and allies have been invited into regional governance activities.

The system of care has identified six key lessons learned from this work:

1. When presented with a clear summary of service barriers, life difficulties, and risk factors for LGBT youth and young adults, people are genuinely concerned about the need for appropriate services and supports for this population.

2. When appropriate services and supports are presented as a professional obligation, human services providers, law enforcement and corrections professionals, and school staff members are genuinely interested in offering those services and supports to youth and families.

3. Faith-based organizations are almost universally interested in providing compassionate services to families and youth to support them through the sometimes difficult passages of life with an LGBT youth. Many of these professionals see this as an issue important to address in keeping families together; keeping children healthy; and reducing the risks of mental and emotional difficulty, suicide, and running away.

4. After receiving training about this topic, many professionals and individuals express a desire for further training and seek that training independently.

5. Agencies and organizations outside the service area also will seek training.

6. Training resources need to be adapted to make them appropriate for regional audiences. Helpful information can be gleaned from a variety of resources, including SAMHSA, Lambda Legal Services; Gay, Lesbian and Straight Education Network; and others.

In the 2 years since launching the LGBT training and social marketing approach, more than 750 professionals from various service sectors have completed some level of training, and the training materials have been presented in numerous statewide and national forums. Two gay–straight alliance groups have opened in local schools. Templates to guide appropriate services for LGBT youth for use in service planning, clinical supervision, and case staffing are under development for use by all participating agencies to embed appropriate service values and practices into these processes. Preservice training conducted on these topics by several regional agencies has been proposed for all newly hired mental health providers and law enforcement professionals.

CONCLUSION

CLC is a journey, requiring a lifelong commitment to learning and personal growth to become more responsive to the cultural and linguistic identities and needs of youth and families. Individuals, organizations, and communities can use strategies and perspectives identified throughout this book to embed CLC throughout their policies, practices, services, and supports. The application of CLC principles in the delivery of culturally and linguistically competent services and supports in systems of care will acknowledge and enhance the dignity, worth, and well-being of LGBT youth and their families, resulting in more positive experiences and clinical, emotional, and behavioral outcomes resulting from the important work of professionals in youth-serving systems.

3

Conducting Cultural and Linguistic Competence Self-Assessment

TAWARA D. GOODE AND SYLVIA K. FISHER

Individual and organizational assessments are key strategies for moving cultural and linguistic competence (CLC) forward in systems of care. The information gathered from a CLC self-assessment can inform strategic planning and decision making relative to service delivery and can help individuals gain personal insight about their commitment and capacity to serve diverse cultural groups. A number of tools and resources to assess individual as well as organizational CLC are available. Self-assessment tools provide an opportunity for organizations to take a critical look at their vision, mission, goals, policies, procedures, governance structure, and service delivery mechanisms to determine strengths and areas that require enhancement to advance and sustain CLC (Goode, Trivedi, & Jones, 2010).

Although there are numerous instruments, tools, and checklists designed to assess CLC, few include items that address lesbian, gay, bisexual, and transgender (LGBT) populations, and even fewer focus on LGBT youth. Moreover, those tools designed specifically for LGBT populations tend to address "gay identity and culture," but typically do not include race, ethnicity, language, socioeconomic status, and other cultural factors that influence within-group diversity. The practice and research literature has not kept pace to address the clear and compelling need to integrate such assessment and measures into the delivery of services and supports for LGBT youth and their families. The form at the end of this chapter provides an example of a checklist for staff of child/youth-serving organizations that integrates CLC to address the needs of LGBT youth and their families.

There are many lessons learned in conducting CLC self-assessment processes that are applicable to organizations committed to serving LGBT youth and their families. An essential CLC element is the capacity to engage in self-assessment at both the organizational and individual levels (Cross, Bazron, Dennis,

& Isaacs, 1989). Organizational self-assessment is a necessary, effective, and systematic way to plan for and incorporate CLC (Goode, 2010; Goode, Jones, et al., 2010; National Center for Cultural Competence [NCCC], 2006). Self-assessment can benefit service providers by heightening awareness; influencing attitudes toward practice and the provision of services and supports; and motivating the development of knowledge, skills, and core competencies (NCCC, 2002).

Equally important, self-assessment can serve as a catalyst to address the social inequities that contribute to disparities in the provision of services and supports to culturally and linguistically diverse populations, including LGBT youth. Self-assessment can help organizations achieve a number of positive outcomes, such as gauging the extent to which they are effectively addressing the preferences, interests, and needs of diverse populations and communities; establishing partnerships that will meaningfully involve diverse populations, communities, and constituency groups; and improving access to, utilization of, and satisfaction with services and supports in youth-serving systems. Implementing such a self-assessment process that includes and/or focuses on LGBT youth and their families can greatly benefit systems of care, organizations, and agencies seeking to provide culturally and linguistically competent services and supports to this population.

Self-assessment at the individual level provides a structured process to examine areas of awareness, knowledge, and skills related to CLC. Self-assessment enables service providers to engage in self-reflection and probe their own cultural values and belief systems to see how these may contribute to disparate care and/or the provision of related services and supports (Goode, Haywood, Wells, & Rhee, 2009). Bias, stereotyping, and discrimination against individuals who self-identify as LGBT, at a conscious or unconscious level, continue to plague many sectors within our society, including those organizations that serve children, youth, and their families. Self-assessment can pinpoint such attitudes which, in turn, can lead to intentional behavior change, ultimately improving services and supports for this marginalized population of children and youth.

Clearly articulated values and principles should guide and underpin the entire self-assessment process, including being strengths based; promoting a safe, nonjudgmental environment for all participants; being inclusive; and using results to enhance capacity (Goode, Jones, & Mason, 2002). A CLC self-assessment should address the values, attitudes, behaviors, policies, structures, and practices of an organization, including but not limited to those of its board, staff, consultants, contractors, advisory groups, and volunteers (Goode, 2010). The process should also elicit the experiences and opinions of the youth, families, and communities served. Self-assessment can involve the administration of a formal instrument or tool. It can also involve conducting focus groups and structured interviews; an analysis of relevant community, regional, state, territorial, tribal, and organizational demographic data; and a critical review of the organization's

---

Box 3.1.   Phases for Conducting a Cultural and Linguistic Competence Organizational Self-Assessment of LGBT Capacity

1. *Establish a structure to guide the work.* Assemble a work group responsible for coordinating the organizational self-assessment of LGBT capacity. The group can serve as the primary entity to plan, implement, and provide oversight to the process. The group should be inclusive and have representation from all levels of an organization, including youth and families. It is essential that the group include youth who self-identify as LGBT and key allies within the LGBT community.
2. *Create a shared vision and shared ownership.* Convene groups to define cultural competence, linguistic competence, and their relevance to serving LGBT children, youth, and their families. Explore the rationale, value, and meaning of these concepts and issues for your organization. Groups may meet face-to-face or via teleconference and web conference. Ensure broad participation and a diversity of perspectives about what it will take to serve LGBT children, youth, and their families effectively and in a manner that is respectful of their multiple cultural identities.
3. *Collect, analyze, and disseminate data.* Many data sources can be tapped for the self-assessment process, such as focus groups, interviews, and state and local data sets on homeless dropout rates, out-of-home placements, bullying, and health and mental health status of LGBT children and youth. The system of care national evaluation also now asks questions about the gender identity and sexual orientation of youth (and children) accessing services and supports. Carefully review and analyze these data. Use findings to create a comprehensive report that can be adapted for dissemination to diverse audiences and constituents.
4. *Develop and implement a plan of action.* Create a plan of action using the results of the organizational self-assessment. Identify priorities. Determine the strategies, activities, partners, resources, timetables, and responsible parties to achieve desired goals of improving services and supports for LGBT youth and their families. Establish benchmarks to monitor and assess progress throughout the implementation of your plan and on a regular basis after implementation.

Adapted with permission from the author and the National Center for Cultural Competence, from "A Four-Phase Approach to Self-Assessment" in *A Guide for Using the Cultural and Linguistic Competence Family Organization Assessment Instrument,* Goode, T.D. (2010). National Center for Cultural Competence, Georgetown University Center for Child & Human Development.

---

values, mission, policies, procedures, practices, budget, research portfolio, web site, publications/print documents, and multimedia resources.

The process of self-assessment is just as important as the associated outcomes. There is no one method for conducting organizational self-assessment. The National Center for Cultural Competence has found the four steps that are presented in Box 3.1 to be useful based on years of experience in planning and conducting self-assessment processes for child and youth-serving systems and agencies (Goode et al., 2002). This four-step process has been modified to integrate LGBT identity, culture, and language. Flexibility is encouraged, and the process should be adapted to the unique considerations of your organization. Box 3.1 also includes key recommendations to assist systems of care in conducting CLC self-assessment.

CULTURAL AND LINGUISTIC COMPETENCE ORGANIZATIONAL SELF-ASSESSMENT: LESSONS LEARNED FROM THE NATIONAL CENTER FOR CULTURAL COMPETENCE

- Ensure a safe and respectful environment for work group members to share their thoughts, perspectives, and feelings (e.g., about sexual orientation, gender identity or expression, or stigma).

- Let the group "be" before it "does." All groups go through a process of "storming, forming, and norming." Ensure that the "storming" phase is neither harmful to individual group members nor to the group process (Tuckman, 1965).

- Attend to members' cultural practices, different experiences, and preferences for getting work done.

- Reach agreement on approaches for communication, conflict resolution, and decision making to help the group do its work.

- Attend to and address issues of language. This includes, but is not limited to, 1) literacy and language preferences and needs of all group members; 2) appropriate and preferred terms for the continuum of experiences and multiple cultural identities under the umbrella of LGBT, including the use of self-identified gender pronouns and preferred proper names; and 3) culturally defined colloquialisms, including language associated with "youth LGBT culture."

- Acknowledge and address issues associated with power (i.e., historical, perceived, actual) among and between group members.

In conclusion, some may view conducting a CLC organizational self-assessment as a challenging undertaking. Integrating LGBT capacity in such an assessment process may be seen as even more challenging. This chapter provides guidance, tools, and lessons learned on how to approach this type of assessment process within systems of care and other child/youth-serving organizations. When fully implemented, this integrated approach to self-assessment has the potential to substantially improve outcomes for LGBT children, youth, and their families, and to enhance the capacity of systems that deliver services and supports to this population.

PROMOTING CULTURAL DIVERSITY AND CULTURAL AND LINGUISTIC COMPETENCY

Self-Assessment Checklist for Personnel Providing
Services and Supports to LGBTQ[1] Youth and Their Families

RATING SCALE: Please select **A, B,** or **C** for each item listed below:

A = I do this *frequently*, or the statement applies to me to a *great degree*.

B = I do this *occasionally*, or statement applies to me to a *moderate degree*.

C = I do this *rarely* or *never*, or statement applies to me to a *minimal degree* or *not at all*.

PHYSICAL ENVIRONMENT, MATERIALS, AND RESOURCES

1. I display pictures, posters and other materials that are inclusive of LGBTQ youth and their families served by my program/agency. ☐ A ☐ B ☐ C

2. I ensure that LGBTQ youth and families across diverse racial, ethnic, and cultural groups:

   - have access to magazines, brochures, and other printed materials that are of interest to them. ☐ A ☐ B ☐ C

   - are reflected in media resources (e.g., videos, films, CDs, DVDS, Websites) for health and behavioral health prevention, treatment, or other interventions. ☐ A ☐ B ☐ C

3. I ensure that printed/multimedia resources (e.g., photos, posters, magazines, brochures, videos, films, CDs, Websites) are free of biased and negative content, language, or images about people who are LGBTQ. ☐ A ☐ B ☐ C

4. I screen books, movies, and other media resources for negative stereotypes about LGBTQ persons before sharing them with youth and their parents/families served by my program/agency. ☐ A ☐ B ☐ C

COMMUNICATION PRACTICES

5. I attempt to learn and use key words and terms that reflect 'youth culture' or LGBTQ youth culture, so that I communicate more effectively with youth during assessment, treatment, or other interventions. ☐ A ☐ B ☐ C

6. I understand and respect that some youth may:

   - choose not to identify as LGBT or prefer to use other terms to identify themselves. ☐ A ☐ B ☐ C

   - abandon use of all terms associated with sexual orientation/ gender identity or expression so as to remain "label-free." ☐ A ☐ B ☐ C

---

[1]L=Lesbian; G=Gay; B=Bisexual; T=Transgender; Q=Questioning

[2]Sexual orientation and gender identity or expression are not synonymous. As used in this checklist, "sexual orientation/gender identity or expression" means and/or.

Adapted from Goode, T.D. (2009). *Promoting Cultural Diversity and Cultural Competency: Self-Assessment Checklist for Personnel Providing Behavioral Health Services and Supports to Children, Youth and Their Families.* Washington, DC: National Center for Cultural Competence (NCCC), Georgetown University Center for Child and Human Development (GUCCHD). © 2009 NCCC GUCCHD.

Reprinted with permission in Tawara D. Goode, M.A. and Sylvia K. Fisher, Ph.D. (2012). *Self-Assessment Checklist for Personnel Providing Services and Supports to LGBTQ Youth and Their Families* © 2012 NCCC GUCCHD.

In *Improving Emotional and Behavioral Outcomes for LGBT Youth: A Guide for Professionals* by Sylvia K. Fisher, Jeffrey M. Poirier, & Gary M. Blau (2012, Paul H. Brookes Publishing Co.).

(continued)

Communication Practices   (*continued*)

7. I understand and apply the principles and practices of linguistic competence as they relate to LGBTQ populations within my program/agency, including the use of:
   - preferred gender pronoun(s). ☐ A ☐ B ☐ C
   - preferred proper names. ☐ A ☐ B ☐ C
   - terms that reflect self-identity about sexual orientation/ gender identity.[2] ☐ A ☐ B ☐ C

8. I advocate for the use of linguistically appropriate terminology for LGBTQ populations within:
   - my program/agency. ☐ A ☐ B ☐ C
   - systems that serve children, youth, and their families. ☐ A ☐ B ☐ C
   - professional and community organizations with which I am associated. ☐ A ☐ B ☐ C

VALUES AND ATTITUDES

9. I avoid imposing values that may conflict or be inconsistent with those of LGBTQ youth cultures or groups. ☐ A ☐ B ☐ C

10. In group therapy or treatment situations, I discourage the use of "hate speech" or slurs about sexual orientation/gender identity or expression by helping youth to understand that certain words can hurt others. ☐ A ☐ B ☐ C

11. I intervene appropriately when I observe others (i.e., staff, parents, family members, children, and youth) within my program/agency behave or speak about sexual orientation/ gender identity or expression in ways that are insensitive, biased, or prejudiced. ☐ A ☐ B ☐ C

12. I understand and accept that family may be defined differently by LGBTQ youth (e.g., extended family members, families of choice, friends, partners, fictive kin, godparents). ☐ A ☐ B ☐ C

13. I accept that LGBTQ youth, parents/family members may not always agree about who will make decisions about services and supports for the youth. ☐ A ☐ B ☐ C

14. I recognize that LGBT identity has different connotations (negative, neutral, positive) within different racial, ethnic, and cultural groups. ☐ A ☐ B ☐ C

15. I accept that culture heavily influences responses by family members and others to youth who are LGBTQ, and to the provision of their care, treatment, services, and supports. ☐ A ☐ B ☐ C

Adapted from Goode, T.D. (2009). *Promoting Cultural Diversity and Cultural Competency: Self-Assessment Checklist for Personnel Providing Behavioral Health Services and Supports to Children, Youth and Their Families.* Washington, DC: National Center for Cultural Competence (NCCC), Georgetown University Center for Child and Human Development (GUCCHD). © 2009 NCCC GUCCHD.

Reprinted with permission in Tawara D. Goode, M.A. and Sylvia K. Fisher, Ph.D. (2012). *Self-Assessment Checklist for Personnel Providing Services and Supports to LGBTQ Youth and Their Families* © 2012 NCCC GUCCHD.

In *Improving Emotional and Behavioral Outcomes for LGBT Youth: A Guide for Professionals* by Sylvia K. Fisher, Jeffrey M. Poirier, & Gary M. Blau (2012, Paul H. Brookes Publishing Co.).

Values and Attitudes   (*continued*)

16. I understand and respect that LBGTQ youth may conceal their sexual orientation/gender identity or expression within their own racial, ethnic, or cultural group.   ☐ A ☐ B ☐ C

17. I accept and respect that LGBTQ youth may not express their gender according to culturally-defined societal expectations.   ☐ A ☐ B ☐ C

18. I understand that age and life cycle factors, including identity development, must be considered when interacting with LGBTQ youth and their families.   ☐ A ☐ B ☐ C

19. I recognize that the meaning or value of health and behavioral health prevention, intervention, and treatment may vary greatly among LGBTQ youth and their families.   ☐ A ☐ B ☐ C

20. I understand that family members and others may believe that LGBT identity among youth is a mental illness, emotional disturbance/disability, or moral/character flaw.   ☐ A ☐ B ☐ C

21. I understand the impact of stigma associated with mental illness, behavioral health services, and help-seeking behavior among LGBTQ youth and their families within cultural communities (e.g., communities defined by race or ethnicity, religiosity or spirituality, tribal affiliation, and/or geographic locale).   ☐ A ☐ B ☐ C

22. I accept that religion, spirituality, and other beliefs may influence how families:
    - respond to a child or youth who identifies as LGBTQ.   ☐ A ☐ B ☐ C
    - view LGBTQ youth culture.   ☐ A ☐ B ☐ C
    - approach a child or youth who is LGBTQ.   ☐ A ☐ B ☐ C

23. I ensure that LGBTQ youth:
    - have appropriate access to events and activities conducted by my program/agency.   ☐ A ☐ B ☐ C
    - participate in training (i.e., panel presentations, workshops, seminars, and other forums).   ☐ A ☐ B ☐ C
    - participate on advisory boards, committees and task forces.   ☐ A ☐ B ☐ C

24. I ensure that members of "families of choice" identified by LGBTQ youth:
    - have appropriate access to events and activities conducted by my program/agency.   ☐ A ☐ B ☐ C
    - participate in training (i.e., panel presentations, workshops, seminars, and other forums).   ☐ A ☐ B ☐ C
    - participate on advisory boards, committees and task forces.   ☐ A ☐ B ☐ C

Adapted from Goode, T.D. (2009). *Promoting Cultural Diversity and Cultural Competency: Self-Assessment Checklist for Personnel Providing Behavioral Health Services and Supports to Children, Youth and Their Families*. Washington, DC: National Center for Cultural Competence (NCCC), Georgetown University Center for Child and Human Development (GUCCHD). © 2009 NCCC GUCCHD.

Reprinted with permission in Tawara D. Goode, M.A. and Sylvia K. Fisher, Ph.D. (2012). *Self-Assessment Checklist for Personnel Providing Services and Supports to LGBTQ Youth and Their Families* © 2012 NCCC GUCCHD.

In *Improving Emotional and Behavioral Outcomes for LGBT Youth: A Guide for Professionals* by Sylvia K. Fisher, Jeffrey M. Poirier, & Gary M. Blau (2012, Paul H. Brookes Publishing Co.).

Values and Attitudes (*continued*)

25. Before visiting or providing services and supports in the home setting, I seek information on acceptable behaviors, courtesies, customs, and expectations that are unique to:
    - LGBTQ youth and their families. ☐A ☐B ☐C
    - LGBT headed families. ☐A ☐B ☐C

26. I confer with LGBTQ youth, family members, key community informants, cultural brokers, and those who are knowledgeable about LGBTQ youth experience to:
    - create or adapt service delivery models. ☐A ☐B ☐C
    - implement services and supports. ☐A ☐B ☐C
    - evaluate services and supports. ☐A ☐B ☐C
    - plan community awareness, acceptance, and engagement initiatives. ☐A ☐B ☐C

27. I advocate for the periodic review of the mission, policies, and procedures of my program/agency to ensure the full inclusion of all individuals regardless of their sexual orientation/gender identity or expression. ☐A ☐B ☐C

28. I keep abreast of new developments in the research and practice literatures about appropriate interventions and approaches for working with LGBTQ youth and their families. ☐A ☐B ☐C

29. I accept that many evidence-based prevention and intervention approaches will require adaptation to be effective with LGBTQ youth and their families. ☐A ☐B ☐C

HOW TO USE THIS CHECKLIST

This checklist is intended to heighten the awareness and sensitivity of personnel to the importance of cultural diversity and cultural competence in human service settings. It provides concrete examples of the kinds of values and practices that foster such an environment. There is no answer key with correct responses. If, however, you frequently responded "C", you may consider advocating for values-based policies, and implementing practices that promote a diverse and culturally and linguistically competent service delivery system for LGBTQ children/youth and their families who require health, behavioral health, or other services and supports.

Adapted from Goode, T.D. (2009). *Promoting Cultural Diversity and Cultural Competency: Self-Assessment Checklist for Personnel Providing Behavioral Health Services and Supports to Children, Youth and Their Families.* Washington, DC: National Center for Cultural Competence (NCCC), Georgetown University Center for Child and Human Development (GUCCHD). © 2009 NCCC GUCCHD.

Reprinted with permission to Tawara D. Goode, M.A. and Sylvia K. Fisher, Ph.D. (2012). *Self-Assessment Checklist for Personnel Providing Services and Supports to LGBTQ Youth and Their Families* © 2012 NCCC GUCCHD.

In *Improving Emotional and Behavioral Outcomes for LGBT Youth: A Guide for Professionals* by Sylvia K. Fisher, Jeffrey M. Poirier, & Gary M. Blau (2012, Paul H. Brookes Publishing Co.).

4

Sexual Identity Development and Expression in LGB Youth

CORETTA JACQUELINE MALLERY AND JEFFREY M. POIRIER

This chapter reviews literature on *sexual identity development,* or the self-awareness, self-conception, and expression of sexual orientation. It is intended to provide a foundation for this book, with basic information about how youth may understand, identify, and express their sexual orientation and related experiences. This information is valuable for providers and other professionals so they can work to effectively address stigma and support lesbian, gay, and bisexual (LGB) youth and their families. System of care community members can apply this information by first understanding why some youth differ from others in their sexual identity development and, second, by equipping those who work with youth with information to help youth understand and positively develop their sexual identity. Finally, providers can share this information with families to describe the experiences that youth may be grappling with so that families can support youth as well. This chapter provides an overview of key information related to sexual identity development and expression, including several models of identity development. This chapter does not address all facets of the sexual identity development literature, and it does not address gender identity development (which Chapter 5 examines).

IMPORTANT CONSIDERATIONS

Sexual orientation can be defined as an "enduring pattern of emotional, romantic, and/or sexual attractions" to others (American Psychological Association [APA], 2008, para. 2). Youth may not necessarily express their sexual orientation in their behaviors or relationships (e.g., they may not be sexually active or dating, or they may engage in sexual behavior that does not align with their orientation). Moreover, sexual behavior does not necessarily define a person's sexual orientation. It is important to remember that each youth's sexual identity development is a unique, individual experience.

Research has not found any definitive evidence about the causes of sexual orientation such as genetic, hormonal, developmental, social, and cultural influences (APA, 2008). We choose *how* to express our sexual orientation, but we are likely biologically predisposed to our sexual orientation. Although social factors do not likely cause sexual orientation, they can either foster or inhibit expression of this predisposition. One theory (*interactional theory of homosexual identity development*) proposes that sexual orientation develops through the intersection of biological, psychological, and social factors. Inhibiting sexual orientation development or expression does not change one's sexuality, but constraining social and environmental factors can make the process of identity development more difficult to navigate (Ryan & Futterman, 1998). Furthermore, negative childhood experiences such as neglectful parenting and sexual abuse do not affect sexual orientation (Ryan & Futterman, 1998).

Research shows that sexual identity can be fluid and that even if individuals identify as lesbian, gay, or heterosexual, they can have other sexual/emotional attractions that do not necessarily fit their expressed sexual identity (Diamond, 2006; Ryan & Futterman, 1998). Youth may experience same-sex behaviors while having a heterosexual identity, whereas youth with an LGB identity may have limited or no sexual experience. Human sexuality is a spectrum that ranges from attraction to solely the opposite sex to attraction to solely the same sex (Kinsey, Pomeroy, & Martin, 1948; Kinsey, Pomeroy, Martin, & Gebbard, 1953) and includes emotional and social aspects (Klein, Sepekoff, & Wolf, 1985). It is important to note that research on sexual identity development has been limited by methodological issues, such as an underrepresentation of particular ethnic groups, youth, women, and individuals who are bisexual (Diamond, 2006).

SEXUAL IDENTITY DEVELOPMENT MODELS

Theorists have proposed multiple models to describe sexual identity development. This chapter introduces multiple models because identity development is an individual process and one may resonate more with a particular youth's journey of sexual identity development than another. This section briefly describes several stage and life-span models.

Stage Models

Early models focused primarily on lesbian and gay development, which some critics argue are more applicable to gay men. The early models, influenced by linear human development models (e.g., Erik Ericson's model of psychosocial development), are organized around stages, meaning that development is seen as occurring linearly over time. These models all share an approach that emphasizes a proposed sequence of events that results in a lesbian or gay identity. Although these models have been criticized and may have limitations, they can also be very useful tools to understand sexual identity development in youth. Even though some models refer to identity confusion, this should not be construed as suggesting that LGB identity is inauthentic. Youth may feel uncertain about their identity for a number of reasons, including a lack of positive opportunities to understand LGB identity.

The first lesbian and gay identity development model in the late 1970s was a foundation for many subsequent stage models showing the development of a healthy lesbian and gay identity (Cass, 1979). It comprises six stages that are commonly referred to when discussing lesbian and gay identity development (it did not account for bisexual identity). These include 1) beginning to consider having same-sex attractions (*identity confusion*), 2) tentatively committing to a lesbian or gay identity (*identity comparison*), 3) beginning to form friendships and connections with the lesbian/gay community (*identity tolerance*), 4) integrating lesbian/gay identity into one's life and becoming part of the community (*identity acceptance*), 5) immersing oneself in LGB culture (*identity pride*), and 6) integrating one's public and private selves so that lesbian or gay orientation becomes part of one's identity (*identity synthesis*).

An alternative four-stage model that emphasized the social context in which a youth develops emerged in the late 1980s (Troiden, 1988, 1989). Although this is a stage model, it is not necessarily linear, and development may not occur in sequential order. This model is currently considered one of the primary stage models of lesbian and gay identity development. The Troiden stages include when 1) children notice feeling "different," typically occurring before puberty (*sensitization*); 2) adolescents begin to have sexual thoughts and possible arousal toward others of the same sex, typically after puberty (*identity confusion*); 3) youth self-identify and begin coming out to a select few trusted others, typically during mid-to-late adolescence (*identity assumption*); and 4) sexual identity is incorporated throughout multiple contexts of one's life, typically in adulthood (*commitment*).

A third model, similar to Cass's model, has six stages and a greater focus on developmental tasks and milestones (Coleman, 1987). First, youth may deny and repress any feelings of being lesbian or gay and may have internalized heterosexist attitudes/feelings, which can lead to negative feelings toward themselves (*pre-coming out*). Next, youth may disclose their sexual identity to others (*coming out*) and then experiment in social and sexual relationships (*exploration*). This exploration is normative in adolescent development; however, it is important to consider that this may occur later than adolescence for some individuals. Finally, individuals enter a stage when they are ready to begin a committed relationship (*integration*).

Life-Span Models

As previously stated, sexual orientation is fluid and develops across the life span within a sociocultural context. Many scholars have questioned the stage models of sexual identity development because these models are predicated on the assumption that sexual identity development occurs in a predetermined order. These models may minimize the importance of individual differences such as personality, race, gender, socioeconomic status, culture, family, and religion that can significantly influence sexual identity development. Individuals may choose to express their sexual identity to different groups of people at different stages in life; thus, it is a constant cycle of negotiating and renegotiating identity. Hence some have proposed a life-span approach to identity development with six interactive processes (D'Augelli, 2006). These processes are not necessarily linear and may happen repeatedly in multiple contexts.

One life-span model proposes six steps. These steps include when individuals 1) realize they are not heterosexual and share this realization with trusted others; 2) develop a personal LGB identity within a social context with individuals who support this identity; 3) develop a social LGB identity by forming a network of supportive family and friends who know and affirm their LGB identity, including others with whom individuals feel safe disclosing their LGB status; 4) renegotiate relationships with family members as a member of the LGB community (i.e., become an LGB offspring); 5) experience physical and emotional LGB relationships; and 6) become involved in social advocacy and become more actively part of LGBT communities. These processes may be navigated and renegotiated across the life span in varying order; for example, some individuals may negotiate most of the steps before coming out to family.

Some theorists argue that the previously described models were developed for men and did not account for the experiences of lesbian or bisexual individuals. Partly in response to this, a continuous model of lesbian development that incorporates attitudes from self, among other considerations, has been proposed (McCarn & Fassinger, 1996). In addition, although bisexuality is included in other models, one model has been proposed that is specific to bisexual development (Weinberg, Williams, & Pryor, 1994). This model similarly begins with an initial *confusion stage,* or feeling anxiety or confusion about one's sexual identity. The second stage involves adopting the bisexual label, and the third stage involves committing to the label and settling into the bisexual identity. The fourth stage involves continued uncertainty and doubt about identity, which may be unique to being bisexual, because other models typically end in a commitment to gay or lesbian identity. For example, a woman who identifies as bisexual may enter into a long-term committed relationship with another woman and, after a time, question her bisexual identity.

The process of identity development also involves negotiating multiple milestones. One study of these milestones in LGB youth examined timing and ages at which they navigated 10 developmental milestones, including first aware-

Table 4.1. Timing of coming out events for Floyd and Stein study sample

	M Age (Standard Deviation)	Median Age	Age Range	n^a
Aware of same-gender attraction	10.39 (3.39)	11	3–18	72
Wondered about orientation	13.38 (3.68)	13	3–22	72
Sex with opposite gender	15.47 (2.96)	16	8–26	51
Considered self gay/lesbian/bisexual	16.14 (3.86)	16	3–24	72
Sex with same gender	16.31 (4.46)	17	4–25	63
Told someone	17.32 (2.45)	17	11–24	71
Told a parent	18.06 (2.69)	18	11–26	54
"Came out"	18.07 (2.90)	18	8–24	67
Same-gender serious relationship	18.48 (2.70)	18	13–25	58
Told other family member	18.72 (2.53)	18	11–25	47

[a]Number of participants who completed the milestone event.

From Floyd, F.J., & Stein, T.S. (2002). Sexual orientation identity formation among gay, lesbian, and bisexual youths: Multiple patterns of milestone experiences. *Journal of Research on Adolescence, 12*(2), 167–191. doi:10.1111/1532-7795.00030; reprinted by permission. Copyright © 2003, John Wiley and Sons.

ness of same-sex attraction, first sexual experiences with same-sex partners, self-identification as LGB, disclosure to someone other than a parent/caregiver, disclosure to mother, and disclosure to father (Floyd & Stein, 2002). Of 72 individuals ages 16–27 years who were interviewed as part of the study, all were aware of same-sex attractions and had disclosed to someone close to them, yet 7 had not yet had a same-sex sexual experience, and 18 (25%) had not come out to a parent. Although the order of events was typically consistent with the sequence in many stage models, many youth did not follow this same pattern. These results demonstrated the individual nature of the identity development process and challenged the linearity of some of the models. Table 4.1 provides more information about the coming out events and ages of occurrence.

This research also identified five different clusters of developmental paths linked to key supports (Floyd & Stein, 2002). The group with the latest path (i.e., who disclosed their LGB identity later) reported lower levels of satisfaction in life, lower connections to gay/lesbian social networks, and lower comfort in their sexuality. Conversely, the youth with early paths (i.e., who disclosed their LGB identity at younger ages) were the most comfortable with their sexuality. These results are not surprising because those with earlier trajectories have had more time to develop a sense of identity and supportive social networks. This research does not suggest, though, that youth with later trajectories will become adults without integrated sexual identities and fulfilling social networks; this may just happen later than youth with supports in place as adolescents.

THE COMING OUT EXPERIENCE

Coming out, or acknowledging and disclosing one's sexual orientation, is a life-long process. It is also an important developmental and psychological milestone for youth, indicating a commitment to LGB identity (APA, 2008; Clarke, Ellis, Peel, & Riggs, 2010). Individuals who are LGB also "come in" to themselves when they begin to self-identify as LGB and acknowledge to themselves these attractions. They also may choose to come out as LGB or share that they are questioning their sexual orientation with family, friends, classmates, colleagues, neighbors, members of their places of worship (e.g., religious leaders), and others in their community. The coming out experience may be especially concentrated in a particular period of an individual's life, such as during adolescence. As of the 1990s, research suggested that the average age of coming out was approximately 15 to 17 years old (Savin-Williams & Diamond, 2000), but this age may be decreasing. For example, children and youth in recent research came out as LGB, on average, at approximately 13 years of age (Ryan, 2009). Research also shows that youth typically disclose their same-sex attractions to peers first, before their families (Clarke et al., 2010). The coming out process does not end during adulthood, although it may become less intense. LGB youth will need to continually decide whether and how to share their LGB identity with others in different situations throughout their lives.

Bolstering Resilience

Earlier coming out experiences may affect how later coming out experiences occur, as well as how youth experience and interpret them. For example, positive early coming out experiences can be a source of resilience and smooth the process of future disclosure. Families, peers, and communities, including professionals in youth-serving systems, can be critical protective factors for youth during their identity development and expression. Affirming communities, continuity with cultural groups, and positive role models can also bolster the resilience of LGB youth as they come out. A supportive environment is important because adolescents may have internalized negative beliefs about LGB identity due to heterosexist attitudes of parents and caregivers, teachers, peers, and the media.

Supporting Parents and Caregivers

Parents and caregivers experience various emotions and thoughts when their child expresses a nonheterosexual orientation. For example, parents and caregivers may experience a process of learning about their child's LGB identity, communicating this with others, understanding and changing their inner perceptions, and eventually taking a stand about this revelation (Griffin, Wirth, & Wirth, 1986; Muller, 1987). These stages can include various behaviors and emotions. For example, the learning stage may include various emotional reactions, as well as denial, rejection, and acknowledgment of a child's LGB identity. Parents and caregivers may eventually move toward acceptance if this is not the case when their child first comes out. Some parents and caregivers may ultimately reach a level of comfort that enables them to address heterosexism, inform others about LGB identity, and come out as parents or caregivers of an LGB child or youth. Importantly, increased family acceptance can positively shape the outcomes of LGB youth, so it is critical for systems of care and professionals to fully support their families (Ryan, 2009).

Reducing Stigma

Chapters throughout this book reference the large and growing body of evidence demonstrating that family and peer rejection, stigma, and bias can contribute to emotional and behavioral health and other challenges. Youth may refrain from coming out because of concerns about their personal safety or other risks such as rejection, which some youth, regrettably, experience in varying degrees when they disclose their LGB identity. Some youth also experience stigma from various sources, including other groups associated with their cultural identity (e.g., ethnic cultural groups), youth-serving systems (e.g., schools, juvenile justice settings, residential care), and their larger communities. Experiences of rejection and stigma, which can change over time, can cause stress and anxiety, can exacerbate other mental health challenges youth may be experiencing, and can contribute to substance use and other negative outcomes. Hence it is important for systems of care to implement strategies and practices that decrease stigma, increase help-seeking behavior, and foster more positive experiences for LGB individuals including acceptance, if not celebration, of LGB identity. Some youth experience acceptance and affirmation—and the coming out process is an opportunity for youth to find comfort in their identity and connect with supportive adults and youth (Ryan, 2009).

Ethnic and Cultural Considerations

Currently, there is little research on the intersection of sexual identity development and ethnic development. One community-based study of Caucasian, African American, and Latino youth found no difference in the acceptance of sexual identity among the three groups (Rosario, Schrimshaw, & Hunter, 2004). There was, however, a difference in disclosure of sexual identity, with Caucasian, African American, and Latino youth being most to least open about disclosure, respectively. Recent research has found that ethnic and sexual identities develop concurrently, but are not necessarily related (Jamil, Harper, & Fernandez, 2009). Ethnic identity development is often a social development process shaped by awareness of one's ethnic and cultural background. This process is supported by peers, family, and the cultural environment. Although sexual identity development is often a more private process, it is likewise supported by peers, a youth's community, and information from the Internet.

RECOMMENDED PRACTICES

Although research on the benefits of LGB disclosure to peers and families is lacking, it is commonly assumed that expressing this identity is "a positive step" (Clarke et al., 2010, p. 164). An APA task force conducted a systematic review of literature on conversion therapy and found no evidence supporting the effectiveness of this technique, which can harm individuals by causing depression, distress, and increased internalized stigma (APA Task Force on Appropriate Therapeutic Responses to Sexual Orientation, 2009). Most of the nation's prominent, credible mental health and medical professional organizations oppose using conversion or reparative therapy to "change" an individual's sexual orientation. The APA recommends affirmative, culturally competent therapy with youth (and children) questioning their sexual identity or experiencing challenges related to their sexual identity development (APA Task Force on Appropriate Therapeutic Responses to Sexual Orientation, 2009; also see Chapter 9). Providers working with LGB youth or those questioning their sexual orientation can support positive identity development by using affirmative counseling techniques and providing a supportive organizational climate. Related strategies are shared throughout this book, and a full list of APA guidelines for working with LGB clients is available at http://www.apa.org/pi/lgbt/resources/guidelines.aspx.

Professionals in system of care and other communities can appropriately support and ease the coming out process for LGB youth (and children) by understanding the related experiences, challenges, and opportunities. Importantly, professionals should work to ensure delivery of the culturally and linguistically competent services and supports included throughout this book. Professionals should provide safe, confidential spaces for youth to come out as LGB or to discuss their questioning of their sexual orientation. Professionals should also proactively work to address issues related to stigma, bias, and rejection that LGB youth may experience (e.g., by using cultural and linguistic competence self-assessments to identify areas of need and provide information, professional development, and other supports to address these needs; see Chapter 3). Positive LGB role models can help address shame or stigma that LGB youth may experience. Furthermore, connection to supportive adults, whether LGB or not, during a youth's sexual identity development can facilitate expression of their feelings and identity to others.

In particular, professionals should work to support families of youth who come out as LGB or are questioning their sexual orientation. It is critical for professionals to be knowledgeable about LGB and LGB-affirming organizations in their communities that may offer family (and youth) opportunities for supportive engagement (e.g., Parents, Families and Friends of Lesbians and Gays, www.pflag.org). If a group does not exist, professionals should collaborate with system of care partners and allies to create one in a safe space and with an appropriate purpose. These groups should include focused outreach efforts to partners and allies to build awareness of them and encourage participation. It is also important to have family friendly information about LGB issues readily available and to provide this to parents and caregivers. Moreover, it is important for professionals to be familiar with LGB-affirming faith-based communities and to reach out to religious leaders of these groups, who can be partners in this work. LGB youth and their families may benefit significantly from the support of faith communities.

CONCLUSION

This chapter reviews different conceptions of sexual identity development and provides a foundation for this book by describing how youth may understand, identify, and express their sexual orientation and identity. The coming out process, which may be ongoing throughout life, is psychologically and developmentally significant and occurs when youth disclose their LGB identity. Systems of care should ensure that those working with youth can help them understand and positively develop their sexual identity and connect LGB youth to affirming resources and supports. Informed families, providers, and other constituencies in system of care communities can ease the complexities and challenges of LGB youth who are navigating their sexual identity development in social environments that are not always accepting or understanding. The information provided here can help guide professionals in systems of care and other communities that support the well-being of these youth so they achieve developmental milestones in a healthy manner and in a safe, supportive climate.

5

Transgender and Gender Nonconforming Children and Youth

Developing Culturally Competent Systems of Care

ARLENE ISTAR LEV AND LAURA ALIE

System of care communities provide a multitude of services and support for transgender and gender nonconforming children and youth; however, a comprehensive understanding of the complex service needs of these youth and their families is essential to ensuring that they receive appropriate, culturally informed, and linguistically competent services and support. This chapter provides substantive information for providers and others who are engaged in systems of care about this population of youth and offers recommendations to address the needs of these youth and their families.

Although the term *lesbian, gay, bisexual, and transgender* (LGBT; or *lesbian, gay, bisexual, transgender, queer, and questioning* [LGBTQ]) has increasingly become part of the social and political vernacular, the *T* (i.e., transgender) is often subsumed within larger discussions of sexual orientation and same-sex attraction. LGBTQ individuals have much in common with one another: Their social and political communities overlap, and their struggles for civil rights follow a similar trajectory. Gender identity and sexual orientation are different aspects of identity however, and gender identity struggles are different from those involving sexual orientation in substantial and consequential ways, especially when exploring the psychological issues that affect gender nonconforming children and youth. This chapter examines the unique issues that affect transgender and gender nonconforming, or gender "atypical," children and youth (i.e., children whose behavior, mannerisms, clothing choices, or choice of pronouns conflicts with societal expectations), with the goal of developing systemic and culturally sensitive approaches to their care.

HISTORICALLY EVOLVING
PERCEPTIONS OF CROSS-GENDER BEHAVIOR

Cross-gender behavior has been recognized throughout history, on all continents and within all nations and tribal communities (Bullough & Bullough, 1993; Roscoe, 1998). In many cultures, gender nonconforming behavior was viewed as a part of normative human diversity, although there is also evidence of cruelty and violence directed at people who deviated from expected gender norms. People who are now called *transgender* have been documented in native cultures worldwide, as well as in modern nation-states (Blackwood & Wiering, 1999; Feinberg, 1996). Despite the ubiquity of cross-gender expression, it has also remained relatively rare, representing a small but stable subset of the human family.

With the establishment of the modern psychomedical community in the 19th century, atypical sexual and gender behaviors became scrutinized by sexologists searching for etiologies and treatments (Dreger, A., 1998). Emerging views of the era, grounded in heterosexist assumptions, conflated sexual orientation and gender identity, assuming that people who were attracted to people of the same sex would "naturally" manifest a cross-gender identity (Hekma, 1994). Although same-sex sexual orientations have increasingly become more acceptable in the past 40 years, cross-gender expression has remained a pathologized identity.

Cross-gender expression is currently classified as a psychiatric disorder in both the psychiatric and medical nosologies (*Diagnostic and Statistical Manual of Mental Disorders,* 4th ed., text rev. [*DSM-IV-TR*]; American Psychiatric Association [APA], 2000a; World Health Organization, 2007). Within the past few decades, this view of cross-gender expression has been challenged by the burgeoning transgender community, which is battling to depathologize gender nonconforming identities (Denny, 2006; Lev, 2005; Winters, 2009). In recent years, they have been joined by professionals allied with their cause who have been equally committed to changing the perception of cross-gender identities and behaviors as an illness (Lev et al., 2010). In response to this advocacy, in 2011, the World Professional Association for Transgender Health (WPATH) updated its internationally recognized Standards of Care, stating that "Being transsexual, transgender, or gender nonconforming is a matter of diversity, not pathology" (WPATH, 2011, p. 4). Reminiscent of the struggle to depathologize homosexuality, atypical gender expression exists at an intersection where social justice struggles are competing with psychosexual medical theories, and in many ways, vulnerable children and youth are caught in the crossfire of these struggles (Lev, 2004).

DEFINING TERMS

Providing culturally and linguistically competent services to children and youth who are gender nonconforming requires greater understanding about the *T* in

LGBTQ. The term *transgender* generally includes a wide spectrum of nontraditional gender identities and expressions, whereas the term *transsexual* is most often used to describe a smaller subset of people who experience persistent distress and incongruence with their assigned sex and anatomical bodies (Lev, 2004) and may more accurately describe adult gender trajectories. Gender nonconforming identities can manifest early in life or first appear during adolescence or later adulthood. As a result of the extreme social pressure to conform to societally based gender expectations, many people do not give voice to their gender concerns until they are older. This pattern, however, may be changing as transgender issues are more represented and fully explored in the media, and possibilities for earlier gender actualization are increasingly available.

The term *trans* is commonly used to include transgender, transsexual, and gender nonconforming expression and may include those who identify as male-to-female transsexuals (MTFs/transsexual women) and female-to-male transsexuals (FTMs/transmen), male cross-dressers, androgynes, and those who identify as third-sex, or *genderqueer* (Lev, 2004; Lev & Sennott, 2012). Language, identity, and questions of inclusion continue to shift and evolve; they vary across culture, nation, community, and age cohorts as transgender people continue to define themselves, and communities emerge with their own unique description and inclusion criteria (Lev, 2006b). Genderqueer, for example, is an emerging self-identity descriptor increasingly used within the LGBTQ communities, representing an overlapping of gender expression and sexual orientation (Lev & Sennott, 2012). It is an especially common self-descriptor for youth who reject the simple binaries of both male/female identities and gay/straight dichotomies. As the transgender community grows and becomes more visible, increasing numbers of people are identifying outside a binary definition of gender (i.e., male or female) and feel they do not want to "cross over" to the other sex; rather, they identify as blending genders (e.g., androgynous, bigendered), or without any gender (Nestle, Wilchins, & Howell, 2002).

Sexual identity encompasses a complex matrix of components, including natal or biological sex, gender identity, gender role, and sexual orientation, which all function independently, despite overlapping and interacting with one another. *Gender identity* is distinct from biological sex and sexual orientation, as well as gender role expression. *Biological sex* refers to the physiological or anatomical body that is determined, or assigned, at birth, whereas gender identity reflects a core or inner sense of knowing oneself to be a "man" or a "woman," or a "boy" or a "girl." Gender identity commonly, but not definitively, conforms to the sex assigned at birth. If a child is born with a penis, the child becomes a "he" within the eyes of society and is expected to develop—and experience himself—as a boy. If that male child sees himself as a girl, is interested in girls' toys or clothes, or behaves in a more feminine manner, this is considered a gender identity or gender role incongruence. Although most children develop a gender identity that is congruent with their birth-assigned sex, many do not.

Some children are born without a clearly identified natal sex, described as *intersex*, and are assigned to either a male or female sex at birth; often they undergo surgery to appear as the sex to which they have been assigned. Surgical treatments, as well as arbitrary social assignments, are currently being challenged by many intersex activists (Dreger, A., 1998). Once children have been assigned a sex, they then experience the same set of social expectations as other children with that assigned sex. Children born with intersex conditions have been an invisible population, and their psychosocial and psychosexual needs have been poorly addressed (Lev, 2006a). People with intersex conditions may experience distress with their assigned sex, or they may feel that their assigned sex is the right designation for them. Some children with intersex conditions may present with atypical gender expressions and as they mature may seek services similar to those sought by transgender individuals.

Gender role is the socialized aspect of gender that affects appearance, behavior, and the manifestation of masculinity or femininity, as defined societally and culturally. Although gender role behavior and expectations have become increasingly flexible since the influence of feminist child-rearing practices, expectations for children, especially boys, still remain rigidly proscribed. Deviations from those behaviors can cause distress for individuals, their families, and those in their social environment. Gender *role* nonconformity may or may not signal gender *identity* incongruence and may or may not coexist with gender dysphoria. *Gender dysphoria* is broadly defined as discomfort or distress that is caused by a discrepancy between a person's experience of his or her gender identity and the sex to which he or she was assigned at birth (Knudson, De Cuypere, & Bockting, 2010; WPATH, 2011). It can also refer to an individual's distress at having to conform to binary gender role expectations. Some children and youth express gender nonconforming behaviors without any gender dysphoria, and others may experience gender dysphoria and still conform to social expectations regarding gender expression.

Sexual orientation describes a relational aspect of identity involving sexual and/or emotional attraction to either men or women, or both men and women (bisexual). It can also include attraction to a wide variety of sexual and gender expressions (pansexual), or having no sexual attraction (asexual). Assumptions about sexual orientation in children and youth are often based on their atypical gender expressions (i.e., boys who are interested in stereotypically girls' toys or games and girls who eschew traditionally feminine clothes are often assumed to be exhibiting early same-sex preferences). Emerging research suggests that many children who exhibit cross-gender behaviors and preferences do grow up to identify as gay, lesbian, or bisexual in high numbers (Drummond, Bradley, Peterson-Badali, & Zucker, 2008; Green, 1987; Zucker & Bradley, 1995). Indeed, many LGB adults retrospectively recall cross-gender experiences, behaviors, and feelings (Bailey & Zucker, 1995; Rottnek, 1999). Although gender identity and sexual orientation are two distinct aspects of identity, their early manifestations may be similar. This distinction between sexual orientation and gender identity is more difficult to discern with prepubescent and young adolescent children and youth, whose sexual orientation and gender identities are still forming. It is unclear exactly what gender nonconforming behavior means for young children, and it may not be until puberty when clear distinctions between sexual orientation, gender expression, and gender identity can be determined.

GENDER NONCONFORMING CHILDREN AND YOUTH: GENDER IDENTITY DEVELOPMENT

Gender identity, as described in the preceding section, is the sense of knowing oneself to be a "man" or "woman," or a "boy" or "girl," and is a core sense of identity. Presumably everyone has some concept of their gender identity, even if it is a negation of the available options (Ekins & King, 2006; Rachlin, Dhejne, & Brown, 2010). Although gender identity commonly aligns with natal sex, it is not an automatic or simple biological process that "naturally" unfolds. Certainly, biochemical and physiological processes influence sexual dimorphism, that is, the biological differences between males and females; however, these complex genetic and hormonal blueprints are affected by psychological and societal expectations that vary cross-culturally. These processes are mitigated in different ways for gender nonconforming children, and for youth in puberty who are dealing with gender dysphoria.

Early Childhood

All children are socialized by the cultures in which they live and are taught the gendered expectations of that society. Although there is greater freedom of expression in contemporary Western cultures, particularly for girls, gendered expectations remain powerful societal determinants. When children cross the acceptable lines of gendered play, or exhibit mannerisms, behaviors, and emotional displays associated with the "opposite" sex, questions are raised about both their sexual orientation and gender identity.

Theories of "normative" gender development (Kohlberg, 1966) describe how gender identity develops over time, and children experience developmental stages through which they come to know themselves as gendered beings. Children as young as 2 years of age can identify a person's sex by his or her gender presentation; by age 3, they can differentiate between males and females and begin to articulate whether they themselves are male or female (Kohlberg, 1966). Zucker and Bradley (1995) identified an affective component of gender acquisition, and Egan and Perry (2001) suggested that there are multiple facets of gender identity, including, for example, knowing that one belongs to a particular gender category, one's satisfaction with that category, pressure to conform to gender expectations, and the sense that one is like others in the same category. Full gender constancy—knowing that one's assigned sex is permanent and unchanging—is not a completed process until age 6 or 7 years old (Yunger, Carver, & Perry, 2004). Children then begin to align their behaviors and verbal expressions with those that they understand to be culturally approved for the gender with which they identify, seeking out same-sex role models for cues about how to act according to one's gender and socializing more with peers of the same sex. By preadolescence, beginning at approximately 9 or 10 years of age, children clearly understand social gender roles, can articulate how much they are permitted to explore cross-sex roles and behaviors, and understand social mores regarding gendered behavior. Perhaps most importantly for gender nonconforming youth, they can articulate how happy or disappointed they are with their gender assignment (Egan & Perry, 2001).

Children generally experience this developmental process without struggle when emerging gender identity is congruent with societal expectations. Children who express gender nonconformity or experience gender dysphoria, however, commonly feel societal and parental pressure to conform to "appropriate" gender roles and likely experience these developmental processes as negative (Yunger et al., 2004). Research reveals that preadolescents experience more distress in relation to the pressure they feel to conform to gender roles than they do regarding a self-perception that they are gender nonconforming (Egan & Perry, 2001). If the adults in a child's life invalidate his or her internal sense of gender, this difficulty can intensify (Ehrensaft, 2011).

Adolescence

Youth naturally begin exploring their sexuality and gender during adolescence. For transgender youth, this can be a difficult time. There may be a sense of newfound urgency as a child's body continues to develop characteristics associated with a gender that does not feel like an adequate reflection of his or her internal sense of self (Drummond et al., 2008; Wallien & Cohen-Kettenis, 2008; Zucker & Bradley, 1995). A prepubescent transgender boy (assigned female), for example, may view pubescent adolescent boys with envy or admiration, either wishing for or believing that one day his shoulders will broaden, his arms will become muscular, and he will grow facial hair. The physical changes that mark the realization that this will not happen can be devastating for a child.

Parents are also challenged as it becomes increasingly obvious that their "gentle" son or "tomboy" daughter is expressing increasingly significant atypical gender characteristics (Krieger, 2011). In addition to the pressure felt by unwanted physical changes and parental anxiety, adolescence is often a time when social pressures increase dramatically for gender nonconforming youth. School, the basis for most social interactions during this age, is often the first place where a gender nonconforming child experiences social conflict, including bullying or physical violence (D'Augelli, Grossman, & Starks, 2006). Sometimes youth begin to socially withdraw to manage increasing anxiety or depression.

The more one strays from socially proscribed gender norms at school during this stage, the more likely one is to be victimized or abused at school (Grossman, D'Augelli, Howell, & Hubbard, 2005). Ninety-six percent of gender nonconforming youth experience physical harassment, and 83% report being verbally harassed (Sausa, 2005). Perhaps largely as a result of this victimization, trans youth are at risk for dropping out of school, becoming socially isolated, or turning to substances to cope (Grossman & D'Augelli, 2006). Emerging research regarding male-to-female transgender youth reveals that gender-related abuse strongly influences psychological health, increasing depression and suicidality (Nuttbrock et al., 2010). Professionals are in agreement about the seriousness of these challenges; there is, however, considerable disagreement about how to manage them.

TREATMENT OF GENDER DYSPHORIA IN CHILDREN AND YOUTH: EMERGING PARADIGMS

Cross-gender expression in both adults and children has been viewed as a manifestation of a mental illness within the modern psychiatric field. Adults struggling with pervasive and persistent gender dysphoria have been able to find relief through medical and social transitions since the mid-1960s (Denny, 2004). This psycho-medical model requires a mental health diagnosis as a prerequisite for receiving medical treatment (Lev, 2009). Diagnoses for transsexualism are outlined in the *International Classification of Diseases* (WHO, 2007) and the gender identity disorders (GID) are outlined in the *Diagnostic and Statistical Manual of Mental Disorders,* initially introduced in the *DSM-III.* The current *DSM-IV-TR* criteria for children include a "strong and persistent cross-gender identification" (APA, 2000a, p. 581), marked by preferences for play, clothing, and peers, as well as either a discomfort with one's sex or a "sense of inappropriateness in the gender role" (APA, 2000a, p. 581) that has been assigned.

There is considerable controversy over this current diagnosis of GID (Lev, 2005; Lev et al., 2010; Winters, 2009), with one major point of dissension being the classification of an identity as a psychiatric disorder. The *DSM-V,* due to be released in 2013, will likely focus less on a cross-gender "identification"—which may simply be the divergence from cultural and socially proscribed gender norms—and center the diagnosis more explicitly on gender dysphoria or gender incongruence (APA, 2010). The *DSM* criteria have not yet been determined at the time of this writing, but the focus will likely include "a marked incongruence between one's experienced/expressed gender and assigned gender" that is "associated with clinically significant distress or impairment in social, occupational, or other important areas of functioning" (APA, 2010). This change will allow gender nonconforming individuals who are experiencing distress related to their gender incongruence to receive appropriate services while minimizing psychological stigma, diagnosis, and treatment of those whose gender nonconformity may be atypical, but does not cause distress.

There are currently two distinct treatment models for working with gender nonconforming children and transgender youth (Hill, Menvielle, Sica, & Johnson, 2010). The first is based on assisting children in accepting their natal sex as their true gender based on the supposition that gender nonconformity emerges from parental influences, especially related to difficulties with attachment and proper gender role acquisition (Coates, 2008; Zucker & Bradley, 1995). Proponents of these theories represent different theoretical orientations ranging from psychoanalysis (Susan Coates) to psychodynamic and behaviorally based treatments (Kenneth Zucker and Susan Bradley), although they have much in common in terms of treatment strategies (Wallace & Russell, 2010). These treatments are all rooted in the idea that therapeutic intervention can eliminate cross-gender behavior and that eliminating these behaviors is in the best interest of children. The focus is on changing children's cross-gender behaviors and assisting them to develop more socially normative expressions on the basis of their assigned sex; these theories have sometimes been referred to as "reparative" therapies.

There are complex politics regarding the use of the term "reparative" therapy (Drescher, 2010)—a term commonly used to describe interventions purporting to change sexual orientation, not gender identity, hence the use of quotation marks. It is, however, undeniable that the focus of certain treatment strategies has been to "change," "fix," "cure," and "repair" what are perceived to be faulty gender expressions. As new models are developed grounded in acceptance of cross-gender behavior and promoting the nurturance of the child's authentic sexual and gender potentiality, these older treatment protocols have become highly scrutinized and increasingly discounted as appropriate interventions for these youth, as outlined later in this chapter.

The second model is an affirmative one (Pleak, 2009) that accepts the cross-gender identity as authentic and indicative of the child's emerging identity (Brill & Pepper, 2008; Ehrensaft, 2011; Krieger, 2011). This model is newly emerging and remains controversial, in part because of the limited research demonstrating successful outcomes. Zucker, a strong proponent of the first model, stated, "there is a large empirical black hole in the treatment literature for children with gender identity disorder (GID). As a result, the therapist must rely largely on clinical wisdom" (2008, p. 359). Clinical wisdom, without empirical evidence, is very much in the eye of the beholder, or as Zucker himself said, "one person's wisdom may be deemed ignorance by another" (2008, p. 359).

The position adopted in this chapter is that recommended practices are embedded in 1) nurturing the emerging gender identity of children and youth, regardless of whether it is typical or atypical; 2) developing protective strategies to support children and youth who are living in hostile environments; 3) supporting families and social institutions to become more gender flexible, so that gender nonconforming children are integrated within their families and communities; and 4) supporting those parents and institutions that are already advocating for their children, because they are often isolated and under public scrutiny. These emerging models contrast significantly with decades of interventions focused on eliminating cross-gender expression in young children and teens. This is consistent with current shifts in cultural and clinical beliefs that increasingly view multiple pathways to healthy gender identity and expression.

RECOMMENDED PRACTICES FOR WORKING WITH TRANSGENDER AND GENDER NONCONFORMING CHILDREN AND YOUTH

Treatment for children and youth who are expressing nonconventional gender identities and expressions must be based in a holistic and systemic modality. Children and youth depend on family and community, even if they often assert their desire for increasing independence. Gender nonconforming children and youth are especially vulnerable to violence and mistreatment, increasing the need for strong community safety nets and familial advocacy and support (Krieger, 2011; Stone Fish & Harvey, 2005).

Potential outcomes vary for gender nonconforming children (Lev, 2004). Gender nonconformity can, first of all, shift and change, increase or disappear with increasing age. Some gender nonconforming children will begin to express their gender in more conventional ways, as part of their natural development as well as in response to social pressure. Other children will persist in gender nonconforming behavior and desires and might experience increasing discomfort as they enter puberty. For children expressing gender dysphoria at young ages, research has indicated that approximately 25% of these children will continue to experience gender dysphoria into adulthood (Wallien & Cohen-Kettenis, 2008).

Research has also long indicated that the most common outcome for gender nonconforming children may be a gay, lesbian, or bisexual identity (Green, 1987; Zucker & Bradley, 1995; Zuger, 1984). This is supported by retrospective studies of adult gay men and women reviewing their own childhoods (Bailey & Zucker, 1995; Rottnek, 1999). It is, however, important to remember that the majority of these studies were completed long before the newly emerging transgender identity movement; indeed, they were completed during the then-exploding lesbian and gay liberation movement. Transsexuality was a rare public occurrence 20–30 years ago, and the word *transgender* had yet to be coined. The idea of "changing sex" would have been unknown to most children, whereas today transgender possibilities are part of the public discourse. One can watch television shows and explore the Internet and easily find examples of transgender experience. This means it is not (quite) as shocking for parents, and it is within the consciousness of children that they can "change sex." It is also worth noting that many trans people retrospectively remember "always feeling this way" and note with envy the choices available to young children today. There are currently no evaluation tools to discern the difference between children who are likely to grow up to be gay and those who are going to grow up trans; for that matter, there is no way to know how gender nonconforming behavior will evolve.

For some children, gender nonconformity will be expressed as gender dysphoria, a discomfort with their assigned gender that will increase during puberty. Some evidence suggests that extreme gender nonconformity in childhood will lead to persistent gender dysphoria in adolescence (Wallien & Cohen-Kettenis, 2008; WPATH, 2011). There is no way to discern outcomes for specific children; accordingly, recommended practices assume that all children, regardless of the extent of their nonconformity or dysphoria, be treated with respect for their chosen gender presentation (Ehrensaft, 2011). The Standards of Care (SOC), published by WPATH, outline guidelines for medical and psychological professionals working with transsexual, transgender, and gender nonconforming individuals, including children and youth (WPATH, 2011). In one study, professionals identified that the most important needs for gender-variant children and youth are 1) to be accepted and supported; 2) to be heard, respected, and loved; 3) to have professional support; 4) to be allowed to express their gender; 5) to feel safe and protected; 6) to be treated and live normally; 7) to have peer contact; 8) to have school support; and 9) to have access to puberty-delaying hormones (Riley, Sitharthan, Clemson, & Diamond, 2011). These values can help guide professionals in developing treatment plans adapted to the individual service needs of each child or adolescent.

Children

Gender nonconformity in very young children is often noticeable, but viewed as "cute." When little boys wear their mother's high heels or little girls place their baseball cap backwards and want to help Daddy fix the car, most modern parents find the behavior within acceptable limits and perhaps even congratulate themselves for raising such gender-neutral children. However, as children begin to mature, if these behaviors and actions increase (or do not decrease), many parents become anxious, sometimes anxious enough to seek out therapeutic services.

There is no doubt that little girls currently have more room to explore a spectrum of gender behaviors than little boys; boys are referred for treatment significantly more frequently than girls (Zucker & Bradley, 1995). Little boys are severely restricted in their gender behaviors, and the social punishment remains stiff, as evidenced by the media flurry when one mom "allowed" her son to wear a traditionally female Halloween costume (Manley, 2011). Even the language of the *DSM-IV-TR* (APA, 2000a) urges clinicians contemplating a diagnosis of GID to think more strictly about cross-dressing behaviors in boys than girls. Although girls must demonstrate an "insistence on wearing only stereotypical masculine clothing" (p. 581), boys must merely exhibit a "preference for cross-dressing or simulating female attire" (p. 581).

Parents range in their reactions to children's gender nonconforming behavior. Some can accept it if little Oscar wears a princess dress to the dining room table, and it does not invoke any more anxiety than letting him wear his Batman outfit, whereas other parents can become very anxious if their son prefers cooking to rough-and-tumble sports. Fathers may have more difficulty accepting a gender-variant child than mothers (Alie, 2011), perhaps as a result of the same societal forces that constrict boys and men into narrower gender roles than girls and women. Fathers who have difficulty accepting their child may use shame or threats in an attempt to change a child's behavior more often than mothers do (Brill & Pepper, 2008).

Children whose parents adhere to strict gender roles may be difficult to assess and diagnose. For example, an assertion by a child that he or she is the opposite gender may be a result of the negative reactions by parents to his or her cross-gender interests and behaviors. In other words, it may be easier to say, "I am a boy" than to be a girl who wants very short hair (D'Augelli et al., 2005).

Nonetheless, there are children who have expressed gender nonconformity since early childhood and clearly insisted on a cross-gender identity as soon as they were old enough to speak. As they develop, their interests, clothing choices, games, and toys continue to lean toward those traditionally associated with the opposite sex. When the child expresses strong discomfort in the gender expectations of his or her assigned sex and parents or guardians discern that these expressions are consistent across environments and persistent over time, they may choose to foster a social transition for the child (Hill et al., 2010; Vanderburgh, 2008). Social transitions are rarely initiated without long, thoughtful processes between families and mental health professionals.

Regardless of whether a gender nonconforming child transitions socially, it is in the best interest of all children expressing gender nonconformity to have their authentic expressions of gender supported by peers, parents, teachers, and other adults in their lives (Riley et al., 2011; Stone Fish & Harvey, 2005). The SOC state: "Acceptance and removal of secrecy can bring considerable relief to gender dysphoric children/adolescents and their families" (WPATH, 2011, p. 15). Children whose emerging gender identity is affirmed will be more likely to have positive mental and physical health outcomes (Brill & Pepper, 2008; Ehrensaft, 2011; Pleak, 2009).

Adolescents

As children enter puberty, they are faced with physical and environmental situations in which gender identity issues cannot be avoided. This creates a sense of urgency for many youth, for as puberty progresses, they continue developing sex characteristics of their biological sex, which may feel alien to them (Pleak, 2009). Although it seems like common wisdom to suggest that transgender teens wait until they are older and more mature to make such a large, life-changing decision as publicly and medically changing sex, there are serious reasons to suggest a more proactive treatment approach. If biological development is not halted and the sex-linked characteristics develop, it will seriously affect the ability to successfully "pass" (i.e., be viewed as the gender that matches one's identity) in adulthood, especially for MTFs. This can interfere with self-esteem, as well as social acceptance and work opportunities. Once a natal male child develops into male puberty (including facial hair, height, muscle development), these are permanent effects, not easily (or inexpensively) ameliorated.

As Pleak noted, "There is a growing international consensus that once kids pass through the period of pubertal changes that begin...around the age of 11–13, gender atypicality or gender variance is not going to change much going forward" (2009, p. 286). It is important to note the difference between a social transition, which can happen at any age, and a medical transition, which is not available until the child enters puberty. Social transitions, which include children changing their clothes and their name, and being referred to in cross-gender pronouns, are not permanent and can be reversed, although some suggest that these reversals may be psychologically challenging for children (Steensma & Cohen-Kettenis, 2011).

Medical protocols include the use of gonadotropin-releasing hormone analogues, which are puberty blockers that halt the progression of secondary sex development and place the adolescent in a temporary suspended latency by blocking the action of the sex steroids, therefore stopping the masculinization or feminization of the body (Delemarre-Van de Waal & Cohen-Kettenis, 2006; WPATH, 2011). Generally, it is most effective to start puberty blockers at the early stages of puberty (i.e., Tanner stage 2). The effects of puberty blockers are fully reversible, and if the medication is stopped, the hormonal activity of (natal sex) puberty is resumed. This treatment essentially "buys time" for the teen to mature enough to make life-changing decisions such as the initiation of full cross-sex hormones, but also serves to buy time for parents or guardians and medical providers to become comfortable in allowing these decisions to be made. It also serves to postpone unwanted puberty, which can be experienced as a trauma for a gender-dysphoric teen. Although more than 20 years of research have documented the success of these medical interventions (Cohen-Kettenis & Pfäfflin, 2003), these remain difficult and challenging decisions for parents and medical personnel to make, evoking numerous ethical questions (WPATH,

2011). As Gooren and Delemarre-Van de Waal wrote, "It is to be remembered that giving, but also withholding endocrine treatment is a momentous and responsible decision" (1996, p. 69); accordingly, one cannot sidestep the ethical dilemmas by merely avoiding them, especially given the devastating impact puberty can have on this population.

Each adult with whom a transgender youth comes in contact, including his or her parents, teachers, therapists, medical doctors, social workers, and other care providers, plays a vital role in helping that child form a positive self-image and keeping him or her safe from potential social victimization; medical interventions may be a part of ensuring recommended practices.

RECOMMENDATIONS FOR FAMILIES

Gender nonconforming children, like all children, need parental and caregiver acceptance to thrive (Stone Fish & Harvey, 2005). Caitlin Ryan and her team at the Family Acceptance Project, using innovative community research and intervention strategies, have identified specific behaviors of parents and the impact these behaviors have on their LGBT youth. Children whose parents more often engage in accepting behaviors (e.g., talking with a child about his or her gender identity, expressing affection when the child discloses his or her gender identity, and advocating for the child when he or she is mistreated) have significantly more positive long-term mental and physical health outcomes than youth whose parents do not exhibit accepting behavior (Ryan, Huebner, Diaz, & Sanchez, 2009). Positive outcomes include lower levels of depression, lower incidents of drug use, a reduced risk of HIV infection, and fewer suicide attempts (Ryan et al., 2009). There are dramatically more positive outcomes for youth with accepting parents (Krieger, 2011), and not surprisingly, gender nonconforming children with parents who are more accepting are also more likely to believe they can be a happy adult (Ryan et al., 2009).

Younger children and teens differ with regard to their parental needs. Parents have greater access to the institutions in which their children spend time when children are younger, so it is easier to advocate in schools than when children enter their teen years. Although parents may still want to intervene to protect their children, adolescents may be embarrassed or uncomfortable with their families' efforts to intervene, preferring to try and "handle things" themselves. Young children may be best served by parents and schools who will support them in their exploration and nonconforming presentations. Adolescents, on the other hand, may need advocacy with medical personnel. Parents of older children may struggle to understand how intensely their children despair when puberty starts and may not believe or comprehend the authenticity of their child's emerging identity, and consequently, transgender youth may receive fewer natural supports in schools and other social venues, such as camp.

Regardless of a child's age or specific needs, the focus remains on acceptance of the child as he or she is and helping "him or her adapt to the constraints of a gendered culture while simultaneously working to change the social system" (Lev, 2004, p. 346). Recommendations for parents and caregivers of gender nonconforming children and youth include the following:

1. *Seek support.* Parents and families with gender nonconforming children often struggle with isolation, believing they are the only families to face these difficulties. Parents are often torn between supporting their child's unique identity and protecting the child from negative social experiences (Hill & Menvielle, 2009; Malpas, 2011). Individual and family therapy can help family members more clearly understand the emotional impacts of having a gender nonconforming child in the family, as well as help facilitate communication between family members and assist the family in navigating social environments (WPATH, 2011). Support groups for parents of gender nonconforming children can also be helpful for parents in the process of coming to accept their child (Malpas, 2011; Menvielle & Tuerk, 2002), as well as providing families with valuable information. When local groups are not available, online support groups can also offer guidance and support. For example, Parents, Families and Friends of Lesbians and Gays (PFLAG) includes the Transgender Network (TNET), which provides information, resources, and support for families (www.community.pflag.org). TransYouth Family Allies (TYFA; www.imatyfa.org) also offers online support, as does the Children's Gender and Sexuality Advocacy and Education Program (CGSAEP) at the Children's National Medical Center in Washington, D.C., under the directorship of Edgardo Menvielle, M.D.

2. *Move toward acceptance.* Research with families of gay and lesbian teens illustrates that parental adjustment moves through stages when a child is coming out; these may include family sensitization, discovery, family recovery, and family renewal (LaSala, 2010); these stages can be similar for parents of gender nonconforming children. Lev (2004) identified stages of family acceptance (referred to as the *family emergence model*), which have been adapted for work with parents and children (see Box 5.1). These stages include "Discovery and Disclosure" of gender variance, including the family's realizations that their child is gender nonconforming (which can be difficult even if the family has suspected it for some time), or the child's statement that he or she does not identify with the gender to which the child has been assigned. Stage two, "Turmoil," includes difficult emotions between family members, such as anger, depression, and anxiety, and may be the time families first seek out therapeutic assistance. Stage three, "Negotiation," is the realization that the gender issues are permanent and that family adjustments must be made. This stage can include negotiations about how to disclose and manage the gender variance in social situations. Stage four, "Finding Balance," refers to the time when gender issues are no longer a secret and the gender nonconforming person is integrated back into the family in his or her authentic gender identity.

Although it is common for families to progress according to these stages, it is also important to remember that paths toward acceptance are varied and will be idiosyncratic to each family (Hill & Menvielle, 2009). Small movements toward acceptance, such as using the gender noun and pronoun that the child is using to self-identify, have been linked to higher levels of acceptance in parents of gender nonconforming children (Alie, 2011), and strides by parents toward accepting their children have been shown to be correlated with large increases in positive mental and physical health outcomes for their children (Ryan et al., 2009).

3. *Encourage gender exploration and expression.* Gender nonconforming children may feel they cannot embody their true identities at school, with peers, or in most social environments. "Most youth who know themselves to be trans live in environments where the prevailing message is that such persons are not lovable and trans lives are not possible" (Hill & Menvielle, 2009, p. 269). As parents begin to create environments that support their children's authentic gender development, the children are "reassured…that they will be loved unconditionally" (Hill & Menvielle 2009, p. 269). Making home a place where the child can be who he or she is without restriction can bring a much needed respite for the child (WPATH, 2011). Behaviors such as enforcing a zero tolerance rule for negativity toward the child within the family, welcoming the child's friends into the home, and connecting the child to resources and others in the transgender community can have significant long-term positive effects on a gender nonconforming child (Ryan et al., 2009).

Questions about gender and sexuality are part of normative and healthy childhood and adolescent development (Israel & Tarver, 1997). Although parents do not have an influence over a child's gender, they do influence the gender *health* of the child (Ehrensaft, 2007). Embracing gender exploration with curiosity and support, rather than attempting to steer a child in a specific direction, will allow the child to embody a strong sense of self (Vanderburgh, 2008). This differs significantly from older models that focused on trying to assist children in increased gender conformity (Zucker & Bradley, 1995). Many parents state they tried to police and mold their children's behavior and that the results caused depression and withdrawal. Depressive and anxiety-related symptoms, in fact, are common for gender nonconforming individuals who are experiencing prejudice and discrimination by family members as well as by society at large. The WPATH SOC clearly distinguish these psychological manifestations from a gender nonconforming identity, explaining, "these symptoms are socially induced and are not inherent to being transsexual, transgender, or gender nonconforming" (2011, p. 4).

4. *Advocate.* Parents must often be advocates for their children. For parents of gender nonconforming children, this includes helping children understand gender norms and roles, as well as what to expect when one deviates from these mores. Parents can also provide the child with language for managing potentially

---

Box 5.1. Family Emergence Stages for Gender Nonconforming Children and Youth

---

Stage One: Discovery and Disclosure

When a very young child exhibits gender nonconforming behavior, it is rarely a concern for parents. However, as a child matures and continues to prefer cross-gender toys and games or seek out primarily "opposite sex" friends, parents may begin noticing the ways their child is different from same-sex peers. Some children may express interest in wearing cross-gender clothing, either for play or simply because they enjoy them; others may change their name to a more gender-neutral or cross-gendered name. Children may reveal a cross-gender identity at a young age, saying, "I am a boy," or "Please say *she*, not *he*." As puberty develops in adolescence, cross-gender expression and identity may become increasingly established. Parents may begin to suspect that their child has a gay or lesbian sexual orientation, or wonder about transgender expression, especially as more information is available in the media. Gender nonconformity in young children is often "discovered" by the parents who witness the child's differences; during adolescence some teens may be able to disclose that they are transgender, which may surprise parents if the gender differences have not been obvious previously. Parents begin to process what it means to have a child who is "different"; for some parents this is shocking and perhaps in conflict with their religious or moral values, whereas others may be able to adapt and become advocates for the child.

Stage Two: Turmoil

After the disclosure, discovery, or revelation of transgenderism, there is often a time of stress and anxiety for the trans child, as well as for the rest of the family. Parents are often at odds with one another, increasing the stress on the marital relationship or with extended family. In some families, gender issues are silenced, and in other families, the child can become the focus of extreme pathologization. Family members sometimes "pick sides," and subsystems form, creating or reinforcing triangulated dynamics. Parents are often anxious about their child's safety and trying to manage their child's emerging needs with the expectations of the social world in which they reside. Not all families experience this upheaval, and some are able to adapt to their child's authentic identity with relatively little strife and become advocates. However, sometimes family members may be supportive and open about a young child's identity, but when questions of physical transition begin to become obvious, the family is often thrown into a state of distress. Families often seek out therapeutic support at this stage.

Stage Three: Negotiation

This stage is noted by the realization that the gender issue will not simply "go away" and will have to be adjusted to in some manner. At this stage, parents often wonder whether their child is gay or transgender, and questions of their child's unknown future can be frightening. The negotiation process often involves questions of whether or not parents can "handle" their child expressing his or her gender identity and how the parents are able to adapt to the changes. The process of limit setting is fundamental to transitioning or even accepting transgenderism within families, and young people often want to move at a faster pace than parents are able to accommodate. Both parents and children or youth need to examine what their bottom lines are: what they can and cannot compromise about and what is—and is not—negotiable. Questions about what clothing a child can wear out of the house or whether or not he or she can change a name or pronoun often become the focus of discussion. Addressing the child's needs in schools is vital, and generally parents require a lot of support so that they are able to be effective advocates for their children.

Stage Four: Finding Balance

Balance does not necessarily infer transition; it does not infer permanent resolution of the gender issues. It means that transgenderism is no longer a secret, that the family is no longer in turmoil and has negotiated the larger issues involving transgenderism. The family has learned that there is a difference between secrecy and privacy; they will negotiate their own unique balance of revealing information if privacy is a concern, but they are not sworn to a painful secret. Balance means the family is now ready to integrate the transgender child or youth—*as* a transgender person—back into the normative life of the family. Balance might mean a child can cross-dress at home but not at school or beginning to reveal the child's identity to relatives. Parents (and sometimes children) may join a support group (online or in a local community). For many families, it might mean living with the uncertainty of not knowing the trajectory of the gender nonconformity and living with the "unknown." However, depending on the needs of the transgender child or youth and the willingness to compromise and experiment for the parents, families can find a healthy balance. Families that are capable of moving through their fear, shame, and ignorance regarding gender variance are often able to find contentment and satisfaction in their daily family lives.

difficult encounters with peers, family members, adults in authority positions, and strangers.

Meeting with school officials, including principals and teachers, either before a child enters school or before a new school year for returning children and older youth, will lessen the likelihood of the child being misunderstood and mistreated. It may also enable the child to be assigned to the most appropriate teacher and provide the teacher an opportunity to ask questions and become more informed about how to support the child and integrate the child into the classroom (Brill & Pepper, 2008).

RECOMMENDATIONS FOR PROFESSIONALS

When a parent is concerned about a child's gender presentation, or when a gender nonconforming youth seeks hormone therapy or gender-related surgery, the medical doctors, teachers, and parents of the child look to the therapist for clear answers, as if the therapist can (or should) know the answer to the question, "Is my child a girl or a boy?" The answer is, however, not always so clear, and the psychological community has yet to create an official assessment tool that therapists can use to form the answer to this and other questions parents may have. Clinicians vary wildly in their beliefs about gender transitions, and even those who specialize in transgender care rarely have experience working specifically with gender nonconforming children and youth. The WPATH SOC (2011) remain cautious in recommending social transitions for young children, and the guidelines for youth transitions are painstakingly detailed to ensure proper assessment and follow-through.

Some who believe the diagnosis is pathological may have a tendency to underdiagnose (Ehrbar, Witty, Ehrbar, & Bockting, 2008). The WPATH SOC (2011) caution against either minimizing or pathologizing gender nonconforming behaviors. However, there is also a concern that some may overdiagnose by viewing all children with gender nonconforming behavior as transgender and in need of social and medical treatment. Consultation with, or referrals to, gender specialists are recommended when the therapist lacks experience working with this population to avoid both extremes. Collaboration with developmental psychologists can be useful for gender specialists accustomed to working with adults. Guidelines for the care of gender dysphoric children and youth are available from the WPATH SOC and are adapted here:

1. *Provide gender-specific competent clinical care.* Gender specialists should be trained in childhood developmental psychology, including competence in diagnosis and treatment of childhood mental health problems and the ability to differentiate these from gender-specific concerns (WPATH, 2011). Clinicians are advised to avoid concepts and terms based on a binary view of gender and to encourage a wide variety of gender expressions while supporting the child's authentic expression. Therapy should focus on reducing gender-related stress for the child and supporting the family in navigating the relational and social dynamics affected by the child's gender (Malpas, 2011). Working with gender nonconforming children often means long-term therapy with children and their families, especially if gender dysphoria develops. As the child matures, different developmental issues will surface, and ongoing therapeutic support is encouraged throughout the child's social and medical processes. Caution is needed when labeling a child with a gender-related diagnosis, because this label will become part of their permanent medical record.

2. *Complete a comprehensive assessment of the child and family.* An assessment for children exhibiting gender dysphoria should include intrapsychic issues, personality, cognitive ability, social relationships, personal strengths, and a thorough assessment for any coexisting mental health issues (WPATH, 2011). Corroborative views of the child's gender presentation should be obtained from family members, teachers, coaches, camp counselors, and others in contact with the child, looking for gender identity consistency over time and across situations (Vanderburgh, 2008). The family's history, environment and culture, beliefs about gender, and level of acceptance they have for the child should be assessed. The family should also be assessed for dysfunction that might exacerbate gender difficulties, such as communication issues, power conflicts, parental disagreements about child rearing (Vanderburgh, 2008), or socioeconomic or other hardships. Unique family strengths and resources that may assist them in working toward acceptance should also be assessed.

3. *Provide informed support.* Provide information to the child and family about gender variance, gender identity versus sexual orientation, and the impact culture has on gender roles and identities (Vanderburgh, 2008). Make clear the distinctions between gender nonconformity and gender dysphoria. Parents may need support accepting the ambiguity of their child's gender or the unknown potential future outcomes for the child; adolescents and their parents may require information about different physical treatments (WPATH, 2011). Parents may also need support recognizing that gender issues are not merely acts of defiance. Parents may need assistance facing the normative stages of grief associated with the shock or disappointment that their child may not be who they thought he or she was.

Social transition. Families will need support when their children desire changes in dress, a change of name, or the wish to be called by a different pronoun. Parents may be concerned about how a child will be received by family and peers or be concerned for the child's safety (Krieger, 2011) and can benefit from a discussion focused on how to answer questions from family and community members, as well as how to advocate for the child at school (Mallon & DeCrecenzo, 2006).

Physical transition. Families will need support when navigating difficult decisions regarding physical changes to a youth's body, especially when the youth's desires for changes do not align with caregivers wishes (Krieger, 2011). Information regarding the pros and cons of puberty suppression and eventual use of cross-sex hormones should be provided. Conversations about surgical interventions often begin in late adolescence. "Top" surgery, which includes mastectomy and chest reconstruction for transsexual males (FTMs), is rarely done for youth younger than 18 years, but may be considered in some cases at age 16 years. "Bottom" surgery, or genital reconstruction, and other surgeries (facial feminization, breast augmentation) are hardly ever performed before the age of legal consent. For youth contemplating or planning on sex reassignment surgery, therapy should include support for the youth and caregivers before, during, and after surgery (Menvielle & Tuerk, 2002). Youth who socially transitioned at an earlier age may be less likely to experience psychosocial difficulties with physical transition than those who are undergoing both a social and a physical transition simultaneously.

4. *Provide appropriate referrals, information, and resources.* Provide referrals for physical interventions when appropriate, with documentation of assessment of gender dysphoria and the youth's appropriateness for these interventions (WPATH, 2011). Provide the family with resources for organizations that support families (e.g., PFLAG, TYFA) and other supportive service providers in their area (Vanderburgh, 2008). Assist them in finding support groups for parents, role models for their child, and resources for advocacy at their child's school.

5. *Advocate.* Mental health providers are encouraged to take an active role in the education and advocacy of their gender nonconforming clients in the

larger community, including schools, extracurricular programs, school boards, and courts (WPATH, 2011).

RECOMMENDATIONS FOR PEDIATRICIANS

The pediatrician is often the first professional to come in contact with a gender nonconforming child whose parents are concerned or who is experiencing distress related to gender. The pediatrician's initial reaction is likely to have a significant effect on the parents and should therefore be supportive and informative. Including gender-related questions on standard paperwork and during intake appointments can normalize this potentially sensitive discourse for a family hesitant to disclose difficulties in this area (Holman & Goldberg, 2007) and can assist pediatricians in identifying gender dysphoria early. Physicians must be able to reassure parents about the range of normative gender expressions, as well as recognize gender dysphoria. To ensure these services, pediatricians are encouraged to follow these guidelines:

1. *Seek training and consultation.* Pediatricians and those working in family medicine should seek out specialized training in gender issues and/or seek consultation with a gender specialist or pediatric endocrinologist trained in gender issues.

2. *Obtain a comprehensive gender assessment for gender dysphoria.* Pediatricians should assess for medical conditions that might have an impact on gender identity such as intersex or endocrine issues, although many children with intersex conditions do not experience gender dysphoria or exhibit gender nonconforming behaviors. Although gender dysphoria differs in its phenomenological presentation, epidemiology, life trajectories, and etiology (Meyer-Bahlburg, 2010), the treatment of children with and without intersex conditions will remain very similar. In addition, a psychological assessment by a knowledgeable mental health clinician, such as a family therapist or developmental psychologist, is advised in addition to the physical assessment if there is persistent gender dysphoria.

3. *Provide medical information and referrals when appropriate.* For families navigating a child's changes in appearance or a name change, referral to a gender specialist is advised. This will normalize the process and provide the family with support for advocacy that may be needed at school and in other social situations. As the child nears puberty and begins to experience physical changes, his or her gender dysphoria may increase. Parents may seek the advice of a pediatrician for their teenagers who are insisting they are the other sex or are requesting medical interventions to stop these pubertal changes. Pediatricians can provide immediate assistance for these families by normalizing their experience, providing information about medical options, and making a referral to a pediatric endocrinologist, hospital, or clinic specializing in working with gender-variant children.

RECOMMENDATIONS FOR SCHOOLS AND RESIDENTIAL FACILITIES

The transition to school often marks the beginning of a time when social influences begin to override parental ones. Teachers, administrators, and peers can create a welcoming and affirmative environment for gender nonconforming children. Schools, camps, hospitals, and juvenile detention and other residential facilities for youth can play a role in supporting gender nonconforming children and youth by following these suggestions:

1. *Create an environment where gender exploration is normative and gender diversity is encouraged.* Children who experience a high degree of pressure to conform to gender stereotypes are more likely to have a negative psychosocial adjustment (Egan & Perry, 2001). Prohibit any type of discrimination, including jokes and name calling, toward youth as well as staff (Wilber, Ryan, & Marksamer, 2006). Encourage gay–straight alliances on campuses, and provide support to groups and social activities that celebrate gender diversity (Toomey, Ryan, Diaz, Card, & Russell, 2010).

2. *Develop gender-affirming policies.* Policies and practices should create an environment where youth are able to disclose gender identity, discuss gender-related concerns, and express gender identity through gender presentation (Wilber et al., 2006). Include gender identity in agency antiharassment policies. Inquire about a child's preferred name and pronoun in routine intake procedures. For children in residential care facilities, gender identity should be treated as confidential client information and should not be disclosed without permission. Inform all staff working with gender nonconforming youth of their jurisdiction's laws relevant to disclosure of such information (Wilber et al., 2006).

3. *Educate staff about gender identity.* Gender nonconforming children should be placed in the care of staff trained in gender issues, including developmental stages of gender identity, educational strategies for teaching age-appropriate gender curriculum, and intervention strategies to prevent gender discrimination.

4. *Use the youth's preferred name and pronoun.* Even when the child's legal name differs from the social name, use the child's preferred name. Inform all staff of this transition, and require correct name and pronoun usage by staff and other youth.

5. *Provide information and resources.* Libraries should have books related to gender that are appropriate to the reading level of students. Provide educational materials for teachers to ensure that gender is included in mandatory curricula.

6. *Avoid gender segregation.* Making gender nonconforming children repeatedly choose with which gendered group they should align themselves can be distracting and emotionally difficult. The Transgender Law Center (www.trans genderlawcenter.org) advises against dress codes, noting that they can be particularly difficult when there are different garments allowed or required on the basis of gender (Cho, Laub, Wall, & Daley, 2004). Avoid gender-segregated class-

room set-ups such as coat racks or desk arrangements, and avoid group assign-ments based on a gender binary. Ensure that extracurricular activities such as sports and clubs are open to all interested students, regardless of gender (Brill & Pepper, 2008; Mallon & DeCrenzo, 2006; Toomey et al., 2010).

For residential facilities, gender segregation is often the standard for sleep-ing arrangements. When facilities are unable to make overnight facilities mixed gender, staff members are recommended to take into account the child's stated gender identity, the child's and family's requests, and the child's gender presenta-tion when placing the child. If difficulty persists regarding placement of the child, allow the child a private room.

Many gender nonconforming students experience harassment in restrooms. Creating gender-neutral bathrooms and locker rooms allows all students a safe and comfortable place to take care of their basic needs (Cho et al., 2004). When this is not possible, single-use bathrooms, privacy doors on bathrooms and showers, or arrangements for gender-variant youth to use the shower before or after others is recommended (Wilber et al., 2006).

7. *Consult.* Consulting with gender specialists can not only create an af-firming environment for gender nonconforming children, but it can also assist administrators and staff members in the creation of welcoming policies for chil-dren of all genders. Trainings such as those provided by Gender Spectrum (www.genderspectrum.org) and Translate Gender (www.translategender.org) can be valuable for staff members. Gender organizations and camps, such as Camp Aranu'tiq (www.camparanutiq.org), a camp for gender nonconforming chil-dren, can also provide consultation for the practical concerns of supporting and integrating gender nonconforming children.

CULTURAL AND LINGUISTIC COMPETENCE FACTORS

Gender nonconforming children and youth, like all children, live within cul-tural, religious, socioeconomic, geographic, linguistic, and ethnic communities. Each of these layers of identity influence how the child is viewed and treated. Some ethnic communities are more rigidly gender stereotyping than others, and the consequences for transgressive behavior might be more harsh. Indeed, in some communities, gender variance might take a backseat to more visceral pressures and issues, such as economics or religiosity. Sadly, there has been very little research, or even discussion, of gender nonconforming children in terms of complex minority issues. Ethnic minority trans youth in urban areas have been the focus of a few studies, portraying a painful picture of lives' of poverty, homelessness, and substance use and abuse. Many of these teens are runaways, engaging in prostitution for their survival.

Garofalo, Deleon, Osmer, Doll, and Harper (2006) found high rates of in-carceration, homelessness, and poor access to health care, as well as high rates of

HIV, among urban, African American trans youth. Nemoto, Operario, Keatley, Han, and Soma (2004) also described high rates of substance abuse and unprotected sex. Rosario (2009) wrote about his experiences working specifically with African American trans youth, many of whom have HIV and work in the sex industry. Beam (2008) wrote about homelessness and sexual assault in the lives of trans adolescents of color. Nuttbrock et al. (2010) and Ryan et al. (2009) also described the impact of violence, abandonment, and rejection of LGBT youth of color. It should not be assumed, however, that all families of color are rejecting of their gender nonconforming children—only that when they are, the outcomes are devastating given the additional impact of racism, poverty, and societal transphobia.

Trans youth of color may express their identities differently from other trans youth, influencing how they seek services and the trajectory of their gender transition process. Of note, Rosario said of the trans youth he worked with:

> Gender identity...is still extremely fluid and is shaped by a variety of complex and often traumatic experiences that these individuals have concerning gender and gender expression which come from society, culture, religion, and especially from the very strong homophobic messages they receive from their families. (2009, p. 306)

Given the nature of minority stress (Meyer, 2003), those who contain multiple signifiers of minority identity are likely to suffer more frequent microaggressions (Sue et al., 2007), as well as blatant acts of violence and oppression. Children and youth struggling with disabilities, those for whom English is a second language, or those who are new immigrants to the United States are likely to be targeted for abuse in higher numbers. Children and youth living in poverty have less access to quality mental and physical health services and competent legal assistance and are at increased vulnerability.

MOVING FORWARD TOGETHER

Gender nonconforming children are born into every kind of family, regardless of race, religion, sexual orientation or gender identity of parents, level of education, socioeconomic level, or geographic region. They are entering every grade of school, attending camps, going to the doctor, and seeking a myriad of other services each day. As their visibility increases as a result of lessening societal stigma of transgender issues, resources to provide them with adequate care are gradually becoming increasingly available.

Each person in a social services system has a critical role to play in providing culturally and linguistically competent and appropriate care for gender nonconforming children and youth. Mental health providers, nurses, and medical doctors need to be informed of gender issues and be prepared to refer to and consult with gender specialists, ensuring adequate psychological and physical assessments of gender dysphoric children and their families. Researchers and clinicians should continue developing innovative psychotherapies and medical interventions to assist gender nonconforming children in their journey toward a healthy gender identity, whether that be family therapy, advocating for a child's rights at school, or providing cross-sex hormones for those with persistent gender dysphoria. Schools, camps, and other residential facilities should effectively support and incorporate gender nonconforming children into the fabric of their organizations, enabling children of all genders to experience normal peer relationships and healthy psychosocial development.

An essential factor in the well-being of transgender youth is support and acceptance by parents and families. Most importantly, these systems must collaborate to ensure effective integration of services and supports (De Vries, Cohen-Kettenis, & Delemarre-Van de Waal, 2006). Pediatricians whose medical interventions take into account the psychosocial implications of those treatments, family therapists whose suggestions for advocacy are informed by the teacher's observations, and school principals who mandate gender-related education as part of the curriculum are but a few examples of the types of collaborations that will allow gender nonconforming children and trans youth to receive the support and services they need and deserve.

6

Disorders or Differences of Sex Development

MATTHEW A. MALOUF AND ARLENE BARATZ

This chapter, which discusses youth who have biological conditions referred to as *disorders or differences of sex development* (DSD)[1] and who may identify as intersex, offers a valuable opportunity for mental health and medical providers, researchers, policy makers, stakeholders, advocates, and other audiences to better understand the needs of families and individuals affected by the various diagnoses that fall under these broad terms. Challenges exist, however, regarding the very language used to describe and discuss the needs of these youth and families affected by DSD. Words surrounding diagnosis and identity labels have reflected the historical marginalization of individuals whose sex falls outside of binary norms (i.e., male and female).

In recent years, advocates and practitioners have made efforts to minimize secrecy, stigma, and pathology historically associated with DSD (Diamond, 2004). Medical terminology has slowly shifted from focusing on genital abnormality (e.g., *hermaphrodite*, a stigmatizing term) to language that is more holistic and clinically precise (e.g., DSD), nomenclature that is now in full use by physicians who treat these conditions. Furthermore, advocacy has led to an increase in stakeholder input and personal choice, and today an individual may choose to self-identify and self-label using any of a host of gendered terms: *male, female, intersex, third-gender, other-gendered, genderqueer,* or other language. It is important to recognize these terminologies to facilitate communication among affected

---

[1]As proposed by the International Consensus Conference on Intersex (Lee, Houk, Ahmed, Hughes, & International Consensus Conference on Intersex organized by the Lawson Wilkins Pediatric Endocrine Society and the European Society for Paediatric Endocrinology, 2006), the initialism DSD stands for "disorders of sex development." Its intended use encompasses a broad range of conditions that affect sex development. As such, DSD is plural but may be made singular when preceded by the indefinite article *a* to reference a singular disorder of sex development. In this chapter we also discuss alternative terminology including *differences of sex development* and use DSD to refer to both disorders and differences of sex development.

people and various clinicians. This proscription holds true even for medical clinicians or those working within medical systems (e.g., a social worker submitting an insurance claim), because it is essential when working with affected youth to respect and use language that reflects their understanding of themselves.

In this chapter, we try to strike a balance between sharing recommendations based on empirical information and recommended practices of care, and recognizing the complexity and diversity of this population. To meet these aims, throughout the chapter, we primarily use the DSD initialism to describe the overall group of medical conditions. As a term that we limit to the conditions themselves, "DSD" allows latitude for the complexity of identity associated with these conditions. It does not capture the full range of individuals' self-perceptions and identities or how they negotiate socially constructed expectations for sex and gender (Bostwick & Martin, 2008). Additionally, although the focus of this chapter is on a larger group of conditions, when discussing a specific diagnosis, we believe it is best to refer to that condition by name. That said, we cannot overemphasize the importance of recognizing the difference between a *diagnosis* and an *individual*. Although using person-first language (e.g., *an individual with a DSD* rather than *a DSD person*) is a good first step, it alone does not fully address the sociopolitical impact of language on identity, power, and choice for affected individuals.

This chapter suggests further recommended practices regarding the use of language, including guidance surrounding the use of terminology related to sex and gender, cultural considerations, and terms suggested by people with DSD. This chapter also clarifies the role of mental health providers in shared decision making regarding sex assignment and treatment options and in supporting families' confidence in parenting, dealing with medical professionals, and supporting adolescents in their development and understanding of their identity. Finally, we provide recommendations surrounding psychosocial support, with an emphasis on empowering individuals and communities.

INDIVIDUALS AND FAMILIES AFFECTED BY DISORDERS OR DIFFERENCES OF SEX DEVELOPMENT

DSD are conditions in which chromosomes, gonads (the organs that usually make sperm or eggs), or reproductive and genital anatomies are not what is usually expected for a person's sex. Recent data note that the overall incidence of DSD is 1 in 500 (Visootsak & Graham, 2006), whereas the birth of a child with genitals that appear neither strictly male nor female (ambiguous genitalia) is approximately 1 in 4,500 (Achermann & Hughes, 2007). The most common DSD is Klinefelter syndrome, in which men have an extra X chromosome in addition to the usual XY chromosomes, with an incidence of 1 in 500 births (Visootsak & Graham, 2006). Some DSD are associated with a serious medical illness, whereas others may require little treatment beyond hormonal therapy. As this chapter explores, although there is great diversity among specific DSD and even among individuals with the same diagnosis, most DSD have been understood through a similar clinical lens, one that emphasizes biology.

Biological sex is often described as having four markers: 1) genetic sex (chromosomes), 2) reproductive sex (e.g., testicles), 3) external genitalia (e.g., clitoris), and 4) secondary sex characteristics (e.g., body and facial hair, breast development). For most youth, these four markers develop and present in a manner aligning with binary sex labels (i.e., male and female). For some youth, however, these markers may not manifest as expected or may be ambiguous. DSD may be caused by prenatal exposure of the fetus to hormones or other substances in the uterus or by conditions in which the fetus produces hormones that disrupt sex development. Genetic causes of DSD arise when there is a variation (or "mutation") in any of the genes responsible for sex development. Genetic mutations, as well as exposure to environmental factors or maternal hormone imbalance, may be the cause of DSD. In many cases, despite thorough investigation, the source of the condition remains undiagnosed.

Some conditions, including diagnoses such as congenital adrenal hyperplasia or partial androgen insensitivity syndrome, may cause the external genitals to have an appearance somewhere between completely male (i.e., penis and scrotum) or female (i.e., clitoris and vagina). This is known as *genital ambiguity.* Within each diagnosis, there may be various forms or degrees of manifestation and/or causes (e.g., types of congenital adrenal hyperplasia are more or less severe or may be caused by deficiencies in different enzymes). In general, these variations are noted by the qualifying language (e.g., "complete," "partial") and may lead to unique outcomes and recommendations for medical care. Although we cannot overemphasize how important it is to recognize the differences between and within DSD diagnoses, this chapter focuses on the promotion of a collaborative system of care for individuals with DSD in general. As such, we defer to medical literature to fully describe the many specific DSD, their varying forms, and related implications for specific outcomes and clinical recommendations.

Individuals are often first diagnosed with a DSD in infancy when a newborn presents with ambiguous genitalia or genitalia that are inconsistent with sex chromosome results obtained via prior amniocentesis or other testing. A comprehensive assessment to establish a diagnosis includes conducting a clinical review and evaluation, obtaining body hydration status as well as a karyotype, and conducting hormone and imaging studies (Migeon, Krishnan, & Wisniewski, 2007). These steps are critical not only to determining the nature of any DSD but also to treating any immediate health concerns caused by the underlying condition.

Individuals with DSD and their families have particular needs that may have implications for behavioral health and quality of life (Cohen-Kettenis, 2010;

Johannsen, Ripa, Mortensen, & Main, 2006; Kuhnle, Bullinger, & Schwarz, 1995; Kuhnle, Bullinger, Schwarz, & Knorr, 1993; Malouf, Inman, Carr, Franco, & Brooks, 2010; Schober, 1999). Symptoms and concerns vary widely for those children and family members whose lives are affected (Slijper, Drop, Molenaar, & De Muinck Keizer-Schrama, 1998; Warne et al., 2005). Individual concerns may be caused by, intersect with, or be completely unrelated to a DSD diagnosis. As with all other children, youth, and adults, those with a DSD experience typical challenges in life and are able to overcome them. The cultivation of resilience, individual strengths, and external supports can facilitate the ability of individuals with DSD to maintain emotional and physical well-being.

Disorders or Differences of Sex Development and Transgender Identities

It is important to distinguish between DSD and related constructs. When newborns with DSD demonstrate extreme genital ambiguity at birth, best medical practice requires making a sex assignment based on multiple biological factors; this sex assignment of the child will affect how parents and caregivers raise the child (Lee et al., 2006). Even when the process is extremely thoughtful, sex assignment is a "best guess," and some youth (and adults) may experience a disconnect between their assigned sex or "sex of rearing" and self-perceived gender identity (gender dysphoria), leading to gender transition. For this reason, DSD is often confused with the term *transgender* or with gender identity disorder (GID), which, in turn, is often conflated with atypical gendered behavior (e.g., boys playing with dolls).

The general public and most practitioners are perhaps less familiar with DSD as a concept, often associating anything having to do with *biological sex* and *sex assignment* with transgender identities. On the basis of the American Psychiatric Association's *Diagnostic and Statistical Manual of Mental Disorders* (4th ed., text rev.; *DSM-IV-TR;* 2000a) criteria, DSD and GID are mutually exclusive (American Psychiatric Association, 2000a). Individuals with a DSD, in rare instances, may still personally identify as transgender. Intersections between gendered behavior, GID, and DSD are discussed in greater depth in the following sections.

Disorders and Differences of Sex Development and Sexual Identities

Although some evidence suggests that DSD diagnoses may influence components of psychosexual development and identity, such as sexual attraction, experience, fantasy, and satisfaction (Hines, 2004; Kuhnle et al., 1995; Malouf,

Wisniewski, & Migeon, 2003; Slijper et al., 1998), sexual orientation and DSD are distinct concepts. Similar to individuals without a DSD, individuals with a DSD describe their sexuality in many different ways, such as heterosexual, gay, lesbian, bisexual, queer, or other language. Previous DSD treatment approaches considered nonheterosexuality a treatment failure. However, since the removal of homosexuality as a disorder from the *DSM* in the early 1970s, same-sex attraction and behaviors are no longer seen as innately unhealthy (Conger, 1975). Therefore, individuals with a DSD may have same-sex attractions and behaviors and still be psychologically healthy.

CULTURAL AND LINGUISTIC COMPETENCE CONSIDERATIONS

When working with individuals and families who are affected by DSD, it is important to consider cultural implications that may affect individuals or inform care. These include those aspects of identity, background, and experience that may be unique to individuals (e.g., ethnicity, socioeconomic status). However, there are also shared experiences that may contribute to an overall DSD culture, to specific diagnoses, or to individuals who were raised during specific eras of treatment for DSD. Because many cultural beliefs, values, assumptions, or biases are conveyed through language, the terminology used when discussing DSD necessitates special attention. This section provides a discussion of linguistic competency and examples of common cultural considerations for working with those affected by DSD.

Language

Conversations about DSD have historically been secretive and vague, reflecting the discomfort of both society and the medical community with the ambiguity inherent in talking about conditions that challenge traditional notions of sex and gender. Yet language, especially that used to label groups or people, provides opportunities not only for marginalization but also for empowerment. Sensitivity to the nuances of language used to describe sex and gender has been and remains critically important in advocating for the rights of those affected by DSD. Understanding the context in which language is used is just as essential, however. It is crucial that providers working with youth and families who live with a DSD recognize and accept coexisting terminologies used by medical and affected communities, because each language has its own host of cultural and linguistic implications.

Although the terminology of "disorders" used by physicians may be critical to advocating for health care, youth and families may find it pathologizing or dehumanizing. Even when intended to be open and precise, medical jargon may also be hard for the general public to understand and conveys inherent messages regarding power dynamics and expertise. Using clear and specific language tailored toward age, knowledge level, and culture is essential in empowering families and individuals to make educated choices about their care.

The term *intersex,* an alternative to DSD, also has several challenges and cannot serve as an umbrella term for people with DSD. It remains popular in some settings, particularly among academics and social justice advocates, and the media often prefer this term because it can be more sensational than DSD. However, this term may not effectively capture diagnosis–specific concerns (e.g., certain diagnoses inherently lead to infertility; others are life-threatening if not medically managed). As medical terminology, *intersex* is currently outdated, and the DSD terminology has almost completely replaced it in medical practice.

When working with youth and families, providers should be mindful to differentiate between diagnosis and identity labels as well as among individual diagnoses. Both *DSD* and *intersex* should also be used cautiously, because affected people may not identify as "disordered," "different," or "intersex." Also, a specific diagnosis (e.g., androgen insensitivity syndrome [AIS]) should *not* be assumed to be an appropriate or even welcome way to describe someone's identity.

To maintain effective communication, providers should invite an individual to identify the appropriate language or terminology to use when talking about identity versus diagnoses and outcomes. Furthermore, language regarding these topics will not be the same for all situations or individuals. In particular, adolescents (and young adults) may struggle with terminology themselves. As youths' self-understanding evolves over time, providers should remain open to ongoing exploration of language and context with each individual.

Age

Age is among the most important cultural considerations when treating DSD conditions. This chapter provides recommendations for working with families, children, and adolescents, some of which may also be extended to the care of youth as they transition to adulthood. Caregivers of infants and children are responsible for much of the care surrounding issues related to DSD. A provider who is working with family as part of the first line of care that family receives has the benefit of knowing an infant's or child's full history. However, when working with older children and adolescents, it is important not only to tailor interventions to their developmental levels and comprehension abilities, but also to recognize that each youth may have experienced varying degrees of support and have vastly different levels of awareness/knowledge of their diagnoses. Similarly, youth with the same diagnosis may have had different surgical and medical care based on family choices and prior treatment. As such, it is important to *not* make assumptions about an individual's experiences.

Geography, Socioeconomic Status, and Race/Ethnicity

Geographical location and socioeconomic status are additional cultural considerations, as both may have implications for access to care. Poor access to care, either because of a lack of trained providers (especially in rural areas) or because of a lack of insurance, can affect the time to initial diagnosis, which may occur in infancy, childhood, or even adulthood. It can also affect treatment, including whether or not affected individuals have surgery, the type and quality of medical care they receive, and how much they and their families understand about their diagnosis. This history also has implications for current and future treatment. For geographically isolated individuals or those who cannot afford care, providers should be mindful not to make unattainable recommendations. Every effort should be made to help youth and their families receive and advocate for their care locally and find alternatives when such care is unavailable. Online, physician-moderated support groups of high quality are accessible to most family and youths and often provide financial subsidies for attendance at their meetings (e.g., www.aisdsd.org, www.heainfo.org, www.dsdfamilies.org).

Finally, ethnicity and national origin are important considerations for several reasons, especially because certain types of DSD are known to be more prevalent in particular ethnic populations (Harper, 2007). First, given the general lack of providers specializing in DSD, fewer providers are available for non-English speakers. Second, cultural factors may have an impact on parental decisions about the sex selected for an infant identified with a DSD at birth. For example, certain ethnic or national communities may place different values on having male or female children (Gupta & Menon, 1997; Warne & Raza, 2008; Zucker, 2006). Despite the lack of clear guidance regarding cultural factors, providers are *strongly* encouraged to respect them when sharing information about the outcomes of various decisions. Although it is critical to assess all families' degree of awareness and knowledge on an ongoing basis, it is also important to maintain extra sensitivity toward those families for whom cultural or religious factors have special importance. Lastly, when working with youth previously treated in other countries, it is important to recognize that cultural factors, as well as overall access to care, may have resulted in different standards of care than might be expected (Gupta & Menon, 1997; Warne & Raza, 2008).

EVOLVING RECOMMENDED PRACTICES

Since international leaders in DSD care published the *Consensus Statement on Management of Intersex Disorders* in 2006 (Lee et al.), the standard of multispecialty team care with abundant psychosocial support has seldom been achieved in clinical practice. The following sections provide a discussion of specific ways a system of care model could expand on that standard and include provision of services by mental health practitioners to affected youth and families.

Standards of Care

Current standards of care for infants and children with a DSD diagnosis call for holistic care by a multidisciplinary core team consisting of various pediatric subspecialists in endocrinology, surgery, and/or urology; psychology/psychiatry; gynecology; genetics; neonatology; nursing; and, if at all possible, social work and medical ethics (Lee et al., 2006). In a holistic system of care, this team is responsible for communication with the family, primary care physicians, and other health care staff. The team is also responsible for working with families on issues related to sex assignment, surgery, and male or female (androgen or estrogen) steroid hormone replacement. Given that the significant degree of uncertainty about choices and outcomes makes health care interactions stressful for parents, we recommend that one clinician provide direct support to the family, especially during initial conversations about a DSD diagnosis. Providers should also include addressing the family's psychosocial needs among immediate concerns at the time of diagnosis, referring them to appropriate supports and helping them manage social and cultural expectations about their child's assigned sex and behaviors with which there may be implicit societal gender assumptions or associations, such as childhood play with dolls or trucks.

We summarize and extend these recommendations in several ways, beginning with an emphasis on the importance of mental health professionals in a system of care model. We then discuss ways to guide families raising a child with a DSD through the decision-making process, from initial decisions surrounding sex assignment to communication with other systems in a child's life. We further develop guidelines for working with youth undergoing puberty and through the transition to adulthood. Finally, we describe various types of psychosocial support available to families and individuals.

The Role of Mental Health Professionals

Care for individuals with a DSD has traditionally been the domain of pediatric endocrinologists who work with pediatric surgeons and urologists. Generally, as the medical providers who are asked to respond to an infant with ambiguous genitalia at birth, these physicians and their staff serve as care coordinators. Highlighting the lack of a collaborative system of care across the life span, it is not surprising to find adult patients still returning to their original pediatric endocrinologist for consultation regarding all aspects of their ongoing care. Although this might suggest a positive and enduring relationship between individuals and their treating physicians, difficulty achieving independence from pediatric medical providers highlights the limitations of a medical model of care. Increasingly, mental health professionals are called upon to serve the emotional needs of children and parents affected by DSD (Pfäfflin & Cohen-Kettenis, 2006). A system of care model includes practitioners as essential facilitators of care. In addition to providing mental health counseling, they are responsible for engaging systems of psychosocial support and assisting caregivers and individuals in navigating other systems within the community (e.g., schools, insurance), a need affected families often discuss in support groups.

Still, access to care is a major hurdle for youth and families affected by DSD and is perhaps the largest one in transitioning from current practice to a system of care approach. It is not unusual for families to drive for hours to find an endocrinologist who specializes in DSD; finding a knowledgeable and informed mental health practitioner is even more difficult. Although the lack of DSD training for mental health professionals is a barrier to treatment that parents identify (Leidolf, Curran, & Bradford, 2008), adult women with a DSD rank actual knowledge of DSD conditions as less important than basic therapeutic helping skills (Malouf et al., 2010). Similarly, biological expertise in the endocrine system is not required to assist families and youth in advocating for care and insurance coverage or to connect them with support.

GUIDELINES FOR SUPPORTING FAMILIES AND YOUTH

Sex ambiguity is often difficult to understand and causes families significant distress (Gough, Weyman, Alderson, Butler, & Stoner, 2008; Lev, 2006a; Zeiler & Wickstrom, 2009). When a baby's sex is uncertain, physicians order consults and diagnostic tests. If only minimal contact with parents is maintained until those results are available, the resulting isolation and uncertainty may be traumatizing for families. Yet, although providers in a collaborative care system are responsible for offering immediate education and support (Lee et al., 2006), research has found that only 58% of larger facilities with pediatric endocrinology training programs have a mental health professional available to support families through the initial stages of coping with a DSD (Leidolf et al., 2008). Moreover, only 19% of patients and families actually receive any form of psychological support during diagnosis, and only 15% receive support after a diagnosis (Leidolf et al.).

Furthermore, families may need ongoing assistance with decision making about their child's care, medical advocacy, integration of their child's DSD into family life, and ongoing parenting strategies. In many cases, limited or biased information from providers or their own anxiety about raising a child with genitalia different than binary norms compromises parents' abilities to make informed choices about treatment (Leidolf et al., 2008; Lev, 2006a; Zeiler & Wickstrom, 2009). There is no argument against life-saving treatments such as the creation of a urinary opening. In cases of genital surgery and hormonal treatments, however, providers may feel that parents are incapable of processing complex scientific information or that parents prefer to defer to medical authority (Karkazis, 2008). Yet, when parents are empowered self-advocates, they are role models for their children to achieve psychosocial and medical independence.

A Model of Shared Decision Making

In the now-standard informed decision-making model of providing services and supports, the physician's role is primarily to share information (Charles, Gafni, & Whelan, 1997). For children born with ambiguous genitalia, there are persistent controversies regarding surgery known as *genitoplasty,* which is performed to modify ("normalize") the appearance of the external genitals. As a preferred approach, *shared decision making* is a gradual process requiring mutual interchange of reasoning, understanding, values, and biases between providers and families (Karkazis, Tamar-Mattis, & Kon, 2010). As described specifically for decision making in DSD treatment, it is a six-step model: 1) set the stage and develop an appropriate team, 2) establish preferences for information and roles in decision making, 3) perceive and address emotions, 4) define concerns and values, 5) identify options and present evidence, and 6) share responsibility for making a decision.

This model enables providers to meet legal and ethical standards for informed consent (American Academy of Pediatrics, Committee on Bioethics, 1995) that require practitioners to provide the parent or child with information they need to make an informed decision, including all available options, and in an unbiased manner. In the case of DSD, the potential reversibility of each treatment (hormonal or surgical) should be clearly explained. Mental health providers play an important role in clarifying parents' feelings about surgical treatments and procedures by exploring risk tolerance and discussing feelings and concerns. A child or adolescent with a DSD should also participate in shared decision making about medical care and potential surgery; mental health providers are critical in providing age-appropriate information to them.

When alternatives to surgery are considered following this approach, psychosocial and peer support are imperative, especially because the relative effectiveness of surgical and psychosocial intervention is unknown (Hurwitz, 2010). In our experience, parents' and clinicians' discomfort with discussions of sexuality limits thorough discussion of future consequences of genital surgery, and a mental health services provider can advocate for the adult psychosexual needs of the child before irreversible interventions are performed. In the age of electronic media, as modern understanding of sex, gender, and gender identity for individuals with DSD evolves rapidly, discussions of what is and is not known about surgery should reflect the most currently available information.

Helping Families Become Self-Advocates

Learning how to become an advocate for their children is a gradual process for most parents. Participating in shared decision making and obtaining peer and psychosocial support help empower parents, and ultimately affected individuals, to advocate for themselves. To lay the groundwork for self-advocacy, it is critical to provide families with information about their right to medical privacy and to unlimited access to medical records. Reassuring them that they are the ultimate experts on their child's well-being helps parents develop confidence and improve communication skills. During medical visits, parents should share a personal vignette to remind providers that their child is much more than a medical condition. They should prepare their questions for physicians and medical providers before medical appointments on issues such as their child's physical development, testing, and medications, which will enable them to focus on the answers when engaging providers.

In the past, patients with DSD were often objectified as anomalies and were subjected to frequent medical photography and display of their genitals to large groups of students and clinicians (Dreger, A.D., 1998). Mental health providers can support parents in insisting on limiting both the number of genital exams and the number of people in the room during medical examinations. Parents have a right to know how much experience a provider has with DSD, including the number of operations a surgeon has performed and whether or not the provider has tracked the long-term outcomes of treatment. If their experience with a health care provider is unsatisfactory, parents should be able to change providers without fear of negative repercussions such as being labeled as difficult or maladjusted.

Self-advocacy also plays a role in helping parents and youth engage with systems of care. Parents and youth who are informed are better able to pass along accurate information to others who may provide services to them, including nonspecialized doctors or mental health providers, schools and educators, legal services, or insurance agencies. This is especially important as families and youth relocate away from current services because of work, school, or other reasons.

Integrating a Child's Disorders or Differences of Sex Development into Family Life

In the continuing process of integrating a child's DSD into family life, understanding complex developmental physiology and anatomy can be difficult for families. Parents have responded very positively to the interactive video education tools regarding child physiology available at SickKids (www.sickkids.ca). Families and providers have found two resources developed by the Consortium on the Management of Disorders of Sex Development in 2006 to be extremely useful. Both the *Handbook for Parents* (Consortium on the Management of Disorders of Sex Development, 2006b) and *Clinical Guidelines for the Management of Disorders of Sex Development in Childhood* (Consortium on the Management of Disorders of Sex Development, 2006a) are available online (www.accordalliance .org/dsd-guidelines.html). Although interdisciplinary team care is described in the medical literature, the *Clinical Guidelines* provide an insider's perspective on what family-centered care means. The guidelines include narrative scripts for talking to families in difficult situations, which can help mental health providers prepare themselves and educate other team members. The *Handbook for Parents* addresses specific family concerns. When isolated, some families may be "stuck" in the initial stages of grief, anger, and shame. In our experience, mental health and peer support rapidly accelerate acceptance and engaged and empowered parenting, which promotes the well-being of their children.

Parenting Strategies

As part of holistic care, families also need parenting strategies and psychosocial support in raising children with DSD. After diagnosis, family members begin to learn to adjust their ideas about and goals for their child outside of the male–female gender norm while learning what sex of rearing/gender role, gender identity, and sexual orientation mean for navigating throughout daily life. They also begin to learn to communicate about DSD with other family members, friends, schools, and eventually their own children. During this stressful period, families should be screened for maladaptive coping such as denial and conceal-ment of the child's diagnosis (Kazak et al., 2003). Currently, there is a great need for the development of DSD-specific tools to assess families' levels of adaptation and resilience when raising a child with a DSD (Cohen-Kettenis, 2010). To re-duce the detrimental effects of unrecognized family distress, families may also need counseling and training in problem solving by psychosocial or behavioral staff. To minimize hospital visits, families should receive supports in outpatient family counseling settings, or, where available, in the home using a trained mo-bile therapist. In addition to this individualized support, parents may benefit from exploring some of the themes discussed in the following sections.

Acceptance of Some Ambiguity Regarding Sex, Behavior, and Gender Identity

As stated earlier, a model of shared decision making can help empower parents of children with genital ambiguity to make informed choices when deciding the sex in which they will raise their child. Critical in this process is addressing the parents' anxiety about the uncertainty of their child's sex. Parents often want a clear outcome where one may be unavailable (Gough et al., 2008). Parents may be better able to tolerate ambiguity when providers equip them with ef-fective coping skills to allay and address any underlying fear or concerns (e.g., bullying) that may result if the child's difference is discovered by others and by helping to normalize their experience. Support from mental health and other practitioners and peers is important in this process.

Once the family and clinical team decide on a sex assignment and a child's future manifestations of gender are discussed with parents, they may be told to expect that their child may exhibit more gender-atypical behavior, such as "tomboyishness" in girls. Psychosocial support is crucial for creating a context in which parents can realistically experience a child's gendered behaviors. Families may not understand that there is a wide spectrum of gender expression for boys and girls and that their child's behavior probably does not indicate their child's comfort level with their assigned sex at older ages. Constantly scrutinizing their child's behavior and trying to figure out what it might mean can exhaust parents. Parents should instead focus their energy on encouraging their children to enjoy a variety of activities, regardless of the gender primarily associated with an activity.

For parents who have concerns about their children's gender identity, it is helpful to emphasize that although there can be similarities between DSD and GID, DSD is distinguished by specific physical, genetic, and hormonal differences that may require lifelong medical care, and that a DSD diagnosis does not necessarily imply that there will be gender dysphoria (Dessens, Slijper, & Drop, 2005; Gastaud et al., 2007; Wisniewski, Migeon, Malouf, & Gearhart, 2004). Dealing with their child's sex assignment and observing whether the assignment aligns with a child's developing gender identity can be quite challenging, and these families may need especially close support. With modern care in which the child's and family's well-being are primary considerations, the need for an individual to self-determine (self-reassign) their sex may be less frequent. When self-reassignment is desired, gender transition may also be less traumatic than in the past, particularly if parents, providers, and others within a system of care receive ongoing support that includes more flexible attitudes toward gender presentation and expression.

Communication with Family, Friends, Schools, and Other Institutions

Families may have difficulty deciding how to share information about their child's sex anatomy and physiology with family and friends. They may worry about how others will react to their children or how they will be treated by family and friends, or they may lack the language to communicate about DSD and associated issues (Gough et al., 2008). When a newborn's sex is unclear, parents can explain that although more will be known soon about a baby's gender, the love of family and friends will be most important in supporting their child throughout the developmental process. Some parents have difficulty disclosing a DSD diagnosis to friends, family, and others involved in their children's lives and express their uncertainty with how others will react to their children or their lack of ability or language to talk about DSD and associated conditions (Gough et al., 2008). It is important for families to realize that addressing the needs of children and youth with DSD is an ongoing process requiring psychosocial support for all affected parents, and new challenges will continue to emerge over time.

A theme that is common in family discussions is how to work with child care providers who may be changing a child's diaper or helping with toileting.

In an AIS/DSD Parents Group, with which one of the authors is affiliated, parents have found success in stating calmly and simply that they and their doctor are aware that the baby's genitalia are atypical, but that the child is normal and healthy. For older children, informing school and other institutions that the child has a condition that requires access to private bathroom facilities should suffice. For children with conditions that may cause life-threatening crises, interacting with school staff may be aided by providing parents with information kits containing letters from doctors and information on how to administer related emergency care or by having someone from the care team visit the school or institution in person (Schaeffer et al., 2010). Parents may also consider sharing these recommendations with grandparents, nannies, or others who will be responsible for communicating with child care providers or other institutions.

As their children spend more time out of the home, parents may also have concerns about their child being bullied because of a DSD. Although schools recognize bullying as a serious issue, parents can receive legal assistance with bullying and other issues from Advocates for Informed Choice (www.aiclegal .org). They are the first, and only, organization in the United States to focus on legal advocacy for the rights of children with DSD.

Information Management and Age-Appropriate Discussion of Condition Details

Although health care professionals advocate gradual discussion of the details of a DSD to a child (Allen, 2009), usually referred to as *disclosure,* families struggle with when and how to do so because resources providing concrete guidance are limited. In our experience, most clinicians feel ill-equipped to provide specific advice to parents regarding this process. A chapter in the aforementioned *Handbook for Parents* (Consortium on the Management of Disorders of Sex Development, 2006b) is devoted to a discussion of child development and sharing of information with children from ages 12 months to 18 years. It provides useful examples of possible questions and answers.

A very important role of peer support and psychosocial support professionals is preparation of parents for sharing information, emphasizing that it is a process, not an event. By using sample scripts and role playing, for example, parents can rehearse various scenarios before they arise. Despite this effort, no matter how parents plan for discussing a DSD, children and adolescents ask questions about themselves when they are ready and often at completely unexpected times. Parents often do not realize that these conversations are variations of discussions that they would be having with their children anyway on subjects such as physical differences, puberty, self-esteem, dating, emotional and physical intimacy, sexuality, and relationships. It is especially comforting for families to understand that children are resilient and that continuing family emphasis on a child's strengths and accomplishments will instill self-confidence. Parents should expect a child with a DSD to thrive, not just adapt.

Supporting Families and Youth
Through Puberty and Adolescence

Puberty and adolescence are crucial times during which youth with DSD need increased psychosocial support. Their physical difference can leave them feeling isolated when peers discuss their development. When girls in a peer group begin to menstruate, it is a topic of intense interest and discussion within the group. Girls with absent or variant menstrual cycles associated with DSD conditions may be concerned about exposure and teasing from their peers. Role playing and enacting potential responses in situations, such as being asked whether they have started their periods or if they have a tampon, can lessen anxiety. In the experience of one author, who is a member of the AIS/DSD Parents Group, parents of young children frequently express fear of the school locker room as a reason for normalizing children's genitalia. This fear may be reinforced by clinicians who are unaware that today's physical education programs do not require children to take public showers. Families should be informed that their children can be excused by their care team from potentially stressful activities (e.g., swimming) that require clothing that could reveal atypical genitalia or development.

As their sexuality emerges, youth with DSD may require extra reassurance of their attractiveness and lovability. Physical activities and nutrition education promote positive body image. Families and providers should recognize that dating and relationships are part of life for youth with DSD and should reinforce expectations for healthy relationships and sexuality regardless of sexual orientation. Parents should understand and be tolerant of adolescent experimentation with sexual activity and sexuality as part of the process of identity development. Education about safer sex is important for all youth.

In talking about sex, adolescents may also have questions surrounding fertility. It is important to note that for some individuals with a DSD, biological parenthood may be an option. For those for whom it is not, parents and practitioners can share that there are many individuals, both with and without health conditions that cause infertility, who achieve parenthood through adoption or surrogacy.

As adolescents with DSD engage in relationships, reinforcing self-esteem is especially important because feelings of inadequacy or unworthiness can place them at risk of sexual abuse. Interacting with other teens online or at support group meetings normalizes their feelings and can improve self-confidence. Affected youth especially enjoy having access to successful young adult role models who share their own stories and strategies for overcoming challenges, such as initiating sexual activity and sharing details about their condition with a partner. Some youth may avoid sexual activity or intimacy because they have to prepare for sexual contact in advance with urinary catheterization or vaginal dilation. They may need referral to clinical providers with the ability to educate youth regarding issues of sexuality and intimacy.

Identity Development

An important task for adolescents and young adults is separating and individu-ating from their families and developing their own unique identities. McCarn and Fassinger (1996) provide a phase model of sexual identity development that we believe is helpful for supporting individuals with DSD. Although it does not specifically address DSD or intersex identities, this model offers considerable room for individuals to understand themselves in the context of their own ex-perience, their own gender, and their own body. The model also provides an approach to informing individuals about how to understand their role within a larger group of people with some degree of similar experience. We believe this is critical given the diversity between and within diagnoses; varying connection with other individuals who have similar experiences; and differences in decisions about and quality of care, awareness, and knowledge. Future theory and research should further explore how this or other models might provide a foundation for a model on DSD identity development.

Transitioning Care

Although adolescents and young adults are tasked with developing their iden-tity, at the same time, a system of care team is tasked with helping them transi-tion to adult care. Depending on insurance requirements, school/college enroll-ment and emancipation status, at some point an individual will no longer be eligible for care by a pediatric endocrinologist. Team management by a provider other than a pediatric endocrinologist is optimal to facilitate transition to adult care. Holistic care teams should include experts in social work and/or case man-agement because providers who function in these roles play an important role in maintaining consistent care for families and individuals affected by DSD.

THE ROLE OF PSYCHOSOCIAL SUPPORT

Regardless of the age at which their child is diagnosed, in our experience, many parents who participate in support groups describe contact with other families as their single most important stress reliever in the mix of emotions after a diag-nosis of DSD. In contrast to the negative information sometimes conveyed by providers to families, stories from other parents and caregivers that confirm that children with DSD grow up to have healthy and fulfilling lives can greatly im-prove parents' and caregivers' expectations that they have the efficacy to suc-cessfully support their child. Although peer support is accessible at the national and often local levels, in situations in which clinical psychosocial support is not prioritized, many families and individuals who might benefit from peer sup-port are not referred to peer services because of providers' perceptions that sup-port groups provide misleading information (Meyer-Bahlburg, Dolezal, Baker,

& New, 2008) or advocate confrontation with medical providers (Lee & Houk, 2010).

One of the authors of this chapter, a physician and long-time online discussion group moderator, has observed that physicians and other clinicians considering referral to support groups frequently do not differentiate between sites on which anyone is free to make an unmonitored posting and professionally moderated support groups that provide high-quality information such as Accord Alliance, the AIS/DSD Support Group, and DSD Families. All of these groups address concerns of families of both boys and girls who are affected by any kind of DSD. Clinicians should understand that many families of children with rare conditions desperately seek to learn all they can outside the doctor's office, and they frequently search the Internet for additional information, where they may encounter frightening web sites that politicize "intersex" for their own purposes. Rather than denying families peer support by omitting their mention in lists of resources, clinicians should familiarize themselves with support groups and provide feedback for improvement.

Holistic health care providers who work with support groups can direct families to reliable sources of information and experience that provide practical, reassuring parenting information. As a standard of practice, clinicians should quickly provide the families of newly diagnosed children with peer support contacts who can immediately provide personalized support. This can help lessen the crisis mentality that accompanies isolation. Definitions of peer support should also be broadened to include a host of local, national, and Internet-based models, as some families prefer to engage in private interaction with other parents and caregivers rather than join a larger online support group.

Inclusion within a System of Care

In a truly patient-centered, holistic system of care, inclusion of adults with DSD or parents of children and youth with DSD on the collaborative care team can help provide timely and expanded access to effective peer support. As initial connections with the affected community, they can facilitate gradual contact, first individually with others who have experience with DSD and later with support groups that can provide nonjudgmental support and coping strategies. The participation of individuals with DSD also expands treatment team consciousness of relevant issues, including how affected people are sometimes objectified in impersonal ways. In addition to advocating for inclusion of individuals with direct experience with DSD on the care team, mental health providers should assume major roles as team participants functioning as "cultural brokers" of experience within the clinical context. This is especially important in areas where teams may not have individuals with DSD available to serve on the team.

Making Referrals to Support Groups

Support groups are often excellent resources for families, adolescents, or even adults looking for information about DSD. Support groups offer a degree of anonymity and privacy (through registration requirements) and can help individuals find referrals, answer questions about insurance coverage and care, and connect with others in varied geographic locations. However, when making a referral, practitioners should consider several factors that impinge on the identification of a support group that is an appropriate match for a particular family. For example, some existing groups may not regularly update their web sites with the latest information on rapid and ongoing developments in the field of DSD care. Some groups are moderated by health care providers, whereas volunteers may run others. Some groups may serve the needs of parents and families, whereas others focus on adults. Similarly, there are often unique groups for varying diagnoses. Providers who refer families or individuals to support groups are advised to always conduct an updated search/site review before referral. Maintaining connections with other professionals and support organizations can ensure that providers maintain the most current information.

Even without a specific referral, families or individuals may discover support groups through their own efforts. As such, it is also important for providers to talk generally about support groups, message boards, and web sites. Families and individuals should be informed that members within each organization are likely to share different experiences and views. Practitioners should facilitate each family's or individual's comfort in developing their own personal views and opinions. Those who participate in support groups should also be aware that recommendations made through these web-based sources regarding specific providers, approaches to care, treatment, and/or participation in research studies should be cautiously considered and evaluated for their appropriateness for each individual.

CONCLUSION

Improving long-term outcomes in DSD care will be difficult to achieve without access to mental health providers as part of a multidisciplinary system of care team that responds to family and individual needs across the life span. Although an international consensus group (Lee et al., 2006) endorsed patient-centered care for DSD in 2006, the actual availability of services for families and individuals to access lags far behind the original vision of collaborative care. Lack of access to psychosocial support is an ongoing barrier to optimum health and functioning for those affected by DSD. Those centers that do have designated care teams are challenged by lack of institutional funding and insurance reimbursement for mental health care. Systems of care with defined mechanisms for abundant psychosocial support could be adapted for DSD care. Medical, emotional, psychosocial, peer, and clinical case management support should go hand in hand.

Inclusion of individuals with DSD on a care team enhances the connection of teams to the DSD community as whole. These relationships in turn enhance follow-up as the community gains confidence in and endorses team care. Full inclusion of individuals with DSD on the team also enriches its collective cultural and linguistic understanding and provides immediate personal support to families with children newly diagnosed with a DSD. This process expands family access to support by cultivating new local volunteers to meet with families. By maintaining contact with local and national support groups, individuals with DSD can offer personalized connections to experienced individuals in support groups that can meet families' specific needs.

As parents and caregivers begin to share information with children and youth, youth increasingly have full knowledge of their DSD, and children are learning the full details of their condition at younger ages. As recently as 2009, the AIS/DSD Parents Group recommended that parents wait until their daughters were 15 or 16 years old to tell them about their karyotype and gonads, which is a prerequisite for attendance at the national meeting. However, in 2010, girls as young as 12 and 13 years old who were fully informed attended the meeting. One result of this ongoing decrease in age is the emergence of role models and leaders who are encouraged to participate in organizational support and advocacy activities. Advocates for Informed Choice (http://aiclegal.org) is currently organizing the first peer-led youth leadership program in the country for youth with DSD. In addition, Inter/Act (http://inter-actyouth.tumblr.com) provides youth with DSD opportunities to network, create a peer community, and articulate their needs, developing a cadre of youth leaders with DSD to take the movement forward. The continuing move to empower youth in their own care and to promote youth leadership in advocacy efforts aligns with the youth-guided approach integral to the success of service delivery in systems of care.

The last few decades have seen a number of positive changes for individuals with DSD: increased awareness and education, creation of support groups, improved treatment choices and outcomes, and efforts to standardize care. There are, however, multiple additional opportunities to maximize the well-being of affected youths, necessitating the full implementation of truly holistic care that embraces the value of mental health, peer support, and shared decision making. We hope that the recommendations presented in this chapter will help systems of care in their efforts to provide culturally and linguistically holistic care and to meaningfully support the affected community. Key recommendations include the following:

- Contact with mental health providers should be immediate when a DSD is detected to be sure that families begin to receive adequate psychosocial support and help tolerating uncertainty. Receiving this support helps ensure that families' and youths' social and emotional needs are met as they develop.

- Mental health providers should assume major roles as team participants functioning as "cultural brokers" of experience within the clinical context and advocating for inclusion of individuals with direct experience with DSD on the care team. They have a primary role in promoting a thoughtful process of shared decision making regarding any treatment and assure team sensitivity to language, cultural and linguistic facts, developmental considerations, and clinicians' own unconscious assumptions about gender.

- All providers should advocate for thoughtful referral to peer support and for the inclusion of people affected by DSD on teams in a system of care approach for families and youth with DSD.

- Although guidelines for care exist, increased empirical research on mental health is needed to better guide providers in their practice with families and youth affected by DSD. Similar to recommendations for holistic care, it is imperative that this research be multidisciplinary and reflect the experience and needs of individuals.

7

Becoming Who We Are Meant to Be

Native Americans with Two-Spirit, LGBT, and/or Related Tribal Identities

MIRIAM L. BEARSE

Regardless of whether you are a practitioner, systems expert, or family or community member in your system of care, you are most likely interacting with or caring for American Indian and Alaska Native (AI/AN) youth, even if there is not a tribe in your area.[1] If you are providing services/supports to AI/AN youth, you most likely have at least some AI/AN youth who are not heterosexual and/or who do not identify or express themselves as their birth-assigned gender. Similarly, if you are part of a tribal or urban Indian system of care or circle of care, you may identify youth with diverse sexual orientations and gender identities once they feel safe to talk about and express themselves. Furthermore, your community may have youth who are not yet identified as lesbian, gay, bisexual, and transgender (LGBT) or another nonheterosexual, gender-variant identity, perhaps because you and/or the youth may lack the language to express these identities. These AI/AN youth often have complex and specific needs and may require support to develop emotionally and physically in healthy ways. To help address their needs, this chapter

- Explores cultural and linguistic terms and identifies conceptual distinctions among identities
- Describes the development of two-spirit identity and antecedent AI/AN tribal-specific terms that continue to define traditional sectors of AI/AN communities

---

[1]For the purposes of this chapter, definitions of *tribe, urban Indian organization,* and *Native American* are based on community usage, rather than a more restricted federal definition. *Tribe* refers to a traditionally recognized sovereign government and its community. A tribe may or may not be federally recognized. An *urban Indian organization* is a nonprofit or not-for-profit organization in a metropolitan (urban) area that serves Native American individuals and families. A definition of *Native American* is in the next section.

- Reviews the overall developmental trajectory for AI/AN youth with varying sexual orientations and gender identities, compared with non-Native youth
- Summarizes common challenges that stem from experiences of bias, resulting in harm to mental health and well-being
- Draws on examples to explore how some individuals have experienced empowerment, even in the midst of numerous challenges
- Offers recommendations for Native and non-Native providers in varied settings

CULTURAL AND LINGUISTIC TERMS

The proliferation of terms used to refer to families and communities that have always resided in what we now refer to as the United States can be confusing. Continued usage of the term *American Indian* is often questioned because *Indian* comes from usage among colonists who intended to go west from Europe to reach the Indian subcontinent of Asia. Many indigenous Americans prefer this term, however, despite its origins.[2] Although the term *Native American* is more accurate, it does not necessarily include those who are indigenous to the geographic area that is now Alaska (or Hawaii). People from Alaska tend to use the term *Alaska Native;* the term *Native Hawaiian* is generally used to refer to indigenous populations in and from Hawaii.

To reflect the terms preferred by most indigenous individuals in the United States (and to minimize confusion), *AI/AN* is used throughout this chapter, except when information comes from a source that uses an alternate term. The AI/AN term includes Native Hawaiians, even though their traditions may vary significantly from what is presented in this chapter. The term *Native* is used occasionally and reflects a combination of AI/ANs and related aboriginal/ indigenous communities. Many AI/ANs today are multiracial, as indicated by the increased number of AI/ANs recognized by the U.S. Census in 2000, when it became possible for individuals to self-identify as members of more than one racial or ethnic category. Note that most AI/ANs see themselves as part of an indigenous community that is continuous at least through the Americas, if not the world, irrespective of modern national borders.

---

[2]*Indigenous* refers to communities 1) whose traditions and history are tied to the land on which they live and/or 2) who existed on that land before colonial contact. If you are in a system of care in a U.S. territory, you may find similarities between the experiences of AI/AN youth and the youth of the indigenous population(s) in your territory.

TRIBAL MEMBERSHIP

Membership in a tribe confers citizenship in that tribe or nation. The Bureau of Indian Affairs (BIA), a federal agency, was legally charged in the 1800s with determining who could be a member of a given tribe, a right not fully restored to tribes until the 1970s. Some tribes retain the BIA criteria for membership, based on percentage of Indian blood or "blood quantum," but other tribes have revised their membership requirements and use a range of criteria such as lineal descendance and residency in the community, among other requirements. Although the BIA keeps centralized records on members of federally recognized tribes, the tribes themselves determine who may be a member. Although many AI/AN individuals are enrolled in a tribe, this is increasingly not true for many individuals with Native heritage due to numerous factors, including intermarriage; changing enrollment criteria; dislocation of families from reservations or tribal areas; the forced relocation of families because of federal relocation programs in the 1950s and 1960s; and the federal termination policies in the 1950s, which ended federal recognition of some tribes (Ulrich, 2010).

The concentration of AI/ANs in rural versus urban areas is changing as well. There are now more AI/ANs in urban areas (approximately 70%) than in reservation or rural areas (National Urban Indian Family Coalition, 2008; Ogunwole, 2002). Diverse, multi-tribal Indian communities exist in most urban centers.

ORIGIN AND DEVELOPMENT OF TWO-SPIRIT IDENTITY

Although the experience of AI/AN individuals may vary significantly across communities,[3] it is necessary to consider several issues to better understand the experience of two-spirit youth. These issues include varied traditions on the identity terms used by two-spirit youth, why some people prefer some terms over others, and the history of AI/ANs in the United States. Additional concerns include the various traumas AI/AN nations have experienced over time related to the rise of homophobia and heterosexism and the historical reduction of two-spirit roles in Native nations due to colonization.

Many tribes' languages contain or historically included terms for those who were two-spirit. Sexual orientation was often less relevant for AI/ANs than other issues in defining identity. Often a person's nontypical gender/sexual

---

[3]Throughout this chapter, you will see terms that are translated from Native languages. Because these terms are not in their original tongue, their spelling as they are translated into English may vary. For correct pronunciation and usage, please refer to a current speaker of the original language or a tribal elder from the tribe referenced. Before colonization began in the 1500s, Turtle Island (a term used to refer to what is now called the Americas) contained an estimated 800 nations. Linguists have identified some 150 language families and 1,500–2,000 dialects. In the United States alone, approximately 200 indigenous languages continue to be spoken today (Anguksuar, 1997).

identity had less to do with one's partner choices and more to do with how one dressed, acted, and interacted with others in one's community, as well as the community role one was given. Tribes' terms for these individuals have varied: *nadleeh* (Navajo), *kwido* (Tewa), *winkte* (Lakota Sioux), *dubuds* (Pauite), *aayahk-wew* (Cree), and *ogokwe* (Ojibwa) (Roscoe, 1998). An estimated 168 (remaining) Native languages have terms for people who are not typical "men" or "women" (Garrett & Barrett, 2003). Many cultures had or have distinct roles for these community members, including marriage brokers, preparers of the dead, treaty negotiators, medicine people, and those who take in orphans. Not all tribes, however, have the same perspective regarding two-spirit people. According to researcher Will Roscoe (1998), former coordinator of the Gay American Indians History Project, there is no single belief about two-spirits among Native nations. Two-spirits may be respected within one tribe and ostracized in another, whereas the topic of sex and gender may be ignored altogether in yet another tribe (Rahimi, 2005).

Furthermore, two-spirit identities have been suppressed over time. For example, when colonists arrived on Turtle Island in the Lake Erie area, many missionaries and colonists targeted nontypical men and women in tribal communities for death because they were considered offensive to the church's sensibilities. Many AI/AN communities hid these individuals from the colonists. In some communities, people and their roles went underground (i.e., kept them hidden), whereas in other communities, these identities disappeared as a result of murder of these individuals. Many anthropological texts record two-spirit life before colonial alteration or destruction, and in some communities, elders still recall the old traditions. As anthropologists and colonists encountered AI/AN cultures, they observed and described the diverse gender and sexual identity roles in Native nations. Many texts recording these roles refer to nontypical men as *berdache*. This term is from the Persian *bardaj*, originally a derogatory term meaning a passive homosexual partner, usually a "pretty" or feminine young boy (Anguksuar, 1997). Nowadays, *berdache* is seldom used because it is usually considered culturally inappropriate and offensive. In the words of Navajo anthropologist Wesley Thomas:

> Homophobia was taught to us as a component of Western education and religion….we were presented with an entirely new set of taboos, which did not correspond to our own models and which focused on sexual behavior rather than the intricate roles Two-Spirit people played. As a result of this misrepresentation, our nations no longer accepted us as they once had. (Rahimi, 2005, p.1)

The federal government, through colonization and Christianization, inserted Western gender and sexual orientation norms into tribal communities where there was previously an array of roles and definitions. Two-spirit people live with this history every day. It is reflected in their overall distrust of mainstream (non-Native) providers, in the hostility they may face on Native reservations, and in the struggle to reclaim and honor their Native identity and the Native traditions that respect two-spirit individuals (Jacobs, Thomas, & Lang, 1997).

In addition, many communities are unaware of their own history regarding nontypical men and women or have adopted a colonial or missionary perspective shared by the dominant society that characterizes these people as shameful. This has created loss and trauma not only for individuals, but also communities. Acceptance and recalling of traditions, however, strengthens communities and helps reclaim traditional values that support two-spirit people (Roscoe, 1998).

TWO-SPIRIT IDENTITIES TODAY

In 1990, AI/AN LGBT people who came together at the International Two-Spirit Gathering created the *two-spirit* term as an "umbrella" term to include those AI/ANs who are not heterosexual and/or who do not identify their gender following Western cultural practice. *Two-spirit* includes tribal-specific terms used to refer to those who are "not male and not female" or who "take on" the other gender (Anguksuar, 1997). It comes from a Northern Algonquin (Ojibwe) word *niizh manitoag* (two-spirits), meaning those with male and female spirit(s) in them. The term *two-spirit* is a "contested compromise to move forward the debate in eliminating culturally inappropriate terms" and includes a wide variety of Native persons: "cross-dressers, transvestites, lesbian, gay, transgendered, or [those] otherwise 'marked' as 'alternatively gendered' within tribes, bands, and nations where multiple gender concepts occur" (Jacobs et al., 1997, p.7).

Not all AI/AN individuals who have a gender-variant or nonheterosexual identity identify as two-spirit. In some languages, *two-spirited* can mean "two-faced," or someone who lies, so some avoid this term because of negative associations with the English translation. Others identify themselves using traditional terms from their tribe. Others do not identify as two-spirit because of a lack of awareness of the term or the historical importance in Native nations of people who were/are nontypical men and women. Others do not identify as two-spirit because they prefer terms from dominant culture (i.e., LGBT). Other Native people may identify using two-spirit as well as LGBT terminology, depending on how these identities are understood within particular contexts (Monette, Albert, & Waalen, 2001).

Two-spirit experience and identity can vary by a person's expression of his or her biological sex (male, female), gender identity (man, woman, other identity), traditional role (if any), partner choice (sex, gender of partner), and acculturation (type of cultural background and expression). Often a person's spiritual experiences are central to the formation of his or her identity and expressions. In the words of a young woman who identifies herself as a two-spirit female:

What it means to me, certainly, it doesn't mean my sexuality only, it means my spirituality, it means…accountability to the community, and the roles that I'm supposed to perform…it comes from something that is remarkable. And not evil and not bad…the Creator made us, you know. (O'Brien-Teegs, 2008, pp. 23–24)

The term *two-spirit* is used throughout the remainder of this chapter as a term that includes two-spirit/LGBT Native youth as well as Native youth who identify with traditional tribal terms.

TRADITIONAL TERMS AND ROLES

There is considerable variety, both historically and currently, in the roles that two-spirit people have in AI/AN nations. In some nations, two-spirit people are identified in childhood or early adolescence by elders, family members, or spiritual leaders. In other traditions, two-spirit people are identified through visions or dreams that they recount to others. Sometimes people who might identify as a two-spirit may hesitate to identify themselves as such because they may not be fulfilling their nation's traditional role associated with individuals who are not typically male or female (Fieland, Walters, & Simoni, 2007; Jacobs et al., 1997). For some communities, knowledgeable elders and community members instruct others about the two-spirit traditions in their nation.

The retraditionalizing trend within the modern two-spirit movement, coupled with new examinations of historical writings and cultural practices, can help identify traditions that existed before colonization. Similarly, these trends can identify the traditions that are continuing and may be reintegrated in the present day. For example, in Lakota tradition, a *winkte* is a physical male who has male partners and performs some female tasks, as well as fulfills particular spiritual roles (Calimach, 2000).

Epple (1998) described four Navajo genders: female-bodied women, male-bodied men, female-bodied nadleehi [two-spirit or alternate gender], and male-bodied nadleehi. Male nadleehi same-sex sexual practices therefore differ from Western gay relationships, because nadleehi partners are of a different gender than nadleehi, although both are physically male. In most Native nations, in contrast to Western ideas, sexuality itself is seen as integrated within the individual's and community's spiritual interconnection with the natural world. Nadleehi also historically can have particular spiritual roles in family and ceremony. For the Mojave, the hwame role is historically filled by individuals with female biological sex who take on some typically male responsibilities and have female partners. For women who became hwame, Mojave culture included an initiatory ritual that provided the hwame with a name and the right to marry a woman. A hwame's wife retained the typical female role and status.

A basic understanding of terms and language is necessary for systems of care to understand the commonalities and diversities within two-spirit identities and the Native nations to which they belong. It is also important to fully understand the effects of colonization on Native nations and two-spirit people, in particular. Furthermore, practitioners, family members, and system of care partners should be informed about the complexity of two-spirit identity and how identity can vary depending on nation, acculturation, individual identity, role, behaviors, and other factors. This awareness can inform efforts to help youth develop and express their sense of self in healthy and empowering ways, both individually and as part of their communities.

CHALLENGES EXPERIENCED BY TWO-SPIRIT YOUTH

Two-spirit youth encounter significant challenges in accessing health care, obtaining employment, finding adequate legal assistance, and avoiding or recovering from violence. They also experience a complex blend of historical traumas, contemporary traumas, systemic biases and, frequently, extreme poverty and lack of access to services and supports. When thinking about the ongoing effects of historical traumas, contemporary Native social workers and psychologists often conceptualize these effects as a "soul wound" or "spirit wound" that affects both individuals and communities (Brave Heart & DeBruyn, 1998; Duran & Duran, 1995). Unhealed grief from traumatic events does not go away; rather, it is passed between generations, affecting and interacting with the different traumas of each generation, often referred to as *intergenerational* or *historical trauma*. Current and historical traumas have led to a spectrum of health problems evident in most AI/AN communities across the continent.

For two-spirit youth, it is often most appropriate for providers and supporters to rely on a trauma-focused and culturally relevant treatment approach based on the youth's own narrative of identity and strengths, within the context of historical trauma, community soul wounding, and community cultural strengths. It is important to remember that youth seeking support come from or exist within a community with both a complex trauma history and particular cultural strengths. Specific challenges and particular risks two-spirit youth can experience are described in the following sections to provide a meaningful context for how practitioners and community members can help two-spirit youth experiencing serious mental health challenges or related concerns.

Challenges to Receiving Culturally and Linguistically Competent Health Care

Many institutional challenges affect and limit the ability of AI/ANs to obtain adequate health care. Even though tribes were promised health care (as well as education and other services) in exchange for land, federal follow-through has been insufficient to meet the need. The U.S. Commission on Civil Rights in

2004 recognized this problem when it stated that "persistent discrimination and neglect continue to deprive Native Americans of a health system sufficient to provide health care equivalent to that provided to the vast majority of Americans" (p. 6). The Indian Health Service (IHS, 1997), a federal agency, was developed to provide health services on or near reservations, but the system is severely underfunded (Forquera, 2001). IHS also has a severe lack of funding for mental health services/supports and an inadequate number of providers (Smith, 2005). Although more than half of all AI/ANs live in urban areas, just 1% of the IHS budget is reserved for urban Indian health centers (Brown, Ojeda, Wyn, & Levan, 2000). When AI/ANs do access urban or rural non-Native health providers, they can experience discrimination based on their ethnicity (Monette et al., 2001), as well as heterosexism or gender stereotyping. Addressing health problems is also complicated by the complex web of jurisdictions across tribal and reservation communities. There is commonly a blend of providers, with mostly IHS services and a few private agencies, combined with tribal social services in some areas and county and state systems, with the IHS as the "payer of last resort" for health care. This can limit access to services and cause frustration for those trying to access health supports.

Moreover, rates of diagnosed mental health disorders are high, and the suicide rate of AI/ANs represents 190% of the rate of the general population. Suicide is the leading cause of death for AI/ANs 15–24 years of age (U.S. Commission on Civil Rights, 2004). Frank and Lester (2002) found that 32.2% of AI/AN females reported suicide attempts in the previous 12 months, as did 22.2% of Native males (compared with 10.5% of Caucasian and 9.7% of African American females, and 4% of Caucasian and 5.2% of African American males). Challenges to receiving health care impede the ability of AI/AN individuals to receive needed services and supports, including behavioral health services.

Bias and Lateral Violence in Native Communities

Attitudes toward two-spirit youth on reservations and in tribal communities can vary greatly. Some communities maintain traditional openness and acceptance. Other communities can be intolerant and even violent toward their two-spirit relatives. Although most communities lie somewhere along this continuum, many two-spirit youth and adults leave reservation or rural communities because of open or subtle intolerance and fear. Two-spirits can also sometimes be the victims of *lateral violence,* a term used to refer to violence between two members of a stigmatized group, which is related to the heritage of bias and violence experienced at the hands of colonial and missionary forces.

Some AI/AN communities are unaware of the historical existence of two-spirit people or the generalized acceptance of differences that was found in many tribes before colonization. Other communities or individuals may have a belief that same-sex relationships are a "White thing" that is foreign to Native cultures.

Christianized Native communities that have partially or fully abandoned traditional ceremonies may see two-spirit people as impure or immoral.

For many AI/AN communities, sex and sexual behaviors are not discussed openly, which inhibits conversations about gender and sexual attraction. Community norms may result in avoiding the topic altogether and shunning or ignoring those who bring it up or who, by their very existence, illustrate that gender and sexual orientation are complex issues in communities. In many rural communities, rumor and gossiping is a key method of communication. Shame is rendered for inappropriate social behavior and can affect whether an individual is allowed to participate in key social and spiritual ceremonies. In some communities, being open as a two-spirit may bring shame not just to the individual but also to the individual's family (Arviso, 2008).

Many young people who leave reservations or rural AI/AN communities move to urban areas to find environments in which they are accepted. Life in these urban areas is often tougher than anticipated, and some youth turn to drugs, the sex trade, or other risky activities to self-medicate or survive. In the words of one youth, "homophobia drives youth away from reserves [reservations] and other rural communities…sometimes they are kicked out for whatever reason, then they find their sexuality down here…youth move to the city to 'hide' and end up isolating themselves" (Youth Migration Project of Toronto, 2010).

Some youth do find that they can make a life for themselves in urban areas, particularly when they are able to connect with supportive relatives. There is a reservation–urban migration pattern for some two-spirit people; they live in urban areas so they can be openly two-spirit and then return periodically to their reservation or rural Native community to reconnect with their culture and family. They often end up expressing themselves as Native while at home and then expressing themselves as two-spirit or "gay" while in urban areas, but sometimes they have difficulty finding places to be comfortable as both.

There are instances in which two-spirit youth (and adults) have experienced violence in reservations and rural areas when they have expressed themselves openly as two-spirit. One example of this is the life and death of Fred Martinez, Jr., an openly identified two-spirit youth of the Navajo Nation who was murdered in 2001. At age 16, Martinez often carried a purse. He identified as gay, and as transgender, refusing to hide. Fred's mother said he called himself a nadleehi, recalling the traditional acceptance of men with feminine attributes. Martinez "took comfort in that history," his mother said, "until they killed him" (Duggan, 2001).

Homelessness and Child Welfare Involvement

As mentioned previously, many two-spirit youth leave home to seek acceptance and freedom in urban areas. Urban centers are "magnets" for two-spirit youth from reservation communities that run away or are thrown out of their homes. Young people who run away, are thrown out of their home, or experience physical abuse to "cure" them of being two-spirit have an elevated chance of ending up in the foster care system, including group homes and transitional living homes. In some areas, AI/ANs are represented at a rate nearly twice that of non-Natives, or higher. Additionally, nonheterosexual youth in foster care report experiencing high levels of physical violence while in care (approximately 70% in one study; Mallon, 2001).

Drug and Alcohol Abuse

Cultural alienation, bias, trauma, and related experiences can help lead two-spirit youth to use alcohol and drugs early in their lives to self-medicate grief and loss or manage mental health problems. As stated by a two-spirit focus group participant:

> When you're two-spirit you're different and unaccepted and everybody in the family wants to make sure that fact is hidden. The only way you can be yourself is to leave the place, essentially [stop being] Native, which is to leave your family and try to find something elsewhere. Or you try to abandon that part of you, you drown it. And literally drown it. I think a lot of people drown themselves in alcohol, to try and suppress it and not to think. (Brotman, Ryan, Jalbert, & Rowe, 2002a, p. 20)

Two-spirit adults reported having their first drink at an earlier age (12.6 versus 14.7 years old) than their heterosexual peers and were also more likely to have used illicit drugs other than marijuana (78.3% versus 56%, respectively; Fieland et al., 2007). AI/AN youth have higher rates of alcohol and substance abuse than any other ethnic group, as well as the highest rate of alcohol abstention (Substance Abuse and Mental Health Services Administration, 2001).

Suicide, Violence, and Mental Health Challenges

As a result of historical trauma, bias, stigma, abuse, and/or isolation that can result from the previously described experiences, many two-spirit youth have mental health and wellness needs and are at risk for negative outcomes. In 2004, the Urban Native Youth Association of Canada released a report of a survey conducted among two-spirit youth indicating that 38% of respondents did not feel accepted in their communities; 43% of respondents reported they were suffering from depression. Other survey self-report data (Pablo, 2008) indicated that:

- 34% were more likely than non–two-spirit people to think about and attempt suicide

- 34% were more likely to become dependent on either alcohol or drugs
- 80% stated that a better understanding of two-spirit issues is needed in their own Native communities

In one study, Native men younger than 25 years who identified as "not heterosexual" had a high risk of suicide (25% versus 8% for heterosexual Native men). More than half of two-spirit adults surveyed reported at least one lifetime suicide attempt. The rate (66%) increased if they had been in foster care or experienced boarding school (82%; Walters, Simoni, & Horwath, 2001).

Two-spirit individuals are also at high risk for being victims of violence both because of their LGBT/two-spirit identity and their Native identity; both groups experience higher rates of violence exposure compared with that of the general U.S. population. A comparison of sexual orientation bias experienced by two-spirit individuals and a predominantly Caucasian group of LGBT individuals indicated that two-spirit individuals reported higher rates of physical assaults (36% versus 5%–13%, respectively) and sexual assaults (29% versus 3%–7%, respectively; Walters et al., 2001).

High Rates of Historical Trauma

Emotional and spiritual effects of historical trauma include internalization of the oppressor, unresolved grief and mourning, and suicidality. Mental health diagnoses such as posttraumatic stress disorder often fail to capture the extent and depth of the wounding of the spirit associated with such traumas. As a two-spirit woman who identifies as a male-to-female transsexual stated, "there is a place within the circle that had been an empty hole for a lot of communities and for a lot of families for the better part of 100 years, people like me got killed or had to go way underground" (Honor Project cited in Bearse, Fieland, & Stately, 2007, p. 18).

Some research studies have found that Native American youth are more likely than non-Native youth to identify as LGB and to suffer abuse and run away from home. Overall, two-spirit youth start having sex earlier than heterosexual peers, and young AI/AN women who identify as lesbian or bisexual are more likely to have opposite-sex sexual experiences than non-Native lesbians/bisexuals, illustrating the gender and sexual behavior fluidity that can characterize two-spirit identities and the cultural importance placed on bearing children (Saewyc, Skay, Bearinger, Blum, & Resnick, 1998).

IDENTITY DEVELOPMENT

Two-spirit youth need support in their families and communities to stay within their family and culture, counter internalized bias, gain a positive sense of self, and be protected from making harmful behavioral choices. They often, however, have challenges speaking openly about their identity as a result of potential rejection and exclusion from family as an integral source of support and concerns regarding violent reactions and confidentiality. The sociopsychological context, with its lack of positive two-spirit role models, stereotypical images of AI/ANs in LGBT cultures, and negative stories about LGBT people in Native communities, can lead to negative self-images and additional trauma for two-spirit youth, who may find it difficult to envision a positive future.

In general, there are a few typical developmental pathways for two-spirit youth. Some are raised as two-spirit within their culture and to some degree find traditional acceptance, roles, and responsibilities that promote respectful behavior from others in the community. This outcome still occurs, but far less often than before colonization. Other two-spirit youth experience a lack of acceptance in their home community and leave to find support elsewhere. Still others make the decision not to be open about their identity, continuing to live in their home community either fully or partially hidden or "closeted." Some two-spirit youth were primarily raised in an urban, non-Native, or mixed culture environment and found early acceptance in the mostly non-Native LGBT community. They sometimes also find acceptance in AI/AN organizations or two-spirit networks (Arviso, 2008; Frazer & Pruden, 2010; Gilley, 2006).

For two-spirit people, the narrative of "coming out" makes more sense if the process is viewed as a lifetime progression of identity development relative to the environment in which the individual exists. Coming out can be an individual's one-time choice to claim one's identity; however, the narrative of two-spirit people coming out into their identity can vary greatly from that pattern. A two-spirit person can be "out" about their two-spirit identity and not out about their Native identity or vice versa. Sometimes a two-spirit person can avoid speaking openly about their identity with anyone, when it is clear that their entire community knows. In other situations, a two-spirit person comes out when their grandparent or elder identifies them as a two-spirit person when they are a child. This last example points to the fact that two-spirit people always exist in relation to their tribe or Native community and their traditions, and identity is defined by a combination of the community and the individual. Two-spirit people can also "come in and out" over time as their relationship with different identity terms changes and they move within and between different communities.

Relationship Between Alaskan Indian/American Native Two-Spirit/LGBT Life and Non-Native LGBT Society

When two-spirit youth and adults contact or participate in LGBT communities, they may be seeking acceptance and a social life in which to find partners and friends and access services from LGBT community agencies. Two-spirit people, however, often do not experience LGBT communities as fully accepting, sometimes discovering that AI/AN people are objectified or eroticized as "different," as "other," and/or as sexual objects. They may also find themselves vastly outnumbered by non-Native people and may feel invisible in LGBT settings. Unfortunately, two-spirit youth often find themselves trapped between the heterosexism and transphobia they experience in Native settings and the racism or bias they experience in non-Native settings.

Two-spirit youth often end up turning to AI/AN agencies in cities only to learn that agency staff may be heterosexist or transphobic. Further, LGBT agencies often discriminate against or lack knowledge about Native people. As one youth noted, "either the non-Aboriginal culture is discriminating against you on the basis of your culture [or] the Aboriginal culture is discriminating against you on the basis of what they think are your activities or behaviors" (Youth Migration Project of Toronto, 2010, p. 2). One statewide survey found that some AI/AN LGBT and two-spirit people were comfortable seeking services and social opportunities within the LGBT community, whereas others were uncomfortable because they experienced stereotyping and fetishism (i.e., they were viewed as objects of intrigue rather than being respected as individuals). A lack of two-spirit programming in the mainstream LGBT community and the experience of stereotyping demonstrate that two-spirit people often do not have culturally and linguistically appropriate services and supports available to meet their needs. Tellingly, in a recent survey, AI/AN respondents were less likely to report having visited an LGBT-specific venue for health and human services in the past year than respondents of other races/ethnicities (Frazer & Pruden, 2010).

In response to these experiences, two-spirit people have created a network of groups, associations, and gatherings over the past 30 years to create space in which to find full acceptance as both Native and two-spirit individuals. In 1987, AI/AN LGBT individuals who attended the Gay and Lesbian March on Washington, D.C., organized a conference called "The Basket and the Bow, A Gathering of Lesbian & Gay Native Americans." This gathering was the first of the annual international two-spirit gatherings; additional gatherings were held in 1988 in Minnesota and 1989 in Wisconsin. The International Two Spirit Gathering has been held at sites in Canada and the United States annually since 1987, offering an opportunity for two-spirit people of many nations to meet, socialize, and learn about traditions for personal healing and growth (Arviso, 2008).

Two-spirit organizations and networks exist in most major urban areas across the United States. The Internet also offers multiple opportunities for two-spirit adults and youth to communicate and learn about two-spirit events and history. Although some non-Native LGBT organizations have become more aware of Native culture and two-spirit identities, and many Native organizations have become more accepting of two-spirit people, ongoing challenges with bias persist in both cultural spaces. Many two-spirit people believe the return of two-spirit people and roles to Native communities is essential for tribes and communities to overcome challenges forced on them by colonization, return to or renew traditions, and become stronger and healthier communities that fully express the sovereignty of Native nations (Roscoe, 1998).

Cultural Considerations for Providers

Although generalizing about AI/AN cultures and two-spirit people is difficult, providers and community partners need to be aware of some crucial areas of general cultural difference between AI/AN and non-Native cultures. These cultural concepts and values represent some common cultural strengths that have enabled communities to continue to survive and thrive despite the sustained effects of historical trauma. Many AI/ANs today have a "blended" cultural style that integrates some Native concepts from their tribe, some pan-Indian concepts, and some mainstream non-Native values and practices. Others may "code-switch" by expressing different values-based behaviors at different times depending on context to express and show due respect in different settings.

AI/ANs' conceptions regarding who constitutes family varies from those of non-Native cultures. Family members can include not only aunts, uncles, and grandparents, but also other adults. In some cultures, cousins are literally your brothers and sisters, whereas uncles or aunts can play parental roles. Often all elders in the community are counted as grandparents, whereas all women of parental age are "aunties" and men are "uncles" to the children in the community. Households are often composed of multiple generations living under one roof, and it is typical and acceptable in many cultures for adult children to remain in their parent's home and raise their children there so that three generations are living in one home (Swinomish Tribal Mental Health Project, 1991).

Another common cultural difference lies in concepts of time and causation. Many AI/AN people and indigenous people in other areas (e.g., Australia) do not have a purely linear sense of time. Time is often seen more as cyclical or spiraling. Likewise, the mainstream worldview's linear perspective that specific causes are linked to specific effects, and altering the cause will lead to a different effect, is not part of most Native cultures. Things occur in relation to one another in multiple ways, and what one sees, for example, as mental health symptoms, could be tied to a number of physical, spiritual, and environmental concerns, and interventions can be determined only after time is taken to understand how the different concerns interrelate and how balance can be restored (Duran & Duran, 1995; Evans-Campbell & Walters, 2004).

Communication patterns for Native peoples can differ from non-Native communication patterns. For example, non-Native practitioners can misinterpret a young Native person who consistently looks at the floor or anywhere but a counselor's eyes as a sign of disrespect or low self-esteem, when in fact this is often a sign of respect toward the counselor. Likewise, many cultures have rich traditions of storytelling, in which humor and engaging stories are used to teach lessons about the world and how to act in it. Humor and other verbal exchanges are often used to give subtle hints or say something indirectly. Teasing and similar forms of humor can be used to send messages of acceptance and also provide indirect feedback to the recipient. Handshakes are often gentle and are more of an exchange of spirit by lightly touching the hands of the other (Swinomish Tribal Mental Health Project, 1991).

Indigenous Wellness and Healing Practices

AI/AN tribes, communities, and individuals engage in a range of healing interventions and ceremonies that draw from traditional sources or blend traditional sources and other religious beliefs, such as Christianity. AI/ANs in both urban and rural areas report using traditional healing practices in addition to mainstream, non-Native health providers (Gurley et al., 2001; Waldram, 1990). Healing through ceremony is generally intended to remove any negative influence that could be harming the individual (or the community) and help restore the individual to a healthy balance physically, mentally, emotionally, and spiritually. Often illnesses are regarded as being due, at least in part, to spiritual harm, either from a spiritual entity or from ill-intentioned medicine directed at the individual from another person. Therefore, the person needs to be cleansed and healed from that harm, and strengthened, so that the individual is no longer vulnerable to further harm (Swinomish Tribal Mental Health Project, 1991).

The many types of traditional ceremonies include sweat lodges ("sweats"), naming ceremonies, pipe ceremonies, Sun Dance ceremonies, stomp dances, and potlatches or giveaways. These and other ceremonies vary by region, tribe, clan, or family. Spiritual and religious activities to promote healing also take place in arenas that blend traditional and Christian beliefs, such as the Native American Church and the Shaker Church. Spiritual involvement and religiosity can be predictive of improved mental and physical health (Hill & Pargament, 2003).

Two examples of the movement to integrate traditional healing into social services systems are the Systems of Care and Circles of Care grant programs funded by the Substance Abuse and Mental Health Services Administration. Tribal communities that receive awards from either of these federal grant programs to develop wraparound mental health systems for youth and families in their tribes and communities have developed innovate ways to blend mainstream mental health services and traditional health and healing services, including developing culturally and linguistically specific diagnostic terms for mental health disturbances and the process of healing or rebalancing (Cross, Earle, Solie, & Manness, 2000). Within indigenous spiritual beliefs, the spirit and physical worlds intermingle, and the sacred is not separate from the secular (Grim, 2000; Hazel & Mohatt, 2001). In this vein, tribal programs that use traditional activities such as canoe carving and journeying from tribe to tribe (as in the Pacific

Northwest) help teach youth skills to regulate their behaviors and actions and provide mentorship from elders and teachers (Cross et al., 2000).

These tribal grantee communities are also working to develop "practice-based evidence," finding ways to demonstrate the efficacy of traditional practices using tribally controlled research studies to respond to the trend within funding sources of restricting the types of services offered to those that have been empirically studied (i.e., evidence-based practices). Many AI/AN people regard spiritual or religious practices (or both) as deeply private, and participation may be limited to community members, certain families or clans, or those who have had specific instructions from elders or others. Certain songs or other practices may be part of ceremonies, and those songs or traditions may be passed down through families or given by elders to younger people for specific reasons; accordingly, they are meant to be used by those individuals involved in the transfer of this cultural heritage or "gift." Mental health practitioners should also be aware that it is normative in many Native cultures for individuals to receive messages through dreams, speak with deceased relatives' spirits, or receive messages or signs from the spirit world, often in answer to prayer. These are not signs or symptoms of mental health disturbances onto themselves, and practitioners should view discussion of such events with respect (Swinomish Tribal Mental Health Project, 1991).

Strength and Hope

Although roles, traditions, and even names may have changed over time as a result of colonization, two-spirit people today are in the process of learning, reclaiming, or revisioning their roles in tribes and AI/AN communities. Overall, this effort is known as *retraditionalization*. Through learning about and reconnecting with two-spirit traditions, two-spirit youth and adults can recognize their intrinsic value and their importance to their culture and nation. This can provide them with both strength and hope. Even when two-spirits are unable to reconnect with their own tribal community, pan-Indian events such as pow-wows have provided opportunities for two-spirit people to connect to Native traditions and find relevant roles in urban settings. Learning to identify as two-spirit or using specific tribal terms can be helpful in building community and promoting a positive self-image (Straus & Valentino, 2001). Some evidence grounded in both practice and research supports the notion that a positive racial or ethnic identity can build resilience (Noh, Beiser, Kaspar, House, & Rummens, 1999), and participation in cultural activities can mitigate the impact of bias and buffer against mental health symptoms for AI/ANs (Whitbeck, McMorris, Hoyt, Stubben, & LaFromboise, 2002).

Increasingly, many two-spirit people are filling modern versions of roles traditionally assigned to them, including social work, teaching, and negotiation. In some tribes and communities, two-spirit people work in tribal offices and health clinics. They are elected to tribal councils. Some remain at home within families performing a variety of roles as caregivers of the elderly, individuals with disabilities, and youth. In families affected by substance abuse or violence, it is often the two-spirit family member who is at the center of caring for others in the family (Arviso, 2008). In some areas where two-spirit traditions were never fully driven underground or eliminated, some two-spirit people grow up with traditional cultural acceptance. Some tribal spiritual and political leaders have also recognized the need to accept/reintegrate two-spirit people in their nation or community. Robert Joseph, a hereditary chief of the Gwa wa enuk First Nation (Canada), has spoken about how elders need to come forward to revitalize the aboriginal culture of acceptance of two-spirit people (Pablo, 2008).

Interventions with Two-Spirit Youth

Practitioners should consider the multiple cultural, community, and health needs of two-spirit youth to construct new programs by or with Native community partners, or to modify existing LGBT youth programs to make them safe and supportive places for two-spirit youth. Serving this population effectively and appropriately necessitates a review of provider ethics, partnerships, service delivery strategies, and theories of change.

Ethical Considerations for Practitioners

Practitioners should also be aware of and knowledgeable about effective and ethical practices when working with tribal communities. First, practitioners must recognize and interact with tribes as sovereign nations. Tribes often operate their own social service programs, and their decision-making structure is determined by their own laws and traditions, as well as through interactions with other governments. It is also important when working with families to focus on tribal, individual, and familial strengths and identify how these strengths can be enhanced through traditional forms of protection and healing. Service delivery strategies should be designed with the input of tribes or families, and clients should be consulted respectfully to ensure that services are appropriate and individualized to meet their needs. There are many innovative service delivery strategies that have been developed by tribes and Indian organizations, and self-determination of needs and services is an important strategy that can help lessen historical mistrust.

Theories and Practice Strategies

Any theory or practice model used to work with and in AI/AN communities should incorporate an understanding of the effects of historical and intergenerational trauma, discrimination, racism, and poverty on the mental, physical, emotional, and spiritual states of AI/AN communities and individuals. These models should also integrate an understanding of cultural values and strengths and recognize how communities have survived intense traumas. Failure to do so can result in pathologizing individual and community patterns of coping (Browne & Fiske, 2001).

For example, Native psychologist Duran (2006) developed a counseling approach that blends Western and traditional native healing traditions. Based on a spiritual framework, this approach uses Native healing ways to rename challenges such as addictions or mental health concerns as spirits visiting a person and promotes developing a relationship between the person and their visiting spirit(s). This visitation offers a "therapeutic opportunity" for the provider to intervene in a culturally appropriate, proper, and necessary manner to have the spirit leave the individual and to help the person heal from its effects. This naming of addictions and problems as spirits differs from the Western practice of diagnosis and is a "shifting of root metaphors" (Duran, 2006, p. 7). This shifting allows separation of clients from their problem and draws out the relationship between individuals and their challenges. The counselor facilitates the client's own spiritual path to healing so that the client is not pathologized. Great emphasis is also placed on tracing intergenerational traumas to frame clients' healing within the context of healing of their ancestor's pain, as well as the protection of their children and future generations from similar pain and trauma.

Another methodological and theoretical tool used with families and communities to help illustrate and draw out trauma is an intergenerational trauma genogram. This tool has been developed by many practitioners, including the Native psychologist Joseph Stone (2006). It is designed as most genograms are (with a graphic representation of family generations), but the levels of generations can signify generations of either the community or of a family. The traumas experienced by each generation can then be drawn out and discussed, allowing identification of interventions that can help heal not only the client but also the generation presenting with addictions or related concerns. Furthermore, healing can be promoted for the traumas unhealed in each generation that have been passed down and continue to affect latter generations.

Recommendations for Systems of Care

As a minority existing within and between two other minority communities (Native and LGBT), it is very important for both Native and non-Native providers to counter historical mistrust and establish their reputation as individuals two-spirit people can go to for support, understanding, and ethical conduct. Building trust includes becoming familiar with local tribes and their cultures, beliefs, practices, and history; participating in local tribal open community events; and consulting with tribal social services agencies to ensure the availability of coordinated services and supports. Because many two-spirit people fear a lack of confidentiality from providers, it is important to ensure confidentiality in all services and activities. An easily accessible and understandable process for people to report violations of privacy and other concerns should also be available.

Training materials about LGBT issues frequently do not include informa-tion about two-spirit identity. Guidelines for practice include 1) ensuring that the particular issues faced by two-spirit youth are known to providers; 2) pro-viding training to Native and non-Native staff on two-spirit issues and includ-ing Native youth as trainers whenever possible; 3) addressing potential personal biases and stereotypes about both Native Americans and two-spirit individuals, because many non-Native, and some Native, individuals are unaware of basic Native history and culture; 4) ensuring that staff are provided with training on AI/AN history, historical trauma, cultures, and cultural strengths, as well as LGBT issues; 5) posting and enforcing in offices a "no tolerance" policy of any form of discrimination or harassment, including racism, heterosexism, and cul-tural tokenism; 6) encouraging and actively promoting a climate of openness and acceptance with staff and in the community; and 7) ensuring a diversity of im-ages of youth and their families in materials and offices. Some resources that focus on or include two-spirit youth concerns are listed in Chapter 16. Additional guidance for working with youth in systems of care is provided in Box 7.1.

CONCLUSION

Two-spirit people are integral parts of the tribes and Native communities to which they belong and from which they originate. Two-spirit identity, includ-ing the tribally specific terms from which the modern two-spirit label is derived, is inseparable from diverse Native concepts of gender, sex, sexual orientation, cultural and spiritual roles, and individuality. These concepts, although general-izable to an extent, vary significantly on the basis of tribal traditions. Even when Native individuals solely or additionally define themselves using non-Native terms (e.g., gay), they are still a part of the continuum of AI/AN identity within the United States.

To provide two-spirit youth and adults with culturally and linguistically competent services and supports, communities must have basic knowledge about the history of AI/AN communities, including the historical trauma that AI/AN communities have endured over time and the cultural strengths that have en-abled their survival. Much historical trauma relates explicitly to the decline of two-spirit life within tribal communities and the rise of heterosexism and gen-der differentiation in Western terms. Historical trauma continues to have a sig-nificant impact on the emotional and spiritual needs of tribal communities and AI/AN individuals.

Similarly, systems of care should acknowledge the strengths that have al-lowed AI/AN communities and two-spirit people to endure and launch a re-newal of two-spirit roles and traditions in modern times. Systems of care can address the specific needs of two-spirit youth by partnering across the multiple federal, state, county, and tribal systems that serve youth to ensure culturally and

---

**Box 7.1.   Recommendations for Addressing
the Needs of Two-Spirit Youth in Systems of Care**

Identifying Youth and Their Needs

- When speaking with youth and determining their needs, do not assume gender pronouns (e.g., he, she). Use terms and language youth use to reference themselves. If the gender reference is unclear, it is appropriate and acceptable to politely ask the youth what gender term the youth prefers. Recognize that pronoun preference may change over time as youth are often involved in identity exploration.
- Respect and use whatever other identity terms youth use to describe themselves. Ask about and discuss gender, sexual orientation, sexual behavior, and identity as distinct concepts (Walters, Simoni, & Horwath, 2001), because these may vary independently of one another.
- When assessing trauma, use an instrument that inquires about cultural and historical trauma of the client, his or her family, and tribe, as well as individual experiences and traumatic events (Balsam, Huang, Fieland, Simoni, & Walters, 2004). Avoid assuming a trauma history simply because of a youth's ethnic, gender, or sexual identity.
- Inform youth directly and indirectly (through comments, imagery, etc.) that you are open to hearing about their lives and identity. Ask and pay attention to family and parenting, including whether youth plan to have or do have children, or whether they have nieces or nephews for whom they provide care. In Native traditions, there is a strong emphasis on "honoring one's obligation with regard to becoming a parent," which may include parenting children of relatives or friends (Garrett & Barrett, 2003).
- Provide outreach to transit areas for two-spirit youth who are relocating to urban areas or running away, including identifying supportive and affirming resources and safe areas to connect with services and supports for youth who are homeless and/or in out-of-home care.

Building Support

- Become familiar with local two-spirit and/or LGBT-friendly Native societies, and connect clients to these or to youth-appropriate resources on the Internet (Gilley & Co-Cké, 2005). If a local two-spirit group is not available, promote the creation of peer or moderated support groups and self-help groups for two-spirit AI/ANs.
- Offer safe opportunities such as social meetings, ceremonial participation, pow-wows, and Native crafts activities for two-spirit people to express themselves (Gilley & Co-Cké, 2005). When hosting an event for youth or group events for two-spirit individuals, hold events in a "neutral" location where participants are unlikely to accidentally encounter family members or others who may not know about their two-spirit identity (Gilley & Co-Cké, 2005).
- Speak with elders or search for historical or present-day positive role models for two-spirit youth in your community. Share these role models with young people as appropriate, or connect elders and youth, with permission from both parties, to help establish a mentoring relationship to promote the building of healthy youth identity.
- Engage local or nearby AI/AN community leaders in discussions to identify culturally relevant and meaningful ways to discuss sex, sexuality, gender, and two-spirit issues in the local Native community. Pay attention to the variation in

gender, roles, identities, and sexuality that occur between nations (Walters et al., 2001).

- Offer presentations or discussions about the varied history of two-spirit people and their roles in AI/AN cultures and the inclusion of Native people in modern-day LGBT communities. Ensure that present-day two-spirit community strengths are also shared (Brotman et al., 2002a; Garrett & Barrett, 2003).
- Have one or more Native elders or teachers who are accepting of LGBT Native/two-spirit people on staff or to consult with and support two-spirit youth.

Addressing Historical Trauma

- Explore how youth and families "make sense" of colonial trauma and cultural loss. Ask how individuals and families survived periods of loss and what strengths helped them to successfully survive traumatic experiences. It is particularly beneficial to identify and cultivate approaches that emphasize resilience.
- Be conscious of "anniversary dates" of historical and familial traumas, because traumatic symptoms may re-emerge on anniversary dates. Consult with Native elders and/or spiritual leaders in your community to respectfully raise the issue of community and historical trauma, and what role you can play (if any) in providing support to address these traumas. Ask to hear more about what the community has endured and whether they have advice about how to help families in their community recovering from shared trauma.

Building in Spiritual Supports and Holistic Healing

- Facilitate access to traditional health practitioners, as most Aboriginal concepts of health are holistic, with the primary goal of health provision and healing being the rebalancing of the emotional, physical, spiritual, and mental/psychological aspects of the human psyche (O'Brien-Teegs, 2008).
- Ask about and discuss the client's involvement in traditional healing practices. Integrate culturally relevant approaches to healing from substance abuse, mental health problems, and trauma as appropriate (Balsam et al., 2004). Do *not*, however, make assumptions about AI/ANs and their use and/or knowledge of cultural beliefs (McIntosh & Eschiti, 2009). Appropriate querying should facilitate the provider's understanding of the youth's degree of embeddedness within cultural belief systems.
- Although it is appropriate to ask youth about spiritual beliefs and practices, some may elect not to share this information because many AI/ANs keep spiritual beliefs and practices private (Frazer & Pruden, 2010). Integrate cultural and spiritual healing approaches as appropriate and when requested, with approaches ranging from solely traditional spirituality to Western or Eastern religions to an integrated combination of these beliefs and practices.

Reaching Across and within Systems

- Because many two-spirit youth are involved in multiple youth-serving systems concurrently, including child welfare, juvenile justice, mental health, and chemical dependency, it is essential to work across and within systems to reach and support two-spirit youth. Hold discussions with multiple social services and child welfare providers in your community, as well as families, about two-spirit youth issues and promoting wellness for two-spirit youth. Expand or strengthen your system of care to include all of the available child-serving systems as well as formal and informal supports.

(continued)

Box 7.1. *(continued)*

- Determine supportive resources for two-spirit youth within or near your community and advertise those resources across venues and service structures.
- Establish a respectful collaborative relationship with local tribal providers, urban Indian, and/or LGBT providers and organizations.
- Connect Native and non-Native providers to help reduce the incidence of two-spirit youth falling through the cracks, either in terms of insurance/payment issues or awareness of and access to needed services and supports.

Encouraging Youth Empowerment

- Involve two-spirit youth in all stages of planning and communication in the ways they are comfortable doing so, as youth vary significantly in their level of openness about their lives and their identities.
- Encourage and facilitate peer support and rely on feedback from two-spirit youth to help guide the services and supports provided.
- Provide an affirming space for youth to recognize and challenge racism, gender, and socioeconomic class bias in LGBT environments and/or heterosexism/transphobia. Provide a culturally appropriate venue for interested youth to openly share their experiences with the various communities to which they belong.
- Promote a positive sense of self as Native and as LGBT/two-spirit. Find and share the works of two-spirit writers, poets, and artists. Encourage youth self-expression through various mediums, including culturally specific art forms.

---

linguistically competent collaboration and coordination. Systems of care also need to address training needs within systems and providers; find opportunities to support and empower youth on their own terms; provide opportunities for peer support, including culturally specific events or groups; and ensure that youth are able to dictate their degree and level of openness to prevent violent responses or community ostracization.

It is insufficient to simply bring two-spirit youth into systems of care for services and supports. Providers should be aware that AI/AN youth are likely to have historically based mistrust of mainstream providers, including LGBT providers. Providers should both raise awareness of two-spirit issues and cultural differences and provide open and accepting avenues for youth to discuss and challenge racism and tokenism within LGBT and two-spirit groups. AI/AN providers should coordinate two-spirit youth support opportunities in addition to those provided for the LGBT youth community as a whole. LGBT and two-spirit providers should also respectfully partner with tribal or urban Indian providers to prevent systems from overlooking these youth.

Above all, two-spirit youth need

- To know they are not alone and are a part of a long tradition in AI/AN communities of people who vary on the basis of gender, sex, and sexual orientation

- Safe spaces available where they can find support for their entire being, including their personal, psychological, social, and spiritual dimensions, without having to compartmentalize parts of themselves
- Safe and supportive adults and peers to rely on and form families with, because many have been rejected by their birth families due to their identity, and family ties are integral to self-worth within AI/AN communities
- Opportunities and support to connect with family members and tribal members, to reach out to those who are supportive, and explore whether others are supportive as well

If bias and trauma become too intense, two-spirit youth need to know that there are healthy two-spirit youth (and adults) with whom they can connect who offer positive role models of resilience—sources of strength, hope, and psychological well-being. It is incumbent on systems of care to provide positive opportunities for two-spirit youth to be aware of, and have access to, Native and non-Native treatment and wellness approaches to help them heal and find balance.

8

The Resilience U-Turn

Understanding Risks and Strengths to Effectively Support LGBT Youth and Families in Systems of Care

KATHERINE J. LAZEAR AND PETER GAMACHE

M ost of the research literature about lesbian, gay, and bisexual (LGB) youth has historically focused on risk factors and problem behaviors as well as sociocultural and psychological challenges that LGB youth experience. Research on protective factors and resilience for LGB youth is starting to emerge and shows early promise for approaches that will enhance the care and well-being of LGB and transgender (LGBT) youth and their families. Research about transgender youth is nascent, and the highly limited literature demonstrates pronounced gaps about both risk and protective factors and the cultivation of resilience among transgender youth. This chapter

- Introduces assets-based approaches for addressing the needs of LGBT youth through a discussion of resiliency, protection from adversity, and a model of cultural and linguistic competence to develop inclusive programs to serve LGBT youth
- Discusses risks associated with LGBT youth that are in the literature (e.g., homelessness, suicide-related behavior) to demonstrate how LGBT youth are depicted in much of the research and clinical literature and provides a counter perspective with an assets-based approach
- Provides recommendations for a research agenda to develop assets-based approaches to meet the needs of LGBT youth and their families and to help advance evidence-based practices and promising approaches to serving this population

POPULATION OF FOCUS

Few population-based studies have included questions on sexual orientation or other dimensions of sexuality, such as attraction and behavior. Therefore, it has been very difficult to determine the proportion of LGB individuals, including

youth, in the general population and how these dimensions of sexual orientation are expressed in it. In addition, varied and nonstandardized definitions and
measures of sexual orientation that alternately classify participants based on self-
report or same-sex sexual behavior confuse needs assessments, evaluation studies, and program reporting about the total number of LGB individuals in the
population (Sell, 1997). Recently, the American Community Survey of the U.S.
Census Bureau found that 4.1% of adults 18 to 25 years of age openly identified
themselves as LGB; this suggests that there are 8.8 million LGB adults in the
United States (Gates, 2006). Reliable estimates of the population of transgender
individuals are unavailable.

Studies show that children become aware of sexual attraction, on average,
around the age of 10 years (Ryan, 2003), and youth are self-identifying as LGB
at younger ages than earlier generations of LGB youth (Kreiss & Patterson,
1997; Ryan, 2003). The "coming out" process of disclosing one's sexual orientation and gender identity may vary, however, for some subgroups of youth. For
example, one study shows that African American and Latino youth disclose their
sexual orientation to fewer peers as compared with Caucasian youth (Rosario,
Schrimshaw, & Hunter, 2004). Factors that affect disclosure among all LGB
youth may include social support, social adjustment, and accumulation of social
capital (Acevedo-Polakovich, Bell, Gamache, & Christian, 2011).

Families with at least one LGBT member—an LGBT parent, child, or
youth—encounter varying levels of acceptance and support when they access
and use needed services within social services and behavioral health systems.
Regardless of family structure, these families share the experience of interpersonal discovery coupled with social signals indicating varying degrees of exclusion and inclusion. Multidimensional challenges related to the coming out process for families also include uncertainty when acknowledging, disclosing, or
asserting the sexual orientation or gender identity of a family member within
new or unfamiliar settings (D'Augelli, 2002; Fisher, Easterly, & Lazear, 2008;
Oswald, 2002; Rosario, Hunter, Maguen, Gwadz, & Smith, 2001).

RISK FACTORS FOR LGBT YOUTH
AND YOUTH PERCEIVED TO BE LGBT

Over the past 20 years, the behavioral health field has been increasingly moving
away from a deficit-based focus on families of children and youth with serious
emotional and behavioral challenges (Alexander & Dore, 1999; Kamradt, 2001;
Rudolph & Epstein, 2000). This evolution is marked by a shift from blaming
parents for the challenges experienced by their children and youth to a strengths-
based partnering model in which families drive individualized services and supports to identify and address the needs of their children. This strengths-based

approach can guide the tailoring of services for LGBT youth who have similarly been viewed through a lens clouded by deficits, risks, and problems.

Researchers and others have articulated concerns that the overarching focus on problems and negative outcomes in the research literature and mental health field stigmatize LGB youth. An unintended consequence of this focus is that sexual orientation may be pathologized as causing negative outcomes for LGB individuals (Bakker & Cavender, 2003; Harper & Schneider, 2003; Meyer, 2003). Individuals perceived to be gay, typically as a result of gender nonconforming behaviors or characteristics, are also at risk for negative outcomes. They may experience the same types of negative attitudes, stigma, stereotypes, and targeted violence, such as bullying, harassment, and hate crimes, as those who are openly gay (Herek, 2003; U.S. Department of Justice, 2004).

Identifying as a gender other than one's birth-assigned gender may also be pathologized (Vance et al., 2010). Transgender identity remains a gender identity disorder within the American Psychiatric Association's *Diagnostic and Statistical Manual of Mental Disorders* (4th ed., text rev.; 2000a). By comparison, the American Psychiatric Association lifted its characterization of homosexuality as a mental disorder in 1973 (Conger, 1975). Although a disorder/disability label increases access to services (e.g., counseling, treatment) for transgender individuals, attributing negative personal outcomes to these innate characteristics does not account for sources of marginalization of transgender individuals resulting from social stigma and negative social conditions (Hanssmann, Morrison, & Russian, 2008).

The identification, diagnosis, and expectation of at-risk and high-risk pathways for the LGBT population are well-established in the research literature (Mizocka & Lewis, 2008; Rivers & Carragher, 2003). Much of the research literature has focused on HIV/AIDS; homelessness; and alcohol, tobacco, and other drug abuse, as well as suicide-related behavior (Hughes & Eliason, 2002), which are touched on in this chapter; more detail is available throughout this book.

HIV/AIDS

Young people, including a disproportionate share of young men who have sex with men, are at high risk for HIV infection. Several psychosocial factors affect the degree of risk associated with HIV infection, including 1) a lack of awareness and misperceptions about others who are at risk for and have already contracted HIV, 2) social stigma related to homosexuality and AIDS, and 3) a lack of accurate information about safer sex and risk reduction that is presented in ways that are relevant to LGBT youth. Limited opportunities to socialize with other LGBT peers in supportive environments that are normative for adolescents (e.g., school dances) and limited access to positive role models for dating, health promotion, and sexual health may also affect the degree of risk for LGBT youth (Centers for Disease Control and Prevention [CDC], 2008a).

Fifteen percent of individuals with a new HIV diagnosis in 2006 were between the ages of 13 and 24 years (CDC, 2008b). Stigma and homophobia toward men who have sex with men are associated with a lower likelihood to seek HIV testing (CDC, 2008c). Other researchers have noted several risk factors within the transgender population. One study found that male-to-female participants had a higher prevalence of HIV compared with female-to-male participants (Clements–Nolle, Marx, Guzman, & Katz, 2001).

Abuse of Alcohol, Tobacco, and Other Drugs

A number of studies find that lesbian and gay adults experience higher rates of substance abuse than heterosexual adults (Gruskin, Hart, Gordon, & Ackerson, 2001; Hughes & Eliason, 2002; Skinner, 1994). Researchers point out several underlying factors for these higher rates, including younger lesbian and bisexual women's participation in the lesbian "bar culture," coping with the stress of heterosexism by smoking or drinking heavily, and negative stress responses that include depression and anxiety.

A meta-analysis of 18 studies from 1994 to 2006 revealed that gay youth reported higher rates of cigarette and alcohol use, as well as illicit drugs, including marijuana, cocaine, methamphetamines, and injection drugs, compared with heterosexual youth (Marshall et al., 2008). Reback and Lombardi (2001) found that transgender adults were at higher risk of substance abuse when compared with adults identifying as their birth-assigned gender. The research identified a lack of health care provider sensitivity and respect; furthermore, transgender people did not seek help because of reports of discriminatory treatment by other transgender individuals (Lombardi, 2001; Lombardi & van Servellen, 2000; Nemoto, Operario, Keatley, Nguyen, & Sugano, 2005). Accordingly, transgender individuals may be inhibited from seeking assistance with alcohol, tobacco, and other drug abuse issues because of concerns that they will not receive culturally and linguistically competent care from providers.

Suicide-Related Behavior

Researchers have explored the methodological and substantive limitations of conducting research about suicide with LGB populations and identified many challenges, including definitional differences of LGB identities and how suicide attempts are operationally defined, which may or may not correlate with self-harm (McDaniel, Purcell, & D'Augelli, 2001). Another prominent limitation is that "most researchers have examined risk factors but have ignored factors that promote resilience" (p. 86).

Despite these definitional and methodological challenges and limitations, some studies provide meaningful insights about suicide and LGBT youth. A recent, groundbreaking, and extensive review of the entire literature about suicide among LGBT populations concluded that several adolescent studies pointed to links between suicidal ideation and behavior and individual experiences of stigma, discrimination, and victimization based on known or perceived sexual orientation/gender identity (Haas et al., 2011). For example, one study found higher rates of suicide attempts among LGB youth than in heterosexual comparison groups. Identified risk factors included stress, lack of social support, and ineffective coping skills (Safren & Heimberg, 1999); psychiatric and substance abuse disorders; discrimination and homophobia; and a diagnosis of HIV/AIDS (McDaniel et al., 2001; Moscicki, 1997).

Studies have also found that LGBT youth are more likely than their heterosexual peers to report suicidal ideation, intent, and attempts (Goodenow, 2004; Remafedi, French, Story, Resnick, & Blum, 1998). In an earlier study, researchers found that sexual orientation for gay and bisexual male youth was tangential to self-harm (Remafedi, Farrow, & Deisher, 1991). Of particular note is the finding that one third of first attempts occurred within the same year as self-identification as gay or bisexual.

Research has also found an association between parental rejection because of sexual orientation and higher risk of suicide attempts among LGB youth (Ryan, Huebner, Diaz, & Sanchez, 2009). Other literature has reported that gender nonconformity appears to be a more significant risk factor for suicide-related behavior than sexual orientation or gender identity per se (Haas et al., 2011). For LGB students, research shows that sexual orientation is correlated with identified risk factors for suicide; however, sexual orientation is less of a factor after controlling for these risk factors (Lazear, Doan, & Roggenbaum, 2003). Peer victimization and bullying are also reported by a significantly higher percentage of LGBT versus heterosexual youth, which researchers have identified as risk factors for suicide-related behavior (Friedman, Koeske, Silvestre, Korr, & Sites, 2006; Goodenow, Szalacha, & Westheimer, 2006; Haas et al., 2011; Ploderl & Fartacek, 2007).

The reportedly high rates of risk among LGB individuals for alcohol and substance abuse, suicidality, and homelessness, in addition to risks for HIV among gay males and young men who have sex with men, offer significant rationale to advance the knowledge base about this population. In particular, greater attention to factors that promote achievement and resilience in maintaining health and well-being is a necessary focus for both research and practice. Emerging research on resilience theory, which the following sections explore, holds promise for a new approach that transforms risks, deficits, and problems into assets. Although the literature about LGBT youth emphasizes significant risks and challenges, resilience theory and other strengths-based approaches provide a promising and necessary foundation for an assets-based approach to learning about and working with LGBT youth. Chapter 13 explores suicide and self-harming behavior in greater detail.

AN ALTERNATIVE TO THE RISK-BASED LITERATURE: ASSETS-BASED APPROACHES

Risk and resilience factors associated with an LGBT identity are salient to mental health providers and other professionals seeking to uphold system of care principles; improve quality of care; and increase effective outreach, engagement, treatment, and support for this population. Effective services and supports for LGBT youth and their families require that systems of care address both processes and structures. This should include frontline practice shifts that focus on the skills, knowledge, and attitudes of service providers; evidence-based practices and promising approaches; treatment efficacy monitoring; and ongoing evaluations for continuous quality improvement (Pires, 2002).

Resiliency is described as a "phenomenon that some individuals have a relatively good outcome despite suffering risk experiences" (Rutter, 2007, p. 205). Resilience has been defined as a "risk factor that has been averted or unrealized" (Keyes, 2004, p. 224). It is a "phenomenon that some individuals have a relatively good outcome despite suffering risk experiences" (Rutter, p. 205), and a "class of phenomena characterized by patterns of positive adaptation in the context of significant adversity or risk" (Masten & Reed, 2002, p. 75).

Resilience theory, grounded especially within the health sciences and developmental psychology in particular, supports an assets-based approach by 1) identifying qualities of individuals and support systems that explain or predict positive mental health outcomes, 2) describing processes for coping with negative stressors, and 3) creating experiences that move individuals toward reintegration (Masten & Powell, 2003; Richardson, 2002; Zimmerman & Arunkumar, 1994). Findings within the area of resilience research indicate that 1) early and continuous attachment positively shapes relationship development in later years among all young children, adolescents, and adults (Rutter & Rutter, 1993); 2) self-efficacy is contingent on an internal locus of control (Anderson, A.L. 1998); and 3) protective factors in one setting (e.g., home, school) can compensate for risks in multiple settings (Bernard, 2004).

Moreover, studies of resilience among LGBT youth have demonstrated that 1) positive social relationships moderate the relationship between stress and distress (Rosario, Schrimshaw, & Hunter, 2005); 2) affirming faith experiences contribute to less internalized homonegativity, more spirituality, and psychological health (Lease, Horne, & Noffsinger-Frazier, 2005); and 3) family support and acceptance explain adolescent comfort and resilience in later life (Glicken,

2006). Consistent with these findings, compelling new research on LGBT youth and their families shows that families often dramatically influence the health and mental health of their LGBT children. Specifically, researchers found that Caucasian and Latino LGB young adults who experienced a high level of family-rejecting behaviors during adolescence were at much higher risk of negative health problems than those in families who were slightly or not at all rejecting (Ryan et al., 2009). They also found that specific family-accepting behaviors toward LGBT youth during adolescence protect against suicide, depression, and substance abuse; furthermore, LGBT young adults who reported high levels of family acceptance during adolescence had significantly higher levels of self-esteem, social support, and general health compared with peers with low levels of family acceptance (Ryan, Russell, Huebner, Diaz, & Sanchez, 2010). The Family Acceptance Project at San Francisco State University produced this research and is developing strategic family interventions to generate a new evidence-based family model to help ethnically and religiously diverse families decrease rejecting behaviors that put LGBT youth at risk for serious health problems and homelessness. The Family Acceptance Project is also developing interventions to increase supportive behaviors that will help protect against risk and promote well-being.

The social support literature throughout the last 30 years has identified natural helping networks as support systems (Crockett et al., 2007; Gottlieb, 1983; Pancoast, 1980). For example, surveys and studies repeatedly show that individuals first seek friends, relatives, neighbors, and lay helpers such as bartenders and beauticians for information and help (Cohen, Underwood, & Gottlieb, 2000; Cohen & Wills, 1985; Germain & Patterson, 1988; Gottlieb, 1988). This is especially true of racially and culturally diverse minority populations (Lazear, Pires, Isaacs, Chaulk, & Huang, 2008). A review of randomized trials of community-based family support programs for children with chronic health conditions indicated that social support from other families can reduce anxiety in parents (Ireys, Sills, Kolodner, & Walsh, 1996).

By contrast, development of resiliency interventions for the LGBT population is at a comparatively young stage as evolving knowledge related to life stages within the field of developmental psychology intersects with the coming out process for this population. Family dynamics within a support network (e.g., friends as family) can foster resilience (Oswald, 2002; Russell & Richards, 2003). One study of baby boomers (born between 1946 and 1964) found that approximately 40% of LGBT respondents cited that being LGBT helped them to develop positive character traits, resilience, and support networks (MetLife Mature Market Institute, Lesbian and Gay Aging Issues Network of the American Society on Aging, & Zogby International, 2006).

Parents, Families and Friends of Lesbians and Gays (PFLAG) is an example of the effectiveness of family and social support provided by a successful grass-roots organization. PFLAG grew from an organization of parents supporting each other and their LGBT children to more than 500 chapters nationwide with 200,000 members, supporters, and affiliates, representing the largest chapter network addressing the needs of LGBT people. The national organization was launched after receiving 7,000 letters requesting information after a mention of PFLAG in the advice column "Dear Abby" (PFLAG, 2008).

A growing number of youth-run organizations are beginning to provide peer-to-peer support, information, and education for LGBT youth. For a number of reasons, a peer-to-peer approach may most effectively address numerous challenges to the development of resilience in LGBT youth. For example, this approach may help address tensions about age appropriateness for children's education programs that include same-sex relationships, religiosity, and intergenerational differences—topics that necessitate open dialogue rather than avoidance and silence. LGBT programs that emphasize open dialogue demonstrate effective ways to begin dissolving fears and producing actions to protect all youth without fear of controversy or confrontation (YES Institute, 2008).

Looking through the lens of risk and resilience associated with an LGBT population will uphold system of care principles and move the field in the direction of improved quality of care, effective outreach, engagement, treatment, and support for this population. It is possible and necessary to address both processes and structures to provide effective services and supports to LGBT youth and their families by focusing on the skills, knowledge, and attitude of frontline professionals; implementing evidence-based practices and promising approaches; and monitoring treatment efficacy.

FOSTERING RESILIENCY THROUGH CULTURAL AND LINGUISTIC COMPETENCE

In a system of care, cultural and linguistic competence incorporates several concepts and definitions. First, *culture* has been defined as a broad concept that reflects an integrated pattern of a wide range of beliefs, values, practices, customs, rituals, and attitudes that make up an individual, family, organization, or community. Second, *cultural competence* is accepting and respecting diversity and difference in a continuous process of personal and organizational self-assessment and reflection (Cross, 1995). Lastly, linguistic competence is the capacity of an organization and its personnel to communicate effectively to diverse audiences (Georgetown University Center for Child and Human Development, National Center for Cultural Competence, 2011). Addressing issues of cultural and linguistic competence with individuals, families, organizations, and community provides a framework for an assets-based approach for the LGBT population. Chapters 2 and 3 discuss linguistic competence in detail.

Individual/Family Cultural Competence

A longitudinal study comparing African American, Latino, and Caucasian LGB youth found that cultural factors do not impede sexual identity formation. Cultural factors such as silence and avoidance, however, delay identity integration, including internal and external acceptance and comfort in being identified as LGB, in addition to positive engagement in LGB social activities (Rosario et al., 2004). These cultural factors affect internalized anxiety as they relate to LGB individuals' experiences with others to whom they feel close or attached. For example, secure attachment during the coming out process enhances an individual's ability to cope with prejudice and challenges to self-acceptance and self-esteem (Griffin & Bartholomew, 1994; Mohr & Fassinger, 2003). Recent research shows that LGBT youth who were rejected by their families because of their identity had much lower self-esteem, had fewer people they could turn to for help, were more isolated than those youth who were accepted by their families, and were at very high risk for health and mental health problems when they became young adults (Ryan et al., 2009). Conversely, LGBT young people who were accepted by their families reported better overall health, higher self-esteem, and reduced rates of depression, substance use, and suicidality (Ryan et al., 2010).

Organization-Focused Cultural Competency

Figure 8.1 illustrates a model of cultural competence that details an organization's/ system's combined policies, structures, and processes (Hernandez, Nesman, Mowery, & Gamache, 2006). The infrastructure domain on the left supports staff conducting outreach and engagement, whereas the direct services domain to the right functions to enable community access, availability, and utilization of mental health services. *Access* encompasses the mechanisms that facilitate entering, navigating, and exiting appropriate services and supports as needed. *Availability* includes having services and supports in sufficient range and capacity to meet population needs. *Utilization* is the rate of service use or its usability by a population.

Compatibility is enhanced through acceptance, ally development, and institutionalization of affirmative policies for LGBT individuals. These components function to increase access, availability, and utilization. For example, LGBT diversity-training curricula, used within programs such as Safe Zone (www.lgbt campus.org/old_faq/safe_zone.html), Safe Space, Safe Harbor, and Safe On Campus, are being implemented at a number of colleges and universities and center on recognition and awareness of the particular needs of LGBT individuals, as well as their challenges and experiences of difference. Participants can become an ally and display a sticker on their office door or other location indicating a safe zone for LGBT individuals to dialogue. Because the sticker functions

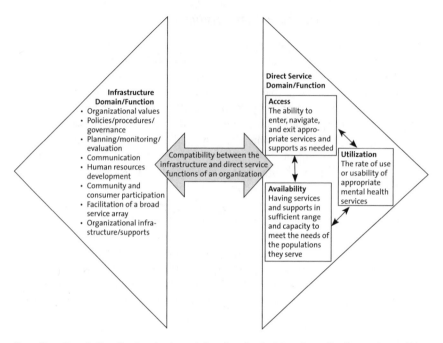

Figure 8.1. Organizational/system implementation domains for improving cultural competence. (From Hernandez, M., & Nesman, T. [2006, February]. *Conceptual model for accessibility of mental health services to culturally/linguistically diverse populations.* Presented during the grantee communities workshop "Operationalizing cultural competence for implementation in systems of care" at the 19th Annual Research Conference: A System of Care for Children's Mental Health: Expanding the Research Base, Tampa, FL; reprinted by permission.)

to increase access, recognition and awareness, capacity, and availability, LGBT individuals are more likely to engage with and use services.

Community-Focused Cultural and Linguistic Competency

Community-focused cultural competence also provides a framework for an assets-based approach for the LGBT population. Early cultural competence scholars defined this as a set of congruent behaviors, attitudes, and policies that come together in a system, in an agency, or among professionals and enable that system, agency, or those professionals to work effectively in cross-cultural situations (Cross, Bazron, Dennis, & Isaacs, 1989). They maintain that it is essential that cultural competence efforts of any organization or system include working in partnership with the community. Although the authors' work focuses on delivering culturally relevant services to children and youth of color, the philosophical framework is relevant for meeting the needs of LGBT youth and their families. For example, the Family Support Organization of Burlington County,

New Jersey, introduced the idea of a book club because of some uneasiness with addressing LGBT issues. They began with a book about American Indian experiences as a way to engage the family organization staff, service providers, and community. The success of their first meeting empowered them to take on a book about LGBT experiences (Dunne & Goode, 2004).

A second premise of community-focused cultural competence is found in other literature that recognizes the importance of systems of care developing a population of focus, that is, being clear about the children, youth, and families for whom a system of care exists and serves (Pires, 2002). Pires stated, "system builders must be thoughtful about the characteristics, strengths, and needs of subpopulations within the population [of focus] so that relevant strategies will be pursued and responsive structures built" (p. 172).

Figure 8.2 indicates the compatibility between an organization's/system's structures and processes and the community's characteristics. Effective outreach

Definition: Within a framework of addressing mental health disparities within a community, the level of a human services organization's/system's cultural competence can be described as the degree of compatibility and adaptability between the cultural/linguistic characteristics of a community's population AND the way the organization's combined policies and structures/processes work together to impede and/or facilitate access, availability, and utilization of needed services/supports.

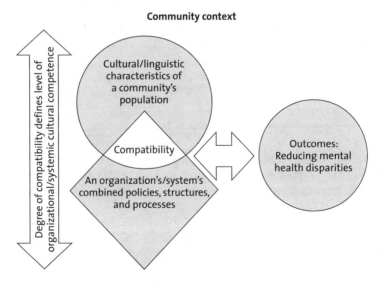

Figure 8.2. Conceptual model for adaptability of mental health services to culturally/linguistically diverse populations. (From Hernandez, M., & Nesman, T. [2006, February]. *Conceptual model for accessibility of mental health services to culturally/linguistically diverse populations.* Presented during the grantee communities workshop "Operationalizing cultural competence for implementation in systems of care" at the 19th Annual Research Conference: A System of Care for Children's Mental Health: Expanding the Research Base, Tampa, FL; reprinted by permission.)

to and engagement of the LGBT population, for example, includes an awareness of "youth language" around LGBT issues and topics, in addition to both their struggles and achievements. Specific practices, such as those that employ messaging (e.g., risk awareness and health maintenance messages) also incorporate a shared understanding of labeling and self-identification. This is especially important with LGBT youth from non–English-speaking groups or for whom English is not the primary language. Messaging is a good example of why linguistic competence is important with the LGBT population.

Reduced behavioral health disparities for youth and their families are the expected outcome of organizational cultural and linguistic competence. The model in Figure 8.2 illustrates that this outcome is the product of joint organizational and community efforts. Taken together, these domains contribute to cultural and linguistic competence when they ensure that LGBT youth and their families share all aspects of decision making.

Child and Family Team Service Planning

An assets-based approach is also consistent with the values and principles of a child and family team approach to providing comprehensive and coordinated service provision, such as the wraparound process (Walker & Bruns, 2007). The wraparound process is based on 10 core principles: 1) family voice and choice, 2) team-based decision making, 3) natural supports, 4) collaboration, 5) community-based participation, 6) culturally competent personnel, 7) individualized services, 8) strengths-based approaches, 9) persistence, and 10) an outcome-based focus (Miles, Bruns, Osher, Walker, & National Wraparound Initiative Advisory Group, 2006). This approach to service planning includes conducting strengths-based assessments. Recent research revealed that child functioning outcomes were significantly better for youth with serious emotional or behavioral disturbance who received a strengths-based assessment, guided by the Behavioral and Emotional Rating Scale, versus typical deficit-based assessment protocols (Cox, 2006). In addition, recent literature suggests that the wraparound process and services promote positive outcomes for both youth and systems (Cox, Baker, & Wong, 2010; Rauso, Ly, Lee, & Jarosz, 2009; Suter & Bruns, 2009).

RESILIENCY RECOMMENDED PRACTICES AND RESEARCH NEEDS

Prevention, treatment, and care interventions for LGBT individuals ideally incorporate awareness of the social determinants of health as well as individual behaviors to reduce disease, illness, injury, and disability across communities (Marmot, 2005; World Health Organization, 2003). Social inequality among LGBT individuals weakens a service system's ability to engage communities in a common dialogue, which is intensified if race, gender, sexual orientation, eth-

LGBTQI2-S individuals and their families have limited opportunities for resiliency education and a need for prevention and treatment of adverse conditions.

LGBTQI2-S individuals and their families receive a Resiliency Collaborative Readiness Assessment (RCRA), and identified resiliency barriers/facilitators inform the tailoring of all education curricula, on-site trainings, and technical assistance.

Communities have an important role in addressing stigma associated with LGBTQI2-S and crossing cultural opportunities for resiliency approaches for LGBTQI2-S individuals and their families.

Communities will identify, develop, implement, and evaluate cross-cultural opportunities for resiliency approaches for LGBTQI2-S individuals and their families.

LGBGTQI2-S inclusive service system administrators are seeking to enhance cross-group resiliency outcomes and resources.

The Provider Support Network team of experts refine and monitor resiliency program work plans in partnership with organizational stakeholders.

Figure 8.3.   LGBT, questioning, intersex, or two-spirit (LGBTQI2-S) theory of change. (From Gamache, P.E., & Lazear, K.J. [2009]. *Asset-based approaches for lesbian, gay, bisexual, transgender, questioning, intersex, two-spirit [LGBTQI2-S] youth and their families in system of care.* [FMHI pub. no. 252]. Tampa, FL: University of South Florida, College of Behavioral and Community Sciences, Louis de la Parte Florida Mental Health Institute, Research and Training Center for Children's Mental Health.)

nicity, and culture are perceived as mutually exclusive and noninteractive across groups (Halperin et al., 2004). With respect to HIV in particular, this unbalanced social equation is marked by poverty and disparities that perpetuate minority status (CDC, 1992). Identifying opportunities to cross social boundaries and encourage health-promoting behavior is an important strategy to more fully develop resilience-based interventions.

Interventions that use resiliency provide a framework not only for risk re-duction, but also for community development of behavior change expectations. Figure 8.3 illustrates the theory of change that drives this framework. In this theory, change progresses along focal points that originate with the needs and opportunities of LGBT individuals and their families, communities, and LGBT-inclusive service providers and system administrators. To meet the need for prevention and treatment of adverse conditions for LGBT individuals, it is im-portant to determine the degree of resiliency barriers and facilitators and then tailor program activities (e.g., on-site trainings, technical assistance, curricula) and promote the facilitation of resiliency among LGBT youth.

To reduce and eliminate stigma and culturally defined barriers associated with LGBT individuals and their families at the community and organizational levels, an informed process is necessary to identify, develop, implement, and evaluate resiliency-based approaches and interventions. Systematic understanding of LGBT-inclusive service provider practices can be developed through a supportive network of LGBT individuals and their families, service personnel, family members, and communities who understand and share service adaptation lessons learned, common teaching methods, opportunities for improvement, and interpersonal growth.

Integrating evidence and practice and establishing practice-based evidence with LGBT community and organizational interventions is integral to assets-based approaches for LGBT individuals. Four key areas of emphasis for effective integration of evidence and practice include 1) research efficacy to examine whether a particular intervention has a specific measurable effect; 2) effectiveness research to identify whether efficacious treatments can have a measurable, beneficial effect when implemented across broad populations; 3) practice research to examine how and which treatments are provided to individuals within systems and how to improve treatment; and 4) service system research to examine large-scale organizational, financing, and policy questions (Barkham & Mellor-Clark, 2003). Placing these four areas within the paradigms of evidence-based practice and practice-based evidence illustrates the complementary relationship between the two as a way to further clinical practice and intervention (Barkham & Mellor-Clark).

Assets-Based Research and Recommendations

"Despite the increase in visibility, gay, lesbian and bisexual youth are still one of the most under-researched groups of children and adolescents" (Miceli, 2002, p. 199). As a result of this relative degree of invisibility within the research literature, limited systematic information is available about disparities in treatment outcomes for this population. This chapter proposes a framework for LGBT research that focuses on assets because the assets-based research on this population is minimal, necessitating an adaptation of assets-based research from other populations. Furthermore, the focus of LGBT research has historically focused so intently on the problem/harm approach that erroneous conclusions can be drawn regarding harm and negative outcomes associated with merely being an LGBT individual, particularly among detractors of LGBT inclusion. Finally, an assets-based approach to research might identify effective clinical practices and interventions that promulgate hopeful and effective strengths-based approaches that can be implemented with LGBT youth.

All of the assets-based approaches presented in this chapter can be structured within a population-based, public health approach. Primary health has taken a lead in this approach, as evidenced by a recent Institute of Medicine (IOM) report focused on developing a more complete understanding of LGBT health issues. The IOM report (2011) recommends applying the following cross-cutting perspectives to research to further the evidence base on LGBT health:

- The *minority stress model* calls attention to the chronic stress that sexual and gender minorities may experience as a result of their stigmatization.
- The *life course perspective* looks at how events at each stage of life influence subsequent stages.
- The *intersectionality perspective* examines an individual's multiple identities and the ways in which they interact.
- The *social ecology perspective* emphasizes that individuals are surrounded by spheres of influence, including families, communities, and society.

A public health approach focuses on the health of all people, including their relationship to physical and built environments (Cummins & Jackson, 2011), in addition to psychological, cultural, and social environments in which people live, attend school, work, engage with others, and continue to grow and thrive. A growing body of literature is moving in this proactive direction. Research shows that positive youth development programs produce positive behavior outcomes and prevent youth problem behaviors (Catalano, Berglund, Ryan, Lonczak, & Hawkins, 2004). Youth programs may benefit from research on the positive aspects of lesbian or gay identity by describing the following: belonging to a community, creating families of choice, forging strong connections with others, serving as positive role models, developing empathy and compassion, living authentically and honestly, gaining personal insight and sense of self, involvement in social justice and activism, freedom from gender-specific roles, and exploring relationships (Riggle, Whitman, Olson, Rostosky, & Strong, 2008). These psychosocial dimensions afford extensive opportunities for developing services and supports that are proactive in cultivating resilience in LGBT youth and their families.

It is especially encouraging to see the larger systems involved with policy and the provision of services addressing the issues and needs of LGB youth. For example, the Child, Adolescent and Family Branch in the Center for Mental Health Services of the Substance Abuse and Mental Health Services Administration (SAMHSA) established a national work group to address the needs of children and youth who are LGBT, questioning, intersex, or two-spirit (LGBTQI2-S) and their families who receive federally funded services and supports through the administration's programs.

Using an assets-based approach to examine the complex biological, psychological, and sociological dynamics of sexual orientation and gender identity can inform efforts to address the needs of LGBT children and youth by policy makers, frontline service providers, parents, other caregivers, youth, and community members (Espinoza, 2008; Lazear & Gamache, 2008; National Institutes of Health, 2007; SAMHSA Center for Mental Health Services, Child, Adolescent, and Family Services Branch, 2008; SAMHSA Center for Substance Abuse Treatment, 2001). Research that examines assets-based approaches, such as the impact of positive development programs, stigma reduction strategies, positive role models and adult mentors, and supportive family settings, should be planned, funded, and implemented. A better understanding of how peer-to-peer support organizations reduce stigma, social withdrawal, and isolation is especially needed.

Research efforts can be proactively focused on strengths-based approaches and the identification of the critical variables in promising practices that function effectively with this population. Studies examining the successful infusion of inclusionary and assets-based approaches into existing systems of care and professional training can yield meaningful findings to support systems of care in adapting specific treatment modalities, direct service programs, and other community supports. An assets-based research program is likely to have significant practice implications throughout systems of care and ultimately benefit LGBT youth and their families.

CONCLUSION

Assets-based approaches hold considerable potential for addressing the needs of LGBT youth and their families, and we recommend developing a research agenda to identify effective assets-based approaches. To make the "resilience U-turn" that we have discussed in this chapter, all levels and components of a system of care providing services and supports to LGBT youth and their families should be examined; opportunities exist within every process and structure to positively affect LGBT youth. Key recommendations include

- Committing to a systemwide focus on the needs and issues of LGBT youth and their families, including societal and family stigma
- Understanding both the risk *and* protective factors of LGBT youth
- Rethinking interventions through an assets-based lens
- Reducing behavioral health disparities for youth and their families by incorporating cultural and linguistic competence in all aspects of services and supports

9

Building Systems of Care to Support Effective Therapeutic and Programmatic Interventions and Resources for LGBT Youth and Their Families

KATHERINE J. LAZEAR, SHEILA A. PIRES,
STEPHEN L. FORSSELL, AND CORETTA JACQUELINE MALLERY

Systems of care provide an organizing framework and a set of values for providing mental health services. A system of care is more than a network of individual service components; rather, it is a philosophy about how communities should deliver services to youth and their families (Stroul & Friedman, 1996). These principles emphasize the role of youth and families in the care of youth, as well as culturally and linguistically competent services for children, youth, and their families (Stroul, 2002). Reflecting this value system, it is imperative to provide appropriate culturally and linguistically competent services to lesbian, gay, bisexual, and transgender (LGBT) youth and their families, as well as youth questioning their gender or sexual identity.

Implementing effective services and supports to LGBT youth and their families requires commitment and planning. At every level of its development and implementation, a system of care addresses both its processes and structures to deliver an effective service array. This includes frontline practice shifts focused on the skills, knowledge, and attitudes of service providers; evidence-based practices and promising approaches; access and availability of services; treatment efficacy monitoring; cultural and linguistic competence; partnerships with families and youth; and ongoing evaluations for continuous quality improvement (Pires, 2002; 2010).

Services and supports tailored to the specific needs of youth and families are essential elements of service provision in systems of care. Ultimately, systems of care are guided by several goals, including assessing needs in a holistic manner, providing individualized services to meet these needs, delivering unconditional care, involving families in a meaningful way, and collaborating across agencies. Moreover, "this approach should permeate the entire system of care in a community—a goal that is consistent with, and established by, the current system of care philosophy" (Lourie, Katz-Leavy, & Stroul, 1996, p. 450). This chapter is grounded in the fundamental principle that specific interventions and therapies, including those that are evidence-based, sit within a larger system context that is attuned to its population of focus. Given that focus, this chapter explores individualized service provisions, formal and informal, to meet the needs of LGBT youth and their families through a wraparound approach and the importance of the larger system structure to support these individualized services. Recommendations addressing counseling challenges and practices specific to LGBT youth or those questioning their gender or sexual identity are included. The chapter's framework and conceptual perspectives are based on *Building Systems of Care: A Primer, Second Edition* (Pires, 2010). These perspectives are described briefly, followed by discussion of their relevance to meeting the needs of LGBT or questioning youth and their families.

ENGAGING LGBT YOUTH IN SYSTEMS OF CARE

The system of care concept provides an organizing framework and a value base for organizing services and supports within a coherent structure (Stroul, 2002). Reform of service systems and development of systems of care begins with states and communities defining their populations of focus (Pires, 2010). Initially, the system of care concept was applied to children with serious emotional disorders and their families (Stroul & Friedman, 1996). Over time, states and localities have increasingly acknowledged that system of care values and principles are applicable to many populations. Accordingly, states and localities now apply these values and principles to other populations, such as all children and families in child welfare and youth in juvenile justice systems or adult populations with substance abuse issues whose children are involved in these systems. LGBT youth are a subgroup within most populations of focus in systems of care and require services that address their strengths, challenges, and needs.

With a growing body of research indicating that disparities and disproportionalities exist for LGB and increasingly for transgender youth, the importance of expanding a system of care's population of focus to meet the needs of this population cannot be overemphasized. For example, relative to their heterosexual peers, LGBT youth reportedly experience higher rates of homelessness (Cochran, Stewart, Ginzler, & Cauce, 2002) and substance abuse (Marshall et al., 2008). They are also reportedly overrepresented in the child welfare system (Wilber, Ryan, & Marksamer, 2006). Moreover, racially and ethnically diverse youth are at even higher risk of experiencing these disparities, so these youth who are also LGBT are at especially increased risk for these negative outcomes.

LGBT or questioning youth should be part of the larger population focus of a system of care because of the challenges they experience in meeting basic care and support needs. The following sections explore how systems of care can accomplish this successfully. This is especially important because systems of care structure various functions of the delivery system, such as the pathway to care, the service array, the provider network, and peer supports and natural helpers. Furthermore, systems of care implement processes to plan, carry out, and oversee system reforms, an important role for the improvement of the delivery of services and supports to LGBT youth.

IMPROVING PROCESSES TO ENHANCE SERVICES AND SUPPORTS

When building a system of care for any population, it matters how system builders plan, progress, and respond to the needs of youth; who is involved in every aspect throughout the process; the relationships that are established with youth and their families; and how individuals and organizations in the system conduct themselves in their interactions with youth and their families. These elements are among the key components of effective processes to build and implement effective services and supports in a system of care. At the same time, the system of care approach is a strengths-based philosophy, and processes must seek to identify, enhance, and sustain the strengths and assets of this population, involving individual youth, supportive family members and organizations, and relevant community assets. Although there are a number of elements included in effective system-building processes, we focus on one aspect that is especially critical: leadership and constituency building (Pires, 2002, 2010).

LGBT youth and family leaders can help inform the planning and implementation of services and supports for other LGBT youth and their families. Outreach to, and engagement of, youth who can be leaders and provision of support to help these youth build their leadership capacity is a key element of a system-development process with a focus on LGBT or questioning youth. In one study examining general barriers to youth participation in systems of care, all youth (not just LGBT youth) identified heterosexism as a barrier to participation; interestingly, it was *not* identified as a barrier by adults surveyed (Politz, 1996). Intentionally involving LGBT youth and their allies sends a powerful message that the system-building process is inclusive.

Constituency building fosters supportive partnerships and engages supportive allies. Effective system-development processes strategically map potential allies in the community (e.g., organizations, faith-based groups, family- and youth-run organizations) whose involvement can create a safer, more welcoming environment for LGBT youth and their families. These allies also contribute relevant knowledge. Often, initiatives underway in a state or community can build a focus on LGBT youth and their families within the initial population of interest. For example, primary prevention and stigma reduction campaigns can include a specialized focus on LGBT youth by partnering with those in the community, including youth themselves, who are knowledgeable about this population.

Analysis of other potential partners or activities within a community offers opportunities for valuable linkages, a key strategy in constituency building and creating greater awareness of the needs, strengths, and unique issues of LGBT youth. Examples of these types of fruitful linkages include expanding an existing major suicide prevention campaign to encompass a tailored focus on LGBT youth, bullying prevention efforts that include a focus on youth who are known or perceived to be LGBT, and family-run organizations focused on larger populations partnering with those focusing on LGBT youth and their families. The availability of a strong Parents, Families and Friends of Lesbians and Gays (PFLAG) chapter within the community enables just such an opportunity for important partnerships. Those involved in developing systems of care can partner with local HIV/AIDS clinics and hotlines and local LGBT youth programs (online listings of local LGBT youth services are provided by the National Youth Advocacy Coalition). Collaborating with the local LGBT community provides systems of care with opportunities to build these unique and invaluable partnerships for the benefit of LGBT youth and their families.

STRUCTURING SYSTEM OF CARE FUNCTIONS TO FACILITATE THE PROVISION OF SERVICES AND SUPPORTS

The importance of addressing the challenges of outreach and engagement for LGBT youth and their families cannot be overemphasized. Systems of care should examine how they communicate with and engage the LGBT community, including individuals who may be closeted (i.e., not openly LGBT) out of fear, stigma, or shame. They should also consider how to best communicate with and engage the larger community with an LGBT group, when many in the larger community may prefer that LGBT youth and LGBT organizations remain hidden because of their own fears and/or institutionalized heterosexism/transphobia.

Building systems of care is about not only process but also structure—that is, the deliberate and thoughtful organization of the many functions that need to be addressed when building a system of care (Pires, 2010). Pires identified more than 30 functions within systems of care requiring structure. The following sections focus on four major functions requiring structure: the pathway to services and supports, service planning, service array, and service delivery.

Pathway to Services and Supports

Stroul and Friedman (1996) described the importance of a system of care community providing access to a comprehensive array of services that address the physical, emotional, social, and educational needs of children in all life domains. Access implies a clear pathway to services that is both welcoming and safe, but also, importantly, readily apparent. For any youth and their family, an organized pathway to services should be welcoming. For the LGBT population, it is especially important to also ensure there is an organized pathway to services that is not only welcoming but also respectful and safe. For example, when LGBT youth enter an intake center, are there any visual cues to indicate that this center is a welcoming environment for them, such as posters showing LGBT family members (e.g., same-sex parents)? Do questions in initial screening applications or in-person intake interviews include LGBT youth, friends, and family members? Does the interviewer pay particular attention to the rights of privacy and confidentiality when sharing information in a collaborative process?

Service Planning

In systems of care, service planning is the process for making decisions about which services to provide to youth and their families, how to provide those services, and how to determine success of these interventions. Systems of care use *wraparound* as their service planning approach. Wraparound is based on the following 10 key principles:

1. Guided by family and youth voice and choice
2. Team based
3. Use of natural supports as well as formal supports
4. Collaboration across providers, natural helpers, systems, families, and youth
5. Community based
6. Culturally and linguistically competent
7. Individualized
8. Strengths based
9. Unconditional/persistent
10. Outcome based

Wraparound is a "definable planning process, that results in a unique set of community services and natural supports that are individualized for a child and family to achieve a positive set of outcomes" (Chamberlain, 2002, p. 117). Hence wraparound provides an approach to service planning that can address the complex issues often faced by youth who identify as LGBT (or who are questioning their sexual/gender identity) and their families. A growing body of research supports the effectiveness of wraparound with various populations (Walker & Bruns, 2007). The scenario that follows illustrates selected components of a wraparound planning process and plan for John, who identifies as a gay youth.

John is on probation for breaking into the school after hours and stealing art supplies. He has been referred to the system of care because of his involvement with the justice system and school-related behaviors—physical aggression (he is often in trouble for fighting with other students), high absenteeism, perceived lack of interest, and poor grades. John and his mother, Claire, also report that they often fight at home, and John leaves home for long periods of time without permission.

During the initial strength-based interview, John and Claire identify individuals whom they would like to see on his team. Besides John and his mother, team members include the care coordinator, art teacher, probation officer, school guidance counselor, family partner/advocate, and Claire's live-in boyfriend, Ray. During the intake interview and subsequent team meetings, John and his team identify a vision to get along better with each other in the family and with other students and for John to graduate and get a good job. The team also addresses the family's culture, strengths, and interests. They note that John is a good artist, Claire likes to help others and has strong spiritual beliefs, the family is close, John has a good relationship with the guidance counselor, and John is well liked by teachers at school. The team also identifies team and community strengths; for example, John's probation officer has strong community connections, including a church-affiliated HIV/AIDS clinic.

John and his team then begin to identify needs: John needs to learn to get along with others, increase his self-esteem and confidence, feel safe at school, and attend all his classes for the next 3 months to graduate. In addition, Claire needs to feel like she is not alone and accept John for who he is. Given John's strengths, interests, and needs, the team discusses possible strategies to meet those needs, which also build on his strengths and interests: John will work with other youth to design logos and posters for the HIV/AIDS clinic; the art teacher will introduce John to famous gay artists and other local artists; the family partner will accompany Claire to a PFLAG meeting and the local Federation of Families for Children's Mental Health monthly dinner meeting; John, John's brother, Claire, and Claire's boyfriend will participate in family counseling to explore the family's attitudes toward people who are gay and transgender, in general, and toward John specifically; and the school will provide an in-service for school staff to better understand LGBT issues and to provide education, support, and resources on promoting a supportive school environment and intervention strategies to prevent and intervene to address bullying.

John's story depicts only one aspect of the team process and wraparound plan, but shows how to develop a more culturally and linguistically competent, individualized plan for a youth who identifies as gay and his family. Recent research demonstrates the importance of family support to prevent risk and promote healthy outcomes for LGBT young adults (Ryan, Huebner, Diaz, & Sanchez, 2009; Ryan, Russell, Huebner, Diaz, & Sanchez, 2010). It is, therefore, important that providers ask about family reactions to a youth's LGBT identity, assess the youth's risk for family rejection, and determine treatment goals based on needs for family education and support (e.g., clarification and modification of the family's attitudes to foster a more supportive family environment). The therapist may involve the entire family in activities that promote individual self-esteem and family pride.

Screening, assessment, and evaluation data inform the wraparound process and plan development; therefore, these functions must also put system of care values and principles into practice and respond to the needs of LGBT youth. When a youth transitions out of the formal wraparound process, it is important to implement community-based services and supports that address a youth's ongoing needs (e.g., connection to medical services and HIV education). Further information about these functions appears later in this chapter.

Service Array and Service Delivery

> Successful systems of care blend formal services and natural supports, helping youth and families to access and make use of both. Natural supports are those found within the neighborhoods in which youth and families live and within the affinity groups with which they associate (or would associate if they existed). (Pires, 2010, p. 253)

For this blending of formal services and natural supports to occur, families, youth, and culturally and linguistically diverse constituencies should be involved in the design of the service array and delivery. This approach will help to adequately address the needs of the service population and the entire community.

Systems of care are also giving greater attention to models of effective practice (i.e., evidence-based practices and practice/community-based evidence) in the delivery of services to youth. For example, a 2-day meeting in May 2010 in Washington, D.C., involved multiple constituencies who shared perspectives about how different models of effective practice can be better integrated to improve performance accountability and outcomes. The group came to the consensus that to address issues as complex as disparities within service systems, it is important to identify and implement effective practices that are evidence-based and practice-based and grow out of community-defined measures of effectiveness, including those defined by the LGBT community (Isaacs, 2010). Because clinical interventions tend to constitute a primary intervention for youth in systems of care, the next section discusses recommended counseling practices/challenges and therapist issues specific to LGBT youth.

Recommended Counseling Practices for LGBT Youth

Many well-intended counselors erroneously believe that there is no difference between providing counseling to the LGBT and heterosexual communities. However, they may overlook the diverse characteristics and needs of LGBT individuals, effects of social stigma, and the context and community supports that are available to support them (Carroll, 2010). Further, counselors may not realize that these community supports are available to help support their clients.

Research exploring satisfaction with counseling services demonstrates that the needs of LGBT youth in counseling settings may be insufficiently addressed. For example, one study found that the level of dissatisfaction with counseling services was twice as high among LGBT-identified individuals as a heterosexual comparison group (Avery, Hellman, & Sudderth, 2001). This study also found dissatisfaction rates to be four times as high among LGBT women and racial minorities as their respective comparison groups. Other seminal research sheds light on specific areas of deficiency. In a national survey of psychologists undertaken to identify the spectrum of practices when working with LGB clients, researchers identified 17 biased and discriminatory themes that emerged from the responses (Garnets, Hancock, Cochran, Goodchilds, & Peplau, 1991). Among the more damaging themes were therapists' beliefs that homosexuality is a mental disorder and, therefore, abruptly making referrals to other counselors. Although this research is somewhat dated, more recent research shows that clinicians may have negative attitudes toward LGBT individuals that subsequently affect their ability to provide appropriate care (Kaiser Family Foundation, 2002; Sanchez, Rabatin, Sanchez, Hubbard, & Kalet, 2006; Smith & Mathews, 2007).

These findings highlight the need for counselors to be trained in affirmative counseling practices that value and support sexual and gender diversity and recognize LGBT discrimination and its consequences (Fassinger, 1991). Counselors who practice affirmative counseling support the client's identity development process and recognize that counseling of LGBT clients should be about helping youth achieve their personal therapeutic goals.

Many exemplary graduate programs address this practice model in multicultural counseling classes, and others incorporate these and related topics throughout the curriculum. External training is still often necessary to increase the knowledge base of clinicians providing services to LGBT individuals. Researchers have also identified 14 themes of exemplary practice, including therapists' awareness of heterosexism and how that may affect a client's presenting problem (Garnets et al., 1991). Their findings were the foundation for the American Psychological Association's "Guidelines for Psychotherapy with Lesbian, Gay, and Bisexual Clients," which are accessible online (2000).

More recent research has found two factors that correlate with high levels of affirmative behaviors from therapists in university counseling centers: a counselor's sexual identity and an organization's gay-positive climate (Bieschke, Perez, & DeBord, 2007). Counselors who are gay themselves may be more cognizant of providing affirmative counseling practices and providing a gay-affirming environment. This does not preclude non-LGBT counselors from providing effective affirmative therapy, but it does highlight the dearth in training of counselors regarding the value of affirmative approaches. Additionally, an LGBT-friendly organizational climate can contribute to more affirming therapist behaviors. For instance, displaying LGBT-friendly magazines, posters, and books in a waiting area can signal acceptance to youth and encourage therapists to act more proactively and positively with their LGBT clients. Lastly, it is important to avoid terminology on intake forms that assumes heterosexual or cisgender identity and to train members of the organization to avoid language that reflects these assumptions.

In addition to individual therapy, group counseling and support groups also offer important modalities for working with LGBT youth (Carroll, 2010). These counseling groups may be made up of solely members of the LGBT community depending on who the group members are and where they are in their sexual identity development. Many youth feel alone in their process of self-discovery and identity development. Group counseling may help to validate these experiences and normalize thoughts and feelings. Further, group counseling can help youth work through intimacy issues and build social skills in a safe environment. LGBT youth may hide their true personality in typical environments; group work provides youth the opportunity to try out new behaviors and obtain feedback from peers and providers. This may include sharing personal thoughts with group members before sharing with friends or family members, which offers opportunities to "rehearse" difficult self-revelations. These youth may also have difficulties with peers, so group work can provide a space for interpersonal learning. Support groups are a variation of the group counseling process and are often psychoeducational with a focus on specific topics such as building and enhancing relationships or "coming out."

Transgender youth may visit LGB affirming therapists or other mental health providers. Grossman and D'Augelli (2006) identified several key factors that affect the experiences of youth who identify as transgender, including the following: 1) providers should acknowledge that transgender youth exist and that atypical gender expression is an acceptable way of behaving; 2) providers should address the discrimination and marginalization experienced by transgender youth through intervention, advocacy, and public education; 3) resources should be available to meet the specific needs of transgender youth, such as physical health care, employment, and housing; 4) programs should assist families and communities in creating safe environments with a plan and process for ongoing continuity of care; 5) specialized programs should assist transgender youth in developing plans to achieve their preferred gender identity; 6) all providers should receive training about transgender people; and 7) transgender youth should learn strategies to assist them in building the resiliency they need to live healthy lives as their self-identified gender identity.

Therapist Concerns

A large body of research recognizes that the therapeutic alliance is an integral part of effective therapy, if not the most important factor affecting positive outcomes of therapeutic interventions (Horvath & Symonds, 1991). Therefore, it is imperative for clinicians to be educated about terminology, experiences, and typical developmental issues that may come up when counseling LGBT youth or those who are questioning their sexual orientation or gender identity. Similarly, it is important for therapists to address any personal values or beliefs that may conflict or interfere with their ability to provide appropriate care for LGBT clients and their families.

If a therapist has not received training about working with LGBT clients, it is the therapist's professional responsibility to seek such training. Even without this formal training, it is appropriate for a therapist supporting an LGBT youth for the first time to ask questions, rather than to avoid the topic of sexuality and gender identity altogether. It is also important to recognize that a youth may come to counseling with an issue not directly related to his or her sexual orientation or gender identity. In these instances, the youth's sexual orientation or gender identity should not be the sole focus of therapeutic intervention (Carroll, 2010). The focus of the therapy should be dictated by the youth, and although issues of sexual identity development may emerge, they may not be the center of the youth's issues. Anecdotal accounts by LGBT and questioning youth purport that therapists sometimes attribute challenges in the youth's life to their LGBT or questioning identity or have made their sexual orientation or gender identity the primary focus of therapy.

Although all therapists have personal values and beliefs, it is critical to ensure that any preexisting beliefs that may be LGBT negative are sublimated in the relationship with the client. As such, the therapist must be prepared to deal with countertransference issues. *Countertransference* occurs when a therapist's unconscious and conscious personal reactions, including conflicts, arise in relation to their client's issues. As it relates to LGBT youth, for example, a therapist who grew up in a culture that taught that homosexuality is immoral may have internal conflict when working with LGBT youth. Countertransference can emerge when therapists avoid discussing LGBT issues with which they are uncomfortable. It may also take the form of redirecting the course of therapy to other issues, or a therapist may experience physical responses such as anxiety as a result of his or her own internalized feelings surrounding LGBT youth. A more serious example of countertransference is a heterosexist or transphobic therapist minimizing a questioning youth's feelings or directing a questioning youth to become heterosexual or identify with his or her birth-assigned gender.

Another form of countertransference can occur when a therapist becomes too emotionally involved in the client's issues. If, for example, the therapist was bullied in school for being gay, working with a youth dealing with this issue may trigger deep personal feelings. In this situation, therapy can inappropriately become more about working through the therapist's own unresolved issues than those of the client. Unconditional positive regard is a necessary component in therapy, but overinvolvement is unhealthy, for both the therapist and the client.

Although detrimental to the therapeutic process, many therapists experience these reactions. It is, however, a therapist's professional and ethical obligation to provide the best possible treatment for clients. Accordingly, it is incumbent on the clinician to work through any unresolved personal issues that contribute to countertransference through training, supervision, or their own therapy (Carroll, 2010). Avoiding or directing therapy away from LGBT issues can be harmful to youth because they may already feel that they make others uncomfortable. Once a therapist recognizes that he or she is engaging in this type of behavior, the therapist should immediately seek training and supervision.

Self-disclosure in therapy is often used to build trust, by helping clients to feel more comfortable working with someone who has been through similar challenges in life. Although LGBT therapists who counsel LGBT clients may want to demonstrate their expertise about the LGBT community and their value and support of diversity, some may also choose to identify as LGBT. A youth's underlying question for a therapist, however, may not be, "Are you gay?" but "Will you truly respect, support, understand, and value me?" As such, non–LGBT counselors can also provide effective LGBT-affirming counseling. A non–LGBT counselor may want to share a bit about his or her expertise or experience working with this population. LGBT youth may have experienced discrimination in the past and may need to hear that their counseling setting is truly a safe place for them.

Decisions about whether LGBT therapists openly identify as such are often informed by their approach to counseling or agency policies. Thus, when youth question a counselor's sexual orientation or gender identity, it is important to process a youth's motivations for asking the question, regardless of the therapist's comfort with self-disclosure. Many therapists find that youth are not truly interested in the personal life of the counselor, but are more looking for evidence that therapy will be a safe and supportive environment for them.

Counseling Challenges Common Among LGBT Youth

Some common issues therapists should be prepared for when counseling LGBT youth include violence, developmental issues, mental health concerns, suicide risk, and substance use. This section briefly summarizes these issues, as most are more fully developed throughout this book. LGBT youth may experience violence, including verbal, physical, and sexual assaults from peers, family members, and other adults important in their lives. Research has shown that LGBT youth face higher levels of harassment and bullying and are more likely to feel unsafe at school (IOM, 2011). This violence can result in depression, anxiety, fear, low self-esteem, and posttraumatic stress disorder. In the worst cases, seeking help may result in further victimization from adults (Ryan & Futterman, 1998).

Youth may also face developmental and identity formation issues that they wish to discuss with a therapist. These include issues surrounding coming out to family and/or friends, internalized homophobia, and concerns related to family of origin. Youth may also deal with identity confusion regarding how their cultural, spiritual, or ethnic identity interacts with their sexual or gender identity. Transphobia is another issue therapists should be prepared for when working with youth who identify as a gender other than their birth-assigned gender. It is important for therapists to realize that LGBT youth may experience a sense of grief and loss due to the loss of typical developmental opportunities such as dating and having close trusted friends. Youth may also lack appropriate outlets for normal romantic and sexual experimentation (Carroll, 2010).

Finally, LGBT youth are at increased risk for certain mental health issues, such as suicidal ideation, suicide attempts, depression, eating disorders, and substance use (Carroll, 2010; IOM, 2011). LGBT youth may use alcohol and drugs to cope with stress related to stigma or bullying, which could, in turn, increase the risk for dependency later in life. It is critical for therapists and all others who work with LGBT youth to be aware of these potential risks and include psychosocial assessment (formal or informal) routinely when working with youth. With the assistance of a positive support system that includes affirmative therapeutic interventions (support, acceptance, and understanding), youth can develop positive coping skills and form fulfilling interpersonal relationships.

Negative assumptions about homosexuality may be attributable to internalized heterosexism and transphobia. *Heterosexism* describes hostile or strong negative attitudes and reactions toward LGB people, some of which stem from the perception that lesbian and gay individuals transgress gender norms. *Transphobia* is an irrational fear, dislike, or hatred of people who are transgender or transsexual or who challenge conventional gender categories of male/female (McIlroy, 2009). Research on internalized heterosexism largely, but not totally, supports assertions that it is related to many aspects of LGB individuals' lives (Szymanski, Kashubeck-West, & Meyer, 2008). Thus it is important to review therapies based on negative assumptions of homosexuality.

Reparative or conversion therapies focus on changing one's sexual identity and are rooted in the belief that homosexuality is a mental illness (Ryan & Futterman, 1998). These therapies have been linked to a host of negative outcomes such as self-hatred, confusion, hopelessness, discrimination, difficulties with intimacy, and suicidal ideation. Use of these therapies is seen as unethical for clinicians by most professional organizations. The American Psychological Association commissioned a task force to conduct a systematic review of the research on sexual orientation change efforts and concluded that these techniques are ineffective and may cause harm (American Psychological Association Task Force on Appropriate Therapeutic Responses to Sexual Orientation, 2009). The results of the task force also showed that same-sex sexual and romantic attractions, feelings, and behaviors are normal and positive variations of human sexuality, not a mental disorder.

The American Psychiatric Association's (2000b) position statement expresses its opposition to reparative therapy or any therapy based on the assumption that homosexuality is a mental disorder. In issuing this statement, the American Psychiatric Association joined the American Academy of Pediatrics, the American Medical Association, the American Psychological Association, the American Counseling Association, and the National Association of Social Workers in opposing reparative therapy. Accordingly, most clinicians do not use conversion or reparative therapies, and we strongly discourage them. Chapter 4 in this book explores related issues and sexual identity development in detail.

CONCLUSION

This chapter has highlighted how communities and individuals can apply system of care principles and values, which propel the processes and structures associated with building an effective system of care to ensure a "good fit" for LGBT youth and their families. We have raised significant issues and advanced several concepts, fully anticipating that others will continue to identify and implement promising strategies and effective approaches. Both those building systems of care and individual service providers working with LGBT youth should address the impact of sociocultural development and factors associated with the youth, family, and community in all aspects of their outreach, assessments, evaluations, and interventions. They should also address the effects of negative life events, population-specific assets and resources, sociocultural aspects of clinician–patient interaction, help-seeking behaviors and coping styles, stigma and multiple social stressors, and perceived causes of symptoms and behaviors. There are large individual differences among youth in their degree of exposure to institutionalized heterosexism, transphobia, fear, and ignorance and associated stress and adversity.

All LGBT youth and their families in need of behavioral health services, however, need safe environments in which to access effective services and fully participate as leaders and partners in their care. Just as Walker and Bruns (2007) described the supportive environment for effective wraparound in a system of care—a child and family team nested within a supportive organization, nested within a hospitable policy and funding system—so must a supportive environment exist to move toward true, full inclusion of LGBT youth and their families. The hard lines between individual and community responsibility and between personal and political ideology may need to soften to achieve such a supportive environment. With increasing social acceptance and greater access to accurate information, LGBT people are more likely to self-identify and to come out at all stages of the life course. The confluence of these psychosociological factors is also likely to result in increased help-seeking behavior among LGBT youth; accordingly, it is important for therapists to be prepared to effectively identify, address, and support the needs of LGBT youth.

10

Standards of Care for LGBT Youth

KIM PAWLEY HELFGOTT AND SIMON G. GONSOULIN

esbian, gay, bisexual, transgender (LGBT), and questioning youth who receive services from youth-serving agencies and across service systems— including mental health, education, youth development, child welfare, juvenile justice, and health care—often have their needs unevenly addressed. Sometimes youth-serving agencies fail to recognize and adequately respond to the unique challenges facing these youth, and as a result young people may feel isolated, alienated, and fearful as they attempt to express their emerging LGBT identity. Consequently, all youth-serving agencies, regardless of function, should be knowledgeable about and sensitive to the specific needs of LGBT and questioning youth and equipped to provide competent services (Gamache & Lazear, 2009; Mallon, 2010; Phillips, McMillen, Sparks, & Ueberle, 1997).

For many LGBT youth, victimization in school, home, and community settings is a norm (Wilber, Ryan, & Marksamer, 2006). They are more likely to attempt suicide, suffer depression, use or abuse substances, have HIV/sexually transmitted infections (STIs), drop out of school, and become homeless as compared with non–LGBT youth (Gamache & Lazear, 2009; Hooper, 2004; Larkin Street Youth Services, 2009; Mallon, 2010; Poirier et al., 2008; Ryan, Hueber, Diaz, & Sanchez, 2009). These considerations underscore the need for committed leadership, policies, practices, and staff training that promote safe and supportive agency environments where LGBT youth can flourish. Although the purpose of youth-serving organizations and systems may differ, they share a common commitment and responsibility for providing a safe environment and promoting the healthy development of youth into well-adjusted, productive adults. All young people in youth-serving systems, including LGBT youth, have

For their contributions to this chapter, including examples, the authors acknowledge Joyce Burrell, principal researcher at American Institutes for Research and former deputy commissioner, New York State Office of Children and Family Services; as well as Marketa Garner Walters, senior researcher at American Institutes for Research and former assistant secretary, Louisiana Department of Social Services.

the right to be safe, protected, and welcomed. Youth-serving agencies and systems that support LGBT and questioning youth play an important role in meeting their emotional and social needs, building on personal strengths, and developing an array of skills and competencies (Gamache & Lazear, 2009, Mallon, 1997). Regardless of the type of youth-serving agency or system, standards of care can guide the delivery of services and build staff capacity to implement appropriate practices that foster positive youth development and minimize risks.

This chapter provides guidance to youth-serving organizations for creating an organizational culture that is responsive and sensitive to these youth and their families. Guiding principles, grounded in system of care values, provide a philosophy of practice for youth-serving agencies and systems that seek to meet the needs of LGBT and questioning youth. Strategies are recommended for implementing standards of care, including suggested policies and practices.

1. Conduct an agency self-assessment and ongoing continuous quality-improvement efforts.
2. Enforce nondiscriminatory policies for serving LGBT youth.
3. Promote staff knowledge and development about LGBT youth and their families.
4. Incorporate culturally and linguistically appropriate intake processes, data collection, and information sharing.
5. Promote a safe, supportive, and culturally and linguistically competent environment.
6. Implement practices that support preferences and affirm identity.
7. Promote healthy and supportive peer connections.
8. Strengthen family connections.
9. Promote access to an array of affirming services and supports.
10. Facilitate community outreach and engagement.

Together, these guiding principles and standards of care strengthen youth-serving organizations' capacity to achieve their goals and improve the quality of life and future potential for LGBT and questioning youth and their families.

GUIDING PRINCIPLES FOR SERVICE DELIVERY

Guiding principles for service delivery emphasize quality care for all children and youth, regardless of race, culture, physical capabilities, religion, sexual orientation, or gender identity/expression (Mallon, 1992). When systems of care are guided by principles and values including coordination of care and culturally and linguistically competent, family-centered, youth-guided, individualized, and strengths-based services and supports, they are more likely to result in better outcomes for children, youth, and their families (Stroul, Blau, & Friedman, 2010;

Stroul & Friedman, 1986, 1996). The following four principles are grounded in system of care values and recommended practice guidance (Mallon, 1992, 1997, 2010; Wilber et al., 2006): 1) foster shared responsibility and a common commitment across service systems, 2) create an inclusive organizational culture, 3) implement a family-centered approach, and 4) promote positive youth development outcomes. These principles are relevant for all youth-serving public and private agencies. They provide an important framework for implementing services and supports for all youth, including LGBT youth.

Foster Shared Responsibility and a Common Commitment Across Service Systems for the Well-Being of LGBT Youth and Their Families

Systems that serve youth share a commitment to improving outcomes and reducing risks experienced by all youth. Regardless of the purpose of a youth-serving organization or the roles and responsibilities of staff and caregivers within that organization, each person recognizes that he or she plays an important role in fostering the well-being of all youth, including those who may identify themselves as LGBT.

Fostering a shared commitment to system of care values across youth-serving systems and providing comprehensive and coordinated service delivery for all youth is critical, regardless of youths' LGBT identity/expression. Youth-serving agencies and systems must continuously assess the consistent application of core principles and values throughout the continuum and array of youth services and supports provided for LGBT youth, from investigation, referral, case management, youth development, in-home care, family preservation and reunification, and out-of-home care/confinement to transitional and aftercare or postadoption and independent living services. Gaining a common understanding of how these values should be implemented will not be easy, and system leaders should proactively create opportunities for open communication and ongoing dialogue to ensure that the policies and practices reflect the values they uphold. When there is a shared commitment across youth-serving systems and between agencies, consistency in practice, as well as shared guidance and resources (e.g., policies, practice manuals, training curriculum) to effectively serve and support LGBT and questioning youth is possible.

The goal of every system of care is to create an array of services and supports across youth-serving systems to meet the individualized needs of youth and their families. Services and supports that are needed should be accessible and available for LGBT and questioning youth regardless of the type of service agency or human services system with which they are involved. Although LGBT and questioning youth should have the same opportunities for services and supports that exist for all other youth, there also should be a shared recognition among systems and service providers that, in some cases, they may need additional support due to unique needs and increased vulnerability.

Create an Inclusive Organizational Culture

Youth-serving organizations within a system of care share a commitment to an organizational culture that honors and respects the inherent worth and dignity of every person, treats each person fairly and equally, and values diversity regardless of gender identity/expression or LGBT identity (Mallon, 1992, 1997, 2010). An inclusive and respectful environment benefits all youth by offering safety for youth to explore their own emerging identities—a crucial developmental task for adolescents. This environment also promotes acceptance of individual differences and teaches young people to value different perspectives (Wilber et al., 2006).

An agency's leadership conveys the value of inclusiveness and reinforces this message at all levels of an organization. Every employee, contractor, service provider, caregiver, family member, and youth involved in the system understands the agency's commitment to treating every person with respect, valuing and affirming differences, and preventing harassment or discrimination of any kind (Wilber et al., 2006). In an inclusive organization, rules are fairly and consistently enforced for all youth, including LGBT youth: Certain behaviors are either appropriate or not. For example, if youth are not to engage in sexual activity because of facility rules, regardless of gender identity or expression, that particular rule applies equally to all youth.

Implement a Family-Centered Approach in Services and Supports

All young people benefit from families and significant adults who care deeply about them and help them make a successful transition to adulthood. Healthy development occurs within the context of nurturing, accepting, and supportive relationships. However, LGBT and questioning youth may feel isolated and may have constrained or conflicted relationships with family members. Research has documented the negative outcomes for youth and young adults who are disconnected from their families and other forms of social support (Wald & Martinez, 2003). Family rejection increases risk for abuse, neglect, and self-destructive or antisocial behaviors that can lead to out-of-home placement. Family-rejecting behavior during adolescence contributes to negative health and mental health outcomes, including suicide-related behavior and sexual health risks, and impaired capacity to form future positive, healthy relationships (Ryan, 2010; Ryan et al., 2009).

Historically, providers who work with LGBT youth have not routinely asked about family reactions to an adolescent's LGBT identity (Ryan, 2010). However, many LGBT and questioning youth and families need assistance from youth-serving organizations to heal current relationships among family members. For parents and caregivers, a little change from being less rejecting and a little more accepting can make an important difference in reducing a young person's risk for serious health problems, including suicide and HIV infection (Ryan, 2009). Family support is crucial for LGBT and questioning youth to develop their self-confidence and self-esteem, foster resilience and coping skills to deal with stress, and integrate a positive and healthy identity. A family-centered approach is critical to working with LGBT and questioning youth, and youth should be recognized as part of a family, regardless of whether family engagement is possible.

Promote Positive Youth Development

Youth development is the ongoing growth process in which all youth are engaged in attempting to 1) meet their basic personal and social needs (e.g., to be safe and feel valued) and 2) develop skills and competencies that allow them to effectively function and contribute in their daily lives (Pittman, O'Brien, & Kimball, 1993). Services and supports provided in the context of a positive youth development philosophy offer youth opportunities to take healthy risks, make choices, contribute, and form lasting relationships (Mallon, 1998).

Youth-serving organizations should work toward developing and supporting youth on the basis of individualized needs, rather than "fixing" them according to societal expectations (Mallon, 1997). Youth-serving organizations are intended to provide supports and opportunities that will build personal strengths, promote competence, and facilitate connections with families and communities. Programs and services should be tailored to meet each youth's needs and interests as opposed to a "one size fits all" approach (Mallon, 1997). Regardless of LGB or gender identity/expression, youth should be included in activities, educational opportunities, and jobs for which they qualify and exhibit interest.

Youth also should play an active role at all levels of decision making within youth-serving organizations. Organizations that promote positive youth development authentically and respectfully include the perspectives of LGBT youth, other LGBT community stakeholders, and advocates who represent LGBT youth. Their voices are represented by membership on governance boards and participation as volunteers or agency staff. Services, policies, and practices that are developed with the involvement and input from LGBT youth, their families, and individuals representing the larger LGBT community will be more responsive and effective in promoting the positive development of LBGT youth.

TEN STRATEGIES FOR IMPLEMENTING STANDARDS OF CARE

The following strategies provide guidance to youth-serving agency administrators and direct service staff members about how they can embrace the aforementioned guiding principles in their day-to-day practices and responsibilities. These strategies include policies and practices that specifically address issues that arise around sexual orientation and gender identity (Larkin Street Youth Services, 2009). These strategies are based not only on the existing literature about serving LGBT and questioning youth, but also on our experiences collaborating with communities and working with leaders of systems of care as they sought ways to transform their agencies to be more responsive to LGBT and questioning youth.

These strategies offer various potential starting points. Some may be more feasible for system of care communities and their staff and partners to apply than others. All of these strategies, however, are recommended for systems of care to provide safe environments and promote healthy development in these youth. For some agencies, it may be more realistic to develop a plan for implementing these strategies incrementally, with periodic reviews to assess progress in promoting competent practices, fostering positive youth development outcomes, and minimizing the risks often experienced by these young people. Although not necessarily sequential, these strategies provide guidance in a systematic order, beginning with initial assessment and progressing toward implementing a comprehensive community system of care that promotes policies and practices that are responsive and supportive of LGBT and questioning youth and their families.

Strategy 1: Conduct an Agency Self-Assessment and Ongoing Continuous Quality-Improvement Efforts

A needs-assessment or agency-readiness survey will determine agency policies and practices, as well as the knowledge, skills, ability, and professional development needs of staff to provide culturally and linguistically competent services to LGBT youth (National Network for Youth, 2002). An agency assessment or survey may also help sensitize administrators and staff to the reality that LGBT and questioning youth are most likely receiving agency services, either openly or not.

To ensure that LGBT youth are adequately served, agencies should develop ongoing continuous quality-improvement (CQI) policies and procedures to 1) monitor the effectiveness of agency implementation of services, supports, policies, and procedures; 2) evaluate agency progress toward its goals; and 3) obtain feedback for programs to institute appropriate changes to meet its goals on an ongoing basis. Examples of questions to guide the CQI process may include the following:

- What has the agency done to promote and infuse competence in serving and supporting LGBT youth and their families?
- What are the agency's outcomes for this population?
- What challenges has the agency encountered in meeting the needs of LGBT youth and their families? How has the agency addressed these challenges?
- What action steps are necessary to address the issues identified through the agency self-assessment process?

Throughout the self-assessment process, agencies can assess the appropriateness of services and supports for LGBT and questioning youth enrolled in a system of care. Every agency should ensure that service delivery responds to the needs of these youth by continuously collecting and analyzing data and using these results to support ongoing changes. Agencies can challenge themselves to continue to identify practices, policies, and training that will improve outcomes for LGBT youth and their families. Chapter 3 of this book describes additional considerations for conducting an agency self-assessment.

Strategy 2: Enforce
Nondiscriminatory Policies for Serving LGBT Youth

Systemwide policies and practices should be in place to create safe, supportive, and open environments for LGBT and questioning youth and staff. Policies must be developed that specifically address issues that arise around sexual orientation and gender identity (Larkin Street Youth Services, 2009). In particular, agencies should adopt and enforce nondiscriminatory policies that communicate that "we will protect you." For example, the New York State Office of Children and Family Services (NYS OCFS) policy directive states that the "agency is committed to providing LGBT and questioning youth a safe and respectful environment" (NYS OCFS, 2009). These policies should then be reinforced within the day-to-day practices of the agencies to ensure that staff and youth are safe from embarrassment, harassment, and assault if they choose to openly share their LGB identity or express their gender in ways that do not conform to their birth-assigned gender. This will also help protect those youth who are presumed to be LGBT but who do not identify as LGBT or are not questioning their sexual/gender identity.

Some staff may state that they support LGBT youth but do not intervene to stop disrespectful and threatening or violent actions and words. Staff may be uncomfortable or unprepared to provide appropriate supports and interventions that may be necessary to protect LGBT and questioning youth. However, direction from agency leadership needs to make clear that providing culturally and linguistically appropriate services and supports in a respectful manner is a requirement for remaining employed, and discrimination against LGBT youth or staff by agency employees is not tolerated. The agency should create a system for reporting and responding promptly to any act of discrimination, stereotyping, harassment, disrespect, and/or acts of bullying. All youth, families, providers, staff, and caregivers should be aware of where and how they can seek assistance if they experience abuse, harassment, or discrimination.

Agency policies should apply to all youth being served and all agency personnel, including managers, caseworkers/service coordinators, probation staff providers who contract with an agency to serve some of its youth, and direct care staff, including resource families such as foster parents and relative caregivers. Specifically, agency policies should

- Prohibit all forms of harassment and discrimination, including jokes, slurs, and name calling
- Preclude contracting with service providers that blatantly discriminate on the basis of LGB status or gender identity/expression, as well as providers who do not include LGBT individuals in their antidiscrimination policies
- Inform youth and staff about formal grievance procedures that allow for confidential complaints and neutral third-party investigators
- Designate an office to review complaints and make determinations regarding graduated disciplines (e.g., counseling, loss of wages) for noncompliance with stated policies. Instituting a safe method for reporting noncompliance will assure staff safety and enable policy refinement based on issues that come up during implementation. Reporting another staff member's failure to follow policy related to LGBT issues can make the reporting staff member vulnerable in the workplace, so protections should be in place. In addition to designating an office to review complaints, another option is designating an ombudsman to whom staff can report issues anonymously.

Agencies can ensure that their employees are aware of its nondiscrimination policy by

- Including a copy of the policy in staff training or orientation for every new employee, contractor, and other caregivers (e.g., foster parents, kinship family members, other guardians for the youth)
- Discussing how the policy should be applied to help staff understand what it means to provide nondiscriminatory treatment and services
- Posting the policy conspicuously in agency offices, group care facilities, courtrooms, and other strategic locations
- Including the agency policy in written materials designed for youth and their families, including handbooks or orientation materials provided to youth when they enter a system

Adopting and implementing nondiscriminatory policies that explicitly include sexual orientation and gender identity/expression can help make clear that anti-

LGBT harassment and discrimination is unacceptable, has clear consequences, and is not tolerated.

Strategy 3: Promote Staff Knowledge and Development About LGBT Youth and Their Families

Agencies should begin recruitment, screening, interviewing, and hiring processes by ensuring that staff and volunteers are dedicated to serving youth entrusted to their care respectfully and equitably. Potential, current, and new employees should be screened using tools to assess their perceptions of LGBT youth, as well as their likelihood of intervening appropriately when disrespectful behavior is displayed toward LGBT youth or their families. Agencies should use the results of this screening to guide supervision and training. Writing a short essay in response to a question or role playing responses to real-life scenarios with LGBT youth can also serve this purpose.

The agency should also commit to preparing staff to meet the needs of LGBT youth by determining their knowledge, skills, and staff development needs to adequately and competently provide services and supports to LGBT and questioning youth. Research indicates that training can affect the beliefs and attitudes toward gay and transgender youth and result in more respectful attitudes and more accurate perceptions of these populations (Phillips et al., 1997). Training provides an opportunity to explore how participants currently relate to LGBT and questioning youth and what practice-related changes may be needed.

A training curriculum should educate staff about LGBT youth, developmental issues, challenges they experience, and how to provide support and intervene effectively (Rockefeller College, 2010). The curriculum should include topics such as

- Vocabulary and definitions relevant to LGBT and questioning youth (e.g. *sexual orientation, gender identity*)
- Myths and stereotypes regarding LGBT and questioning youth and adults
- Developmentally appropriate concerns such as dating and sexuality for LGBT and questioning youth
- How families, peers, and other significant adults can support a young person who is "coming out" or deepening their understanding of their LGBT identity
- Issues and challenges experienced by transgender and gender-variant youth
- Approaches to working with the families of LGBT and questioning youth
- Agency and community resources that are available to support and serve LGBT and questioning youth and their families

Training should acknowledge the discomfort experienced by some staff as they balance their knowledge, personal beliefs/attitudes, and feelings for clients. As staff openly discuss and reconcile new information with beliefs surrounding these issues, they will be better prepared to provide competent care to these youth.

Targeted training will enhance understanding and staff competence in effectively addressing youth sexuality, racism, heterosexism, and transphobia, as well as how these negatively affect the well-being of LGBT youth. Additionally, staff should be trained to identify signs of bullying as well as appropriate steps for intervening to address and eliminate bullying of LGBT and questioning youth or those youth who are presumed to be LGBT or questioning. Staff should know that an agency has zero tolerance and that failure to intervene in bullying incidents will result in disciplinary actions. Training should inform staff about the implications of social isolation and the effects of limited or no family connections on LGBT and questioning youth. Training should enable staff not only to recognize the importance of family support on the well-being of LGBT youth but also to build staff capacity to effectively engage families. The training should inform staff of current research that identifies a positive correlation between the experience of family acceptance or rejection and how it affects the ability of LGBT youth to form healthy and loving relationships throughout their lives (Ryan et al., 2009).

Ongoing coaching of staff is highly recommended, as staff may have difficulty implementing agency policies and strategies shared in training. Supervisors must be prepared to provide ongoing support and assure consistent implementation of recommended practices.

Strategy 4: Incorporate Culturally and Linguistically Appropriate Intake Processes, Data Collection, and Information Sharing

The intake process provides an important opportunity to identify the strengths and needs of LGBT and questioning youth so that an agency can assess the most appropriate services, supports, and placement(s) for a youth. Agencies often find it helpful for LGBT youth to provide input into the development and implementation of intake processes and information-sharing policies to ensure that they are responsive to the needs of youth who are receiving services and supports.

Intake forms and screening procedures should be in gender-neutral language and reflect options for various sexual orientations and gender identity/expression, as well as risk factors, family relationships, mental health concerns, and presenting issues (Larkin Street Youth Services, 2009). The health screening conducted during the intake process can help identify the needs and concerns of LGBT youth. Treatments and any specialized medications, including hormone therapy, should be continued for LGBT youth as would be the case for any other youth.

Maintaining confidentiality relative to disclosure of personal information is often an important issue for youth in services and supports, but is particularly a concern for LGBT youth. Although the intake or reception unit provides an opportunity for information sharing, youth may refuse to identify as LGBT until they know that the environment is safe and supportive of individual differences. All staff should receive training in appropriate data collection, sharing, reporting, and confidentiality. An agency's written policies should specifically describe when and when *not* to disclose a youth's identified LGB or gender identity/expression to outside parties, organizations, family members, or other individuals. Policies should articulate how agency staff will use information about LGB and gender identity/expression for program planning and decision making regarding placement considerations.

Strategy 5: Promote Safe, Supportive, and Culturally and Linguistically Competent Environments

A climate of safety and inclusiveness contributes significantly to the demonstration of respect for self and others and alleviates isolation for those who are adjusting to their LGBT status (Sullivan, 1994). To successfully meet the individual needs of LGBT youth, and for youth to be receptive to an agency's efforts, an organizational culture should communicate acceptance and openness (Wilber et al., 2006). In a welcoming and affirming environment, LGBT youth can interact with their peers and staff without fear of harassment or violence. Agencies can promote a culturally competent environment for LGBT youth by

- Placing and authentically engaging LGBT youth and adults on agency boards of directors, advisory groups, and other decision-making bodies
- Encouraging youth to participate in identifying culturally competent policies, procedures, and practices the agency should adopt
- Being sensitive to the ways in which youth self-identify and use language that respects and acknowledges their preferred identity
- Displaying symbols that positively represent the LGBT community (e.g., rainbows, pink triangles) so that youth feel their LGBT identity is accepted and supported. These symbols are associated with the LGBT movement and indicate that the gay community is supported and the agency is a safe haven for LGBT youth and their families.

Agency brochures, promotional materials, and posters should include language about serving LGBT youth and portray positive images of LGBT youth and adults. An agency that displays youth-friendly books and other reading materials indicates that LGBT youth are not only served and supported by the agency, but are also welcomed and encouraged to seek assistance from staff members and others.

A culturally competent environment ensures LGBT youth are protected from harm. Youth should not be put in isolation as a means of keeping them safe from discrimination, harassment, or abuse. Generally, *isolation* refers to an area in the facility usually associated with punishment due to significant acting out behaviors or a contagious illness. Youth may be placed into isolation as a result of a disciplinary action due to their behaviors that are seen as unsafe for staff and for the youth in the facility (e.g., violently attacking staff or other youth, bringing in a weapon, or fashioning a weapon). At other times, a youth may be placed in isolation to quarantine the youth because of a significantly contagious illness. LGBT youth should *not* be placed in isolation on the basis of the fact that they identify as LGBT. Youth may be separated from other youth, however, for their own protection or treatment, especially as an agency considers housing decisions. Agencies can further promote a culturally competent environment that supports the well-being of LGBT and questioning youth by

- Specifically and deliberately defining policies and procedures that affect LGBT youth, including policies for bathroom use, showering, and sleeping arrangements (Marksamer, 2011)
- Anticipating specific risks to the safety of transgender or gender nonconforming youth and implementing safeguards such as individual sleeping quarters, individual stalls for restrooms, and policies that allow transgender youth to shower privately and separately from other youth
- Allowing and accommodating requests from transgender youth to have a particular staff member conduct a strip search, if required

Chapter 2 identifies additional strategies for providing culturally and linguistically competent services and supports to youth.

Strategy 6: Implement Practices that Support Preferences and Affirm Identity

Adolescence is a time of exploration and experimentation when adolescents are defining their identity and a time when they typically experience developmental and social challenges. LGBT and questioning youth who are struggling with their LGBT identity may need support to explore their feelings in a respectful, affirming manner. Youth should be given opportunities to develop skills to adopt healthy behaviors, such as interpersonal coping mechanisms for handling conflict and peer pressure (Mallon, 1992). Prevention education about safe-sex practices, STIs, and personal development should provide accurate and nonjudgmental information about LGBT identity, sexual behavior, and gender identity and expression.

Youth will disclose their LGBT identity if, and when, they are ready to do so. Either pushing youth for premature LGBT disclosure or dismissing the relevance of same-gender attraction feelings can be damaging to youth because it discounts and may stigmatize their experience, feelings, and developing identity.

Although there are different perspectives on how to incorporate this into practice, some literature recommends that staff should *not* directly ask whether the youth is LGBT (Phillips et al., 1997). Youth should decide when and with whom to share their sexual orientation (Hooper, 2004). This approach emphasizes creating an environment that is safe enough for youth to decide for themselves whether to share their and inform staff and peers of their preferences. Youth in threatening and unsafe environments may often deny or hide their LGBT identity for reasons of safety or perceived differential and negative treatment. Youth who fear disclosing their identity are less likely to report experiences to providers and may not seek needed supports to address problems or personal conflicts (Lambda Legal, n.d.).

There should be clear guidelines for staff around how to respond when youth disclose information regarding sexual orientation or gender identity (Larkin Street Youth Services, 2009). If youth disclose that they are LGBT, all agency staff and providers should speak with the youth in an open and understanding manner, including communicating information about the rights of the youth that affirm their identity. Further, agency policies should reflect these rights, so that LGBT youth

- Receive the same services and care as other youth and are *not* treated differently because they have identified themselves as LGBT or questioning

- Are *not* required to participate in religious activities that condemn their LGBT identity or intimidate or force them into adopting certain religious beliefs

- Are able to express their gender identity through clothes, hair, nails, makeup, shaving, jewelry, and undergarments. Rules regarding personal grooming should be the same in male and female facilities and residents should *not* be prevented from, or disciplined for, personal grooming that does not align with typical social expectations for youth expressing their birth-assigned gender (Marksamer, 2011).

- Are referred to by their preferred pronoun (e.g., *he* or *she* or avoiding pronouns altogether in the case of youth who identify as nongender; Marksamer, 2011)

- Are referred to by preferred, rather than legal, names when they are spoken to and when they complete nonlegal documentation

- Have access to counseling for effective interpersonal coping mechanisms for handling conflict, peer pressure, friendships, and information needs related to safe sex practices and other individual, family, and health issues

- Are informed that their LGBT identity will not be shared with family members unless the youth has indicated that preference regarding disclosure; preferences identified by LGBT youth for disclosure to families, friends, and other youth should be duly noted in a youth's records and honored by all staff and providers

All youth should have opportunities to discuss questions or feelings that may arise as a result of youth who may be perceived as "different." Acknowledging, affirming, and respecting a youth's LGBT identity expression is critical for healthy development (Marksamer, 2011).

Strategy 7: Promote Healthy and Supportive Peer Connections

To experience mutual support, caring, and personal development, all youth, including LGBT and questioning youth, should have opportunities to participate in social support groups and recreational activities with their peers. Opportunities to socialize with other LGBT or questioning youth reduce a sense of isolation, stigmatization, degradation, and continual self-denial (Sullivan, 1994). Especially for LGBT youth, locating support and building social connections strengthens their positive self-concept (Hooper, 2004). As positive youth development is more likely within the context of nurturing, accepting, and supportive relationships with peers, all youth-serving agencies should play a role in fostering these relationships. Opportunities should offer LGBT youth a safe place to meet and support each other.

Strategy 8: Strengthen Family Connections

Family acceptance and support are critical to the positive development and overall well-being of LGBT and questioning youth. Some families, however, respond negatively when they learn that a youth is LGBT and resist efforts from service providers and others that encourage them to discuss and support their child's LGBT identity openly. Rather than uniformly excluding rejecting families from their LGBT children's lives, parents, other caregivers, and family members may need support and guidance to help them understand the impact of their negative reactions on the health and mental health of LGBT youth.

To capitalize on opportunities to resolve those challenging issues, it is important to ask youth about family reactions to their LGBT identity (Ryan et al., 2009). Many adolescents in out-of-home care or placement, including LGBT and questioning youth who may not be able to live with their parents, still need those relationships, although these relationships may be conflicted, they give continuity to their lives and open the prospect of eventual reconciliation (Mallon, 1997). Given the importance of family connections and relations with youth, youth-serving organizations should support youth and their families by ensuring that service providers

- Educate and inform families about the emergence of LGBT identity in adolescence

- Increase parents' and caregivers' knowledge about the needs, interests, and perspectives of LGBT and questioning youth and the importance of family connections for youth regardless of LGB and gender identity

- Advise parents and caregivers that negative reactions to their child's LGBT identity can have a serious effect on their child's health and mental health as young adults (Ryan et al., 2009)

- Model, encourage, and promote nonjudgmental and accepting attitudes and behaviors toward the youth and communicate with LGBT youth in a non-judgmental manner that shows respect and concern for the youth (regardless of personal views on LGBT identity)

- Identify LGBT support programs and online resources to inform families about how to better understand and support their LGBT youth

- Encourage families to allow youth to participate in family activities, because evidence indicates that family exclusion of LGBT youth is related to significant health risks in young adulthood and affects future interpersonal relationships (Ryan et al., 2009)

Strategy 9: Promote Access to Affirming Services and Supports

Youth-serving agencies within the system of care should assess whether LGBT youth have access to appropriate housing, job placement, and educational and mental health supports. Where there are service gaps, collaboration across youth-serving systems and advocacy for community development will be needed to increase the array and access to services needed to meet the specific needs of youth. Coordination among agencies through multiagency training, policy development, and co-location of staff can maximize limited resources while building capacity among agencies and organizations to effectively and consistently serve LGBT youth across systems and agencies.

Creating collaborative partnerships with service providers in the community who specialize in LGBT and questioning youth facilitates access to needed services (Larkin Street Youth Services, 2009). Staff need to recognize when young people need extra help or when they are struggling with issues that require nonbiased consultation from those with expertise in LBGT youth. These specialized services and supports may include LGBT youth mental health counseling, confidential sexual health education, and testing and counseling for STIs (Phillips et al., 1997; Wilber et al., 2006).

LGBT advocates, LGBT families and youth, and other representatives from the community may offer additional support that meet identified needs of some LGBT and questioning youth and their families. LGBT adults and families in the community could provide potential foster and adoptive homes. LGBT youth groups and other LGBT community organizations may offer opportunities for mentoring, job training, leadership skills development, and peer affiliation in ways that affirm an LGBT youth's identity. Community advocates and LGBT youth programs may offer guidance to LGBT and questioning youth about coming out and managing discrimination and prejudice. Agencies may consider engaging and providing training for LGBT "big brothers" and "big sisters" who can serve as supports and role models for youth. These individuals are often referred to as "cultural brokers" because they can serve as consultants to staff, foster parents, and family members and provide suggestions for enhancing the quality of services and supports for these youth (Sullivan, 1994).

Strategy 10: Facilitate Community Outreach and Engagement

Agencies should identify and distribute local and online resource lists and community contacts for LGBT services and educational materials. Information on agency-sponsored activities, open houses, community presentations, and LGBT events should also be collected and distributed. Youth can also play an important role in facilitating opportunities for community outreach and awareness about issues such as bullying, self-acceptance, identity formation, depression, suicide-related behavior and prevention efforts, tolerance, and community LGBT resources. An organizational culture that encourages opportunities for LGBT youth to become advocates or mentors in the community promotes peer connections and facilitates supportive relationships and leadership development skills (Mallon, 2010). Often youth are more attentive and responsive when information and experiences are shared by other youth, because they are able to understand and relate to "youth voice." Forums of this type provide supportive venues to eliminate or lessen myths and stereotypes.

CONCLUSION

When system of care principles guide the vision and practices of youth-serving organizations, *all* children, youth, and their families receiving services and supports benefit. Service delivery built on the principles outlined in the beginning of this chapter can help ensure that LGBT and questioning youth will be part of a system of care that affirms their identity and encourages their individuality. All youth-serving agencies should ensure that services and supports for LGBT and questioning youth not only meet their needs, but also create safe environments for them to begin to understand and embrace their LGBT identity.

The guiding principles are intended to provide a foundation upon which leaders can create and implement standards of care for LGBT youth. Conducting an agency self-assessment is a critical first step and becomes the catalyst for ongoing continuous quality improvement efforts. Implementing policies and practices that respect LGBT youth and ensure safety and confidentiality will not always be easy. All staff members will need to examine their beliefs and attitudes about LGBT and questioning youth and their abilities to provide culturally and linguistically competent care. Fostering healthy and supportive peer and family connections and ensuring access to supportive services may also be challenging. Therefore, ongoing review of policies, practices, and training will be essential to ensure that culturally and linguistically competent services and supports are de-livered and that safe, supportive agency environments for LGBT and question-ing youth are sustained.

Youth-serving agencies within a system of care will need to collaborate to achieve these standards of care. Each youth-serving agency plays an important role in helping LGBT youth remain in their homes and communities safely and productively. By working together and sharing common goals, youth-serving organizations and the systems in which they operate can ensure that LGBT youth experience dignity and affirmation and receive supports and services that foster their well-being, development, and successful transition to adulthood.

11

Fostering Welcoming, Safe, and Supportive Schools for LGBT Youth

JEFFREY M. POIRIER

"When someone with the authority of a teacher, say, describes the world and you are not in it, there is a moment of psychic disequilibrium, as if you looked into a mirror and saw nothing."

—Rich, 1994, p. 199

Youth spend much of their lives in schools, where their experiences, personal development, and educational outcomes are shaped by the attitudes and behaviors of peers and adults as well as what they learn in their classrooms. As this chapter describes, the school experiences of youth have important relationships with their perceptions of school, likelihood to attend, academic achievement, educational aspirations, and well-being. Schools may reinforce assumptions and beliefs that all youth are, or should be, heterosexual and conform to expectations for "appropriate" gender behavior and expression. Lesbian, gay, bisexual, and transgender (LGBT) students may also be victimized in various ways because of their identity and expression. These ongoing challenges and inequities, and their negative effects on student outcomes, should raise serious concern in communities and schools.

This chapter illustrates the deep significance of schools, which are a critically important sector supporting youth in systems of care and are important settings of social change in communities. All youth, including those who are LGBT, should learn and thrive in schools where they are welcomed, respected, supported, and emotionally and physically safe. Addressing anti-LGBT bullying[1] and making schools safer for LGBT students can benefit *all* youth. Moreover,

---

[1]Bullying includes 1) physical, psychological, or verbal attacks or intimidation intended to distress or harm another person; 2) an imbalance of physical or psychological power; and 3) repeated behavior between the same individuals over a period of time (Center for Mental Health in Schools at UCLA, 2011).

curricula that give fair recognition to LGBT individuals and identity can help youth feel more included and create safer schools. Systems of care can help further progress toward these improved conditions by collaborating with school systems and schools. It is important for all professionals working in schools, including athletic coaches, cafeteria workers, guidance counselors, school psychologists, security personnel, social workers, and even bus drivers to be meaningful partners in efforts to make schools safer, more supportive, and more respectful for LGBT students. School-based professionals should enhance their cultural and linguistic competence relative to LGBT topics and value and accept LGBT youth, if they do not already. Expressed school staff attitudes and beliefs, decision making, and behavior should demonstrate respect for LGBT youth, regardless of professionals' individual opinions about LGBT identity.

SCHOOL CLIMATE AND CONDITIONS FOR LEARNING

Schools present key challenges but also valuable opportunities for systems of care and professionals to enhance the experiences of LGBT youth and improve their emotional, behavioral, educational, and other outcomes through improved school climate. *School climate* includes conditions that affect how school staff, students, and parents and caregivers experience various aspects of the school community (Center for Social and Emotional Education, 2010). Researchers commonly point to four components of school climate that create conditions which maximize a student's ability to learn: 1) emotional and physical safety, 2) positive relationships with adults and peers as well as school connectedness, 3) a teaching and learning environment that emphasizes social–emotional and civic learning, and 4) a higher quality physical school environment (Center for Social and Emotional Education; Osher & Kendziora, 2010; Osher et al., 2008). Figure 11.1 displays four conditions for learning, including academic challenge, connection and support, safety, and social–emotional learning (Osher et al., 2008). Research shows that student connection and a sense of belonging to their schools, as well as respectful, supportive relationships, are important to student well-being and success in school (Goodenow, 1993; Resnick et al., 1997; Wentzel, 1997).

A growing body of empirical data and research points to the conditions necessary for learning to prosper in schools, including student support and connectedness to caring adults, emotional safety, and physical safety (Center for Social and Emotional Education, 2010; Collaborative for Academic, Social, and Emotional Learning, 2003; Learning First Alliance, 2001; Osher & Kendziora, 2010). Students feel supported and connected to their schools when they believe that adults and peers care about their learning and well-being (Center for Social and Emotional Education, 2010). Positive relationships and caring interactions with adults and peers, positive role modeling, and access to needed ser-

Academic challenge	Connection and support
• High expectations • Strong personal motivation • Rigorous academic opportunities	• Meaningful connection to adults • Positive peer relationships • Strong bonds to school

Safety	Social–emotional learning
• Emotionally, physically, socially safe • School is orderly • Treated fairly and equitably	• Cooperative teamwork • Emotionally intelligent • Responsible and persistent

Figure 11.1. Four conditions for learning: 1) academic challenge, 2) connection and support, 3) safety, and 4) social–emotional learning. (From Osher, D., Kendziora, K., & Chinen, M. [2008, March]. *Student connection research: Final narrative report to the Spencer Foundation.* Washington, DC: American Institutes for Research; reprinted by permission.)

vices and supports, among other factors, contribute to a school climate that promotes student well-being and academic achievement (Osher, 2011). Bullying, peer rejection, stigma, and social exclusion—challenges LGBT youth experience disproportionately compared with non-LGBT youth—all negatively affect student experiences of school climate and can counteract other school-related assets, such as strong instructional quality. It is important for school leaders to understand and address this connection with teachers and other school professionals so that they understand how a safe, supportive school can enhance efforts to improve academic outcomes including school attendance and achievement.

Unsafe school environments (e.g., due to student harassment and bullying) can lead to a range of challenges for all youth, including those who are LGBT, which can affect their development into healthy, successful adults:

- Negative academic outcomes (e.g., lower achievement, postsecondary aspirations, and levels of school attendance and completion)
- Mental health concerns (e.g., increased anxiety and depression, decreased self-esteem)
- Self-harm and suicidal thinking (Center for Social and Emotional Education, 2010; U.S. Department of Education, Office for Civil Rights, 2010a)

LGBT students may feel disconnected from adults in schools because of biased language that they hear or because of the behavior of adults themselves, which may suggest to LGBT students that the adults in the school do not care about them. Moreover, students may be verbally or physically harassed, or even physically assaulted by peers, because of their LGBT identity and expression—or because of *perceptions* that they are LGBT. These experiences create emotionally and physically unsafe, unsupportive learning environments for these students. These negative experiences are detrimental to the academic success and healthy development of LGBT youth. The next section describes some related research findings.

SCHOOL EXPERIENCES OF
LGBT YOUTH: FINDINGS FROM RESEARCH

"Classrooms lay the experience for an inclusive and safe society....Any adult interested in creating safe spaces for LGBT youth needs to consider the impact of schooling on the social and psychological development of young people" (Vaccaro, August, & Kennedy, 2012, pp. 83–84). LGBT youth often experience unwelcoming—if not outright hostile and unsafe—school environments where they receive inadequate supports and disproportionally encounter peer rejection, harassment, and stigmatization because of their LGBT identity/expression.

Research demonstrates that heterosexism (bias against non-heterosexual individuals), heteronormativity (institutional and individual assumptions that heterosexuality is superior to nonheterosexual identity and all people are heterosexual), and transphobia (fear of transgender and gender diverse individuals) are ongoing challenges in schools, contributing to unsafe, unsupportive school environments and negative emotional, behavioral, and academic student outcomes. For example, school curricula often continue to overlook the LGBT identity of important individuals in history and literature, and school social events (e.g., proms) do not necessarily welcome same-gender couples. Furthermore, heterosexism continues to contribute to victimization among LGBT youth (Chesir-Teran & Hughes, 2009). According to Russell (2010a):

> There is clear scientific consensus that LGBTQ[2] youth are, indeed, a vulnerable group....research from multiple disciplines and perspectives, based on multiple methods, and from samples across the world continues to show that LGBTQ youth are a group that is at high risk for preventable negative outcomes. (p. 4)

LGBT-related incidents of physical and verbal assault of students abound for students across all ages. One shocking story of kindergartners physically and verbally assaulting two peers because they were pretending to be a lesbian couple during play time is shared in a *School Psychology Review* article (Henning-Stout, James, & Macintosh, 2000).

LGBT youth experience particular stresses in school relative to other students (Hunter & Schaecher, 1987); heterosexist behavior, for example, is a significant safety-related concern in schools (Birkett, Espelage, & Koenig, 2009). The Gay, Lesbian & Straight Education Network (GLSEN) provides a valuable

---

[2]In this citation, the Q in the LGTBQ acronym Russell uses refers to queer/questioning youth.

national snapshot of LGBT youth experiences of school climate. In its recent survey of 7,261 demographically diverse LGBT students[3] in Grades 6–12, GLSEN (2010) found that more than 72% reported hearing anti-LGBT remarks often or frequently in their school. Most reported feeling distressed by these experiences. A large majority also reported being verbally harassed because of their sexual orientation (84.6%), including almost 4 in 10 students who reported this happening often or frequently during the past school year. Physical harassment and assault because of sexual orientation were less prevalent during the previous school year, but still alarming: 40.1% reported being physically harassed (shoved or pushed) at some time (more than 1 in 10 often or frequently) and more than 1 in 10 students reported being physically assaulted (kicked, punched, injured with a weapon) at least sometimes. Of those students who were harassed/assaulted, 62% did not report the incident because they believed their school would take little or no action or their situation would worsen (unfortunately, that was the experience of the one in three students who reported incidents).

GLSEN and Harris Interactive (2012) also completed the first survey of elementary school students and teachers, using a national sample of 1,065 students in Grades 3–6. They found that approximately half of responding students heard others make comments such as "that's so gay" or "you're so gay" sometimes (25%), often (13%), or all the time (7%). Approximately half of teachers reported hearing students use the word "gay" in a negative way sometimes (31%), often (11%), or very often (7%).

Another study using survey data from 7,559 adolescents 14–22 years of age found significant differences in reports of bullying and victimization based on sexual orientation (Berlan, Corliss, Field, Goodman, & Austin, 2010). Among male respondents, 26% of heterosexual respondents reported being victims of bullying compared with 35% of mostly heterosexual,[4] 36% of bisexual, and 44% of gay respondents. Among female respondents, 16% of heterosexual females reported being bully victims compared with 25% of mostly heterosexual, 26% of bisexual, and 40% of lesbian respondents (Berlan et al., 2010).[5]

---

[3]On average, participating students were 16.3 years old. They came from all 50 states and the District of Columbia, representing 2,723 school districts. Approximately two thirds (67.4%) of respondents were White; 14.1% were Hispanic or Latino; 10.4% were multiracial; 4.0% were African American; 2.6% were Asian or Pacific Islander; 1.0% were Middle Eastern or Arab American (any race); and 0.5% were Native American, American Indian, or Alaskan Native. The sample included students from communities in various geographic regions (25.3% from the Northeast, 29.0% from the South, 23.4% from the Midwest, 22.3% from the West), with varying urbanicity (30.1% urban, 45.0% suburban, 24.9% rural or small town) and levels of poverty (21.5% with more than half of students eligible for free or reduced price lunch).

[4]The survey adapted its sexual orientation question from the Minnesota Adolescent Health Survey. The question asked respondents to select one of six responses that reflected their feelings of attraction, including completely heterosexual, mostly heterosexual, bisexual, mostly homosexual, completely homosexual, and unsure.

[5]The researchers note that the study is limited by small sample sizes of LGB respondents and a nonrepresentative sample. These findings did not include transgender students.

These negative experiences can have serious implications for the well-being of LGBT youth. For example, a study using data from the Oregon Health Teens Survey from 2006 to 2008, which 31,852 public school 11th graders completed, examined the association between the social environment for LGB youth and attempted suicide after controlling for individual predictors of suicide attempts such as depressive symptoms and peer victimization (Hatzenbuehler, 2011). As part of its index of five characteristics of the social environment, the researcher included the proportion of schools with 1) gay–straight alliances (GSAs),[6] 2) antibullying policies protecting LGBT students, and 3) antidiscrimination policies that include sexual orientation. The study found that 4.4% of students self-identified as LGB and concluded that although LGB identity was a strong predictor of suicide attempts in the past 12 months, *LGB youth in negative social environments* were more likely than those in more positive environments to attempt suicide in the previous year (Hatzenbuehler, 2011).[7]

Furthermore, GLSEN'S (2010) analyses of its aforementioned student survey data found that higher levels of in-school victimization based on sexual orientation of gender expression correlate with 1) higher school absenteeism, 2) greater depression and anxiety, 3) lower self-esteem, 4) less of a sense of belonging to their school community, 5) lower grades, and 6) lower postsecondary educational aspirations. For example, participating students were three times as likely to miss school in the past month if they experienced high levels of victimization related to their sexual orientation or gender expression. Students experiencing higher levels of victimization also reported lower grade point averages (2.7) compared with students experiencing less victimization (3.1; GLSEN, 2010).

Experiences of unwelcoming, unsafe, and unsupportive conditions in schools can affect the likelihood that LGBT students attend and eventually graduate at the high-school level. Research points to this relationship, with students who are LGBT (or are perceived to be) and who are victimized being less likely to attend school (GLSEN, 2010; Kim, 2009). Other research has added to the growing evidence that LGBT and youth questioning their sexual/gender identity are at greater risk for unexcused absences from school, as early as middle school (Robinson & Espelage, 2011). It is important that systems of care and school-based professionals acknowledge and understand the connection between negative school experiences and the well-being of LGBT youth, including anxiety, depression, substance abuse, and academic performance. Enhancing

---

[6]GSAs are student-led clubs that include all students regardless of their sexual orientation or gender identity/expression and are intended to provide an emotionally and physically safe space for students.

[7]The study found that 19.6% of lesbian and gay self-identified youth, 22% of self-identified bisexual youth, and 4.2% of heterosexual youth reported suicide attempts in the past 12 months. The interaction between LGBT identity and social environment characteristics were not statistically significant, although variation was evident in the results.

school conditions for LGBT students can benefit school, district, and state efforts to improve student achievement and other outcomes—which can further system of care efforts to foster healthy, positive outcomes for youth. The next section explores some specific strategies that school-based professionals can implement to create more positive learning conditions.

STRATEGIES TO IMPROVE SCHOOL CONDITIONS AND PRODUCE MORE EQUITABLE OUTCOMES FOR LGBT YOUTH

The stigma and victimization that LGBT youth may experience in schools and the fact that youth spend a large proportion of their time in school necessitates including schools as part of system of care and other community efforts to improve the lives and well-being of LGBT youth. Systems of care should partner with schools to address the conditions that can negatively affect LGBT students and the inequities they may experience relative to social acceptance, support, and safety. The growing body of research on LGBT youth in schools shows that particular policies, programs, and practices promote the safety and well-being of these youth, including:

- School nondiscrimination and antibullying policies that enumerate actual and perceived sexual orientation as well as gender identity and expression
- Staff professional development on how to intervene when students are harassed
- A supportive school environment with information and resources and an LGBT-inclusive curriculum
- Availability of school-based support groups or clubs such as GSAs (Russell, 2010b)

A GLSEN survey found that students in schools with LGBT-inclusive policies and available GSAs report feeling safer in their schools (GLSEN, 2010). More inclusive policies and programs can also positively affect the experiences of LGBT students in high schools by making them feel more supported and welcomed (Chesir-Teran & Hughes, 2009; Szalacha, 2003). These policies should be clearly stated in student handbooks and information families receive about school discipline expectations.

The National Education Policy Center, Williams Institute (a sexual orientation law and policy think tank), and Great Lakes Center for Education Research and Practice recently identified key policy recommendations for proactively improving school environments for LGBT students (Biegel & Kuehl, 2010). These recommendations included strategies intended to address school climate, curriculum and teaching, and school sports and called for 1) proactive school climate initiatives that demonstrate a commitment to inclusion, 2) implementation of LGBT programs (e.g., GSAs, safe zones), 3) professional development on LGBT topics, and 4) inclusion of age-appropriate LGBT content in school curricula (Biegel & Kuehl). In addition to a greater need for safe spaces for LGBT youth in schools, LGBT youth themselves have pointed to the need for more lesbian and gay counselors in schools (and in the mental health system) to facilitate positive relationships with adults and access to unbiased supports (U.C. Davis Center for Reducing Health Disparities, 2009).

Furthermore, all professionals working in or with schools should be prepared to talk about sexual orientation and gender identity with youth and other adults in a positive, informative way. School-based professionals can assess their cultural and linguistic competence and develop their knowledge and skills to become more competent for their LGBT student populations (see Chapters 2 and 3). In *The School Services Handbook: A Guide for School-Based Professionals*, Diane Elze (2006) identifies core traits of an approachable practitioner. These include 1) self-awareness about personal beliefs and attitudes, 2) knowledge and appreciation of LGBT youth, 3) competent social work skills, and 4) prioritizing professional (rather than personal) values. Among other suggestions, she proposes various recommended practices, including enhancing students' problem-solving, decision-making, and adaptive coping skills and creating more affirming, safer school environments. Elze notes that school social workers are "uniquely positioned to provide counseling, information, and referrals" to LGBT students, to facilitate school-based support groups, to help students with establishing GSAs, and to deliver "training and consultation on sexual orientation and gender identity diversity to students, teachers, administrators, support staff, and parents" (p. 861).

Others note that school counselors also have an essential role in ensuring more positive school experiences for LGBT students. School counselors can effectively support the personal development of LGBT students (a core counseling function) by providing accepting, nonjudgmental support; building competence among school personnel through professional development on LGBT topics; forming partnerships with LGBT-affirming organizations; and sponsoring the creation of GSAs when there is student interest (Brinkley & Hawley, 2012). Systems of care should partner with these valuable school-based professionals to foster cultural and linguistic competence and support school climate improvement efforts.

These strategies align with a three-tiered framework for creating safe, supportive schools including schoolwide promotion and prevention, targeted prevention, and intensive supports for students at higher levels of risk or need (Dwyer & Osher, 2007). Staff professional development, more culturally and linguistic competence language, and availability of GSAs—because of their positive effects on school safety—should be part of schoolwide prevention (Brinkley & Hawley, 2012). For those students who participate in them, GSAs can become a form of targeted prevention for students who are experiencing challenges related to their sexual orientation or gender identity (although GSAs are valuable supports for students not experiencing these challenges as well). School counselors can also provide intensive supports for students experiencing severe challenges and families experiencing serious struggles with students' sexual orientation or gender identity/expression.

Gay–Straight Alliances, Safe Zones, and Other Supportive Spaces

As discussed previously, school staff can proactively support LGBT students by creating physically safe, caring, and respectful school environments. This should include provision of safe zones/spaces (e.g., classrooms or other places where students are safe to talk about their sexual/gender identities), GSAs, and educational media addressing LGBT concerns (Biegel, 2010). A GSA is a student-led club that includes all students regardless of their sexual orientation or gender identity/expression and is intended to provide an emotionally and physically safe place for students to 1) access resources and information, 2) connect with supportive peers and a caring adult, 3) develop a positive sense of self, and 4) address heterosexism and transphobia to make their schools and community safer by building awareness of LGBT-related concerns (Gay-Straight Alliance Network, n.d.; GLSEN, 2011; Griffin, Lee, Waugh, & Beyer, 2005; Holmes & Cahill, 2005; Macgillivray, 2007; Miceli, 2005; Sears, 2005). Some GSAs may also serve a counseling role when the GSA advisor is a school counselor who provides students with individual counseling and psychological support to address stressors they are experiencing (Griffin et al., 2005). GSAs should be part of efforts to enhance the cultural and linguistic competence and safety of schools, but they also can be valuable, proactive tools for providing leadership opportunities for LGBT youth (and their allies), developing their resilience and building school community.

In its research brief on GSAs, GLSEN (2007) identified several major findings from the literature, including an association between safer, more supportive, and more respectful school environments and GSAs. Research shows that GSAs enhance student self-esteem, including pride in their LGBT identity, and foster their resiliency and coping skills for dealing with heterosexism (Draughn, Elkins, & Roy, 2002; Lee, 2002). Peer-reviewed research has also found that LGBT students in schools with GSAs are more likely to feel that adults in their schools support LGBT students and to know supportive adults in their schools than students in schools without GSAs (Szalacha, 2003; Walls, Kane, & Wisneski, 2010).

The previously mentioned GLSEN survey also found that having a GSA in school correlated with more positive experiences for LGBT students (e.g., less victimization because of sexual orientation and gender expression, a greater sense of belonging to the school community). This growing body of research warrants increased action to improve school climate for LGBT students and acknowledge the unique function GSAs (and other welcoming spaces) can serve to create—or be part of—safe, supportive learning environments. GSAs are protected free speech (Broberg, 1999; U.S. Department of Education, Office of Elementary and Secondary Education, 2011), and the National Education Association, among other organizations, has also called for the removal of institutional obstacles to creating GSAs (Kim, 2009). School-based professionals, in particular administrators and counselors, should meaningfully work to address any barriers to GSAs in their schools.

There also is evidence that principals believe GSAs can positively affect school climate. Other GLSEN research has examined the school experiences of LGBT youth from the perspectives of principals, including a nationally representative survey of 1,580 K–12 public school principals (GLSEN & Harris Interactive, 2008). Survey analyses found that 45% believed allowing clubs at schools where LGBT and heterosexual students come together to promote tolerance would help create safe environments for LGBT students and students with LGBT parents; 67% felt that antibullying/harassment and antidiscrimination policies that explicitly protect LGBT students also contribute to a safe environment for LGBT youth.

In addition to addressing the overall climate of schools, systems of care should collaborate with LGBT community partners (e.g., local GLSEN chapter), schools, and students to establish or provide additional support to GSAs and other safe spaces in middle and high schools. The GSA Network (www.gsanetwork.org/resources) and GLSEN (e.g., Jump-Start Guide for GSAs at www.glsen.org/cgi-bin/iowa/all/news/record/2226.html) offer supports for implementing and sustaining GSAs. It is also important to access and apply other resources, and address LGBT invisibility in school curricula, which are discussed further in the next section.

Resources and Curriculum

Regardless of whether a GSA is available to students, school-based professionals should provide affirming, appropriate LGBT resources for students in various locations in schools (e.g., main offices, guidance counselor offices, libraries). This could include, for example, information about local LGBT youth and family groups. School libraries should also have LGBT reading materials for students, including age-appropriate literature about LGBT youth and families with same-sex parents. School curricula should be inclusive and fairly represent the experiences and contributions of LGBT people. LGBT youth rarely have the opportunity to "see themselves as wise or powerful main characters or heroes worthy of celebration and emulation," which can make them "feel validated, included, and safe inside their classrooms" (Vaccaro et al., 2012, p. 85). It is paramount to address this experience of invisibility, which can negatively affect the well-being of LGBT youth, and systemwide change can facilitate this progress.

Moreover, numerous national organizations, including those not specifically focused on advocacy for LGBT students, have called attention to the significance of providing safe, supportive school environments for LGBT students. These professional organizations include the American Psychological Association (1993), American School Counselor Association (2007), American School Health Association (2009), Mental Health America (2012), National Association of School Nurses (2003), National Association of School Psychologists (2006), National Education Association (2006), and School Social Work Association of America (2009). All have issued guidance to their members about the importance of providing appropriate services and supports to LGBT students and have recommended strategies to accomplish these goals. Systems of care can leverage these professional resources when collaborating with school-based professionals, LGBT youth, their families, and other stakeholders.

Strategies for Systemwide Change

It is critically important to include schools within the larger set of cultural and linguistic competence strategies of systems of care to facilitate systemic change. As already mentioned, GSAs and safe zones should be part of strategies for creating safe, supportive school environments for LGBT youth. Systemic change, though, is needed to address the school-related experiences of LGBT youth in the long term (Griffin et al., 2005; Griffin & Ouellett, 2002). To sustain the positive effects of GSAs and other safe zones on school climate, an iterative planning process is needed to effectively enhance policies, programs, and practices at the organizational level (Griffin et al., 2005). This is important given that GSAs are led by students, who will eventually leave their schools, as well as GSA advisors who are not permanent members of the school community.

Several strategies for developing long-term positive change and more equitable outcomes for LGBT students in schools include supportive statewide policies and programs (which is more relevant for statewide systems of care), active support of key administrators (e.g., principals) and other adults, student involvement in the change process, and participation of LGBT community organizations (Griffin & Ouellett, 2002). This more comprehensive approach is consistent with a culturally and linguistically competent set of strategies for addressing the needs of LGBT students (Poirier et al., 2008). LGBT students (and LGBT-headed families) should be part of school improvement plans related to climate, in particular emotional and physical safety.

School district leadership, school principals, teachers and other school-based professionals (e.g., school counselors), and school parent organizations should partner in system of care efforts to reduce stigma and bias and improve the experiences of LGBT youth. They should participate in school climate assessment efforts, strategic school improvement planning, and implementation of interventions and resources. To enhance learning conditions, school leadership should assess school climate through multiple measures including valid, reliable student surveys and student data (e.g., attendance, behavior; Osher, 2011). Importantly, all school staff—from leadership to bus drivers—should receive meaningful, on-going professional development on LGBT topics and areas of need identified through the review of school climate data. These supports can be formal (e.g., having external trainers come in and facilitate learning opportunities) or more informal (e.g., topics regularly discussed as part of ongoing school improvement and staff meetings, sharing of resources and information briefs). School-based professionals should complete self-assessments (see Chapter 3) to understand their level of competence and values related to supporting LGBT youth. This information should then help inform identification of the most valuable learning opportunities. School leaders and support personnel (e.g., counselors) can create discussion groups, provide resources that help address particular areas of need or interest, and facilitate guest speakers including youth to discuss relevant issues with school staff and students.

To improve emotional and physical safety, school-based professionals can also proactively address bullying and harassment of all students, using evidence-based bullying prevention and intervention programs that include a focus on sexual orientation and gender expression. Antibullying policies should enumerate sexual orientation and gender expression to be clear about who is targeted for bullying. Bullying policies and interventions should be part of a comprehensive system that addresses barriers to teaching and learning—and not fragmented from other school initiatives that can foster positive conditions for learning (Center for Mental Health in Schools at UCLA, 2011). Educators can infuse lessons into their curricula that address how students are treated by their peers (e.g., the 2003 GroundSpark documentary, *Let's Get Real,* which includes a curriculum guide, and the 2009 GroundSpark documentary, *Straightlaced: How Gender's Got Us All Tied Up*, both directed by Debra Chasnoff). School-based professionals can also apply a range of strategies and resources. These include 1) GLSEN (www.glsen.org), which has numerous resources for educators and students (e.g., toolkits and grade K–12 curricula and lesson plans); 2) the Safe Schools Coalition (http://safeschoolscoalition.org/safe.html), an international public–private partnership working to make schools safe for LGBT youth with resources for all types of school staff from school administrators, counselors, and teachers to library media specialists, nurses, and school security personnel; and 3) the Human Rights Campaign's Welcoming Schools Project (www.welcomingschools.org). Furthermore, school-based professionals can ensure that LGBT-affirming information and resources are accessible.

Every professional working in schools can help to reduce stigma. They should be equipped to address myths, stereotypes, and other misinformation that adults or students may express (Elze, 2006). They should also normalize LGB sexual orientation and gender variant behavior by talking about these in positive ways and infusing the experiences and contributions of LGBT people into curricula and lesson delivery (Elze, 2006; Vaccaro et al., 2012). Strategies to build cultural and linguistic competence (see Chapter 2) can help increase acceptance of LGBT identity and expression, foster a more welcoming school environment, and contribute to more positive student outcomes. For example, use more inclusive (gender neutral) language when discussing students' dating interests, and include images and examples of same-sex parents in lessons or conversations with students and families. School-based professionals should access, share, and integrate strategies from resources that can help reduce stigma of LGBT identity (e.g., Elze, 2006; GLSEN, n.d.b; Vaccaro et al., 2012).

EXAMPLES OF RECENT FEDERAL EFFORTS TO ADDRESS SCHOOL EXPERIENCES OF LGBT YOUTH

Significantly, there is increasing attention given to school safety for LGBT students at the federal level—such as the U.S. Department of Education, Office for Civil Rights letter sent to school districts on October 26, 2010, which noted that Title IX prohibits harassment based on LGBT status (U.S. Department of Education, Office for Civil Rights, 2010b). The letter and accompanying fact sheet noted that when "harassment has occurred, a school must take prompt and effective steps reasonably calculated to end the harassment, eliminate any hostile environment, and prevent its recurrence....regardless of whether the student [experiencing the harassment] makes a complaint" (U.S. Department of Education, Office for Civil Rights, 2010a, p. 2). In addition, a recent federal LGBT Youth Summit, hosted by the U.S. Department of Education and cosponsored by the U.S. Department of Health and Human Services in Washington, D.C., on June 6 and 7, 2011, brought together various stakeholders, including federal leaders and program administrators, researchers, advocates, and youth to discuss the experiences of LGBT youth, including unsafe schools. In addition, the Interagency Working Group on Youth Programs, which is a collaboration of 12 federal agencies that support programs and services focused on youth, has school-related LGBT resources on its web site (www.findyouthinfo.gov).

CONCLUSION

School-age youth spend much of their time in settings that may be demonstrably oppressive, if not tacitly unwelcoming, environments where they may worry about their safety. At the same time, they may also experience school curricula that exclude the contributions and experiences of people that represent who they are, whether these are women, racially/ethnically diverse individuals, or LGBT people. Schools, including the adults working in them, may reinforce gender norms and assumptions that all youth engage in opposite-sex relationships and identify with their birth-assigned sex. School climate and learning conditions may not be conducive to maximizing the ability of LGBT youth to fully succeed and contribute to their school communities. Whenever and wherever this happens, there is a loss—both for LGBT youth themselves, their schools, and their larger communities. Accordingly, district and school leaders should implement, monitor, and sustain LGBT-affirming policies, programs, and practices, including GSAs and safe zones, proactive efforts to eliminate bullying and harassment, and staff development to enhance LGBT cultural and linguistic competence. They should also collaborate with the larger community, to ensure that curricula fairly represent LGBT people, including their history and contributions to society.

Schools can provide rich opportunities for LGBT youth to learn, express themselves, feel celebrated, and thrive. Systems of care should partner with school districts and schools to create safe, respectful, and welcoming schools for all students and implement strategies that will yield positive systemic change in learning conditions for LGBT youth. The benefits will be great for LGBT youth, their families, and the larger community if these youth feel positively connected to the world around them—and not "looking into a mirror and seeing nothing," as the opening quote by Adrienne Rich poignantly expresses. I call on all systems of care and professionals working in schools, including school leaders, teachers, school social workers, and guidance counselors, to be proactive change agents and further their school efforts to comprehensively enhance learning conditions and ensure more respectful, more inclusive school experiences for all LGBT students and their families. District leaders, including superintendents, deputy superintendents, department directors, and school board members, also should articulate and reinforce district visions, principles, strategies, and goals that address the challenges LGBT students may experience—and should guide, support, monitor, and hold accountable school administrators so that these goals are attained and meaningful improvements are sustained. The fairness of our educational system depends on this—and LGBT youth deserve this positive treament like any other student.

12

Improving Outcomes for LGBT Youth in Out-of-Home Care Settings

Implications and Recommendations for Systems of Care

MARLENE MATARESE

R esearch examining the experiences of lesbian, gay, bisexual, and transgender (LGBT) youth who have formal involvement in child-serving systems and/or out-of-home care (OHC) settings is limited, but there is evidence to support the notion that LGBT youth experience considerable disparities in OHC settings. Misperceptions and institutionalized heterosexism are manifested in OHC settings through discriminatory treatment of LGBT youth and a lack of access to culturally and linguistically responsive resources. Employing system of care values and principles across systems to support LGBT youth in OHC settings benefits LGBT youth and leads to improved behavioral and emotional outcomes. This chapter provides policy, research, practice, and community-level recommendations designed to help system of care communities take the next steps in supporting the needs of LGBT youth in OHC settings.

For the purposes of this chapter, OHC includes living environments outside of an adoptive or biological family home that require formal child-serving system involvement. Accordingly, OHC includes foster homes and congregate care settings such as juvenile detention facilities, group homes, and treatment facilities. The current, albeit limited, literature has primarily illustrated that LGBT youth have negative experiences and receive limited culturally appropriate support in OHC settings (Majd, Marksamer, & Reyes, 2009; Mallon, Aledort, & Ferrera, 2002; Woronoff, Estrada, & Sommer, 2006).

Much of the practice and research literature, as well as the actual work within systems of care, focuses on community-based services and supports, with less concentration on OHC settings. This is due largely to the system of care philosophy that youth and their families should receive services and supports within their community and reduce the likelihood of youth placement in OHC whenever possible. In general, systems experts, researchers, and many family members and youth view OHC as a less desirable outcome for those participating in system of care services and supports.

Study findings suggest, however, that OHC settings continue to be a part of the system of care service array. Researchers have examined use and predictors of OHC for youth in system of care grantee communities funded between 1998 and 2000 using data from the National Evaluation of the Comprehensive Community Mental Health Services for Children and Their Families Program (also known as the Children's Mental Health Initiative or CMHI program) that funds systems of care (Farmer, Mustillo, Burns, & Holden, 2008). They found that of 3,066 youth receiving services from system of care grantee communities, 32% had been placed in an OHC setting at some point between 6 and 24 months after enrollment in grantee services and supports. The majority of these placements were in more restrictive settings, including group homes, residential treatment facilities, hospitals, jails, or juvenile detention facilities; 12% were in foster care, a less restrictive setting and often community-based OHC placement. Of this entire group, 75% experienced multiple OHC placements during the 2 years after enrollment in systems of care. Furthermore, 34% of the 3,066 youth in the sample resided in an OHC setting when they first enrolled in system of care services and supports, although these youth were not included in the aforementioned findings (Farmer et al., 2008).

These findings reinforce the need for system of care leadership to assist in practice and policy enhancements to support all young people residing in OHC settings using a culturally and linguistically responsive approach grounded in system of care values and principles. Although estimates of the number of LGBT youth are unavailable, a review of recent literature about LGBT youth in OHC indicates that they may disproportionately access some OHC venues (Curtain, 2002; Irvine, 2010; Majd et al., 2009). This disproportional representation in OHC likely stems from the lack of family and/or caregiver support, resulting in the need to reside in OHC placements that may or may not be a good fit to their needs. System of care principles dictate that youth have access to a comprehensive array of culturally and linguistically appropriate community-based services and supports that address their unique needs and potential (Stroul & Friedman, 1986). Furthermore, system of care principles are applicable to OHC settings, including the right for youth to be protected and for families, providers, and youth to advocate on behalf of the well-being of youth who receive OHC services and supports. OHC settings may need to institute specific policies and procedures designed to protect LGBT youth and tailored to addressing their needs.

One objective of the system of care approach is to minimize or reduce altogether the need for youth to receive services and supports in OHC settings so that a youth remains at home and receives services and supports in school, work, and the community. Youth in systems of care, however, sometimes have a history of OHC placements before entering them (Farmer et al., 2008). A proportion of youth who receive community-based system of care services and supports are placed in OHC for a variety of reasons. Accordingly, although OHC is not traditionally the purview of systems of care, this topic still pertains to this book because a complete array of services and supports for youth in systems of care sometimes includes OHC. It is essential for the well-being of LGBT youth to operationalize system of care values and principles in meaningful ways for application to OHC settings. This operationalization should effectively shift practice and policy to foster a more culturally and linguistically responsive approach to serving and supporting LGBT youth and their families in these environments.

LGBT YOUTH WITH FORMAL SYSTEM INVOLVEMENT

Because current studies estimate highly disproportionate representation of LGBT youth in OHC, as well as a large degree of involvement with youth-serving systems, it is imperative to assess the experiences of LGBT youth in these settings. Research has found that between 20% and 40% of homeless youth identify as LGBT (Ray, 2006). Studies that accurately estimate the number of LGBT youth in the child welfare system are unavailable, however, at least partly because of the invisibility of these youth in this system (Majd et al., 2009). The Equity Project,[1] however, has estimated that between 20% and 60% of youth in child welfare are LGBT (Majd et al., 2009). Other current research suggests that upwards of 13% of youth in detention facilities identify as LGBT (Irvine, 2010). Schaffner (1999) found that between one fifth and one third of girls in the juvenile justice system identified as lesbian or bisexual.

Disparities span beyond mere statistics and are also related to the experiences of LGBT youth in detention settings. For example, LGBT youth are twice as likely as their heterosexual peers in detention settings to have been removed from their homes as a result of being hurt by a member in that home, almost twice as likely to have lived in a foster home, more than twice as likely to have been detained for running away from their home or placement, and four times as likely to have been detained in juvenile facilities for prostitution (Irvine, 2010). LGB and questioning youth are also more than twice as likely to have been detained for substance-related offenses (Irvine, 2010). The underlying reasons for this level of disproportionality are not clear; however, several studies have made the connection between a young person's sexual orientation, gender

---

[1]The Equity Project is an initiative that ensures that LGBT youth "in juvenile delinquency courts are treated with dignity, respect, and fairness. The Equity Project examines issues that impact LGBT youth during the entire delinquency process, ranging from arrest through post-disposition" (The Equity Project, n.d.).

identity/expression, and their connection to the juvenile justice and child welfare systems (Curtain, 2002; Mallon, 2001; Rosario, Hunter, & Gwadz, 1997; Savin-Williams, 1994). Himmelstein and Brückner (2010) reported that although LGB youth are nearly 40% more likely than other youth to receive punishment from the legal system and school authorities, these disparities are not explained by differences in misconduct; in fact, LGB youth reportedly engaged in less violence than their heterosexual peers.

Experiences within the education system can also influence the placement of LGBT youth in OHC settings. For example, LGBT youth were reported to have been adjudicated on assault charges when using self-defense in response to bullying. In addition, studies have found that youth who experienced regular bullying and harassment at school about their sexual orientation or gender identity did not attend school, which can lead to truancy charges or violations of probation that require regular school attendance (Curtain, 2002; Freundlich & Avery, 2004; Majd et al., 2009; Mallon, 2001; Mallon et al., 2002; Willging, Salvador, & Kano, 2006; Woronoff et al., 2006). Many of these youth are not siloed in singular systems, but often receive services and supports across multiple systems. Their experiences in these systems can potentially increase risk factors that researchers have identified across the general population of LGBT youth. Chapter 11 explores educational settings in more detail.

Similarly, research on outcomes for the general population of youth in OHC has reported findings of significant concern. Many youth experience considerable challenges in making the transition from an OHC setting to independent living, including minimal employment experience; lack of access to medical care; financial hardship; lack of affordable, stable housing; increased likelihood of mental health and substance abuse problems; incarceration; adjustment difficulties; and early pregnancy (Barth, 1990; Blome, 1997; Cook, 1991; Reilly, 2003). These challenges are compounded by child welfare's response to LGBT and questioning youth, including the lack of key adults during their transition into adulthood and the persistent problem of youth living in congregate care facilities where permanency is not addressed (Jacobs & Freundlich, 2006).

These findings indicate that young people involved with OHC are potentially at increased risk for abuse, victimization, and negative outcomes. Chapter 4 reports that the average age for youth to "come out" as LGBT is decreasing to lower ages in recent years. Accordingly, LGBT youth may be ready to identify and seek support during their placements in OHC as they begin their transition to adulthood at earlier ages than has been true historically. Barriers to a successful transition, along with increased challenges and risk factors, are more likely for LGBT youth who are living in OHC settings without proper services and supports from important and caring adults. Young people in OHC often rely on their providers for formal support because there are often limited opportunities for these youth to develop informal and natural support systems. Providers may include clinicians, case managers, probation officers, child protective services workers, foster parents, and residential or corrections staff. Provider perceptions about and attitudes toward LGBT youth may influence their provision of service and support delivery, which, in turn, may affect the experiences that youth have in OHC settings. When these attitudes are negative toward LGBT youth, there can be irreparable harm to young people who are in OHC and not cared for by their families.

MISPERCEPTIONS ABOUT LGBT IDENTITY AND INSTITUTIONALIZED HETEROSEXISM

Once in the care of youth-serving systems, LGBT youth frequently experience more discrimination and abuse than their heterosexual peers. Much of the research focused on LGBT youth with youth-serving system involvement records pervasive misperceptions about LGBT youth held by professionals responsible for the care of these youth. These misperceptions by staff, foster parents, social workers, case managers, probation officers, and other care professionals range from a lack of awareness and understanding about LGBT language and culture to the belief that LGBT youth will sexually offend heterosexual youth; an equally damaging belief is that LGBT youth do not exist in the youth-serving systems, creating a sense of invisibility of this population (Clements & Rosenwald, 2007; Curtain, 2002; Freundlich & Avery, 2004; Majd et al., 2009; Mallon, 2001; Mallon et al., 2002; Willging et al., 2006; Woronoff et al., 2006).

These misperceptions are potentially a result of inadequate knowledge about LGBT youth, lack of training, and limited or no access to resources about LGBT people. Across multiple studies, religiosity is a factor in professionals' attitudes toward LGBT youth and has been identified by researchers as a justification for harassment. Additionally, religious-based providers sometimes affect access to resources because they may hold beliefs that identifying as an LGBT youth is morally unacceptable, which permeates through to the practice level (Clements & Rosenwald, 2007; Curtain, 2002; Freundlich & Avery, 2004; Majd et al., 2009; Mallon, 2001; Mallon et al., 2002; Willging et al., 2006; Woronoff et al., 2006). This belief may affect practice if agencies prevent youth from receiving culturally and linguistically appropriate services and supports if they openly identify as LGBT. In other instances, LGBT youth may be denied access to supportive services, restricted from dating peers, forced to attend church services, or required to participate in other activities or behaviors that conflict with their sexual orientation and/or gender identity and expression. The literature has not yet determined that attitudes and misperceptions lead to abuse in OHC settings, but abundant anecdotal evidence exists to support the notion that LGBT youth experience abuse in these settings.

EXPERIENCES OF ABUSE IN OUT-OF-HOME CARE SETTINGS

Majd et al. described LGBT experiences in confinement and secure facilities as "egregious" (2009, p.16). In a qualitative study, Curtain (2002) found that the juvenile justice system is, conceivably, a dangerous system for lesbian and bisexual girls and that their needs are notably overlooked. Staff in juvenile detention facilities have been found to perpetrate verbal, physical, and sexual abuse and tacitly permit these forms of abuse by other youth in facilities (Curtain, 2002; Majd et al., 2009). There have been reports of physical violence by staff under the auspices of behavioral restraint, which have led to physical abuse (Mallon, 2001).

The literature also abounds with anecdotal evidence from affected youth and mental health professionals describing risks related to sexual abuse, as well as actual events when LGBT youth were sexually abused and raped by peers and staff in detention centers and other congregate care settings (Clements & Rosenwald, 2007; Curtain, 2002; Majd et al., 2009; Mallon, 2001). Findings have shown that providers and staff framed many of these sexual abuse reports as attempts to change the youth's sexual orientation and/or gender identity/expression (Clements & Rosenwald, 2007; Curtain, 2002; Majd et al., 2009; Mallon, 2001). Care providers were found to subject LGBT youth to punishment or ridicule, particularly transgender youth who expressed their non–birth–assigned gender through clothing, language, and/or mannerisms. Some researchers have also noted that transgender youth placed according to their biological sex in congregate care settings were also at higher risk for physical, sexual, and verbal abuse from peers (Clements & Rosenwald, 2007; Majd et al., 2009).

PROTECTION, SUPPORT, ACCESS, AND VOICE

LGBT youth in OHC settings, regardless of system involvement, reportedly do not trust that their care providers will protect them (Curtain, 2002; Freundlich & Avery, 2004; Majd et al., 2009; Mallon, 2001; Mallon et al., 2002; Ragg, Patrick, & Ziefert, 2006; Willging et al., 2006; Woronoff et al., 2006). This belief, reportedly, has been fostered by repeated experiences wherein adults have failed to provide protection against abuse, including staff and other care professionals allowing and even encouraging verbal, physical, and sexual abuse of LGBT youth. These studies report that LGBT youth did not believe adults charged with their care and protection would intervene and help them when they witnessed abuse transpiring; that sense of a lack of protection from adult staff created fear in these youth and prevented them from disclosing their sexual orientation or gender identity (Curtain, 2002; Freundlich & Avery, 2004; Majd et al., 2009; Mallon, 2001; Mallon et al., 2002; Ragg et al., 2006; Willging et al., 2006; Woronoff et al., 2006).

A common challenge for LGBT youth in OHC is their lack of access to equal treatment and supportive services. Both youth and professionals report barriers to accessing information about sexuality or gender that would help them to understand LGBT youth and their needs and experiences (Curtain, 2002; Freundlich & Avery, 2004; Majd et al., 2009; Ragg et al., 2006; Ware, 2010; Willging et al., 2006). LGBT youth have reportedly experienced differential treatment, including isolation and placement in cells identified for individuals with a sex-offending history or HIV/AIDS, despite having no sex-offending history or communicable diseases (Majd et al., 2009; Ware, 2010). LGBT youth may be inappropriately pathologized in the system and perceived as a risk for preying on heterosexual youth, leading to punitive actions against LGBT youth. LGBT youth may also be subjected to a lack of supportive relationships, extended lengths of time in placement, multiple placements, prolonged psychiatric hospitalization stays, and disproportional detainment pending trial (Curtain, 2002; Freundlich & Avery, 2004; Majd et al., 2009; Ragg et al., 2006; Willging et al., 2006). Furthermore, LGBT youth are sometimes court ordered to receive inappropriate services, including reparative/conversion therapies (Majd et al., 2009).

Lack of access to culturally and linguistically competent services and resources contributes to differential treatment and unacceptable practice; in some instances and regions of the United States, these types of resources are minimal or nonexistent. Bias, misperceptions, and negative attitudes toward LGBT youth have led care providers to create barriers to access of supportive health and mental health services (Curtain, 2002; Freundlich & Avery, 2004; Majd et al., 2009; Ragg et al., 2006; Willging et al., 2006). Health care has been identified repeatedly as a critical issue for transgender youth who are denied hormone treatment when they enter OHC settings (Freundlich & Avery, 2004; Majd et al., 2009; Mallon et al., 2002; Ragg et al., 2006; Willging et al., 2006). State agencies that contract with faith-based organizations have reduced access to supportive resources because these organizations may not accept youth who openly identify as LGBT (Majd et al., 2009; Mallon et al., 2002; Ragg et al., 2006; Willging et al., 2006). Overall, a lack of access to supportive resources has created barriers to permanency and placement stability for LGBT youth. This lack of access and acknowledgement of LGBT youth in youth-serving systems has created a loss of voice for some young people.

The unfortunate invisibility of LGBT youth in OHC settings is promulgated by the failure of some youth-serving systems to acknowledge the existence of LGBT youth, as well as the persistent and purposeful silencing of these youth (Curtain, 2002; Majd et al., 2009; Mallon et al., 2002; Ragg et al., 2006; Willging et al., 2006). In rural communities, there are examples of therapists using practices that discount the possibility that LGBT status could be a factor in the mental health or substance abuse problems of clients or discouraging discussion of sexual orientation or gender identity in therapeutic settings (Willging et al., 2006). A study of these same rural communities found that mental health providers assumed that all of their clients were heterosexual; if LGBT youth did happen to disclose, they were frequently encouraged to "live quietly" for their own protection, despite the effects of reinforcing negative messages about being LGBT (Willging et al., 2006).

Ignoring the sexual orientation and gender identity of youth in care fosters the invisibility of LGBT youth and their needs. This invisibility remains true in the juvenile justice system, where the lack of culturally and linguistically competent counsel to advocate for the needs of these LGBT youth has further fostered a loss of youth voice in the justice system (Majd et al., 2009). LGBT youth reportedly fear disclosure of their sexual orientation or gender identity, because youth fear the power and authority that staff have over them while they are placed in congregate care settings. LGBT youth also fear that disclosure of one's sexual orientation or gender identity increases their vulnerability in OHC settings, leading to removal from foster homes or other placements or being targeted for abuse or differential treatment. This process of silencing and increasing invisibility includes disclosure related to LGBT-specific victimization (Curtain, 2002; Majd et al., 2009; Mallon, 2001; Ragg et al., 2006; Willging et al., 2006). In contrast, youth in OHC who choose to remain silent about their identity may feel safer by remaining invisible because they can control and have ownership over access to their LGBT identity (Majd et al., 2009; Mallon et al., 2002; Ragg et al., 2006).

Young people are also losing ownership over their sexuality and gender. There are reported instances of care professionals attempting to control and change a youth's sexual orientation or gender identity (Curtain, 2002; Majd et al., 2009; Mallon et al., 2002; Ragg et al., 2006; Willging et al., 2006). This has been particularly true for transgender youth who were pressured into being biological gender conforming in OHC through efforts such as preventing these youth from having access to medically necessary hormonal treatment and requiring gender-conforming clothing, hairstyles, and name choice (Majd et al., 2009; Mallon, 2001). Transgender youth have reported punishment across OHC settings for not conforming to dictated mandates related to gender expression (Majd et al., 2009; Mallon, 2001). LGBT youth have also reported that they are perceived to be oversexualized and that their sexual orientation became the focus of every conversation and decision made about them without their permission. LGBT youth have also reported concerns about their portrayal in agency files that were given to every new provider (Curtain, 2002; Majd et al., 2009; Mallon et al., 2002; Ragg et al., 2006; Ware, 2010; Willging et al., 2006). As a result, LGBT youth report they are unable to control disclosure about their sexual orientation and gender identity, which increases their sense of vulnerability in OHC settings.

OUTCOMES FOR LGBT YOUTH IN OUT-OF-HOME CARE SETTINGS

When assets are lacking, the extensive range of these experiences and associated outcomes can affect the sense of self-worth and self-esteem in LGBT youth (Curtain, 2002; Mallon, 2001; Ragg et al., 2006; Willging et al., 2006; Woronoff et al., 2006). Youth have described feelings of shame and stigma about their sexual orientation and noted that these feelings lead to challenges in building future relationships (Curtain, 2002; Mallon, 2001; Ragg et al., 2006; Willging et al., 2006; Woronoff et al., 2006). Some youth have felt further stigmatized due to repeated messages of care professionals that are disparaging and stereotype LGBT individuals; this stigma can result in further trauma for young people in OHC settings (Curtain, 2002). LGBT youth who experience rejection related to their sexual orientation and/or gender identity/expression often actively avoid opportunities for future rejection by remaining closeted (i.e., silent about their identity), even when this choice negatively affects their mental and physical well-being (Curtain, 2002; Mallon, 2001; Ragg et al., 2006; Willging et al., 2006; Woronoff et al., 2006).

Although studies abound with evidence that LGBT youth have negative experiences while in OHC settings, youth also report positive experiences. Studies have reported positive experiences in OHC settings where LGBT youth were supported and empowered by the professionals responsible for their care (Freundlich & Avery, 2004; Mallon et al., 2002; Ragg et al., 2006). These positive experiences occurred when the professionals and other care providers protected and listened to them, helped them work through problems, and advocated for them (Mallon et al., 2002; Ragg et al., 2006). These youth were able to feel validation by gaining a sense of pride in their difference and being connected to supportive community resources that provided connection to the LGBT community (Mallon et al., 2002; Ragg et al., 2006).

Some youth in studies have also described supportive staff that individualized their care, were affirming, and helped to counter stigma about being an LGBT youth. Supportive care professionals were accepting of LGBT youth and remained open and supportive and allowed youth to openly explore their sexual orientation or gender identity (Freundlich & Avery, 2004; Mallon et al., 2002; Ragg et al., 2006). LGBT youth who described supportive professionals and other adults in their lives reported feelings of empowerment, validation, pride in who they are, and safety and protection, which may affect their social support connections, sense of autonomy, and power over their own lives, as well as their general well-being (Mallon et al., 2002; Ragg et al., 2006). These positive experiences can enhance the development and implementation of policy and practice guidelines within a system of care to better support LGBT youth currently or previously in OHC settings and dealing with the consequences of negative experiences.

RECOMMENDATIONS

Systems of care are funded to enhance, integrate, and coordinate the systems, services, and supports that young people and their families receive. It is imperative that systems of care implement practice and policy shifts through the lens of system of care values and principles by providing culturally and linguistically appropriate and individualized services and supports for LGBT youth placed in OHC settings. Furthermore, a key tenet of system of care values and principles—meaningful youth involvement and engagement in their own care—includes youth participation in decision making about interventions and approaches. LGBT youth should have an ongoing and active voice in the enhancement of youth- and family-guided systems to create and implement more services and supports to address the needs of LGBT youth.

System of care values and principles can be operationalized in OHC settings through the action steps identified within the subsequent recommendations grounded in both the literature and practice. These recommendations can be useful to policy makers, researchers, administrators, practitioners, caregivers, youth, and other community members and include strategies for implementation at the policy, practice, and community levels.

The policy recommendations in Box 12.1 are intended for agency administrators and policy makers at the state or local levels or within community-based organizations; they are also relevant for larger national organizations that provide OHC treatment for LGBT youth. These recommendations encourage administrators and policy makers to develop explicit policies for supporting LGBT youth and their families. They emphasize how policy components and implementation of specific strategies can be integrated throughout the work of a larger provider community to actively support LGBT youth in OHC settings within a system of care.

This chapter highlights the lack of research focusing on LGBT youth in OHC settings or LGBT youth with youth- (or child-) serving system involvement. There is a significant need for researchers to continue addressing these gaps in the literature. The research-level recommendations in Box 12.2 are aimed at administrators, policy makers, researchers, and academic institutions within system of care communities.

The practice-level recommendations in Box 12.3, primarily directed at administrators, supervisors, direct-care staff, caregivers, and youth, support individuals responsible for providing care for youth in OHC settings. They are also aimed at the youth and caregivers who are entitled to voice their concerns and serve as active leaders in creating change within OHC settings.

Although OHC settings are not typically at the center of system of care approaches, LGBT youth in system of care communities may experience OHC settings while still enrolled, before enrollment, or after enrollment in services. These facilities may be community-based and are chosen to keep a child safe and

---

Box 12.1.   Policy Recommendations for Supporting LGBT Youth

Develop, integrate, and (or) implement

- LGBT-appropriate language into documents and materials and forms that agencies and organizations use to provide OHC (e.g., admissions forms, exit forms)
- Policies of agencies and prospective and current providers to ensure inclusive language and protections for LGBT youth
- Policies to include protections from bullying, harassment, and discrimination for LGBT youth in OHC settings
- Policies that are specific to meeting the needs of transgender youth or youth who express nonconforming gender
- Policies that are shared across child-serving agencies and that foster broad respect for diversity and that specifically acknowledge the LGBT community
- A mandated screening process for staff hires and agency program contracts to ensure they will be safe and affirming supports for LGBT youth
- An agency grievance procedure with explicit protections noted for youth who make any reports of abuse, bullying, and so forth
- Policies that require training and other educational opportunities designed to help staff understand and better meet the unique needs of LGBT youth in a culturally and linguistically responsive manner
- Spaces and OHC facilities that are designed to meet the needs of LGBT youth, including housing that does *not* segregate these youth from heterosexual and gender-conforming peers
- Policies that allow LGBT youth to self-determine regardless of whether they are integrated with heterosexual and cisgender peers or provided with segregated facilities or accommodations
- Unisex bathrooms, showers, and accommodations for transgender and gender nonconforming youth whenever possible
- Education curricula within OHC settings that include LGBT youth experiences (e.g., books and stories that include same-sex relationships)

Box 12.2.   Research-Level Recommendations for Supporting LGBT Youth

Support and conduct research that

- Enhances understanding on how to better meet the needs of LGBT youth in systems of care
- Includes identification of LGBT youth in all studies supported within a system of care community
- Focuses on recommended practices in supporting LGBT youth in OHC settings that can be replicated in other communities
- Builds understanding about work force attitudes toward LGBT youth in systems of care and the training and support needed to ensure quality care for LGBT youth in OHC environments

---

Box 12.3.   Practice-Level Recommendations for Supporting LGBT Youth

---

Require internal agency and contracted provider staff to

- Participate in training and ongoing educational support to understand and address the needs of LGBT youth, including education about culturally and linguistically responsive resources available in the community for LGBT youth
- Intervene in harassment and bullying by peers or other staff
- Implement diversity training and other learning opportunities for all youth residing in OHC settings

Provide

- Training and ongoing educational opportunities to peers and caregivers of LGBT youth to increase their understanding of the importance of offering acceptance and support
- Individualized housing and placement options according to a youth's identified gender or where a youth feels the most safe
- Positive resources, information, and support related to sexual orientation and gender identity to youth, their family members, and staff

Ensure

- Programming does not negatively affect LGBT or questioning youth by conveying negative attitudes about nonheterosexual, gender nonconforming youth
- Staff are held accountable for nondiscriminatory practices with specified consequences for discriminatory behaviors
- Youth who are transitioning to a different gender have access to quality health and mental health care, including hormone treatment under the care of a qualified physician
- LGBT youth are not forced involuntarily into isolation or segregation, are connected to supportive family members or other adults, have access to programs that support their cultural identity, and are treated respectfully in all interactions with staff, providers, and so forth

Respect a youth's right to

- Confidentiality and self-disclosure around sexual orientation and gender identity
- Nonconforming gender expression, including hair, clothing, accessories, and so forth
- Self-define "family" and identify who constitutes membership in the youth's family and friends, so the youth can have contact with those individuals
- Determine how and when they have contact with the people they have identified as family; denial of family visitation rights as punishment should never occur for LGBT youth because they may experience social isolation in OHC settings and need contact with supportive "family"

Create opportunities for

- LGBT youth to be involved in leadership opportunities that affect practice and policy
- Family members of LGBT youth to be involved in developing practice approaches and policies to create and institute supportive environments for LGBT youth

---

**Box 12.4.   Recommendations for System of
             Care Community Members and Stakeholders**

Community members and stakeholders building the foundation of a successful system of care should

- Take a stand on behalf of LGBT youth and advocate for equality and culturally and linguistically responsive treatment and living environments
- Enhance their own understanding and that of others around them about LGBT people and the experiences of LGBT youth in OHC settings
- Organize educational opportunities at community centers, libraries, and so forth to share information and correct "misinformation" about LGBT youth, their needs, and how these needs can be addressed respectfully and meaningfully
- Help organize local LGBT pride events that LGBT youth in OHC can attend
- Help develop community-based, LGBT-supportive resources that youth in an OHC setting can connect with in the community
- Connect with OHC provider organizations and facilities to provide training and information about community resources for LGBT youth
- Connect with welcoming and affirming faith-based organizations to raise awareness of the need for ongoing support for LGBT youth
- Encourage places in the community to display symbols of support (e.g., rainbow flags, pink triangles), including OHC provider organizations and facilities
- Work with local LGBT-affirming community organizations such as Parents, Families, and Friends of Lesbians and Gays (PFLAG) to secure support for LGBT youth
- Advocate for antibullying policies and protections for LGBT youth within schools, as well as other LGBT-affirming policies that affect their community

---

supported while remaining connected to the community. Because these settings have a place within the service array available to youth in all communities, system of care community/stakeholders are responsible for helping to foster safe and supportive OHC for young people living outside of a family home. Box 12.4 provides related recommendations.

CONCLUSION

As documented earlier, the limited available research and anecdotal evidence substantiate the considerable disparities that LGBT youth experience in OHC settings. A more in-depth analysis of the literature strongly suggests that supporting LGBT youth in OHC settings through a system of care approach can result in improved behavioral and emotional outcomes commensurate with those achieved by other groups of youth in systems of care. These positive outcomes include reductions in the number of suicide attempts, increased connections to the community, increased levels of self-esteem, and decreased levels of self-reported suicidal ideation.

System of care values and principles dictate that young people should have access to, and receive, a wide array of culturally and linguistically responsive services and supports that are tailored to meet their individualized needs. To ensure family-driven care, family members should have a leading role in determining the care of their children. Further, these families deserve to be secure in knowing that youth will be respected and supported while outside of their home environment. The operationalization of family-driven care within a system of care can result in conflicts with respect to parents of LGBT youth. Parents or caregivers may recommend that their LGBT child *not* receive culturally and linguistically responsive care and access to supportive LGBT resources. Caregivers may even request reparative therapies for their LGBT youth.

When these situations arise, it is critical that practitioners working with the family refer to their professional code of ethics for guidance. Most professional boards, including the National Juvenile Defender Center (2009), the National Association of Social Workers (1999), and the American Psychological Association (2002), for example, have stated the ethical responsibilities and level of protection staff must provide to their clients. These include protection from abuse, harassment, and discrimination, as well as access to necessary medical and mental health treatment and advocacy if a young person's rights are violated. Although the value of family-driven care is critical to successful planning for LGBT youth in youth-serving systems, it does not preclude a practitioner's ethical responsibilities to a youth's well-being.

The principle of youth-guided care asserts that young people should have a voice in matters related to disclosure about their sexual orientation or gender identity. Caregivers and youth should be able to determine how their needs will best be met, including the identification and selection of appropriate placement and culturally and linguistically relevant supports and services. Youth who are guiding their care have a right to refuse discriminatory treatments or practices and should have access to supportive resources related to their sexual orientation or gender identity. Youth deserve to be protected by the systems designed to provide them with care, protection, and support. Box 12.5 describes one state's efforts to promote a full-inclusion approach to care for LGBT youth and their families in its system of care communities.

Supportive adults in the lives of LGBT youth make a difference by helping these youth achieve positive outcomes (e.g., Ryan, 2010). LGBT youth may experience victimization and increased risk in OHC settings, and providers and other professionals responsible for their care are often the key supports in a young person's life. Their attitudes toward individuals who are not heterosexual and who do not identify as their birth-assigned gender can affect how they support, protect, and foster resiliency among LGBT youth. LGBT youth who have supportive professionals and other adults in their lives feel empowered, validated, pride in who they are, safe, and protected, which affects their social support connections, sense of autonomy, power over their own lives, and general

---

Box 12.5: An Example of Full Inclusion: Maryland Integrates Services and Supports Specifically for LGBT Youth in Systems of Care

Through system of care grants and interagency support, the state of Maryland has taken important steps to improve the quality of supports youth experience while participating in its system of care. The state has received two system of care grants, one focusing on Baltimore City and another that is concentrated on the Eastern Shore, a nine-county rural region. Through these grants, Maryland has supported statewide training focused on understanding and addressing the needs of LGBT youth and their families in a culturally and linguistically responsive manner. During the two cooperative agreements, more than 1,000 youth, parents, foster parents, providers, case/care managers, and others working within the system of care communities have participated in the trainings. Agencies outside of the system of care communities that participate in informal collaborations with the systems of cares have requested trainings for their entire staff as well as technical assistance to develop policies and practice enhancements to better support the needs of LGBT youth and their families.

The youth-serving state agencies have also made policy shifts to improve the experiences that LGBT youth have while in care. For example, the Maryland Department of Juvenile Services (DJS) has recently begun surveying staff about their attitudes and behaviors toward LGBT youth to better understand staff training and policy needs. DJS has also developed an implementation committee to support these efforts and is concurrently reviewing current policies. Moreover, DJS has conducted an analysis of other juvenile justice agencies to see how their internal policies can be more supportive of LGBT youth. Similarly, the Maryland Department of Human Resources (DHR), the state's child welfare authority, recently requested proposals for providing residential child care services for children in foster care. Within this request, DHR required that prospective contractors describe how they will ensure that every youth has an opportunity to participate in religious services of his or her choice or to refrain from religious practice, if so desired. In addition, the request required that contractors link any LGBT or questioning youth with an organization or other networks that would support the identity and culture of youth. These initial steps are only the beginning for Maryland, but show promise of the evolution of a full-inclusion approach to care for LGBT youth and their families in the state's system of care communities.

---

well-being (Freundlich & Avery, 2004; Mallon et al., 2002; Ragg et al., 2006). It is incumbent upon systems of care collaborating with OHC settings to ensure that culturally and linguistically appropriate services and supports are available for LGBT youth in OHC and that young people are connected to caring adults so that they are safe, supported, and able to thrive.

13

Addressing Suicide and Self-Harming Behaviors Among LGBT Youth in Systems of Care

KEITH J. HORVATH, GARY REMAFEDI,
SYLVIA K. FISHER, AND CHRISTINE WALRATH

In 2010, a spate of news reports covering a series of suicide deaths of youth who were known or perceived to be gay drew unprecedented national media attention to the harassment and bullying of students in day-to-day life as well as in the virtual realities of online social networks. During the 2009–2010 academic year, five students in the Anoka–Hennepin School District (including Minneapolis, Minnesota) alone died of suicide (Draper, 2010). Concern about these deaths and the potential contribution of bullying has triggered an intense national response from parents and other constituents and focused attention on school-based and other risks to the well-being of youth who are gay, perceived to be gay, or gender nonconforming. Addressing the causes and consequences of self-harming behaviors among lesbian, gay, bisexual, and transgender (LGBT) youth (and adults) is a national priority and requires a multifaceted response from individuals, advocacy groups, service-providing organizations, and communities.

Suicide ranks third as the leading cause of death (surpassed only by unintentional injuries and homicides) for U.S. youth ages 1–21 years, accounting for 2,658 deaths in 2007 (Centers for Disease Control and Prevention [CDC], 2009). Self-harm is defined as behaviors, thoughts, or feelings resulting in negative physical health, mental health, or social outcomes for an individual or a group of people, and self-harming behaviors contribute significantly to morbidity and mortality in LGBT youth communities. Critical information is needed to help resolve lingering doubts and debate about the link between sexual identity and suicide or self-harm; the availability of this information has significant implications for preventing and responding to individual deaths and outbreaks of suicide in LGBT youth.

This chapter examines causes of self-harming behaviors within a system of care approach, beginning with a conceptual framework within which to explain self-harm behaviors among LGBT youth. Although self-harm behavior may take many forms (e.g., sexual risk behavior, alcohol and drug use), we focus here on youth suicide because it potentially carries the gravest consequences. We review what is known about self-harming behavior, as well as the complexities of defining the population and scope of the problem, to illustrate why gaps in understanding persist despite the recognition that self-harming behavior is a crisis among LGBT youth. The bulk of this chapter reviews current literature on causes and identifies recommended practices to address suicide among this highly vulnerable group of youth.

MINORITY STRESS PROCESSES AMONG LGBT POPULATIONS: A CONCEPTUAL FRAMEWORK

Models in the literature that help describe and understand negative health outcomes and disease offer insight into how to address suicide-related behaviors in LGBT youth both nationally and in systems of care. Both individual-level (e.g., experiences of discrimination) and societal-level (e.g., stigma of LGBT identity, legal disaffirmation of intimate relationships) environmental stressors unique to minority status are associated with less than optimal health outcomes. Furthermore, these environmental stressors contribute to a causal chain of events that can lead to a variety of self-injurious behaviors.

Consistent with this framework, Ilan Meyer proposed a theory of minority stress that "positions the source of stress, and therefore mental health problems, as stemming from prevailing societal-level sexual stigma, prejudice, and discrimination and not a reflection of individual traits" (2010, p. 1218). Figure 13.1 illustrates the moderating effects of (d) distal (e.g., prejudice events) and (f) proximal (e.g., internalized homophobia) minority stress processes on the association between minority status and mental health outcomes and how these relationships can be altered by community- and individual-level coping and social support factors. To extend the minority stress model, studies consistently show that negative mental health outcomes (e.g., depression) are associated with self-harming behaviors among adolescents, including suicide (for a review, see Spirito & Esposito-Smythers, 2006). Although this model does not account for all self-harming behaviors, it provides a useful framework for addressing these concerns, as it suggests environmental factors that may be modified to reduce the occurrence or impact of self-harming behavior among LGBT youth.

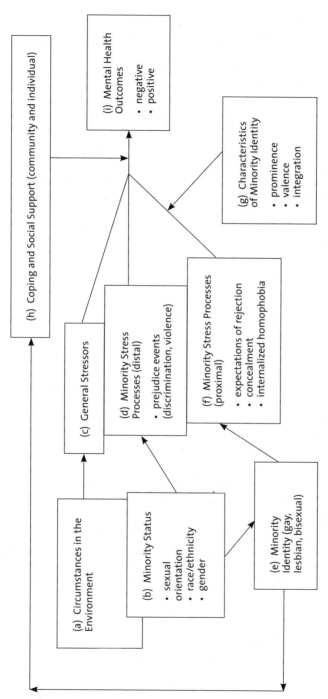

Figure 13.1. Minority stress processes among LGBT populations. (From Meyer [2003]. Prejudice, social stress, and mental health in lesbian, gay, and bisexual populations: Conceptual issues and research evidence. *Psychological Bulletin, 129*[5], 674–697.)

HEALTH DISPARITIES RELATED TO SELF-HARMING BEHAVIORS

Self-harming behaviors can take many forms, and we focus here on those behaviors reported to be particularly prevalent among LGBT youth, the most
lethal of which is suicide. Suicide-related behavior, including suicide attempts,
is reported to be prevalent among LGBT youth. Although significant methodological limitations exist to accurately estimate the rate of suicide, surveys consistently find rates of reported suicide attempts to be two to seven times higher
among LGB high school students compared with those who self-identify as
heterosexual (Garofalo, Wolf, Kessel, Palfrey, & DuRant, 1998; Garofalo, Wolf,
Wissow, Woods, & Goodman, 1999; Remafedi, 2002). Furthermore, suicidal
ideation has been associated with elevated rates of substance use among LGB
youth in some studies (Remafedi, Farrow, & Deisher, 1991), but not in all (Silenzio, Pena, Duberstein, Cerel, & Knox, 2007).

Definitions of health disparities vary and can emphasize reducing the morbidity and mortality of negative health consequences and disease within a population and improving survival rates. Alternatively, health disparity definitions
may focus greater attention on health outcomes and health disparities and cor-
recting power imbalances in access to health care and health outcomes. A review of definitions of mental health disparities identified the CDC definition
of mental health disparities as the most unifying because it addresses disparities
1) between the degree of attention a given problem receives relative to the degree of attention other public health issues of comparable magnitude receive;
2) in the health of individuals with mental illness compared with those without;
and 3) with respect to quality, accessibility, and outcomes of care provided to a
particular population (Safran et al., 2009).

Applying this definition to LGBT youth and self-harming behavior provides evidence that disparities exist along each of these dimensions. First, although calls for greater attention to self-harming behaviors among LGB youth
were made more than a decade ago (Remafedi, 1999b), comparatively little research has focused on the needs of this group, and the needs and health concerns
of transgender youth have been recognized only recently. Second, as described
in this chapter, studies comparing rates of self-harming behaviors of LGB youth
compared with their heterosexual counterparts show significant health disparities across a range of topics (see discussion that follows). Finally, despite the
need for services that specifically address the needs of LGBT youth, there is a
clear deficit in appropriate health care providers and programs addressing this
population.

Studies cited throughout this chapter clearly indicate that suicide-related
behavior affects LGBT youth disproportionately relative to other youth populations, presenting a large challenge for systems of care seeking to address the
behavioral health needs of LGBT youth. Accordingly, greater attention on health
disparities faced by LGBT youth is needed to increase access to appropriate

care and preventative services and ultimately reduce health disparity outcomes faced by many in this population.

SOURCES OF INFORMATION ABOUT SELF-HARMING BEHAVIOR

Although self-harming behaviors have serious negative consequences for LGBT youth and health disparities exist for these youth compared with their sexual and gender majority peers, accurately describing their prevalence and seriousness is challenging given current methodological limitations of investigative methods used to inform our knowledge of the area. Sources of information about self-harming behaviors include death records, psychological autopsies, disease surveillance, emergency room and hospital admission data, and quantitative and qualitative survey research.

Although death records can help identify clear cases of suicide, they are limited by the exclusion of the identification of the person's sexual orientation or the likelihood that less obvious cases of suicide may not even be recorded as suicide. To supplement death record information, some researchers have opted to conduct a "psychological autopsy," during which family members and friends of the deceased person are interviewed. Psychological autopsies are conducted postmortem to make a more definite determination of the cause of death in ambiguous situations. Researchers have used this method to assess the association between sexual orientation and deaths by suicide (Rich, Fowler, Young, & Blenkush, 1986; Shaffer, Fisher, Hicks, Parides, & Gould, 1995), although we are not aware of any studies that have done the same for transgender identity. This method may provide greater information about the sexual orientation and/or gender identity of the deceased individual, but actual suicides among LGBT youth may be underestimated when family members and friends underreport sexual or gender identities or were not even aware of the youth's identity. Surveillance of attempted suicide or deaths by suicide and substance use among LGBT youth, however, is not conducted, and therefore, this data source is unavailable for these behaviors.

Because of the limitations of death records, psychological autopsies, and surveillance, researchers have also turned to qualitative and quantitative survey methods to estimate the magnitude and incidence of these behaviors. A number of school-based surveys estimating rates of suicide attempts, substance use, and sexual risk behaviors have included questions about sexual orientation (although not gender identification beyond dichotomous male/female). School-based surveys of LGB youth indicate that rates of suicide attempts are two to seven times higher among this group than non–LGB identified youth (Garofalo et al., 1998; Remafedi, 2002). Survey data may be problematic, however, because they rely on self-reported behavior, often not generalizable to all LGBT youth depending on the sampling strategy, and self-reported rates of problem behavior vary significantly depending on how survey items are written. Accordingly, achieving consensus about the scope of these problems among LGBT youth from survey data remains elusive. To best understand the scope of problem behaviors for LGBT children and youth, conclusions should be drawn from extensive findings stemming from multiple data sources.

COMPLEXITIES OF DEFINING
SELF-HARMING BEHAVIOR AND SEXUAL IDENTITY

Defining the scope of the problem of self-harming behavior is complicated because self-harming behavior can be defined along a number of dimensions, about which there is not broad consensus. For example, should self-harming behavior be defined by its intent, its consequence (i.e., whether or not actual bodily injury was involved), its effect on others, or by an array of interrelated factors? Even among cases of apparent suicidal behavior, for example, there may be instances in which an adolescent primarily is seeking attention (i.e., making a "cry for help") rather than intending to end his or her life. In cases without clear evidence of the intent or reason for self-harming behavior, unreliable interpretations of the cause of death are possible.

Another challenge is that although same-sex sexual behavior during adolescence appears to be relatively commonplace, it is not a robust predictor of sexual identity (Laumann, Gagnon, Michael & Michaels, 1994). Accordingly, it is debatable whether an individual with a history of same-sex sexual behavior that occurs only during adolescence and who subsequently engages in self-harming behavior should be considered a member of LGBT youth at risk for suicide (particularly if this behavior is not concomitant with the youth questioning his or her identity or behavior). Second, many families may be unaware or unwilling to admit that their child or sibling is LGBT. If self-harming behaviors are closely associated with the youth's LGBT identity, it may be difficult to directly address the primary source of self-harm within the family system when parents or siblings are not receptive, understanding, or even aware of the identity.

HETEROSEXISM, TRANSPHOBIA, AND STIGMA

Among the striking findings of early research about the development of sexual identity are the formidable challenges facing youth who are trying to manage same-sex attractions in the context of hostile environments, sometimes leading them to contemplate or attempt suicide or resort to other self-compromising behaviors to relieve or escape stressful situations. As an outgrowth of interest in these early research findings, heightened awareness of the vulnerability of adolescents during the "coming out" process, and U.S. public health goals to reduce mortality from suicide, hundreds of scientific articles on the topic of suicide and sexual orientation have been published (for a review, see King et al., 2008); a disproportionate share of them focus on adolescents and young adults (e.g., Jiang, Perry & Hesser, 2010; Saewyc et al., 2007; Spirito & Esposito-Smythers, 2006).

With some notable exceptions, youth-serving and government agencies have been less than prompt in translating knowledge about the challenges facing LGBT youth into practice. For example, the *National Strategy for Suicide Prevention (NSSP)* (U.S. Public Health Service, 2001) and the Institute of Medicine's *Reducing Suicide: A National Imperative* (Goldsmith & Institute of Medicine Committee on Pathophysiology & Prevention of Adolescent & Adult Suicide, 2002) recognized gay and bisexual youth as populations at risk for self-harming behavior, but barely included any mention of contributing factors and made no recommendations for intervention, prevention strategies, or public health policies.

Recent suicides among gay youth and young adults, however, have increased the public's recognition of risks for sexual and gender minority youth, and there are currently efforts underway to address the problem of suicide among LGBT youth on a national level. The National Action Alliance for Suicide Prevention, launched in September 2010 in accordance with a key recommendation of the *NSSP* (U.S. Public Health Service, 2001), immediately instituted three task forces that focus on addressing suicide among high-risk groups, including one focused on LGBT youth. This dedicated task force has been working to include language and recommendations about reducing suicide among LGBT youth in the revised *NSSP* to be released in April 2012. This new strategy will reflect new developments, advancements in science, and increased knowledge about vulnerable populations since the first edition of the *NSSP* in 2001.

Although the national media has shined a spotlight on schools and the failure to respond to instances of bullying that may have played a role in triggering desperate acts among LGBT youth (or those perceived to be LGBT), schools are rarely the sole or main actors in events leading to suicide deaths. Heterosexism and transphobia are commonly expressed in the music, games, movies, videos, television programs, and web sites that many young people enjoy, despite the pain they cause to the individuals who are maligned. Instruction for students to become savvy consumers of social media and confront bias is seldom provided in primary and secondary educational curricula. Similarly, most parents are no better prepared to combat prejudice than are students and professionals when bullying regarding sexuality occurs at school. Families may avoid taking formal action, worrying that complaints will not be heard, embarrass the victim, and/or invite retaliation. Further, some families may feel trapped in adverse circumstances and compelled to remain silent because alternative placements in safer schools are not readily accessible or affordable (Ryan, Russell, Huebner, Diaz, & Sanchez, 2010).

In the absence of an underlying medical diagnosis or persistent psychiatric disorder (e.g., schizophrenia), psychosocial problems among gay and lesbian youth are best understood as a reaction to stigma and discrimination (Meyer, 2003). At a time in life when peers play a critical role in healthy personal and social development, isolation and stigma are highly traumatic for adolescents struggling with their sexual orientation or gender identity who lack needed supports.

School-based studies have shown that LGB students are more likely to both fear for their safety and to be attacked and injured with a weapon at school as compared with their heterosexual peers (Garofalo et al., 1998). Furthermore, LGBT youth may not seek familial support or assistance because they are concerned about the potential negative reactions of their families; this fear of rejection when seeking support makes LGBT youth especially vulnerable because of diminished or nonexistent family support. Some LGBT youth may not want to worry their families about their well-being and rejection by others outside of the family. Moreover, without family and peer support, some LGBT youth might internalize negative stereotypes and engage in self-defeating or self-harming behaviors.

SUICIDE BEHAVIOR AMONG LGBT YOUTH

Suicide behavior among LGBT youth has been studied with respect to suicide attempts and suicide deaths.

Suicide Attempts

To date, multiple peer-reviewed studies have found unusually high rates of attempted suicide, in the range of 20%–42%, among young bisexual and homosexual research volunteers (Remafedi, 1999a). Initial studies of sexual orientation and suicidality used convenience samples that were limited by participant biases or school-based samples that could not capture out-of-school youths. Since 1997, however, more than half a dozen population-based and controlled studies have corroborated the findings of earlier studies (Garofalo et al, 1998; Garofalo et al., 1999; Paul et al., 2002; Saewyc et al., 2007; Wichstrom, Hegna, Wichstrom, & Hegna, 2003). All have found a significant association between suicide attempts and LGB identity, strongest among males.

Comparable information about suicide attempts and deaths by suicide in transgender young people is unavailable. One study (Grossman & D'Augelli, 2007) of 55 transgender youth reporting on life-threatening behaviors, however, found that nearly half of the sample reported having seriously thought about taking their lives, and one quarter reported suicide attempts. Factors significantly related to having made a suicide attempt included suicidal ideation related to transgender identity; experiences of parental verbal and physical abuse; and lower body esteem, especially weight satisfaction and thoughts of how their bodies were evaluated by others. In sum, there is clear evidence that attempted suicide is disproportionately high among LGB youth, and there is growing evidence that the same is true for transgender youth.

Suicide Deaths

At this time, there is strong evidence that LGBT youth are more likely to attempt suicide than heterosexual counterparts, but there is relatively less evidence that they are more likely to die of suicide. Conclusions about the relative risks of suicide and self-injury associated with sexual or gender identity must be carefully nuanced. There are many remaining questions about the epidemiology of suicide in LGBT populations, and they are not likely to be answered by existing data sets and psychological autopsy studies. Although not without its own set of sociopolitical and methodological challenges, the routine inclusion of sexual identity identifiers in death records offers the best prospects of a breakthrough in understanding morbidity, mortality, and health disparities across subpopulations. Understanding risk and protective factors for suicide among LGBT youth is key to developing effective and appropriate interventions.

SUICIDE RISK AND PROTECTIVE FACTORS IN LGBT YOUTH

To reduce suicide-related deaths among LGBT youth, investigators have sought a unifying explanation(s) for suicide and practical means of suicide prevention. Because suicide is an uncommon event, clear identification of factors associated with suicide is difficult in even the most rigorously designed studies (Low & Andrews, 1990). Studies that contribute to a seminal understanding of risk and protective factors associated with suicide attempts among LGBT youth are described in the next section.

Studies comparing gay-oriented suicide attempters with nonattempters have generally highlighted the importance of social risk factors such as gender nonconformity, early awareness of homosexuality, gay-related stress, victimization by violence, lack of social support, school dropout, family problems, suicide attempts by friends or relatives, and homelessness (Remafedi, 1999a). Psychosocial stressors associated with elevated risk for suicide attempts among LGB youth include gender nonconformity, victimization, lack of support, dropping out of school, family problems, suicide attempts by acquaintances, homelessness, substance abuse, and psychiatric disorders (Kitts, 2005). Further, protective factors that promote resilience may be less available to LGBT youth (e.g., strong family connections, peer support, positive LGBT role models, access to effective health and mental health providers). Suicide attempts often occur in proximity to the developmental period of "identity assumption," as the child or adolescent acknowledges being LGBT (Remafedi et al., 1991). Studies have also examined the protective influence of cohesive families and safe schools (Beaty, 1999;

Eisenberg, Ackard, & Resnick, 2007) and other factors that contribute to resilience among LGBT youth (see assets-based model in Chapter 8).

Sex- and Gender-Related Risk

In a seminal investigation of suicide attempts (Remafedi et al., 1991) involving in-depth interviews with 137 gay and bisexual males 14–21 years of age from the U.S. upper Midwest and Pacific Northwest, 41 subjects (30%) reported a suicide attempt; almost half reported multiple attempts. Twenty-one percent of all attempts resulted in medical or psychiatric admissions. Compared with non-attempters, attempters had more feminine gender roles and adopted a bisexual or homosexual identity at younger ages. Attempters were more likely than peers to report sexual abuse, drug abuse, and arrests for misconduct.

Among the epidemiological studies of suicide and sexual identity in population-based samples, the two largest studies were conducted among students in Minnesota (Remafedi, French, Story, Resnick, & Blum, 1998) and Massachusetts (Garofalo et al., 1999). The former study compared students who identified themselves as LGB with those who identified as heterosexual. The latter study compared students who identified as LGB or "not sure" with those who identified as heterosexual. Both studies found a significant association between homosexuality (or "not sure") and suicidality among males only. The relative risks of attempted suicide for bisexual and homosexual male students were, respectively, 7.1 and 3.4 times higher than those of heterosexual male peers.

An analysis of the results (i.e., meta-analysis) of 25 international population-based studies (King et al., 2008) of suicidal behavior in both adolescents and adults concluded that gay or bisexual males were more than four times as likely as heterosexual males to have attempted suicide at any time in their lives. The relative risk of attempted suicide for lesbian and bisexual women compared with heterosexual women was approximately 1.9. Similarly, depression, anxiety, and alcohol and substance misuse were at least 1.5 times more common in LGB individuals. Findings were similar in men and women, but lesbian and bisexual women were at particular risk of substance dependence, whereas lifetime risk of suicide attempts was especially high in gay and bisexual men.

Academic Engagement

Another study involving young men who have sex with men (MSM) found that school enrollment was singularly associated with a prior suicide attempt among the potential correlates identified in the study (Remafedi, 2002). Specifically, young MSM in school were significantly less likely to attempt suicide, suggesting that leaving school may be a symptom of the underlying emotional and social difficulties predisposing youth to suicide. Conversely, "school connectedness" may operate as a protective factor, accounting for the observed lower attempt rates among students (regardless of sexual orientation). Analysis of data from a statewide survey of 6th, 9th, and 12th grade students in Minnesota found three factors to be significantly protective of reported suicide attempts in youth with same-sex sexual experience: family connectedness, perceived adult caring, and school safety (Eisenberg et al., 2007).

Family Cohesion

Among 224 LGB young adults (21–25 years of age) involved in a study of family rejection and health problems, participants who reported higher levels of family rejection during adolescence were 8.4 times more likely to report having attempted suicide, 5.9 times more likely to report high levels of depression, 3.4 times more likely to use illegal drugs, and 3.4 times more likely to report having engaged in unprotected sexual intercourse compared with peers from families that reported no or low levels of family rejection (Ryan, Huebner, Diaz, & Sanchez, 2009). The results of this study, together with those finding that family connectedness is a protective factor for suicide attempts, suggest that familial support is a critical buffer against suicide among LGB youth.

Substance Use and Mental Health

Several works have found a significant association between reported suicide attempts and substance abuse or mental health symptoms in LGB youth (Wolitski, Stall, & Valdiserri, 2008). Although some investigators have attributed suicidality to psychological disorders, others have found that the association between suicidality and same-gender orientation in adolescent and adult men is independent of the confounding effects of substance use and mental health diagnoses (Cochran & Mays, 2000; Garofalo et al., 1998; Herrell et al., 1999).

REDUCING SUICIDE-RELATED BEHAVIOR AMONG LGBT YOUTH: RECOMMENDED PRACTICES

The primary prevention of self-harming behavior and suicides rests on ensuring that all children and adolescents, regardless of sexual or gender identity, have an opportunity to reach their full potential for physical and emotional well-being. Achieving this goal entails removing personal, interpersonal, and social obstacles associated with institutionalized heterosexism, biphobia, and transphobia and assuring that all young people have ample opportunities to advance personally and contribute to the collective well-being of communities. Building community awareness and capacity is integral to preventing and addressing self-harm and suicide. For example, in response to the recent youth suicides among students in the Anoka-Hennepin school district, school board members passed a resolution in early 2011 that strengthens antibullying efforts, includes LGBT themes in school curriculum, and tracks anti-LGBT related bullying incidents (Birkey, 2011). The new curriculum will include information about ways to increase the safety of LGBT students, offer yearly trainings on LGBT issues to district employees, and revise the sexual health curriculum to address topics relevant to these communities.

Every sector of society that interfaces with youth, including families, schools, faith-based organizations, recreational facilities, social services organizations, employers, clinics, civic organizations, and legal/governmental systems, has an investment in promoting the well-being of LGBT youth. Future efforts to prevent suicide in LGBT youth should include the following:

- Expanded access among LGBT youth and their families, health care providers, and individuals employed in systems that interact with LGBT youth to information, counseling, and support (including gay–straight alliances inside and outside of schools) for specific concerns about sexual and gender identity

- The availability of culturally, linguistically, and developmentally appropriate health care services, including assessment of cofactors and markers for self-harming behaviors, such as deteriorating school performance or drop-out, family conflict or disapproval, exposure to bullying and violence, substance abuse, eating and weight problems, and somatic symptoms of emotional distress

- Provision of outpatient and/or inpatient information, counseling, pharmacotherapy for symptoms of impaired mental health and substance abuse, and other appropriate interventions, as needed, to LGBT youth and their families

- Extensively vetted and appropriate online resources for LGBT youth advocacy and crisis intervention

- Referral of families and youth who have active suicidal ideation and/or attempts, active substance use, or a history of persistent sexual risk-taking to specialized medical and mental health treatment services

- Measures to ensure that schools and clinics are safe and inclusive and that employers and publically funded organizations prevent discrimination on the basis of sexual and gender identity; of particular importance are antibullying initiatives underway within primary and secondary schools, as these activities have a unique potential to reach the majority of children, youth, and families throughout the United States

- Efforts to advance knowledge of disparities in suicide and other causes of mortality by including questions about sexual and gender identity on death records

- Research to develop and evaluate interventions to prevent suicide attempts and deaths, high-risk sexual behavior that may result in infection with HIV or other sexually transmitted infections, and substance use among at-risk LGBT youth

SYSTEMS OF CARE AND SUICIDE PREVENTION

The Substance Abuse and Mental Health Services Administration (SAMHSA)–funded Children's Mental Health Initiative (CMHI), also known as "systems of care," has made an active commitment to reduce suicide-related behavior among all children and youth receiving services and supports in system of care communities. Two documents guide systematic program efforts to address suicide-related behavior among children and youth in systems of care: *A Comprehensive Vision—A Logic Model Addressing Suicide Issues in System of Care Communities* and *A Blueprint for Addressing Suicide Issues in Systems of Care* (SAMHSA Center for Mental Health Services, Child, Adolescent, and Family Services Branch, 2009a, 2009b), as articulated by the following statement:

> To promote and ensure appropriate and culturally and linguistically competent services and supports in the areas of suicide prevention, intervention and postvention (i.e., intervention conducted after a suicide, often in the form of support of the bereaved family, friends, peers and providers, an aspect of which is to reduce the possibility of 'suicide contagion' among affected persons) for children, youth and families within System of Care communities who are at risk for suicidal ideation and behavior. (p. 1)

A goal of this mission is to reduce the stigma associated with help-seeking behavior for youth who are at risk for suicide-related behavior.

LGBT youth are identified as one of several populations of interest that are at risk for suicidal intent and/or suicide-related behaviors. These documents articulate a comprehensive and coordinated vision and plan for addressing suicide in systems of care at both the national and community levels, extending to policies, practices, interventions, services, and supports. Community strengths and challenges are identified, as well as assumptions at the youth and family and system of care community levels, respectively. Short- and long-term outcomes are identified for youth and families and communities, and several programmatic and other strategies are identified to achieve the full set of positive outcomes, beginning with reductions in incidents of suicide-related behavior (e.g., ideation or "thinking about suicide," attempts, deaths) and extending to the sustainability of effective interventions throughout system of care communities.

Developing culturally, linguistically, and developmentally appropriate interventions for children and youth at risk for self-harming behaviors and suicide-

related behaviors necessitates that clinically meaningful data be collected to identify at-risk children and youth. The national evaluation of the CMHI collects
data routinely about suicidal ideation and suicide attempts among children and
youth receiving services and supports through systems of care. Box 13.1 describes what relevant data are collected, how and when these data are collected,
and what the results indicate about children and youth who have received services and supports in system of care communities initially funded from 2002
through 2006.

**Box 13.1.   Suicidal Thoughts and Behaviors Among Youth Served Through
Systems of Care: What Do the National Evaluation Data Tell Us?**

This box examines data compiled through the national evaluation of the SAMHSA–
funded CMHI regarding the presence of suicide-related thoughts and behaviors
among youth who have received services in systems of care. Although the data collected to date through the national evaluation of the CMHI have not included information about the gender identity or sexual orientation of youth entering services,
this data set represents the largest and most comprehensive available to understand suicide-related behavior and risk among youth referred into and served
through mental health systems of care.

Children's Mental Health Initiative National Evaluation Background

Children and youth receiving services in federally funded systems of care range in
age from birth through 21 years and must have a diagnosis of a mental health disorder that meets standardized diagnostic criteria. The information about suicide
attempt history between 1995 and 2010 is based on caregiver report of suicide attempt collected on more than 35,000 children across years. The bulk of the information in this summary is based on the national evaluation of the system of care
communities initially funded from 2002 through 2006 (N = 7,710). These data were
gathered about youth 6–18 years of age via youth self-report and caregiver report.

Prevalence of Suicide-Related Thoughts and
Behaviors Among Youth Served in Systems of Care

National evaluation results indicate that suicide-related thoughts and behaviors are
prevalent among youth referred into systems of care for mental health services. On
the basis of national evaluation data collected between 1995 and 2010 about more
than 35,000 children and adolescents entering services, 14.2% had a caregiver report
of a previous suicide attempt, and more than half of those (52.2%) had made more
than one attempt.
  CMHI national evaluation data suggest that a large percentage of youth entering systems of care have had intra- and/or interpersonal experiences associated
with suicidal behavior (i.e., risk factors for suicide). Between 40% and 50% of youth
entering services have had prior law enforcement contact, experienced sudden
mood changes, or have histories of alcohol/substance abuse, with a striking 41% reporting suicidal ideation. Further, between 20% and 39% of youth have reports of
anxiety, sleeping problems, social isolation, and physical abuse, with 30% reporting
a prior suicide attempt. Furthermore, 17% of youth enter services with a history of
physical abuse, and 14% report feelings of hopelessness.

**In-Depth Summary of Youth Served in System
of Care Communities Funded from 2002 Through 2006**

The following in-depth summary is based on data about 7,710 youth who have re-ceived services in systems of care. Data were collected from the youth themselves and their caregivers and provide insight into the suicide risk profiles of these youth when they entered systems of care and their experiences and outcomes while re-ceiving services.

Of the 7,710 entering services, 81.3% had no prior attempt of suicide, 3.4% had one prior attempt, and 15.3% had multiple prior attempts. Identifying and grouping youth as a function of their previous suicide attempts is important, because a his-tory of prior suicide attempt is considered one of the strongest predictors of future suicide attempt. When this categorization is used to better understand risk profiles, service experiences, and outcomes of youth entering systems of care, some interest-ing patterns emerge from the national evaluation data, including the following:

- *Reason for referral:* An analysis of the reason for referral into service suggests some variation associated with suicide attempt history. Although the frequency of many presenting problems is relatively consistent regardless of suicide at-tempt history (e.g., adjustment, eating disorders, learning and developmental disabilities, conduct and delinquency, school performance), the percentage of children and adolescents referred for reasons of anxiety, depression, and suicide-related problems increases for youth with single and multiple attempts, respec-tively, over those with no suicide attempts.

- *Risk factors:* The average number of risk factors reported for a youth with mul-tiple prior suicide attempts is greatest (i.e., an average of five risk factors), fol-lowed by that reported for youth with a single prior attempt (i.e., an average of four risk factors) and no prior attempts (i.e., an average of two risk factors). With that said, the family characteristics of youth entering services—specifically, family mental illness, number of adults in the home, youth exposure to a house-hold member with drug or alcohol problems, and living in poverty—are similar for youth regardless of suicide attempt history.

- *School absences:* Approximately 45% of youth at the time of service entry had been suspended or expelled from school. There is a steady increase in the per-centage of youth with chronic absences (i.e., had missed three or more times a week) when comparing youth with no prior suicide attempts (11.9%) with those with a single prior attempt (15.9%) and those with multiple prior attempts (19.0%).

- *Service use:* Service experience data during the first 6 months of care suggest that although more than two thirds of all youth in systems of care are receiving individual therapy, the percentage of youth who receive individual therapy is the highest among youth with multiple prior attempts (78.7%). Additionally, al-though nearly 70% of all youth receive wraparound supports during their first 6 months of care, a higher percentage of youth with suicide attempt histories receive medication, crisis stabilization, psychiatric hospitalization services, and family support services compared with youth with no attempt histories.

- *Risk for future suicide attempt:* Once children and adolescents with multiple at-tempt histories enter systems of care, the data indicate that they remain at high risk for future suicide attempt. Specifically, a greater percentage of youth with multiple prior attempts attempt suicide during their first 6 months of service (12.8%) than those with a single prior attempt (8.8%) and no prior attempt (1.6%).

- *Clinical profiles:* Clinical assessment data of behavioral and emotional problems, life functioning, and behavioral and emotional strengths indicate that youth who present to services with suicide attempt histories have more severe clinical

(continued)

Box 13.1.   *(continued)*

profiles (i.e., significantly more internalizing and externalizing behavior problems and functional impairment; significantly fewer overall behavioral and emotional strengths) than those without suicide attempt histories.

- *Clinical outcomes:* All children—regardless of suicide attempt history—demonstrate significant and positive change at 6 months into services relative to problem behavior, functioning, and strengths. An important additional national evaluation finding is that the probability of reporting suicidal thought or attempt (over the prior 6 months) decreases significantly from intake to 6 months after service entry for youth with suicide attempt histories: Accordingly, although 48% of these youth reported a suicide attempt in the 6 months immediately before entering system of care services, only 17% reported an attempt during their first 6 months of system of care service.

Implications of National Evaluation Results

Collectively, the information gathered through the national evaluation of the CMHI to date, and presented in the preceding sections, underscores that systems of care provide essential infrastructure for youth suicide prevention, intervention, and postvention efforts. Youth at varying levels of risk for suicide-related behavior are identified within system of care environments, and the services provided are tailored to meet their individual and family needs. As a result, the clinical and behavioral outcomes for these youth are positive.

Given the patterns that have emerged from these data, there is a continued need to better understand the service array patterns for youth with multiple-attempt histories as compared with single-attempt histories to ensure that youth and families with chronic histories of suicide attempt—those at greatest risk for future attempt—are receiving the same or augmented levels of monitoring and support as those who have attempted for the first time. Finally, although the data available for this summary did not allow for an examination of suicide risk profile, service experience, or outcomes as they relate to gender identity or sexual orientation, future data collected as a part of the national evaluation of the CMHI will provide that opportunity.

This summary was prepared by Christine M. Walrath of the CMHI National Evaluation Team.

CONCLUSION

Self-harming behaviors among LGBT youth represent a complex interplay between individual-, family-, peer-, community-, and societal-level influences. The literature consistently describes empirical results indicating that LGBT youth are at higher risk for a variety of self-harming behaviors. The conceptual framework presented earlier identifies environmental circumstances, minority identity, general and minority-specific stressors, coping skills, and individual and community social support as factors contributing to the incidence of self-harming behaviors and the overall well-being of LGBT youth (Meyer, 2003, 2010).

The aim of primary prevention of self-harming behaviors is to ensure that children and adolescents, regardless of sexual orientation and gender identity, are able to achieve their full potential for physical and emotional well-being. Primary prevention efforts include providing safe and supportive environments, enacting legislation to protect the safety of LGBT youth, reevaluating institutional practices that undermine positive child and youth development, and building community awareness and capacity to understand and address stressors within these communities. Eliminating personal, interpersonal, and social obstacles associated with institutionalized heterosexism, biphobia, and transphobia, as well as ensuring that all young people can advance personally, contribute to the collective well-being of communities, and be included fully in the life of the community, all serve as protective factors for the well-being of youth.

14

Addressing the Needs of LGBT Youth Who Are Homeless

RACHAEL R. KENNEY, SYLVIA K. FISHER,
MEGAN EDSON GRANDIN, JUSTINE B. HANSON, AND LAURA PANNELLA WINN

One day, when I came home after class, the key to my apartment would not work. The landlord changed the locks; I was evicted. It was 9:00 at night and it was cold and dark. My immediate thought was to ride the subway all night since subway cars have heat and that at least would keep me warm. But the thought of being assaulted by strangers or arrested for sleeping on a subway car made me change my mind.

I remembered seeing people waiting for their trains at Penn Station. At 2:00 in the morning I found myself there, settling to go to sleep on a bench. But then a railroad worker asked me for my ticket. I pretended to look in my bag, though it was clear I did not have one. At that time, the worker asked that I purchase a new ticket or get off the bench.

I left the station and began to walk but by 3:00 in the morning I was exhausted. All I wanted to do was to close my eyes and get some sleep. At last I armed myself with enough courage and went to the office where I worked. I was scared. I knew it would be dark and there would be no heat. But I had no other options.

—Vanessa A. Fuentes

Estimates indicate that 575,000 to 1.7 million unaccompanied youth ages 12 to 17 years experience at least one night of homelessness in the United States each year (Hammer, Finkelhor, & Sedlak, 2002; Robertson & Toro, 1998; Toro, Dworsky, & Fowler, 2007). Unaccompanied youth include runaways, street youth, youth who have "aged out" of the foster care system, those exiting the juvenile justice system, and those who are thrown out of their homes (Toro et al., 2007). Although estimates vary greatly, approximately 20%–40% of these youth identify as a sexual or gender minority (Ray, 2006). These youth experience homelessness as a result of multiple, often interrelated factors, and a growing body of literature documents the risks and vulnerabilities they face (Cochran, Stewart, Ginzler, & Cauce, 2002; Gangamma, Slesnick, Toviessi, & Serovich, 2008; Rew, Whittaker, Taylor-Seehafer, & Smith, 2005; Walls, Potter, & Leeuwen, 2009; Whitbeck, Chen, Hoyt, Tyler, & Johnson, 2004). Although many are employed and even have families, these youth are at significant risk for a host of negative outcomes and are in need of culturally and linguistically competent services that can address their complex and multifaceted service needs. Effective services entail, at a minimum, a guarantee of safety, security, and connections to a broader network of services and supports that can meet these needs.

Although few youth participating in system of care services report histories of homelessness, the prevalence of youth who identify as lesbian, gay, bisexual, and transgender (LGBT) among homeless youth in the United States supports the inclusion of homelessness as a topic addressed in this book. This chapter presents research findings, personal anecdotes of formerly homeless LGBT youth, and information about programs that serve this population. This chapter summarizes the work of the Substance Abuse and Mental Health Services Administration's Homelessness Resource Center (HRC) from 2009 to 2011 when HRC reviewed the services available for LGBT youth who experience homelessness. In February 2010, the HRC assembled an expert panel to better understand the needs of LGBT youth who experience homelessness. A core panel recommendation was development of a model program to address the needs of LGBT youth who are homeless or at risk for homelessness. In response to this need, the HRC conducted a listening tour later that year with programs that serve LGBT youth.[1] The third phase of this project, which is currently underway and being piloted in four cities around the United States, entails the development of a training curriculum for homeless services providers about the needs of LGBT youth.

IDENTIFYING AND ENGAGING THE POPULATION OF FOCUS

What exactly constitutes "youth homelessness"? Youth homelessness is difficult to identify; youth who are homeless often do not "look" homeless, and many youth may not consider themselves homeless. As the anecdote at the start of this chapter indicates, many youth who are homeless are employed. Youth may iden-

---

[1]Listening tour programs included: Youth on Fire, Cambridge, Massachusetts; Larkin Street Youth Services, San Francisco, California; Outside In, Portland, Oregon; The Ruth Ellis Center, Detroit, Michigan; UCAN Host Home Program, Chicago, Illinois; and The Drop In Center at Tulane University, New Orleans, Louisiana.

tify as "travelers," "doubled-up," "couch surfing," or "squatting" (Hyde, 2005). Many youth, especially older youth and youth who have been homeless for longer periods of time, do not access services (Robertson & Toro, 1998).

Furthermore, there is no unified definition of *youth* in homeless services; most programs serve youth from ages 12–25 years, and many research studies use this age range to describe their population of focus. A unified definition of homelessness is also lacking in both the research and practice literature; for example, some funding streams and studies include staying with friends or couch surfing, whereas others may not. As an additional wrinkle, programs and studies vary the sexual and gender minority categories they use to collect data for the purpose of service planning and delivery, and many programs may not collect information about sexual orientation and/or gender identity.

Identifying youth is only half the challenge, followed in quick succession by the difficulty of engaging youth in services. One study in Detroit, Michigan, found that only 2% of homeless youth reported accessing soup kitchens or outreach services, whereas 18% reported using inpatient or outpatient mental health services (Toro & Goldstein, 2000). Hyde (2005) noted that youth resist homeless assistance programs that tend to be "deficit-focused," or focus on challenges, rather than strengths.

HOUSING BEFORE HOMELESSNESS

The HRC estimates that there are up to 640,000 LGBT youth who experience at least one night of homelessness each year, which highlights the importance of this issue for the work of advocates for LGBT youth. Youth become homeless for a myriad of reasons, with family conflict topping the list for both LGBT and non-LGBT youth (Ray, 2006). For LGBT youth, existing family conflict may be exacerbated when they disclose their identities; the Center for American Progress asserts that 77% of clients at the Ali Forney Center in New York City reported that they experienced physical or emotional abuse from family members (Quintana, Rosenthal, & Krehely, 2010). In these situations, family reunification may not be an option, but for many LGBT youth, interventions that foster family acceptance can result in reduced risky behavior and more positive health outcomes (Ryan, Huebner, Diaz, & Sanchez, 2009).

Although foster care can be a safe alternative for youth who face an unsafe situation when they "come out" at home, this is not always the case. Foster parents are more likely to request that LGBT youth be removed from the home and placed elsewhere (compared with non-LGBT youth), often as a result of misperceptions about the implications of the youth's sexuality or gender identity (Clements & Rosenwald, 2007; Mallon, 2001). LGBT youth in group foster care report that staff members do not come to their aid when they are abused by other youth and that staff sometimes imply the youth deserves the abuse

(Mallon, 2001). Moreover, for youth who remain involved with social services until they age out of the system, research suggests that 25% experience homelessness (Ammerman et al., 2004; Cook, Fleishman & Grimes, 1991).

Some foster care and supportive group home programs are developed to serve homeless LGBT youth. In Massachusetts, the Waltham House is designed to serve LGBT and questioning youth, with family reunification a goal for some of the youth in this program. In New York City, the Gramercy Residence of Green Chimneys also provides foster care services to youth who identify as LGBT or are questioning their sexual orientation or gender identity, but the program's primary goal is preparing foster youth for independent living. Other examples include the GLBT Host Home program in Minnesota and Uhlich Children's Advantage Network's (UCAN's) LGBTQ Host Home program in Chicago, Illinois.

HOUSING OPTIONS

There are not many housing options for homeless youth, LGBT and non-LGBT alike. Furthermore, many programs have policies in place that make the housing feel too restrictive for youth already living on their own. Hostile housing situations further limit residential options for LGBT youth and increase the likelihood that LGBT youth will live on the street compared with their non-LGBT peers (Ray, 2006). Even when placed in appropriate transitional or permanent housing, the supportive services necessary to meet the unique, age-appropriate needs of LGBT youth may be lacking or underdeveloped. Also, family reunification should not be ruled out as a housing option for homeless LGBT youth.

One response to the lack of safe housing for homeless LGBT youth is the UCAN Host Home Program, pioneered by The GLBT Host Home Program in Minneapolis, Minnesota. Host Home programs recruit, screen, train, and support adults who open their homes to LGBT youth in need of safe and stable housing. Both the youth and prospective host families are screened extensively, and Host Homes are provided with training and support by UCAN's clinical staff.

A different approach is Castro Housing, a transitional housing model developed by Larkin Street Youth Services (Larkin Street) in San Francisco, California to provide a home setting for LGBT-identified youth who are transitioning out of homelessness. Castro Housing is located in a traditionally LGBT neighborhood in San Francisco and offers 22 units of housing with single-room occupancy units in a hotel and scattered site apartments. The program offers services geared to LGBT youth. Housing is based on a "structured home" model, defined as an environment developed in collaboration among youth and house staff.

Many LGBT-identified homeless youth choose to live on the street and not in homeless shelters or group homes/residences due to discrimination, harassment, trauma, abuse, victimization, and exploitation, because it's a "safer" option. In the agency in which I currently work, the Rainbow Heights Club in Brooklyn, New York, a few young adult clients that aren't street living have stated that they would rather live on the street due to discrimination, harassment, trauma, abuse, victimization, and exploitation.

—J. Danée Sergeant

CHALLENGING AND COMPLEX NEEDS OF HOMELESS LGBT YOUTH

Although a roof over one's head may at least temporarily resolve the immediate challenges of homelessness, more than a place to sleep is often needed. Mental health and trauma are some of the most prevalent challenges for homeless youth. Homeless youth are generally more likely than their non-homeless or "housed" peers to have histories of physical or sexual abuse, placing them at further risk for mental health challenges (Ray, 2006; Rew et al., 2005; Whitbeck et al., 2004). For homeless LGBT youth, research suggests that the prevalence of these challenges is even higher: 73% of homeless LGB youth report suicidal ideation compared with 53% of their homeless non–LGB peers. Homeless LGB-identified youth also experience higher rates of conduct disorder, suicidal behavior, and posttraumatic stress compared with their non–LGB peers (Whitbeck et al., 2004).

Trauma

The state of being homeless itself is traumatic, but trauma for homeless youth often begins before they are homeless, and youth are at increased risk of trauma after they become homeless (Whitbeck & Hoyt, 1999). Estimates of trauma for homeless youth are high: One study that compared LGB and non-LGB homeless youth found that 47% of LGB homeless youth experienced posttraumatic stress disorder compared with 33% of their non–LGB peers. Posttraumatic stress disorder is particularly prevalent among homeless lesbian youth, with estimated rates as high as 59% (Whitbeck et al., 2004).

With this degree of prevalence of trauma, Trauma Informed Care, a widespread practice that is implemented to foster a strength-based approach, offers a critical tool. Training in this practice and trauma more generally helps providers understand how trauma affects health and well-being and teaches them how to create safe physical spaces and interact in ways that are not threatening to individuals who have previously experienced trauma. One Larkin Street provider shared, "When people come in who identify as LGBT, we see that as a strength and as an issue. They have been through so much, demonstrating their resiliency. But the trauma that results from it has to be addressed." Understanding and healing from trauma is a first step toward rebuilding self-esteem. Youth on Fire, a program in Cambridge, Massachusetts, agreed: "Radical acceptance is really profound. You are who you are. We assume everyone who comes in here is a survivor."

Substance Use and Survival Sex

Substance use is often, but not always, closely tied to mental health and trauma. Several studies suggest that homeless LGBT youth have higher rates of substance use compared with their non–LGBT peers who are also homeless because they turn to substances as a way of coping with discrimination (Ray, 2006; Salomonsen-Sautel et al., 2008). Anecdotal evidence also suggests that substance use is a survival tool and a coping mechanism for homeless youth. Sleeping in places not meant for human habitation, and even in some shelters, is unsafe. Many youth use stimulants to stay awake and may, despite their best effort to use substances as a tool, become addicted. Others use substances to cope with mental health challenges.

Youth sometimes use substances to cope with *survival sex,* which involves exchanging sexual behavior for necessities such as money, food, clothing, a place to sleep, or drugs. Substances lower inhibitions so youth can use their bodies to get the things they need. Research also suggests a correlation between familial abuse and survival sex (Greene, Ennett & Ringwalt, 1999). Given that LGBT homeless youth experience, on average, 7.4 more acts of sexual violence during their lifetime than their housed peers (Cochran et al., 2002), it is not surprising that LGBT homeless youth are at especially high risk for engaging in survival sex, which can often, tragically, result in sexual assault (Ray, 2006; Van Leeuwen et al., 2006; Whitbeck et al., 2004). A significant amount of anecdotal evidence suggests that homeless youth rarely report or seek treatment for sexual assault and exploitation, suggesting that the already high prevalence is largely underreported.

The complex overlapping needs of homeless LGBT youth can be overwhelming, resulting in the pathologizing of youth who need respect, acceptance, and safety to begin healing from repeated rejection and to build relationships with providers. Staff can foster this feeling of acceptance and safety by respecting and supporting a young person's goals. As a staff member at the Ruth Ellis Center, a program for homeless youth in Detroit, Michigan, stated, "Don't use your views as the goal you're trying to obtain. It's their goals." In addition, a representative of Larkin Street shared that "the thing that the youth would say is most important is that they get to take ownership of their lives. All this time they couldn't call the shots and be who they are. This is an opportunity to be who they are."

MEETING THE SERVICE NEEDS OF HOMELESS LGBT YOUTH

There is a ceiling that they've experienced in their lives before they come here. They have to live a lie. They feel like because of who they are they can only do so much. Then they come here and hear us ask, "Where do you want to go? What do you want to do?" We try to turn all of the past experiences that youth have into real-world skills and strengths. This is particularly true for transgender youth.

—Larkin Street

Complex challenges necessitate coordinated and responsive services. In an ideal world, agencies would have all needed services under one roof because the more services available in the same place at the same time, the more likely youth are to use them. In most communities, however, complex service delivery systems provide disjointed, uncoordinated services and supports. Referrals and access to services, even those within another part of the same agency, need to be as seamless as possible to ensure success, such as providing transportation, accompanying youth to appointments, and helping youth navigate bureaucratic hurdles.

A seamless referral is not the be-all-end-all solution; the referred provider must be appropriately trained to care for the needs of homeless LGBT youth. The Ruth Ellis Center addresses this issue with a "health navigator" who talks with youth about their experiences after referrals. Said the executive director:

> One of our young people preferred to be called Tamara instead of her given name, Thomas, but the doctor was unwilling to do that. We listen to that feedback and take that into account when making future referrals. It's really important to us that the young people's experiences inform how we do our work.

Unlike services in system of care programs, services that homeless youth access can be fragmented and difficult to navigate. Effective referral practices are essential to ensure that youths' needs are met and to help build collaboration among providers who may not otherwise be connected, so they can leverage their shared skills. For example, Youth on Fire partners with a larger organization to conduct outreach, and this relationship helps identify individuals who are eligible for the program. There is still much work to be done to create coordinated systems of care for homeless youth, and the fragmented service delivery system can sometimes lead to uncomfortable situations for the consumer: "When agencies providing services to youth experiencing homelessness have conflict, it can feel like divorced parents, undermining the work that we do. We need to become a true community of care."

Health Care

Homeless youth face many barriers in accessing health care, but for transgender youth, these barriers may seem impossible to navigate. As previously mentioned, some health care professionals may not be well versed in the needs of this population, and when an understanding, supportive service provider is identified, word travels quickly. At the Drop-In Center at Tulane University in New Orleans, Louisiana, staff noted a large increase in requests for health care for transgender youth in transition. They attributed the increase to a new physician who specialized in these services. Staff noted that "by giving our young people access to her [the new physician], they've really opened themselves to receive the medical attention they need."

One of the primary health concerns for youth who are homeless is sexually transmitted infections, including HIV. In one study, 50% of all homeless youth considered it likely or very likely that they would someday test positive for HIV (Wardenski, 2005), and LGB youth are at a particularly high risk for HIV infection (Gangamma et al., 2008). These disturbing results may reflect the lifelong negative experiences and ill treatment endured by these youth.

Education and Employment

Housing requires money. To earn income you need a job. To be employable you need credentials. Homeless youth often have great difficulty obtaining those credentials and therefore may enter into a long-term cycle of homelessness and poverty. For youth who worry about finding a place to sleep at night, attending school during the day is often low on their list of priorities. For LGBT youth, this reality is exacerbated by the fact that they report more academic struggles than their non-LGBT peers and are at higher risk for dropping out of school (Kosciw, Diaz, & Greytak, 2008). To work through these issues, the Ruth Ellis Center builds bridges to schools, meeting with school boards when a young person is reentering class:

> This way everyone, from superintendent to teacher, is on the same page about the student. When we get resistance from educators we try to inform and train the school faculty as much as we can about the issues these kids face, like protecting them from bullying, and listening to their pronoun and name preferences.

Even with a high school diploma, finding consistent employment for any young person who lacks skills and stable housing is a significant challenge. LGBT youth face the additional barrier of discrimination on the basis of their sexual or gender identity/expression. Fortunately, all of the programs that participated in the HRC's listening tour focus on this issue and offer some level of employment services, including skills development, resume support, and placement programs.

Larkin Street creates opportunities by asking youth what they want to do for employment, but their employment services do not stop there. Employment programs for homeless LGBT youth need to go beyond resume building and interview skills and move toward real relationships between the program and employers. As a staff member at the UCAN Host Home program stated, "It's been about finding allies. We know that even if you find a position, it might not be a healthy place for the young person. Even in cases where the supervisor is an advocate for the youth, peers can create a negative experience."

Once initial relationships with employers are solidified, employers need support to help them best work with youth who are or are formerly homeless. At Outside In in Portland, Oregon, staff maintain open lines of communication with employers, but acknowledge that this is time-consuming work. Larkin Street formalizes this process and engages employers in 2 months of training and assessment, recognizing that relationships with co-workers can be just as important as relationships with supervisors. Peer providers, or staff who once met the eligibility criteria for a homeless youth program who now work for the program, are an increasingly popular approach to homeless program employment services. Programs such as Larkin Street, Outside In, and Youth on Fire recruit and employ program participants to serve as youth peer providers, outreach workers, and liaisons to the target population. Youth are often well connected with other youth, and although youth are often resistant to adults approaching them and providing guidance, common experience with a peer may serve as a foundation to build trust. This practice embodies the principle of consumer involvement, helps programs better access potential consumers who may be leery of traditional service providers, and helps youth staff feel more connected to the program. This is also a tremendous opportunity for youth to share what they gained from the program.

RECOMMENDATIONS FOR HOMELESS SERVICE PROVIDERS

The needs of homeless LGBT youth are similar to the needs of LGBT youth who are housed, but the needs often are more complex because of the previously mentioned challenges. One of the salient service delivery considerations for providers is to decide which services for LGBT youth are best integrated with services for all youth or best delivered separately. Consultations with experts suggest that both of these service models are important, and several of the programs offered both models within their agencies. Experts suggest that programs that include LGBT as well as non-LGBT youth play an important role in normalizing diverse sexual and gender identities/expressions. At the same time, programs focused on LGBT youth celebrate these identities and play a vital role in helping LGBT youth accept, celebrate, and take pride in their identities.

Safe Spaces in Homeless Services

Regardless of whether programs are inclusive of or are exclusively LGBT, service providers should ensure that spaces are safe for youth. System of care principles apply to these programs, but the biggest challenges for homeless service programs are often showers and sleeping quarters. Because many programs do not encounter gender-variant youth on a regular basis and are set up as dorm-style living, the result may be segregation for transgender youth. The National Gay and Lesbian Task Force developed a comprehensive, valuable guide, *Transitioning Our Shelters,* to address many of these issues (Mottet & Ohle, 2003). Making these changes, however, requires an organizational commitment to nondiscrimination and cultural competence from administrative to frontline staff and the executive director (Mottet & Ohle, 2003). Sometimes, formally garnering this support is a challenge.

Creating a safe space requires consumer empowerment, including the employment of consumer providers. All of the listening tour programs involve program participants in decisions about service design, delivery, and evaluation in various ways. For example, at the UCAN Host Home Program, two youth who identify as LGBT participate in their advisory council, where all decisions, from the approval of volunteer host families to program policies, are made by consensus. Youth on Fire has an all-youth advisory board that has a significant role in shaping the culture and making decisions at the drop-in center. Programs that seek consumer input should be prepared to respond accordingly. The Ruth Ellis Center learned this through their youth advisory council. Said one staff member:

> We've tried youth advisory councils in the past, but struggled to implement the requests of the youth. It was defeating. We are rethinking our strategy because you can't ask for youth input and ultimately ignore it. They've been through that before, and it's not positive for anyone.

Youth advisory councils have the ability to empower young people, but programs need policies to review and act on their recommendations.

Staffing and Training

Staffing decisions for programs serving LGBT youth can be challenging. It is important that staff be willing to learn, if not already knowledgeable, about culturally competent practices for LGBT youth. Hiring interviews should include questions about applicants' experiences in the LGBT community and comfort level with working with this population to identify whether the candidate is a good fit for working with homeless LGBT youth.

How staff are selected can also have an impact. For example, the Youth on Fire youth advisory board includes an applicant hiring committee. Applicants meet with the committee, which recommends or denies applicants before they are hired. "This level of control is empowering to our members," said one staff member. "You see a side of applicants that comes out in the youth interviews that does not come out in interviews with other staff members. Sometimes members can better tell if the applicant 'gets it' with regard to GLBT issues."

Many homeless service providers, child welfare workers, and youth advocates lack the knowledge, skills, and language needed to discuss issues of sexual and gender identity with youth. Moreover, these adults may feel uncomfortable or unable to adequately identify and care for LGBT youths' needs. There is an urgent need for LGBT cultural and linguistic competence training for all who serve homeless youth (National Advisory Council on LGBTQ Homeless Youth, 2009). Agencies that serve homeless youth can take the first step toward enhancing their cultural and linguistic competence by conducting an agency self-assessment process to assess readiness to serve LGBT youth. (See Chapter 3 for additional detail.)

Bias and stereotypes can persevere, however, despite comprehensive training. For example, Tulane's Drop-In Center found that some providers and youth held religious perspectives that viewed an LGBT identity as a deficit rather than a strength. Multiple staff from conservative religious backgrounds shared that working with transgender youth was a shocking experience for them. The Drop-In Center recognized that such beliefs were detrimental to clients. Staff learned that the more they engaged with LGBT youth, the more they were able to connect on commonalities. Fostering these relationships helped staff put aside their beliefs that limited their ability to provide culturally competent services when they entered the center. They explained that although they had to experience an adjustment in their attitudes and way of thinking, they ultimately believed in accepting youth for who they are.

Community Connections

Partnering with the LGBT community is at the heart of Castro Housing at Larkin Street. "People in the community were seeing kids on the street and asking what could be done. LGB-specific providers, including our Larkin Street Drop-In Center, came together and thought about the youth that we see and the services they need." Larkin Street recognizes that their housing model was a result of collaboration between "queer-centric" organizations in San Francisco. "If we hadn't been in partnerships with these groups, Castro Housing would not have happened."

Positive adult LGBT role models are critical to helping youth realize their own potential. The Ruth Ellis Center recognized the importance of partnering with LGBT adult advocacy groups: "The importance of how integrated we've become with LGBT adult advocacy groups cannot be overemphasized," reports the executive director. "They provide the support, advocacy, and role models necessary to make what we do possible." The Ruth Ellis Center has developed relationships with Black Men Together; Parents, Families and Friends of Lesbians and Gays (PFLAG) Detroit; The Bears; and other community groups. These partnerships help youth to develop mentor relationships with caring adults and find a sense of belonging within the community.

The need for LGBT partnerships includes services specific for transgender youth who represent a small percentage of homeless youth, but who have unique emotional and physical needs. Youth on Fire has worked to provide a higher level of care for these youth through a partnership with TransCEND, a sister program focused on transgender women. TransCEND offers case management, provides support for name changes and gender alterations on identification, makes referrals to doctors who are trans-friendly, and provides physical and emotional guidance during transition.

Working with community partners, including police departments and school districts, is integral to the success of program efforts on behalf of LGBT youth who are homeless or at risk of homelessness. After staff at the Ruth Ellis Center repeatedly reached out to local police and informed the officers about services, staff now say the officers "bring kids to us [Ruth Ellis Center] instead of arresting them." Center staff also emphasized their efforts to build relationships with their department of child and family services. "We've engaged in capacity building with child protective services that was very positive. They have now become the impromptu community ambassador, referring calls from families struggling with their LGBT child to us."

Expanded Public Awareness

Many listening tour programs emphasized that changing community perceptions about LGBT youth is important. Across programs, staff and youth are involved in various public awareness activities. As one provider shared:

> There is such a need for communities to understand the dynamics of LGBT youth homelessness. These young people feel isolation on so many levels—when they look for work, go to school, access social services—it spills everywhere. Increased awareness on a larger scale could help reduce family and community rejection.

A common way to expand awareness is through public education. The Ruth Ellis Center suggests hosting community education panels to support open dialogue. "Broader education for the public is important for improving the lives of LGBT youth. We need to have more discussion forums for providers and parents to work through issues so that there is a community of support. Understanding follows awareness." Larkin Street and the UCAN Host Home Program have focused on increasing awareness with the adult LGBT community.

The Ruth Ellis Center also emphasized the importance of "taking any opportunity we can to educate." Staff often take calls from concerned community members and use the conversations as educative opportunities.

Outreach is also an effective method for enhancing the community's awareness and knowledge. The Ruth Ellis Center reaches out to inform schools, community services, and the child welfare system about their services for LGBT youth. The executive director explained, "We've created a reputation now that if you give us a call, we can help. We get three to four calls a week, from parents who want to remove their kids from home, or from young people who don't feel safe with their families." Many of the programs also conduct outreach with landlords and employers to destigmatize LGBT youth.

SUPPORTING HOMELESS LGBT YOUTH: DATA AND RESEARCH NEEDS

I have been on both sides of the spectrum, one heavier than the other, but that's changing as I am progressing by means of employment experience and by being a research-concentrated MSW student at Fordham. I was an LGBT-identified homeless youth that has, many times, ended up living on the street. And, now, being completely immersed on the other side of that spectrum, I notice gaps in literature left and right, because I know what to look for. Also, having a substance abuse background, both from being a very actively using addict who's now in recovery (over 3 years clean) and having my B.S. in substance abuse, I know why I used and why many other homeless LGBT identified kids use as well. I have these tools that allow me to very easily zero-in on what's missing.

—J. Danée Sergeant

LGBT youth experience homelessness at alarming rates, and there is an urgent need to more accurately document homelessness among LGBT youth. Further, although promising service delivery models for LGBT homeless youth exist throughout the nation, research is needed to substantiate the effectiveness of the programs that serve them. Many programs report heartfelt stories of success, but do not implement rigorous data collection to provide quantitative support for this anecdotal information. Research also needs to identify effective interventions that successfully build, translate, and disseminate current knowledge so that providers can alter their practices to provide culturally and linguistically competent care to homeless LGBT youth. Data help to comprehensively document the scope of the problem, assess needs, advocate for resources, and develop appropriate services.

Some communities are taking steps to improve the quality of data by including information about youth in biannual homeless counts, which are mandated in most communities by the U.S. Department of Housing and Urban Development. This activity does not come without challenges, however. Homeless youth are mobile and difficult to reach. They may not identify as homeless, and they may not feel comfortable identifying as LGBT. Furthermore, large numbers of youth who experience homelessness experience short-term, episodic homelessness that needs to be defined operationally for data collection purposes and that affects the ability to reach this population.

SUPPORTING HOMELESS LGBT YOUTH: POLICY AND PRACTICE

The National Advisory Council on LGBTQ Homeless Youth (NAC) was created to address the needs of LGBT and questioning (LGBTQ) youth by improving national planning and policy, improving local communities' responses to LGBTQ youth at risk of or experiencing homelessness, and enhancing the ability of service providers to meet the needs of these youth (Robertson & Toro, 1998). NAC (2009) has recommended practices for serving homeless LGBT youth, in particular fostering an inclusive environment in which LGBT youth are safe and respected. Other recommendations are included in the following sections.

Improving Practices: Recommendations for Employees Serving LGBT Homeless Youth

- Appropriately address LGBT identity during intake process.
- Support access to education, medical care, and mental health care.
- Support transgender and gender nonconforming youth participants.
- Inform LGBT youth about local LGBT programs and services.

Improving Organizational Culture: Recommendations for Administrators and Supervisors

- Adopt and implement written nondiscrimination policies.
- Adopt confidentiality policies.
- Provide LGBT competency training to all agency employees and volunteers.
- Establish comprehensive recruitment and hiring practices.
- Develop agency connections to LGBT organizations and the LGBT community.
- Collect and evaluate data.

In addition, the Center for American Progress has developed policy recommendations for a federal response to addressing the needs of gay and transgender homeless youth (Quintana et al., 2010). For example,

- Strengthen and support families with gay and transgender children so youth do not become homeless.
- Establish schools as a safe refuge for all children and youth.
- Take concrete steps to expand housing options for gay and transgender homeless youth.

Each state, city, and county is different, and no single one-size-fits-all model exists for programs that serve LGBT homeless youth in these varied jurisdictions. The common thread for programs participating in this listening tour is the provision of a welcoming environment, ranging from the overt display of welcoming symbols (e.g., pink triangle, rainbow flag) to the adoption of welcoming approaches from front desk staff to clinical and service providers. This approach and related efforts are likely to reach and support the largest number of homeless LGBT youth. As Larkin Street staff stated, "We assume everyone who comes in here is a survivor." Youth who identify as LGBT and experience homelessness tend to be fiercely resilient and resourceful. Many will find their way back into housing regardless of whether they engage in services.

I've come a long way since those nights of sleeping in the office. There are still times when I do not have any money, but the difference between then and now is that I have developed close relationships with people at work and through my volunteer work with mental health organizations. These individuals help me, financially and emotionally.

During the time that I was homeless, I never stopped working or going to school. The benefits of my persistence became clear last year when I was promoted to a new position within my organization. A few months later, I moved into a bigger, more adequate room. If all goes well, I anticipate graduating from college in June 2012 with a degree in international relations. My plan is to attend graduate school and pursue a master's in public affairs or public policy.

—Vanessa A. Fuentes

15

Social Marketing Efforts to Promote Social Inclusion and Help-Seeking Behavior

Lisa Rubenstein, Mojdeh Motamedi,
Ryan C. LaLonde, and Cody Mooneyhan

This chapter discusses social marketing as a tool to promote resiliency and help-seeking behavior among lesbian, gay, bisexual, and transgender (LGBT) youth and youth with LGBT parents or caregivers; foster social inclusion; and reduce the discrimination that these individuals often face. Furthermore, social marketing is a valuable strategy for enhancing cultural and linguistic competency in systems of care. The chapter begins with the important considerations related to youth outreach and how social marketing can serve as a strategy to reach out to and successfully collaborate with youth. Five social marketing campaigns[1] are provided as case studies to help you understand your audiences. The following lessons learned from these and other campaigns are discussed:

1. When promoting resilience among LGBT youth, one size *does not* fit all.

2. Collaboration with youth as well as LGBT advocacy and like-minded organizations is crucial for success.

3. Messages for youth should be perceived as authentic, current, and aligned with culture and language; effective messages for youth may be vastly different from what would work with an adult audience and different among subgroups of youth (in particular, youth with LGBT family members as well as American Indian and Alaska Native (AI/AN) LGBT and two-spirit youth).

4. Increase your campaign's impact by optimizing when, where, and how its messages are delivered.

---

[1]A *social marketing campaign* is a course of action that includes planning, development, implementation, and evaluation to effect social and behavioral change (Rodriguez, Rubenstein, & Huff, 2008).

5. Audiences other than LGBT youth should be engaged, ready, and able to accommodate the behavior change that you want them to make (in particular, communities, providers, schools, and families).

The chapter concludes with lessons learned and recommendations for future research.

REACHING OUT TO YOUTH: IMPORTANT CONSIDERATIONS

Despite the need for increased outreach by service systems, youth outreach in general is a difficult task, and reaching out to LGBT youth and youth with LGBT parents or caregivers in particular can be even more difficult. Some communicators focus mostly on how youth are open to learning and using new technologies, but disregard the fact that some youth may have little or no access. Keeping up with these technologies (e.g., the latest web services, portable devices, other media) is very demanding because they are constantly changing.

Another fundamental difficulty in reaching youth is that they are always in transition, with new members coming in from childhood as older members transition to adulthood. Finally, a major challenge in reaching youth has to do with the relatively rapid physiological, psychological, and social changes that occur during this time. These developmental changes make it necessary for communicators to understand that youth are neither children nor adults. Most youth are not yet able or legally allowed to undertake a full range of adult responsibilities and decisions, but they also are not necessarily so young that they completely rely on the decisions of parents or caregivers.

UNDERSTANDING SOCIAL MARKETING

Social marketing is used widely by organizations promoting attitudinal and behavior change in areas ranging from saving endangered species to issues related to LGBT youth and youth with LGBT parents or caregivers. System of care communities often use social marketing strategies to reach out to potential partners in their communities, increase social inclusion of youth with mental health challenges, and create opportunities for long-term sustainability of system of care values and principles. In *Making Health Communication Programs Work*, a highly regarded social marketing manual for communicators working in public health, the National Cancer Institute (1989) defines social marketing as

> The application and adaptation of commercial marketing concepts to the planning, development, implementation, and evaluation of programs that are designed to bring about behavior change to improve the welfare of individuals or their society. Social marketing emphasizes thorough market research to identify and

understand the intended audience and what is preventing them from adopting a certain health behavior, and to then develop, monitor, and constantly adjust a program to stimulate appropriate behavior change. Social marketing programs can address any or all of the traditional marketing mix variables—product, price, place, and promotion. (p. 251)

Social marketing always aims to change *behavior* in addition to attitudes and perceptions. A social marketing effort involves constant evaluation. If outreach through billboards does not work, messages may be adapted for other channels, such as radio stations that community members are likely to listen to in their cars while driving. A social marketing effort is intended to get people to use car seats, for example, rather than simply making them aware that they should use them. This ongoing evaluation and fine-tuning requires the communication tactics to be audience-driven, as well as culturally and linguistically competent, making social marketing much more of a "natural fit" with system of care core values than other types of communication methods. Both social marketing and system of care strategies are guided by the people being served.

One trans-theoretical model of health behavior change details the six stages that an individual or group can undergo before adopting a new behavior (Prochaska & Velicer, 1997). This behavior change model is applicable to the same types of change that social marketing campaigns seek to achieve, especially because many focus on health-related issues. Although it is highly unlikely that all individuals within an audience will start at the same stage, a social marketer's goal ultimately is the same: getting 100% of the intended audience to adopt the new behavior. These stages include the following:

1. *Precontemplation:* Individuals do not intend to take action in the foreseeable future; they may be uninformed of the need to change their behavior or may have tried to change it and have since given up.

2. *Contemplation:* Individuals are aware of the need to change and intend to do so, but they have not yet started to change a behavior.

3. *Preparation:* Individuals intend to take action to change a behavior and have a plan for doing so.

4. *Action:* Individuals have started the change process and are showing measurable signs of progress.

5. *Maintenance:* Individuals have made most, if not all, of the changes that they wanted to make, but are still doing things to prevent losing the progress they have made.

6. *Termination:* The change is 100% complete, and the audience has no temptation to stray from the desired behavior.

We turn now to examining how to apply social marketing principles to collaborate with LGBT youth and youth with LGBT parents or caregivers.

UNDERSTANDING YOUR AUDIENCE

A first step in any social marketing or communication effort is to identify your audience and the behavior that you would like them to do. If you are reading this chapter, your audience is somewhere within or related to LGBT youth and youth with LGBT family members, and you are seeking to reduce discrimination or promote help-seeking behavior, resiliency, social supports, coping skills, engagement, acceptance, awareness, or social inclusion among LGBT youth or youth with LGBT parents or caregivers.

The populations of LGBT youth and youth with LGBT family members include a wide range of different characteristics and needs and many different subpopulations, including questioning, intersex, and two-spirit individuals. These subgroups may vary greatly in their experiences related to stigma and discrimination or when seeking mental health services and supports. Children of LGBT parents or caregivers vary in their family structure, as they may have at least one caregiver (i.e., parent, grandparent, foster parent, guardian) who is LGBT. As a social marketer and communicator reaching out to these audiences, you will need to identify exactly who you intend to reach and then research all facets of message development: who, what, when, where, why, and how.

To ensure that a message is as effective as possible, you should first identify a single primary audience and then learn all you can about that audience. Once you have a firm understanding of what will and will not resonate with your audience, you can then refine messages and develop tools that work for them. Part of identifying your audience involves identifying subgroups within an overall population, referred to as *segmenting* (Turning Point Social Marketing National Excellence Collaborative, n.d.). To segment an audience, you need to identify subgroups according to common characteristics relevant to the behavior to be changed, such as age, culture, race, ethnicity, location, socioeconomic orientation, language, education level, behaviors, attitudes, or physical characteristics (Argenti, Howell, & Beck, 2005).

After you select your audience, it is necessary to learn as much as possible about their characteristics, needs, strengths, and challenges. Review available literature about effective social marketing campaigns that have been directed toward this audience, however limited, to save valuable time and expense in your own campaign development and avoid pitfalls.

Our review of the social marketing literature reveals very little data about campaigns focusing on resiliency in LGBT youth or children of LGBT parents or caregivers as it relates to mental health. There is literature, however, about campaigns that focus on behaviors that identify or reduce risk, such as HIV and suicide prevention. Promoting risk reduction is not the same as promoting resilience or help-seeking behavior, but campaigns focusing on risk reduction serve as valuable case studies and provide important lessons learned to social marketers and communicators looking to reach similar audiences. Although the following description of the Trevor Project's effort is not comprehensive, it does provide an overview of a recent campaign intended for LGBT youth. Additional examples that we have examined are woven into the rest of this chapter and other chapters in this volume (see Chapters 12, 13, and 14). The lessons learned that follow this vignette should be valuable to social marketers or communicators seeking to engage the same audiences.

The following case study is based on personal communication with R. Lombardini on January 4, 2011, and the Trevor Project's (2009) full report of "I'm Glad I Failed."

The Trevor Project emerged from a very unusual and unexpected place. The Trevor Project is the outgrowth of the 1994 Academy Award–winning short film, *Trevor*, a comedy/drama about a gay 13-year-old who attempts suicide after being rejected by friends because of his sexuality. The project was founded by the film's writer (James Lecesne), its director/producer (Peggy Rajski), and its producer (Randy Stone) to support the nation's first and only nationwide crisis and suicide prevention hotline available 24 hours a day, 7 days a week for youth who are LGBT or questioning their sexual orientation or gender identity. In addition to the hotline, the Trevor Project provides support to youth through its web site, as well as resources for educators and caregivers. In September 2008, the Trevor Project launched the "I'm Glad I Failed" campaign to raise awareness about this hotline, now called the "Trevor Lifeline," and about how what people say can seriously harm youth.

The campaign primarily focuses on promoting the lifeline and other messages disseminated through schools and in magazines that LGBT youth are likely to read. The campaign identified these channels through focus groups with youth from around the country, conducted in person by a professional firm with social marketing research experience. The Trevor Project developed the message "I'm Glad I Failed" on the basis of focus group results and consultation with an advisory committee of 20 children and youth ages 6–24 years located across the country. This message accompanied four posters and four online ads, each of which included a youth: one Asian female, one Latina female, one African American male, and one Caucasian male. By design, these individuals appeared neither LGBT nor heterosexual, mostly because the Trevor Project believed that to convey a person's orientation correctly through appearance would have required more resources for testing and development than were available at the time. The campaign also created collateral materials, such as lifeline cards and a curriculum. The cards include basic information about the Trevor Lifeline (e.g., phone number) to share with students. The curriculum is a teaching tool for educators who discuss the subject in their classrooms. These materials and the posters were shipped to ensure that recipients understood the full context and importance of suicide prevention for LGBT students.

The Trevor Project's measures of success for the campaign were straight-forward and relatively easy to track. First, they wanted to measure whether or not more youth were using the lifeline than before the campaign began. Second, the Trevor Project wanted to be sure that the images and messages that the campaign created actually resonated with the intended audience. The Trevor Project saw a 58% increase in call volume from 2008 to 2009. Although the top reason for calling was general inquiries, there also was a noticeable increase in calls from youth who might have a future risk for attempting suicide.

The Trevor Project wanted to ensure that the increase in the suicide lifeline's usage was driven by the campaign, rather than an increase in the number of youth contemplating suicide. The Trevor Project conducted an online survey of LGBT and questioning youth and learned that 1) youth who had attempted suicide or considered attempting suicide strongly identified with the stories and images of the youth on the posters, and 2) most youth were very likely to refer someone to the Trevor Project after viewing its campaign.

WHAT CAMPAIGNS TEACH US ABOUT OUTREACH TO LGBT YOUTH AND YOUTH WITH LGBT FAMILY MEMBERS

Our review of campaigns can be summarized into five lessons about outreach to LGBT youth, which are discussed in the following sections.

Lesson 1: When Promoting Resilience Among LGBT Youth, One Size *Does Not* Fit All

Tailoring messages and channels for individual audiences is fundamental to most of the work that social marketers and communicators undertake, and this is especially true for LGBT youth. As with any campaign, culture and ethnicity play a major role in the effectiveness of messages. Choudhury et al. (2009) illustrated how large of a role race and culture play in message perception. They observed that South Asian LGBT individuals value a sense of being a part of their community and family, but considered "LGBT" to be inherently outside of the South Asian community—a Western "disease" (Choudhury et al., 2009). Because of this perception, Choudhury et al. concluded that many South Asian LGBT youth do not seek services because they do not want to be isolated from their community or be shamed and embarrassed. For social marketers and communicators, this means that they should create messages that reach LGBT youth in ways that are sensitive to their perceptions of community, culture, and race (e.g., develop messages that focus on the entire South Asian community rather than messages that single out South Asian LGBT; Choudhury et al., 2009).

LGBT youth face unique challenges that can make it difficult to be resilient, including the following:

- Some LGBT youth face stress and negative emotions related to being different or marginalized, the "coming out" process, antigay violence and discrimination, and oppression (National Youth Advocacy Coalition [NYAC], 2004). STARS for Children's Mental Health, a system of care grantee, has addressed the stress associated with the coming out process by providing information on their web site, which has been so successful that information related to the coming out process is one of their web site's top three resources (C. Woessnera & T. Freed, personal communication, September 15, 2010).
- Some LGBT youth seeking to find a sense of belonging, socialize within the LGBT community, or find relationships may explore places they should not be legally accessing, such as bars (NYAC, 2004). This challenge could be addressed by fostering a sense of community among and within age-appropriate groups and by creating safe social spaces for youth to come together.
- Addressing the lack of support from peers and family (NYAC, 2004) could possibly help LGBT youth become more willing to seek support and deter them from engaging in unhealthy coping mechanisms to deal with these challenges.
- LGBT youth may be more likely to engage in smoking, which has also been found to correlate with the use of illicit drugs (NYAC, 2004; Zickler, 2000).
- LGBT youth may be less likely to be able (or want) to access health care because of a history of trauma from insensitive providers or a lack of insurance (NYAC, 2004).

Transgender youth face additional and unique stigma. For instance, openly transgender youth may not be able to participate in activities that contribute to their well-being, such as sports, because of stereotypes about transgender athletes (Lambda Legal & NYAC, 2008). This may be important when considering the challenges transgender youth encounter or whether physical activity will be a part of your campaign. To help address this stigma, you may want to call attention to positive transgender athlete role models from the Olympic and professional levels, as well as highly regarded recreational or amateur transgender athletes. The Sports Project at the National Center for Lesbian Rights can assist with finding positive transgender athlete role models to highlight in your campaign.

Understanding how culture, race, and LGBT identity affect how your messages will be perceived will position you to promote a sense of community among LGBT youth. Promoting community among LGBT youth serves to facilitate the ability of your audience(s) to act on your messages because they will have the social supports they need to move from a contemplation stage to a preparation stage and beyond. Several campaigns have found that promoting community has been useful in this way. For instance, focus groups for the "I Love My Boo" HIV prevention campaign (Mathis, 2010; not described in this chapter) show that messages, strategies, and tactics that nurture a sense of self, being cared for and respected, and community belonging increase the potential for developing tight-knit communities among LGBT youth, especially where no such communities currently exist.

Lesson 2: Collaboration with Youth as well as LGBT Advocacy and Other Like-Minded Organizations Is Crucial for Success

Because collaboration is a common theme among all of the campaigns reviewed or featured for this chapter, and because youth interact with many individuals representing numerous groups and organizations, it makes sense that a campaign would attempt to engage youth in as many of these venues as possible and appropriate. After developing relationships with youth, you can begin promoting messages or offering youth–friendly programs, such as youth groups that openly discuss issues related to your campaign's messages.

The Gay, Lesbian & Straight Education Network (GLSEN) and NYAC in particular have found that collaborating with youth and LGBT organizations can help connect LGBT youth with others in the community, create a safe and LGBT youth–friendly environment, gather input for campaign plans and messages, and promote a campaign (D. Presgraves, personal communication, September 15, 2010; J.B. Beeson, personal communication, September 24, 2010). Such collaborations can become the driving force of a campaign, which was the case for GLSEN's National Day of Silence, a day when thousands of students and groups vow to be silent for an entire day in order to bring attention to and end the bullying and harassment of LGBT students (D. Presgraves, personal communication, September 15, 2010; GLSEN, 2009). GLSEN has found that gay–straight alliances and collaborations with adults give youth a sense of being cared for and supported (D. Presgraves, personal communication, September 15, 2010), which can promote resiliency.

Another method of collaboration involves recruiting opinion leaders who combine peer education and social marketing. For example, the Teen Alcohol and Other Drug Abuse Prevention Training program focused on addressing drug abuse among LGBT youth. To reach its population of focus and develop effective campaign materials for "Out. Proud. Sober." (AIDS Action, 2001), the program has collaborated with members of high-risk populations who are popular with other members to advocate behavior change at the community level. Community opinion leaders can be identified through your collaborations with LGBT and youth organizations.

Homeless LGBT youth are among the most difficult audiences to reach, but collaboration may go a long way in helping your campaign engage these individuals. Working with child- and family-serving agencies and organizations may be particularly useful, and working with schools is particularly important, as research shows that missing class contributes to longer term homelessness for LGBT youth (Kosciw, Diaz, & Greytak, 2008). Collaborating with child welfare organizations and family organizations can also help your organization reach homeless LGBT youth or LGBT youth at risk for homelessness. Housing organizations, federal agencies, mental health providers, suicide prevention programs, substance abuse reduction programs, HIV programs, homeless shelters, faith-based organizations, national organizations for homeless youth, and organizations providing services to sex workers share common goals in reaching homeless youth and provide additional sources for collaboration (Helping Individual Prostitutes Survive, n.d.; Homelessness Resource Center [HRC], 2010; Ray, 2006). Organizations addressing trauma, justice, and legal issues may also be able to help provide resources for homeless LGBT youth (HRC, 2010; Livny & Guarino, 2010).

Lesson 3: Messages for Youth Should Be Perceived as Authentic, Current, and Aligned with Culture and Language

Effective messaging covers more than just a single tag line, slogan, logo, image, design, or URL. A campaign's messaging covers all of these items, as well as anything else that communicates a message. The "You Know Different" campaign for increasing HIV testing among African American and sexual minority youth, for instance, shows that a critical aspect of effective messaging is the use of and respect for youth- and LGBT-friendly images (J.B. Beeson, personal communication, September 24, 2010; NYAC, n.d.b). This campaign found that selecting an image that resonates with and reflects youth in their community motivates youth to respond (J.B. Beeson). Interestingly, NYAC found that the youth images used were perceived differently from one location to another, despite the advisory board's belief that sexual orientation needed to be reflected in the images. For instance, urban youth preferred subtle images of youth with an ambiguous gender, reflecting the "fluidity" of gender in urban areas. In rural areas, however, where heterosexism was a barrier making gender less "fluid," the campaign used images of an easily identifiable rural male youth without an explicit sexual orientation. For communities such as those in South Florida, the campaign used images of easily identifiable gay males who could be found in the same place gay youth in that community frequented, such as clubs and bars.

STARS's campaign shows that images are not the only aspect of messaging that can vary widely among audiences. They discovered that even the language in a URL mattered when it came to messaging. They found that the words that resonate for youth may be perceived very differently, even oppositely, by adults who had reservations about the youth's choice of the word *queer* in queerheartland.org.

Effective campaigns intended for LGBT youth have found that it is necessary for messages to retain an edgy and attention-grabbing component. Focus
groups conducted for NYAC have shown that youth prefer hard-hitting and
direct messages related to HIV that captured their attention. In the focus groups,
youth expressed that they believe the reality of HIV is harsh and that messaging
needed to reflect this reality (NYAC, n.d.b). For example, youth said they liked
messages that depict reality such as the "Truth" antitobacco commercial adver-
tisements with their depiction of death as a result of smoking, as opposed to
including messaging with celebrities perceived to be too rich to relate to the
youths' sense of reality. Nevertheless, NYAC was unsure about whether to trust
their focus group's perspectives. Their campaign's advisory committee initially
wanted youth who could be easily identified as LGBT in their campaign images. Focus group results, however, indicated that youth did not prefer that
every image clearly be identifiable as LGBT, so the campaign chose to stay true
to their audience's perspectives and included images that did not suggest a specific sexual orientation (J.B. Beeson, personal communication, September 24,
2010).

Similarly, the Trevor Project conducted focus groups that confirmed that
youth preferred hard-hitting messages because these types of messages best captured their attention. Although the Trevor Project contemplated changing their
overarching message from "I'm Glad I Failed" to something less provocative,
they ultimately sided with their focus group findings and retained the original
messaging. This decision proved successful, as the ironic, hard-hitting message
contributed to a compelling campaign and led to an increase in call volume
to their suicide lifeline (R. Lombardini, personal communication, September 14,
2010).

Getting youth to take the next step and act on a message, however, requires more than just grabbing their attention. The message should also involve
a great deal of creativity to get them to act. NYAC learned this during their
campaign. To have youth attend events where HIV tests were being administered, the campaign did not directly promote them as HIV testing activities.
Instead, these activities were combined with, and promoted as, dances or other
popular events. Once at the event, youth received information on HIV, which
allowed the community-based organizations to gain access to youth who might
not otherwise pay any attention to their messages or act on them. Furthermore,
to ensure that youth actually read campaign messages and information on promotional flyers, these flyers served as tickets into the events (J.B. Beeson, personal communication, September 24, 2010).

Youth with LGBT Family Members

According to Children of Lesbians and Gays Everywhere (COLAGE), many
youth with LGBT family members consider themselves part of the LGBT community, regardless of their own sexual orientation or gender identity/expression.

Some may even refer to themselves as "culturally queer." As members of the community, children with LGBT family members also may have a unique understanding about LGBT issues. Therefore, campaigns should welcome and encourage these youth to take leadership roles when such roles exist. Although they consider themselves part of the same community, there is a tendency to assume incorrectly that LGBT youth and youth with LGBT family members have the same experiences and needs (Bailey, 1995). This means that youth with LGBT family members are likely to have different experiences in school, health care settings, and in the community than those of their family members or counterparts who are LGBT. COLAGE recommends recognizing the unique needs of youth with LGBT family members by providing information and resources regarding their experiences as opposed to only focusing on providing information regarding the experiences of LGBT youth (COLAGE, 2010a).

Youth with LGBT family members may experience exclusion and harassment, especially in schools, because their community may not accept or include their families and LGBT parents or caregivers in some school activities (Kosciw & Diaz, 2008). To overcome this exclusion and isolation, some campaigns may need to offer youth with LGBT family members additional support, for instance, encouraging LGBT family members to express that their family is "normal" by establishing relationships with community members and sharing their story rather than waiting until there is a problem before speaking with others such as school staff (Wooten, 2008).

A campaign should not overlook youth with transgender or gender-variant parents or caregivers who may experience bullying, stigma, and discrimination in public differently than children of LGB parents or caregivers. Transgender identity is based on gender identity, which is almost always visible to other individuals. LGB identity may not always be visibly obvious. COLAGE (2010b) has found that a family with a transgender member may experience a greater amount of bullying and discrimination when they are in public. Youth with transgender parents or caregivers can benefit from information about what it means to be transgender, how to explain their situation to others, and which pronouns to use. Youth may also struggle more with their parent or caregiver coming out and express transphobia because of the social gender norms they have learned. Campaigns can support these youth by focusing on the strengths of the transitioning process, such as becoming more open-minded and learning more about gender identity and expression (Canfeld-Lenfest, 2008).

Campaigns should also be aware that other barriers to care exist for youth with LGBT family members, and these barriers may need to be addressed before youth can make any substantive changes in their behaviors. Youth are concerned that family members could lose their jobs should the youth seek help. This makes it very important for social marketing efforts to direct the youth to safe environments where they can safely share their concerns, such as with peers who have LGBT family members. In addition, some youth who have two parents

of the same gender may avoid seeking help because they are concerned that
if they seek health services for themselves, only one parent will be allowed to
accompany them to the doctor or hospital (B. Teper, personal communication,
September 14, 2010).

American Indian and Alaska Native LGBT and Two-Spirit Youth

Less information is available about AI/AN LGBT and two-spirit youth than
about other LGBT groups. A review of existing literature and web searches revealed very little information, so we consulted with Miriam Bearse, Tribal
Child Welfare Specialist, at the National Resource Center for Tribes, under the
auspice of the Tribal Law and Policy Institute in Los Angeles, California. Miriam has been practicing social marketing to AI/AN audiences, including youth,
for approximately 10 years (M.L. Bearse, personal communication, February 8,
2011).

Bearse identifies several factors that help explain why there are so few social marketing campaigns directed toward AI/AN LGBT and two-spirit youth
or AI/AN youth with LGBT and two-spirit parents or caregivers, including
disenfranchisement, lack of knowledge, and bias. Although the size of the AI/AN
population is relatively small, AI/AN populations can reach 10%–15% or more
of the total population in some areas. Many well-meaning individuals who
design campaigns around LGBT or related issues are unaware of the needs of
AI/AN LGBT and two-spirit individuals, the cultural needs of AI/AN youth
in general, and how to reach out and collaborate respectfully with AI/AN organizations that may serve an AI/AN LGBT and two-spirit population. Sometimes, non-Native individuals may not think about including AI/AN LGBT
and two-spirit individuals in outreach efforts, which may reflect the invisibility
and biased tokenism related to AI/AN individuals in the dominant culture
(M.L. Bearse, personal communication, February 8, 2011).

Bearse also points out that some AI/AN organizations and tribes do not
typically talk about LGBT and two-spirit issues publicly, particularly in non-
urban areas, and most do not have funds to do social marketing campaigns unless directly related to specific grants. As a result, reaching out to AI/AN LGBT
and two-spirit youth may be left to social marketers within broader campaigns.
The responsibility then falls on individual social marketers to become aware of
LGBT and two-spirit youth needs as they relate to the campaign, to find appropriate partners to help with efforts, and to distribute materials through channels
that can reach AI/AN youth.

Once a campaign has identified a need to reach out to AI/AN youth,
LGBT and two-spirit or any other group for that matter, a common pitfall is assuming that a "general multicultural" campaign that includes photos of AI/AN
youth is something with which they will identify. According to Bearse, campaigns that mindfully reach out to AI/AN youth consider the specific needs of
the youth in their community, what tribe(s) they are from, other cultures with

which they interact, and other characteristics. Involving AI/AN youth and local AI/AN providers (tribes or urban providers) in the development of a social marketing campaign can help greatly with successful outreach.

An effective campaign that increases help-seeking behaviors must account for the trauma and stigma that AI/AN LGBT and two-spirit individuals have endured. Colonialism has left a legacy of multigenerational trauma among AI/AN individuals, which has contributed to a devaluing of their native culture (Meyer-Cook & Labelle, 2004). Before colonialism, LGBT/two-spirit individuals were embraced and honored for the gifts they shared with their community, such as listening, sensitivity, softness, and keeping balance. Colonialism forced European values and gender roles on AI/AN individuals, resulting in a dearth of elders who can convey the rich traditional LGBT and two-spirit history that existed before colonialism and serve as positive role models.

As a result of being shunned and oppressed from outside cultures and sometimes within their own culture, some AI/AN LGBT and two-spirit youth resort to leaving their native culture and community in search of acceptance in urban areas. However, even within these communities, LGBT and two-spirit youth encounter difficulties and are still susceptible to unhealthy coping mechanisms. Overall, the numerous challenges AI/AN LGBT and two-spirit youth face has led to a feeling of being devalued and puts them at high risk for engaging in unhealthy coping mechanisms (Meyer-Cook & Labelle, 2004). To address the lack of two-spirit elders, a social marketing campaign can encourage the acceptance of AI/AN LGBT and two-spirit youth through strategies that call attention to the positive history of AI/AN LGBT and two-spirit youth and promote a new generation of related role models.

There is a wide range among AI/AN communities in how AI/AN LGBT and two-spirit individuals are referenced, as well as other cultural differences. Accordingly, some cultural considerations a campaign should undertake include, but are not limited to, the following:

- Take into account the terms youth and AI/AN communities use in their community. Terms may include *LGBT, two-spirit,* or specific tribal terms (e.g., *nadleeh* in the Navajo language). If unclear, use LGBT and two-spirit terminology, but with the awareness that some individuals may or may not use "two-spirit" as an identity.

- Sex, sexuality, and gender are typically not openly discussed in AI/AN culture. This does not necessarily mean, however, that there is a lack of acceptance; rather, it may simply mean that it is not a topic of open conversation. As much as possible, emphasize the acceptance of AI/AN LGBT and two-spirit youth by focusing on commonalities between these and other youth instead of differences; do not use explicit language in discussing sexual practices.

- When partnering with tribal or AI/AN organizations, focus on a goal, use data to show that you are aware that the issue is important to the community, and focus on the potential benefit to their community as a whole. Make sure that you are willing to truly partner, not just have them at the table. There is mistrust in AI/AN communities of non-Native organizations that want an AI/AN representative but that are not necessarily willing to hear and respond to specific AI/AN needs. This is true of interactions with the LGBT and two-spirit community as well.

- Respectfully include elders, youth, and parents from tribal and AI/AN communities, and set aside time to listen to advice from these elders on how to incorporate cultural supports and/or cultural imagery. In some communities, offering a gift to elders when asking for their advice, or a prayer to help set the tone for a meeting, may reflect traditional practice. Check with community members to determine local protocols for gift-giving and other traditional practices.

- There may be a split between those in AI/AN communities who do and do not accept LGBT and two-spirit youth. Those between the ages of 25 and 50 (roughly) may have been brought up with less traditional awareness than their elders and less acceptance than their children. Often LGBT and two-spirit individuals find support in *retraditionalization,* the effort to reintroduce or strengthen cultural traditions, including those of LGBT and two-spirit acceptance that existed before colonization.

To learn the full scope of how a community's culture plays a role in how your campaign and AI/AN LGBT and two-spirit youth are perceived and received, Bearse recommends that social marketing campaigns establish partnerships with existing community organizations and community leaders to accumulate as much information as possible. This strategy can be particularly helpful if these organizations or tribes have previously (or are currently) engaged in services and marketing for service and/or awareness for LGBT and two-spirit youth or AI/AN youth with LGBT and two-spirit parents or caregivers. Once your campaign has identified the right partners who understand the background, you can move forward together to identify the needs for LGBT and two-spirit youth, the services available, the level of safety for LGBT and two-spirit youth in the area, and the types of materials and dissemination plans that would reach the most youth within the overall campaign.

Lesson 4: Increase Your Campaign's Impact by Optimizing When, Where, and How Its Messages Are Delivered

Even the best message is useless if your audience does not hear it or if it is presented through an inappropriate channel. *When* messages are presented is important too, as youth may be easier to reach and mobilize at certain times of the year than others. For instance, the "You Know Different" campaign report found that an overwhelming majority (70%) of youth in focus groups indicated that they preferred that a campaign be launched in the summer, and nearly a fourth (22%) preferred the fall. Nevertheless, a campaign may still consider the fall an ideal time to reach youth because during this time school provides them with daily structured routines, whereas summer months are likely to lack this structure and predictability. This structure makes it easier for a campaign to predict where clusters of youth will be located (i.e., in school) and as a result be easier to reach and mobilize to action (NYAC, n.d.b).

A campaign should be launched with sensitivity given to the current political and social environment at the national, state, and local levels. For instance, Parents, Families and Friends of Lesbians and Gays (PFLAG) changed the initial launch date of its "Claim your Rights" campaign to address LGBT discrimination and harassment in schools because many of its collaborating organizations were focusing on the "Don't Ask Don't Tell" policy. At that time, this policy was being vigorously debated at the national level, making it highly likely that the "Claim your Rights" campaign launch would not have received maximum visibility. The delay lasted only a few weeks, however, because a series of LGBT youth suicides resulting from bullying (J.R. Perry, personal communication, October 8, 2010) brought attention to the issue of LGBT youth's safety and rights. Because of these unfortunate events, PFLAG believed its campaign would make a positive difference, and the campaign's launch sparked a national conversation about the safety of LGBT youth.

"Claim Your Rights" also shows how timing a campaign's launch can be a critical factor to getting off to a good start. In addition to staying abreast of current events related to a campaign's issues, you may also be able to optimize the impact of the launch by scheduling it during partners' special events or annual celebrations (if appropriate). When done correctly, this strategy can bring more attention to both a campaign and a partner's event than if these activities were conducted alone. You can also schedule a launch during an annual celebration, such as Gay and Lesbian Pride Month (June), Gay Pride Day (last Sunday in June), National Coming Out Day (October 11), LGBT History Month (October), National Children's Mental Health Awareness Day (early May), or any local gay pride events. Doing this can be an effective way of bringing like-minded organizations together to support a unified cause. Make sure, however, that when you employ this strategy you work closely with your partners to avoid the misperception that your campaign or organization is attempting to take over another organization's event or celebration. Close collaboration is needed right from the start to prevent such tensions.

The media you use to deliver your message is equally as important as the timing. The Internet is frequently cited as an ideal medium for reaching out to LGBT youth because it offers privacy and because of the frequency and time that youth spend online. A national survey showed that more than half (55%) of gay and lesbian adults (age 18 years and older) use social networking sites, such as Facebook, MySpace, LinkedIn, Plaxo, Twitter, and blogs, at least once a day as compared with less than half (41%) of heterosexual adults. Nearly one third (30%) of gays and lesbians visit social networking sites several times a day compared with less than one in five heterosexuals (17%). They also read blogs more often than heterosexuals (54% versus 40%, respectively; Harris Interactive, 2010).

As social media blurs the lines between the traditional one-way communications that dominated the World Wide Web for more than a decade, the Internet, which includes mobile devices, now serves as a tool for peer networking. Through peer networking web sites, social marketing campaigns have provided tools and information to motivate youth and to place information in the hands of youth in their social environments (NYAC, n.d.b). The importance of peer networking is supported by the Trevor Project's experience when they found providing information online through a chat service with a counselor to be very successful because it allowed for greater anonymity. As a result of this increased privacy, chatting did not feel as daunting to the youth, and they did not have to fear that their phone numbers would be tracked (R. Lombardini, personal communication, September 14, 2010). If an organization chooses to use chat, e-mail, or other forms of online communication, it is helpful to document conversations with clients online, be honest in identifying your purpose, and be ready to provide sensitive counseling and support. For social media profile images for an LGBT organization, using faces of individuals instead of just logos may add a sense of authenticity (NYAC, 2010).

NYAC's focus groups also showed that the World Wide Web's vast collection of informational resources is still very important, as LGBT youth reported they looked online when they wanted information. Focus groups with rural and homeless youth told a different story: They do not go online for information because they have limited or no Internet access. Reaching rural and homeless youth may involve marketing in LGBT newspapers and magazines or partnering with organizations that provide services, such as clinics (NYAC, n.d.b).

Because members of your audience may have limited Internet access, it is still important to identify and include alternate channels in your outreach. NYAC's campaign focus groups identified numerous channels for reaching LGBT youth, such as clubs; movies; providers' offices; LGBT organization's events; billboards; flyers; hip-hop magazines; commercials; and LGBT newspapers, magazines, and other publications (NYAC, n.d.a). NYAC's focus groups also revealed that youth considered peers to be among the most trusted sources of information (NYAC, n.d.a). In addition to peers, youth also want to engage with adults who they know are sensitive to their situations. PFLAG (2010), for instance, recommends providing youth with a listing of providers who are culturally and linguistically sensitive to the needs of LGBT youth.

Delivering your message through a channel tailored to your audience can be especially important in the case of homeless LGBT youth. Homeless LGBT youth are largely considered to be an "invisible" group because they are difficult to identify and reach within a community. Many are resistant to identifying openly as LGBT or as homeless. Rather, they may regard themselves as "travelers" (Hyde, 2005). They may also be unwilling to access services or reveal their sexual orientation because of a history of negative experiences with providers or adults, a history of physical and sexual assault, a desire to avoid unsafe spaces, a lack of financial support, and/or a fear of losing their independence (Hooks-Wayman & Sicilliano, 2009; HRC, 2010; Hyde, 2005).

Given this information, reaching homeless LGBT youth may seem like a daunting goal, but many of the lessons learned for LGBT youth also apply to this audience. For example, helping homeless youth empower themselves is also a key principle among many organizations because homeless LGBT youth have typically experienced a history of not having control over many aspects of their lives (AIDS Action, 2001; HRC, n.d.). Furthermore, you may want to launch your campaign in the winter instead of the fall, as homeless youth may be more willing to go to an indoor event to escape the cold (Crutsinger-Perry, 2009).

Homeless LGBT youth who are wary of services or service providers may be more receptive to messages if those messages are presented in places where they feel safe. Some venues that may be considered safe are places where youth regularly frequent or drop-in centers (Hooks-Wayman & Sicilliano, 2009; HRC, 2010). Be aware, however, that some areas of a neighborhood may be considered especially dangerous by homeless LGBT youth, such as those considered to be a part of a gang's territory, as many homeless LGBT youth consider these territories to be unsafe and, in some cases, lethal (HRC, n.d.).

Lesson 5: Audiences Other Than LGBT Youth Should Be Engaged, Ready, and Able to Accommodate the Behavior Change That You Want Them to Make

Helping an audience reach Prochaska's maintenance stage of health behavior change usually involves more than effective marketing. You also have to have adequate resources and supports within the home and community when your audience is ready and willing to engage in the desired behaviors. This means that when promoting healthy coping strategies, social supports, and other help-seeking behaviors to LGBT youth and youth with LGBT family members, you need to be certain that once they "buy in" to your message, resources will be available within the community to allow them to act on your message and maintain the targeted change in behavior. To do this, you should consider other audiences in environments where these youth are likely to interact. These audiences include members of their greater community (at-large public), providers (service settings for mental health, health, social services, etc.), schools, and families (home). The following are lessons learned from audiences related to campaigns intended for LGBT youth.

Communities

Support for LGBT youth may vary widely from one community to another. Focusing on social justice and fairness appears to be an effective way to open doors and build community collaborations. Because most individuals can understand the need for fair and equal treatment, focusing on fairness and equal rights is a strong premise for gaining the support of a range of community members. The "Fairness Campaign," which focused on passing an ordinance for the civil rights of LGBT individuals in Lexington-Fayette County, Kentucky, epitomizes how focusing on fairness leads to a campaign's success (Otis, 2003). Despite negative perspectives of LGBT identity, the campaign successfully passed the LGBT civil rights ordinance by focusing on a discussion of social justice because the issue resonated with the community.

All of the campaign's representatives were trained to deliver one unified message of social justice to inundate politicians, the media, and the community with a message that countered opponents' arguments. This priority was established not only through messaging but also through the name of the campaign itself. By calling it the "Fairness Campaign," all opponents of the campaign were inherently viewed as anti-fair. Keeping the focus on the common goal of social justice instead of morals, the campaign won the favor of many key religious leaders and politicians who may have otherwise opposed the campaign (Otis, 2003). Similarly, framing LGBT issues as civil rights issues has been effective for reaching racial minorities or other communities who have faced discrimination. Choudhury et al. (2009) showed that members of the South Asian community in California were more responsive and empathetic to needs of LGBT youth when these needs were discussed in terms of human rights and antidiscrimination (Choudhury et al., 2009).

Social justice also is used as a means for community collaborations with others and can be cemented by exemplifying how all social issues matter to the LGBT community. For instance, the "Fairness Campaign" gained support of various human rights organizations because its volunteers also supported other human rights causes. Furthermore, by working on a range of shared causes throughout the year, when appropriate, organizations and campaigns are able to maintain and strengthen relationships once a campaign or an event finishes (Otis, 2003).

Nevertheless, even with the best collaborations, some groups may be more difficult to reach than others, especially if they are unwilling to recognize the spectrum of sexual orientations that exist. The failure of some to recognize that LGBT individuals exist may create differences in world views that seem impossible to reconcile. PFLAG, however, has found that sometimes an organization may only need to implement a few small changes in their communications to create a more welcoming environment for all (PFLAG, n.d.). For instance, Choudhury et al. (2009) found that a South Asian community was confused about LGBT issues and unaware of the existence of the unique needs of LGBT individuals. By reaching out to this community in a comfortable space (e.g., holiday festivals, theaters, media), the organization raised the profile of South Asian LGBT youth, who may have otherwise felt uncomfortable about bringing up LGBT issues in their community. Many community members were receptive to being approached about the issues of sexual orientation and identity, especially when they were discussed in familiar terms such as a human rights issue (Choudhury et al., 2009).

Some faith-based communities are hesitant to engage LGBT youth out of concern that doing so will violate one or more of their tenets of faith. When working with religious communities, focus on their commitment to compassion and the well-being of youth rather than discussing specific beliefs or articles of faith. Religions differ in teachings, but almost all share similar values, such as advocating for compassion and love and supporting a family structure (PFLAG, 1997). Instead of discussing religious interpretations with people of faith, PFLAG recommends focusing on their love for their children and how you can work together around values you share with them, such as compassion, love, and the importance of family (PFLAG, n.d.). When the board of STARS, which includes representatives from a religious community, was reluctant to support the system of care in reaching out to LGBT youth, the system of care focused on providing information about issues the board was invested in, such as how reaching out to the LGBT population is related to mental health. They presented statistics describing how LGBT youth are at high risk for bullying, homelessness, suicide, substance abuse, and mental health challenges, especially because of the family's response to their sexual orientation and/or gender identity/expression. These national data were not specific to their community, but still exemplified how LGBT youths' needs were inextricably tied to the interests of the system of care. As a result, the religious community was more motivated to support the system of care in its efforts (C. Woessnera & T. Freed, personal communication, September 15, 2010).

Good rapport with religious communities, however, goes beyond sharing information. At its core, this rapport should be grounded in respect, not just for the religion of those you are engaging, but for all religions, as well as their beliefs and holidays. PFLAG believes it is important to let religious communities know that you welcome and respect all faiths, as well as those who do not practice organized religion. They recommend that you provide religious organizations and communities with resources and programs addressing LGBT issues by collaborating to include materials in libraries of religious organizations. Resources such as faith-related films that showcase LGBT and family struggles with their faith can be leveraged by organizing educational programs that focus on dispelling myths and stereotypes or through informal discussion groups (PFLAG, n.d.).

In addition to providing information and materials, it is important to talk about the range of faiths, and when possible, to hold events and meetings in spaces that are open to all religions. Assure people of faith that you respect their beliefs by avoiding generalizations about religious perspectives, focusing on common ground, using a respectful tone, and honoring their religious celebrations. Showing respect may require planning events around religious holidays and holding events that are not specific to a religion, such as hosting a "holiday celebration" or "an end-of-the-year celebration" instead of a Christmas party (PFLAG, n.d.). A campaign may need to enlist the help of a cultural guide similar to those used by the STARS system of care to ensure successful outreach to faith communities. Once a good rapport is developed, it is easier to assure religious communities that supporting a youth's well-being does not mean that they will be forced to change their beliefs, or that youth will be forced to identify as LGBT. In fact, PFLAG recommends not trying to change your audience's beliefs at all; rather, you can gradually help them expand their perspectives to include compassion for LGBT youth and those with LGBT family members (PFLAG, n.d.).

Providers

The wide range of providers who offer services and supports to youth in every professional field is an important audience to reach, but you may not have sufficient resources to develop messages tailored to each professional group. Segmenting this audience, identifying those groups most likely to engage the youth you want to reach and most likely to accept your messages, is a good place to start. For instance, if you are promoting help-seeking behaviors among victims of hate crimes, first responders for these situations (e.g., emergency medical professionals, police) are key audiences for outreach and receiving information and training on cultural sensitivity and heterosexism. First responders are likely to be the first, and perhaps only, professionals an LGBT youth encounters, and this engagement sets the tone for how willing the youth is to seek further help from providers (Dunbar, 2006).

The personal perspectives of providers may result in barriers to providing effective services to LGBT youth. Some providers may have conscious or unconscious biases against LGBT individuals, and some may need to be motivated to address specific LGBT needs. Barriers for health care providers may include heterosexism and the perception that LGBT needs are trivial (Scout, Bradford, & Fields, 2001). As many as 5%–10% percent of a provider's patients may be LGB, making it important that providers address and understand their perceptions of these individuals (PFLAG, 2009). Providers should be reassured that efforts are not focused on changing what they believe, but rather on making a practical adjustment in behavior to help those being served feel comfortable and accepted (PFLAG, 2010). Over time, providers may be more willing to move beyond the "what" (i.e., how to behave), to learn the "why" (i.e., why LGBT needs are valid; Lambda Legal, National Alliance to End Homelessness, National Center for Lesbian Rights, & National Network for Youth, 2009).

One way to help providers understand the "why" is to share data on health outcomes—particularly suicide. When STARS provided LGBT cultural and linguistic competency training to mental health centers, clinicians, therapists, social workers, and child-welfare workers, they presented statistics on why LGBT youth are at risk and have a higher likelihood of reporting a suicide attempt, alcohol/drug use, or an HIV diagnosis compared with other students (C. Woessnera & T. Freed, personal communication, September 15, 2010).

Even well-intentioned providers may not realize that their actions and their office may not reflect sensitivity or support for LGBT issues, which can cause LGBT youth to feel uncomfortable or unaccepted and, therefore, less likely to disclose information (PFLAG, 2010). For instance, in health care settings, good rapport with patients is associated with better treatment outcomes, greater patient retention, and more word-of-mouth referrals (PFLAG, 2009). The opposite, however, can make patients feel uncomfortable and unable to be honest with their provider (PFLAG, 2010). This discomfort and lack of openness creates barriers that interfere with a health care provider's ability to offer the best care.

Good rapport is at the core of respect and sensitivity to a person's cultural and linguistic needs. Providers can demonstrate LGBT sensitivity and create an LGBT-friendly environment in various ways. For instance, more than 85% of gay people determine whether a provider is sensitive to LGBT needs by scanning the provider's office for signs of acceptance, such as rainbow signs and LGBT resources and publications (PFLAG, 2010). Box 15.1 provides a general list of practices providers can adopt to improve openness with LGBT youth, including those who may be homeless. In most cases, increasing provider LGBT sensitivity requires more than providing them with tips. Your campaign may need to work with the providers, even if it means working around their busy schedules. PFLAG recommends gradually developing a relationship with providers and integrating LGBT information into their practice by collaborating with professional organizations, exhibiting at professional events, volunteering, and using prepared talking points that resonate with providers (PFLAG, 2010).

Once providers have agreed to work with you, it can still be difficult to schedule time to discuss LGBT cultural and linguistic sensitivity. When STARS wanted to provide trainings for providers, they found that the best time to talk to providers was during their lunch time and time set aside for paperwork. By talking to providers during these times, providers did not lose valuable billable hours. Offering continuing education units for attending trainings also helped increase the number of providers who attended trainings by providing additional incentive (C. Woessnera & T. Freed, personal communication, September 15, 2010).

Finally, the adults' reservations regarding the use of the term *queer* in the STARS web site URL (queerheartland.org) also is a good reminder of why it is important to remember that what may be culturally and linguistically appropriate

---

Box 15.1.   Practices for Providers

- Use gender-neutral language or use appropriate pronouns (Lambda Legal et al., 2009; NYAC, 2009).
- Do not make heterosexist or stereotypical assumptions, such as asking a question about a boyfriend, girlfriend, husband, or wife (Choudhury et al., 2009; Lambda Legal et al., 2009; PFLAG, 2010; Washington & Murray, 2005).
- Listen well and be willing to learn (Choudhury et al., 2009).
- Know the cultural background or have experience working with the population (Choudhury et al., 2009; Washington & Murray, 2005).
- Be comfortable with asking questions regarding sexual orientation (Choudhury et al., 2009; Washington & Murray, 2005).
- Explain confidentiality rights (PFLAG, 2009).
- Display signs of support for LGBT issues such as LGBT materials or publications, unisex signs, or signs designating an area a safe zone (Beeson, 2009; COLAGE, 2010c; Lambda Legal et al., 2009).
- Do not make assumptions in patient intake forms, such as assuming a child has a mother and father (COLAGE, 2010c).
- Do not separate LGBT youth from heterosexual youth (Lambda Legal et al., 2009).
- Do not segregate youth based on their assigned birth gender; instead, make decisions based on the youth's current gender identity (Lambda Legal et al., 2009).
- Post a nondiscrimination policy and support youth when they "come out" (Lambda Legal et al., 2009; PFLAG, 2009).
- Have an LGBT staff member who can help LGBT youth feel safe and can serve as a role model (Hooks-Wayman & Sicilliano, 2009; Ray, 2006).

---

for youth may not be culturally and linguistically appropriate for providers. Significant differences may exist between what youth and providers prefer, and it is crucial to identify differences in perception by testing messages with a sample of your audience before developing a final message for them.

Schools

Although many would consider schools to be part of the "providers" group, we have segmented them out because they are the only provider that serves nearly all youth in any given community. Within the school environment, there are numerous audiences, such as students, parents, teachers, administrators, community volunteers, elected school boards, and other state–level appointees. Furthermore, schools often include professionals who work in areas other than education, such as health, mental health, law enforcement, transportation, and food service. Because so many individuals come together under the general umbrella of "school," you will need to look carefully at exactly which school audiences you wish to reach and then assess each audience's level of readiness for change. You can work with one school or an entire school system and will need to balance your available resources accordingly. If your resources are very limited, it may be most efficient to limit outreach to key stakeholders, which in many instances would be parents, teachers, and school administrators (Lambda Legal & NYAC, 2008).

If your goal is to change an entire school culture, it is likely that you will need to work with as many of the different audiences as possible within the school environment. One way you may be able to extend your reach is to collaborate with other groups that already make contact with one or more of your audiences (e.g., parent–teacher associations, teacher unions). Some of the most influential groups within a school or school system are parent groups, and they can be very powerful allies for your campaign. AIDS and Adolescents Network of New York (AANNY) demonstrated how involving parents over the past 20 years has helped HIV prevention education be implemented in schools throughout New York City's school system. AANNY involves youth service providers, health care providers, teachers, activists, researchers, parents, and youth in all their promotion and education programs (AIDS Action, 2001).

In addition to parent groups, collaborating with or helping students form gay–straight alliances may be beneficial, as these alliances can be used as stepping stones for involving an entire school or community in your campaign (Griffin & Ouellett, 2002). If possible, work with those alliances that include teachers or other adults within the school. Participants from the 2010 Federal Partners in Bullying Prevention Summit emphasized that school culture and climate change requires strong and authentic partnerships between student and adult advocates (Byard, 2010). The National Day of Silence demonstrates the effectiveness of this strategy as it serves as a means for *all* students and teachers to make schools safer for all and make a petition of love and support (as opposed to a protest). Similarly, the participation of straight students and "teacher allies" can play a key role in implementing activities in schools, bringing attention to LGBT needs, and providing a supporting and caring community for LGBT youth (D. Presgraves, personal communication, September 15, 2010). Through this approach, allies can serve the whole child (Byard, 2010).

Allies can also support LGBT students online. Online behavior applies to schools because *cyberbullying,* often an extension of school bullying, leads to the same psychological harm as general bullying, impeding LGBT students' opportunities to have an equal learning experience (Shariff, 2005). The National Day of Silence campaign provides information about the psychological and legal repercussions of students' online and cell phone behavior, as well as about how youth can stop cyber harassment by reporting it to their Internet service provider (Media Awareness Network, 2009).

As is the case with almost any audience, providing schools with relevant and important data is most likely to motivate them to take action. For instance, safety is a significant concern of schools. GLSEN's "ThinkB4YouSpeak," a campaign that works to eliminate the use of heterosexist phrases such as "that's so gay," especially in school settings, highlighted safety-relevant data and then linked

it to additional data showing an extremely high prevalence of heterosexist language being used in schools. Together, these data were enough to motivate educators to take action. In addition to quantitative data, qualitative data, including the
stories of youth and families, can be extremely motivating. "ThinkB4YouSpeak"
also uses personal stories whenever possible and appropriate (GLSEN, n.d.a.).

STARS also uses data to illustrate the types of harassment LGBT youth
face and the impact of the harassment on overall school climate. In particular,
they provide facts about the high prevalence of bullying, harassment, and assault
among LGBT students as well as the consequences, including the increased
likelihood for LGBT students who are harassed to drop out of school, have a
lower grade-point average, and attempt suicide. Equally important, however, is
that they do not just show all of the negative things that can happen to LGBT
students when schools do not intervene. STARS also shows positive outcomes
(e.g., less harassment, less school missed because of safety concerns, greater academic achievement) when there is intervention and support for LGBT students
(C. Woessnera & T. Freed, personal communication, September 15, 2010).

"ThinkB4YouSpeak" and STARS achieved success by linking positive
qualitative and quantitative outcomes related to providing supports for LGBT
students to the goals of their audiences. Ideally, you would use information that
is directly related to the schools you are engaging, but if no data exist, there are
substantive national data that demonstrate that a significant relationship exists
between academic performance and students' perceptions of safety at school
(Hanson, Austin, & Lee–Bayha, 2003). After leveraging data to create mutual
goals and develop relationships with school personnel, you are in a prime position to share tips on how to address the academic success and safety of LGBT
youth and youth with LGBT parents or caregivers.

You may want to inform school personnel about the stigma and discrimination that LGBT youth face, providing data and/or personal stories when possible. Your audience may not be aware that some stigma and discrimination may
be due to their own behavior. By helping your audience increase their awareness
and self-awareness about the prevalence of overt and covert anti–LGBT biases
and behaviors, you will help them take an important step in helping LGBT
students feel safer and more welcome at school. STARS and NYAC have found
that addressing the following can help increase self-awareness and create safe
spaces: prejudiced attitudes; negative language; a lack of inclusiveness and representation; inappropriate and lack of policies; insufficient resources; and overall
support for youth and their rights in the context of their family, school, community, and coming out process (NYAC, n.d.a; C. Woessnera & T. Freed, personal communication, September 15, 2010).

Once a school is committed to your campaign and providing a safe space,
announce it and equip them with LGBT-related resources that facilitate a change
in behavior and meet the needs of youth (Greytak & Kosciw, 2010). These
schools should also be willing to show their commitment to LGBT youth, such

as developing or asking for the institution of an antidiscrimination policy for LGBT students and a plan for how to respond accordingly if the policy is violated (Crutsinger-Perry & Webster, 2009). Simple and direct action steps can also demonstrate support and facilitate change. The "ThinkB4YouSpeak" campaign does this by encouraging youth to pledge not to use heterosexist phrases such as "that's so gay" and empowers LGBT and heterosexual students to say something original instead by providing them with tools and examples. They include 1) how to use humor and 2) when humor is not appropriate, how to simply state why a particular use of heterosexist language is wrong. One popular example the campaign provides is to replace the phrase "that's so gay" with another phrase that also uses a description of a person as a derogatory comment, such as "that's so 16-year-old kid with a cheesy mustache" (GLSEN, n.d.a.).

"ThinkB4YouSpeak" significantly increases its chances of success because it takes an important step beyond simply telling people to find alternatives. It actually provides a wide range of resources, such as videos, how-to language, flyers, web sites, web banners, and guides. It also offers a Twitter application that counts the number of times a heterosexist term is used on Twitter in 1 day, with examples of phrases that can be used in place of heterosexist terms. The success of this effort is reflected in the more than 1,000 unique user-generated phrases posted on their web site as substitutions for heterosexist phrases (GLSEN, n.d.a.). Most importantly, the campaign provides a section of their web site tailored to educators. The section includes an educator's guide that describes how to incorporate the tools together to implement a campaign in their school. The guide recommends that school personnel discuss the tools and how to implement the action steps in a safe space with students (GLSEN, 2008).

Families

Families and parents/caregivers are an important audience to consider because they have a tremendous amount of influence over the attitudes, beliefs, and actions of youth, which can last a lifetime. In some instances, families and parents/caregivers may not know that their child is LGBT and could learn this for the first time because of a social marketing campaign. This means that when reaching out to this audience, it is important to use care in understanding "where" families and parents/caregivers might be in the coming out process. It is likely that families and parents/caregivers will have concerns after learning that their youth is LGBT, but these concerns can be alleviated. Following are some points to consider based on PFLAG's experiences:

- Parents and caregivers may feel that they have lost their child or that their child is a different person after they have come out. A campaign can focus on helping families recognize these emotions and understand that regardless of a child's sexual orientation, children may always surprise their family by doing something different from what the family expects. Remind families that the child has not changed, but rather the vision the family had for the child may change (PFLAG, 1995).

- Parents and caregivers may not believe their child is LGBT and may reject the youth's coming out. Families should be helped to understand that coming out is not an issue to be taken lightly because youth may face stigma when doing so. Youth may share their LGBT identity with their family because they love them and want an open, honest relationship with their family. Focus on a family's concern for their child's well-being (PFLAG, 1995). Share with them that LGBT youth whose parents and caregivers respond negatively when they reveal their orientation are more likely to attempt suicide, experience severe depression, and use drugs compared with those whose families accept them (Ryan, Huebner, Diaz, & Sanchez, 2009).

- Parents and caregivers may feel that they can make their child become heterosexual with treatment. These treatments have been overwhelmingly rejected and have even been found to lead to serious damage, including suicide (PFLAG, 1995).

- Many parents and caregivers become concerned with why their child is LGBT. They should understand that there is no conclusive cause for being LGBT and that such information is irrelevant to supporting or loving their child (PFLAG, 1995).

- Some parents and caregivers become uncomfortable or have negative emotions when their child identifies as LGBT, which may be because of heterosexist beliefs. They may need help to feel comfortable with continuing to support and love their child (PFLAG, 1995).

- Some parents and caregivers may have trouble reconciling their love for their child with their faith. In these cases, encourage the family member to explore and examine their religion and their feelings toward their faith and their child. Remind them that at the core of most religions are love and compassion (PFLAG, 1997).

Once families and parents/caregivers become aware of their child's LGBT identity, they may need resources to help them resolve family conflict and reconcile. Many parents and caregivers, especially foster parents, lack necessary resources for accepting their child's LGBT identity and their corresponding needs. A campaign might help alleviate these concerns by promoting resources that help parents/caregivers to

- Better understand LGBT identities
- Better discuss LGBT identity with the use of appropriate terms
- Resolve their emotions regarding their child's LGBT identity
- Address the other aforementioned concerns that families may have

This is especially important among foster care families, as many LGBT youth continue to be rejected or abused within their foster care home because of their sexual orientation (HRC, 2010; Wilber, Ryan, & Marksamer, 2006).

Another important resource for families and parents/caregivers are other families and parents/caregivers of LGBT youth who can serve as role models and who can guide and support them. By working with families, PFLAG's local chapters are able to promote campaigns and motivate hesitant families and parents/caregivers to support their LGBT children. Families and parents/caregivers that are members of PFLAG are used as examples for others to create a safe space for their children in the home and to accept their children for who they are.

Families and parents/caregivers may also get help from service providers and religious organizations when working through concerns that they may have with their LGBT youth. PFLAG has found that LGBT-accepting providers can give families information about their concerns and help them work through heterosexism (PFLAG, 2009). PFLAG also recommends working with religious organizations that are accepting of LGBT youth because it helps families and other community members reconcile their feelings for their loved ones and their commitment to their faith (PFLAG, n.d.).

Social marketing campaigns also have a role in helping families and parents/caregivers create safe spaces at homes for LGBT youth. Family-friendly language that focuses on the love that families and parents/caregivers have for their youth is likely most effective. According to PFLAG, it is important that campaigns do not use language that blames families for their negative responses to their child's LGBT identity. Families' responses, including anger or guilt, are understandable reactions. PFLAG suggests using language that focuses on a family's love for their child (PFLAG, 1995). PFLAG has a wide range of resources on this subject that were developed with the input of family members (visit http://community.pflag.org/Page.aspx?pid=594). Be aware, however, that language used for LGBT youth may not always be appropriate for their families or parents/caregivers, just as STARS's "queerheartland.org" is problematic for some service providers, but is considered acceptable by youth (C. Woessnera & T. Freed, personal communication, September 15, 2010).

RECOMMENDED AREAS FOR FUTURE RESEARCH

As noted in this chapter, few evaluated and documented social marketing campaigns are available that address the need to create healthy and safe environments for LGBT youth and youth with LGBT parents or caregivers. Even fewer published studies exist describing campaigns proven to affect attitudes and behaviors about LGBT youth in positive ways. More national communication strategies for promoting help-seeking behaviors and reducing stigma should be designed, evaluated, and disseminated to meet the needs of the entire spectrum of LGBT youth and youth with LGBT family members. Evidence is also needed to identify how campaigns can increase acceptance and support among families, school personnel, providers, the juvenile justice system (Ray, 2006), and other community members for LGBT youth and youth with LGBT parents or caregivers. Finally, more evaluation is needed to identify effective social marketing efforts and strategies that should be culturally adapted, disseminated, and replicated throughout system of care communities.

CONCLUSION

System of care communities seeking to engage LGBT youth and youth with LGBT family members with messages that promote resilience, help-seeking behavior, and social inclusion will take part in groundbreaking social marketing work. Key concepts to take away from this chapter as you go forth in carrying out these activities include the following:

- Take time to understand the unique characteristics and needs of your population of focus, whether it is LGBT youth, youth with LGBT family members, LGBT youth with LGBT family members, or two-spirit youth.
- From the outset, collaborate with organizations that have similar goals or focus on youth or LGBT people.
- Tailor your message to your audience by creating authentic messages for youth and aligning your message with the culture and language of your subpopulation of youth.
- Deliver your message using the place, time, and media your audience is most likely to access, such as safe spaces or the Internet for urban youth.
- Engage secondary audiences, such as families, schools, providers, and the community, because they play a vital role in a youth's life and are necessary to completely create behavior change and promote resilience, help-seeking behavior, and social inclusion.

This chapter offers useful tools to aid social marketing efforts as new outreach programs become available for LGBT youth and youth with LGBT family members. The authors caution, however, that much of the information in this chapter is indirectly related to mental health social marketing, and the related literature is still limited. Nevertheless, if a system of care sticks to the fundamentals of social marketing within the context of a system of care's core values, its social marketing work is very likely to succeed given the proper amount of time and resources.

16

Internet-Based Information and Resources for Supporting LGBT Youth and Providing Culturally Competent Services

STEPHEN L. FORSSELL, JEFFREY M. POIRIER, AND RACHAEL R. KENNEY

T
he World Wide Web in the 21st century is a vast, easily accessible source of seemingly limitless information, including a wealth of data, opinions, ideas, products, resources and services. The Internet is a portal to a bounty of resources related to a range of lesbian, gay, bisexual, and transgender (LGBT) topics: gender and sexual identity; health and counseling services; assistance with housing, homelessness, and substance use challenges; cultural and linguistic competence of services and supports; stigma, discrimination, and harassment; and a host of other topics regarding the well-being of LGBT youth. This chapter provides guiding tips for effectively using this ever-evolving, ever-expanding locus of information. Most importantly, we identify 38 credible, useful web sites that provide information and resources related to LGBT youth and their families.

TIPS FOR LOCATING INFORMATION AND RESOURCES ONLINE

You can retrieve information quickly from Google or other similar "search engine" web sites. A *simple search* (i.e., searching with a few key words) often generates a large list of web pages containing those key words. Although the simple search is likely the most common way Google is used, Google, Bing, Yahoo!, and other search engines now have easy-to-use, built-in tools that can help you narrow your searches and generate more useful results. The following hints use the Google search engine as an example, although Bing and other web sites have similar features.

More narrowly defined searches are important because the sheer volume of information in cyberspace can be overwhelming. A recent Google search for *gay lesbian youth* (conducted January 23, 2012), for example, yielded more than 11 million results! Sifting through this information requires time, and many web pages that are listed as a result of your search may be irrelevant to your information needs. Moreover, not all material will be "good" information. Controversial issues or subjects of philosophical or political differences may be particularly likely to spawn content with biased information, including distorted facts and opinions presented as fact, conflicting and contradictory advice, "experts" without appropriate credentials, selectively presented data, misinterpreted findings, pure speculation, and misinformation masquerading as science.

The abundance of unverified information on the Internet results in a confusing, time-consuming, and frustrating environment for fact finding, making it challenging to differentiate good information from bad. Using the Internet to find resources addressing the emotional and behavioral health needs of LGBT youth is no exception. Despite the plethora of available bona fide information about the healthy development of LGBT individuals, considerable misinformation still abounds. Hence effectively navigating the Internet for information necessitates avoiding inappropriate or misleading information and resources.

Google provides tools to narrow your information searches. For example, icons appear on the left side of the web page after you have conducted a simple search in Google. You can use these icons to instruct Google to show you the most recently added or updated web pages or only those web pages that have been updated or posted within a particular period of time (e.g., in the past week). Google also provides results based on your location. Using your Internet address and searches you have conducted previously, Google will prioritize web pages that belong to organizations or providers in your community. If you want results tailored for a different geographic location, you can do this by clicking on the "Change location" link and adding the new city name or zip code. Future searches will prioritize this location.

Google's "More search tools" section at the bottom of the left column allows you to access additional search options. Select "More search tools" and then "Related searches" to see a list of searches similar to the one you most recently conducted or that contain similar content. By clicking on "Reading level," Google will sort sites into three levels of reading difficulty: "Basic," "Intermediate," and "Advanced." By clicking the "Nearby" link on the left column, Google will exhibit web sites of organizations with street addresses that are close to you.

The icon for the useful "Advanced search" feature is in small font and located at the very bottom of the results page after you submit your initial search. (You will likely have to scroll down to get to this link.) In a simple search, Google will pull up only web pages that have all of the words you entered. For example, if you entered *gay lesbian transgender,* only web pages that have all three terms within them will be listed, whereas web pages that do not have *transgender* in them will be excluded. Conducting an advanced search allows you to refine your Internet search criteria. Currently, you can look for web pages that contain all, any, or none of the words you enter—or the exact words you enter. For example, to search for resources for homeless LGBT youth, you can type *homeless* in the "all these words" field, then *gay, lesbian,* and *transgender* in the "any of these words" field to yield results that mention *homeless* as well as *gay, lesbian,* or *transgender.* This will ensure that your search includes all web pages for *homeless* and any of the additional search terms. The advanced search also allows you to look for web pages that contain a specific phrase or set of words exactly as you type them. You can specify that Google find web pages that do *not* contain certain words or terms (e.g., you can potentially eliminate web pages that contain profanity using this tool). The "Advanced search" tool also allows you to limit your list of web pages to those with particular types of documents available for download, such as Adobe PDF or Microsoft Word files, which can expedite your search for downloadable documents.

USING THE INTERNET TO ACCESS *GOOD* INFORMATION

Sorting "good" from "bad" information requires us to think critically, analyze and evaluate complex information, and formulate logical arguments. Critical thinking allows us to recognize bias and flawed reasoning, separate facts from speculation, and have a more complete picture of "what's going on" (Dunn, 2010). Critical thinking can help us evaluate new information about any topic. Fully unbiased information does not exist. Therefore, bias will exist in the information we gather from the Internet or from the media or elsewhere. By thinking critically about information in the ways highlighted in this chapter, you can minimize the impact of bias and find the most appropriate and accurate information. Ground rules and questions to ask to evaluate material on the Internet (e.g., a single statement or an entire web site; an abstract idea or a claim of factual truth; a proposed solution to a problem or the suggested cause of a problem) are discussed in the following sections.

Evaluating the Source

What organization or individual is offering the material, and what are their credible qualifications for making claims or offering resources? Do they have practical experience or higher level training or education in the area? Does the group or person offering the material operate from an underlying value system or even an outwardly stated "mission" that affects the content and approach to resources (e.g., if information comes from an organization, what is its vision and purpose)?

What Are the Underlying Assumptions of the Material?

Does the material include statements that presume facts, without appropriate evidence? Often arguments in favor of a particular position "skip a step" by inserting a flawed assumption or logic into the set of presumed facts.

What Values Have Influenced the Material?

Our world views, experiences, and education influence both how we interpret new material and how we present information to others. Our perspectives are embedded in a value system that may bias how material is presented. Accordingly, we need to ask what value systems or traditions may have influenced the author(s) of a particular piece of information on the Internet. What beliefs might bias this material or how it is presented? In the case of research, what steps were taken to account for or control those biases?

How Does the Material Compare with Other Information?

Is this new information compatible with established facts and findings in the field, or does it contradict existing findings? If the latter, you should carefully consider why this is so. The preponderance of evidence, not just an individual finding or study in isolation, should be considered. For example, although a large number of studies indicate that gay and lesbian parents differ little from heterosexual parents and raise healthy and happy children (e.g., Farr, Forssell, & Patterson, 2010), it is always possible to find studies or parts of studies that suggest otherwise. This is closely related to the next tip.

Is the Material Presented in a Methodologically and Conceptually Appropriate Context?

Even a well-conducted study or a high-quality set of data can be misinterpreted or misrepresented. For instance, small subsets of data within larger studies can be misused to show the opposite of what the study as a whole concluded. Some research may also inappropriately generalize findings to larger groups of individuals, even though methodologically the study was not conducted with the appropriate rigor. For example, a study of 10 youth cannot be generalized to all youth in the United States (or even a state or local community).

Correlation Versus Causation

Claims about "what causes what" are ubiquitous on the Internet and are usually rooted in the co-occurrence of two events. Two phenomena that "go together" or happen concurrently does not indicate that one causes the other. Phenomenon A and phenomenon B may co-occur because A causes B, B causes A, or a third phenomenon that may not even be accounted for causes or affects both A and B. Claims of causality and relationships among events or conditions necessitate that all possible related factors be considered carefully. Claims of causality, particularly those regarding complex behaviors, should always be regarded cautiously and not accepted without significant evidence.

RECOMMENDED RESOURCES

A good approach for accessing new LGBT-related information is to seek it from trusted sources, such as professional organizations or individuals with known expertise and credibility in the LGBT community. The matrix shown in Figure 16.1 presents recommended web sites with LGBT resources and information. Although we have not vetted all information on these web sites, we believe these organizations can be trusted to provide accurate and helpful information. The matrix includes the web site names and current web addresses, short descriptions of the organizations and information about the key topics the web sites typically address, and their intended audiences. The identified topics and audiences reflect the focus of the material on the web sites, and are not intended to reflect all content that may be available from these valuable resources. Further, web sites regularly change, and new information on topics or for audiences we have not identified may be added. We hope this is a valuable resource on your journey to becoming more knowledgeable and supporting more culturally and linguistically responsive services and supports for LGBT youth and their families in your community.

Name	Description	Topic: Family	Schools	Foster care	Homelessness	Violence	Latino	Two-spirit	Policy/advocacy	HIV/AIDS	Trans/intersex	Health/medical	Mental health	Audience: Families/youth	Education	Mental health	Health care	Social work
Accord Alliance www.accordalliance.org	Accord Alliance's mission is to promote comprehensive and integrated approaches to care that enhance the health and well-being of people and families affected by disorders of sex development by fostering collaboration among all stakeholders.	✓									✓	✓		✓		✓	✓	
Advocates for Youth www.advocatesforyouth.org	Advocates for Youth champions efforts to help young people make informed and responsible decisions about their reproductive and sexual health.						✓		✓		✓	✓	✓	✓		✓	✓	
Ambientejoven www.ambientejoven.org	As a project of Advocates for Youth (see above) Ambientejoven provides LGBT information and resources in Spanish.					✓	✓				✓	✓		✓		✓	✓	
American Psychological Association—The Healthy Lesbian, Gay, and Bisexual Students Project www.apa.org/pi/lgbt/programs/hlgbsp	The Healthy Lesbian, Gay, and Bisexual Students Project strengthens the capacity of the nation's schools to prevent the behavioral health risks of LGB students. It focuses on knowledge development, dissemination, and application by working with and through national organizations of school stakeholders.	✓	✓						✓	✓	✓		✓		✓			

Organization	Description																
American Psychological Association—The Lesbian, Gay, Bisexual and Transgender Concerns Office www.apa.org/pi/lgbt	The office's mission is to advance psychology as a means of improving the health and well-being of LGBT individuals; increasing understanding of gender identity and sexual orientation as aspects of human diversity; and reducing stigma, prejudice, discrimination, and violence.	✓		✓		✓			✓		✓		✓	✓	✓		✓
Association for Lesbian, Gay, Bisexual & Transgender Issues in Counseling www.algbtic.org	The association promotes greater awareness and understanding of LGBT issues among members of the counseling profession and related helping occupations.	✓		✓		✓			✓		✓		✓	✓	✓		✓
Association of Gay and Lesbian Psychiatrists www.aglp.org	The AGLP is a community of psychiatrists that educates and advocates on LGBT mental health issues and aims to foster a fuller understanding of LGBT mental health issues and develop resources to promote LGBT mental health.								✓				✓	✓	✓		✓
Center of Excellence for Transgender Health www.transhealth.ucsf.edu	The center's mission is to increase access to comprehensive, effective, and affirming health care services for trans and gender-variant communities and to develop and implement programs in response to community-identified needs.								✓	✓ ✓ ✓	✓				✓	✓	
Children of Lesbians and Gays Everywhere www.colage.org	COLAGE is a national movement of children, youth, and adults with one or more LGBTQ parents. It builds community and works toward social justice through youth empowerment, leadership development, education, and advocacy.	✓					✓		✓								✓

(continued)

Figure 16.1. Recommended web sites for LGBT resources and information.

257

Figure 16.1. *(continued)*

Name	Description	Topic												Audience				
		Family	Schools	Foster care	Homelessness	Violence	Latino	Two-spirit	Policy/advocacy	HIV/AIDS	Trans/intersex	Health/medical	Mental health	Families/youth	Education	Mental health	Health care	Social work
Day of Silence Project www.dayofsilence.org	The National Day of Silence (DOS) brings attention to anti-LGBT name calling, bullying, and harassment in schools. Founded in 1996, DOS has become the largest single student-led action toward creating safer schools for all, regardless of sexual orientation, gender identity, or gender expression.	✓	✓			✓			✓					✓	✓			
Family Acceptance Project http://familyproject.sfsu.edu	The Family Acceptance Project (FAP) is a community research, intervention, and education initiative to study the impact of family acceptance and rejection on the health, mental health, and well-being of youth who are LGBT. The project creates resources to help families provide support for LGBT youth.	✓	✓						✓		✓		✓	✓	✓	✓		✓
Gay & Lesbian Medical Association www.glma.org	The Gay & Lesbian Medical Association aims to ensure equality in health care for individuals who are LGBT and health care providers. It offers resources, including a provider directory.								✓	✓		✓		✓			✓	

Organization	Description														
Gay, Lesbian & Straight Education Network www.glsen.org	GLSEN works to ensure safe schools for all students, regardless of sexual orientation and gender identity. More than 40 GLSEN chapters work closely with the network's national office to work to cover a variety of subjects and issues, from public policy to teacher training to supporting students and educators around the country.		✓		✓			✓							
Gay–Straight Alliance (GSA) Network www.gsanetwork.org	The GSA Network is a youth leadership organization that connects school-based GSAs to each other and community resources. Through peer support, leadership development, and training, GSA Network supports young people in starting, strengthening, sustaining, and building GSA capacity.	✓	✓		✓			✓							
Gender Education & Advocacy www.gender.org	Gender Education and Advocacy is a national organization focused on the needs, issues, and concerns of individuals who are gender variant. It seeks to educate and advocate for all individuals who experience gender-based oppression in all of its many forms.		✓		✓	✓	✓	✓			✓	✓	✓		

(continued)

Figure 16.1. *(continued)*

Name	Description	Family	Schools	Foster care	Homelessness	Violence	Latino	Two-spirit	Policy/advocacy	HIV/AIDS	Trans/intersex	Health/medical	Mental health	Families/youth	Education	Mental health	Health care	Social work
Gender Spectrum www.genderspectrum.org	Gender Spectrum provides education, training, and support to help create a gender-sensitive and inclusive environment for all children and adolescents, including those who are gender variant.	✓	✓	✓					✓		✓	✓	✓	✓	✓	✓	✓	✓
GLBT National Youth Talkline www.glbtnationalhelpcenter.org (800-246-PRIDE or 800-246-7743)	The Talkline provides telephone and e-mail peer counseling, as well as factual information and local resources. Telephone volunteers in their teens and early 20s speak with adolescents and young adults up to age 25 about coming-out issues, relationship concerns, parent issues, school problems, HIV/AIDS and safer-sex information, and other concerns.	✓	✓			✓				✓			✓	✓		✓		
Homelessness Resource Center: LGBTQI2-S Youth www.homeless.samhsa.gov	On this topic page of the Homelessness Resource Center, homeless service providers can access tools such as recommended practices for serving youth who are LGBTQI2-S and a tool for assessing an organization's preparedness for working with this vulnerable youth population.				✓								✓			✓		✓

260

Organization	Description																
Human Rights Campaign www.hrc.org	The Human Rights Campaign (HRC) is the largest national LGBT civil rights organization. HRC envisions an America where LGBT people are ensured of their basic equal rights and can be open, honest, and safe at home, at work, and in the community.	✓					✓					✓	✓				
It Gets Better Project www.itgetsbetter.org	The It Gets Better Project provides an opportunity for the public to submit user-created videos so that 1) children and youth who are LGBT can see with their own eyes how love and happiness can be a reality for them, 2) adults who are LGBT can share the stories of their lives, and 3) straight allies can add their names in solidarity with this effort.	✓			✓				✓	✓	✓						
Lambda Legal www.lambdalegal.org (866-LGBTeen or 866-542-8336)	Lambda Legal is a national organization committed to achieving full recognition of the civil rights of individuals who are LGBT and those with HIV through impact litigation, education, and public policy. Its Out-of-Home Care Project raises awareness and advances reform on behalf of LGBTQ youth in child welfare, juvenile justice, and homeless systems.	✓			✓	✓	✓	✓		✓		✓		✓	✓		

(continued)

Figure 16.1. *(continued)*

Name	Description	Family	Schools	Foster care	Homelessness	Violence	Latino	Two-spirit	Policy/advocacy	HIV/AIDS	Trans/intersex	Health/medical	Mental health	Families/youth	Education	Mental health	Health care	Social work
			Topic											Audience				
National Association of Lesbian, Gay, Bisexual and Transgender Addiction Professionals www.nalgap.org	NALGAP is dedicated to the prevention and treatment of alcoholism, substance abuse, and other addictions in LGBT communities. NALGAP aims to confront all forms of oppression and discriminatory practices in the delivery of services to all people and to advocate for programs and services that affirm all genders and sexual orientations.		✓						✓			✓	✓			✓	✓	✓
National Center for Lesbian Rights www.nclrights.org	The National Center for Lesbian Rights is a legal organization committed to advancing the civil and human rights of LGBT individuals and their families through litigation, public policy advocacy, and public education.		✓	✓	✓	✓			✓		✓	✓	✓	✓			✓	✓
National Center for Transgender Equality www.transequality.org	The National Center for Transgender Equality is a social justice organization devoted to ending discrimination and violence against individuals who are transgender. The center provides education and advocacy on national issues of importance to these individuals.					✓			✓		✓	✓		✓			✓	

Organization	Description
National Coalition for LGBT Health www.lgbthealth.net	The National Coalition for LGBT Health is committed to improving the health and well-being of individuals who are LGBT through research, policy, education, and training.
National Resource Center for Permanency and Family Connections: LGBTQ Issues & Child Welfare www.hunter.cuny.edu/socwork/ nrcfcpp/info_services/lgbtq -issues-and-child-welfare.html	The NRCPFC at the Hunter College School of Social Work LGBTQ Issues and Child Welfare web page provides resources on children, youth, and parents who are LGBTQ. Resources include information packets, PowerPoint presentations, and links to relevant web sites.
Parents, Families and Friends of Lesbians and Gays www.pflag.org	PFLAG promotes the health and well-being of LGBT individuals, their families, and friends through 1) support, to cope with a society that presents challenges to individuals who are LGBT; 2) education, to enlighten those lacking information about individuals who are LGBT; and 3) advocacy, to end discrimination and to secure equal civil rights.
The Red Circle Project www.apla.org/native_american/ RCP	The Red Circle Project is a cultural network for the Native American gay/ two-spirit community and provides various resources, including training materials and links to Native LGBT and two-spirit social and cultural groups in urban and island areas.

(continued)

Figure 16.1. (continued)

Name	Description	Topic												Audience				
		Family	Schools	Foster care	Homelessness	Violence	Latino	Two-spirit	Policy/advocacy	HIV/AIDS	Trans/intersex	Health/medical	Mental health	Families/youth	Education	Mental health	Health care	Social work
Safe Schools Coalition www.safeschoolscoalition.org	The Safe Schools Coalition is an international public–private partnership to support LGBT youth. The coalition works to help schools become safe places where every family can belong, every educator can teach, and every child can learn, regardless of gender identity or sexual orientation.	✓	✓		✓	✓			✓		✓	✓	✓	✓	✓			
Sexuality Information and Education Council of the United States www.siecus.org	SIECUS provides education and information about sexuality and sexual and reproductive health. They help schools and communities develop comprehensive sexuality education curricula, educate policy makers about issues related to sexuality, and produce resources for various audiences to ensure everyone has access to accurate, complete, and up-to-date information about sexuality.		✓						✓	✓		✓			✓		✓	

Straight for Equality www.straightforequality.org	Straight for Equality is a national outreach and education project created by PFLAG National to empower allies in supporting and advocating for LGBTQI2-S individuals.
Technical Assistance Partnership for Child and Family Mental Health, LGBTQI2-S Learning Community www.tapartnership.org/COP/CLC/lgbtqizs.php	The LGBTQI2-S Learning Community provides a forum for systems of care and their partners to collaborate, exchange knowledge, network, and share recommended practices to advance the development of culturally and linguistically competent mental health systems for children and youth who are LGBTQI2-S and their families.
Trans Youth Family Allies www.imatyfa.org	Trans Youth Family Allies empowers children and families by partnering with educators, service providers, and communities to develop supportive environments in which gender may be expressed and respected.
The Trevor Project LGBT Suicide Prevention Hotline www.thetrevorproject.org (866-488-7386)	The Trevor Project operates the only accredited, nationwide, around-the-clock crisis and suicide prevention helpline for youth who are LGBT and questioning their sexual identity. It is the leading national organization focused on crisis and suicide prevention efforts among youth who are LGBTQ.

(continued)

Figure 16.1. *(continued)*

Name	Description	Family	Schools	Foster care	Homelessness	Violence	Latino	Two-spirit	Policy/advocacy	HIV/AIDS	Trans/intersex	Health/medical	Mental health	Families/youth	Education	Mental health	Health care	Social work
							Topic									Audience		
True Colors www.ourtruecolors.org	True Colors works to create a world where youth, adults, and families of all sexual orientations and gender identities are valued and affirmed. It provides education, training, advocacy, youth leadership development, mentoring, and direct services as well as an annual event with youth and professionals.	✓	✓	✓					✓		✓		✓	✓	✓	✓		✓
The World Professional Association for Transgender Health www.wpath.org	WPATH is an international multidisciplinary professional association that promotes evidence-based care, education, research, advocacy, public policy, and respect in the health of individuals who are transgender.										✓	✓				✓	✓	
YES Institute www.yesinstitute.org	The YES Institute aims to prevent suicide and ensure the healthy development of all youth through powerful communication and education on gender and orientation. It provides related resources and education opportunities.		✓								✓	✓	✓	✓	✓	✓	✓	
YouthResource www.amplifyyourvoice.org/ youthresource	YouthResource is a web site created by and for youth who are LGBT or questioning their sexual orientation. It takes a holistic approach to sexual health and issues of concern to these youth.	✓												✓				

17

Where Do We Go From Here?

Next Steps for Research, Practice, and Policy

SYLVIA K. FISHER, GARY M. BLAU, AND JEFFREY M. POIRIER

Institutionalized heterosexism, biphobia, transphobia, and discriminatory treatment of lesbian, gay, bisexual, and transgender (LGBT) youth, as well as inadequate access to culturally and linguistically responsive resources, have resulted in considerable disparities in services and supports for LGBT youth. These social inequities can exacerbate behavioral health challenges because youth do not receive appropriate care from the systems and individuals they and their families turn to for support during times of need. Systems of care provide an organizing framework and a set of values for how communities can deliver effective mental health services and supports to children, youth, and their families (Stroul, Blau, & Friedman, 2010).

This book has adopted a public health approach to highlight how system of care communities and individuals can apply system of care principles and values to ensure that these systems are "good fits" for LGBT youth and their families. In addition to providing a blueprint for approaches to services and supports in systems of care to enhance outcomes for LGBT youth, this book has raised significant issues and advanced several concepts (e.g., assets-based approaches to services and research; LGBT-affirming clinical interventions; culturally and linguistically competent approaches to service delivery for youth who are LGBT, two-spirit, or have differences in sexual development; guidelines for working with LGBT headed families). We anticipate that the content of this book will support the efforts of others to identify and implement additional promising strategies and effective approaches.

Youth participating in systems of care may exhibit large individual differences in their degree of exposure to institutionalized heterosexism, transphobia, fear, stigma, adversity, and violence. Many, if not most, LGBT youth have experienced trauma and may benefit from a trauma-informed approach to the delivery of services and supports from entry into services and throughout their tenure in systems of care (The National Child Traumatic Stress Network, 2006; Savin-Williams, 1994; Stern-Ellis & Killen-Harvey, 2007). Accordingly, those building systems of care and individual service providers working with LGBT youth should address the impact of sociocultural development and factors associated with the youth, family, and community in all aspects of their planning, outreach, assessments, and interventions. Furthermore, Lazear and Gamache (Chapter 8) point out the importance of addressing the benefits of LGBT-specific assets and resources as well as the effects of negative life events, sociocultural aspects of the clinician–patient interaction, help-seeking behaviors and coping styles, stigma and other social stressors, and perceived causes of symptoms and behaviors. Despite these challenges, LGBT youth who experience multiple challenges are often fiercely resilient and resourceful, and it is critical to capitalize on the strengths these youth demonstrate.

NEW DIRECTIONS FOR RESEARCH

Inadequate attention to the behavioral health needs of LGBT youth within the research literature has resulted in limited information about disparities in access to services and supports and effective treatment approaches that can promote positive outcomes for this population. The Institute of Medicine's (IOM's; 2011) groundbreaking report notes that the lack of information about LGBT youth impedes our ability to address these disparities. Furthermore, most of the research literature about LGBT youth has historically focused on risk factors and problem behaviors as well as sociocultural and psychological challenges that LGBT youth experience. Research on protective factors and resilience for LGBT youth is limited but is growing and shows early promise for identifying approaches that will enhance the care and well-being of LGBT youth and their families. In this book and in their 2009 monograph, Gamache and Lazear have articulated an assets-based research agenda that emphasizes a strengths-based approach and an emphasis on resilience and its cultivation in LGBT youth. Assets-based research offers a positive focus on LGBT youth and how services and supports can be tailored to promulgate positive behavioral and clinical outcomes for these youth.

The IOM report recommends that both cross-sectional and longitudinal research be conducted to explore "the demographic realities of LGBT youth in an intersectional and social ecology framework, and to illuminate the mechanisms of both risk and resilience so that appropriate interventions for LGBT youth can be developed" (2011, p. 172). Accordingly, multidisciplinary research efforts should focus on promising service delivery models for LGBT youth to substantiate the effectiveness of the programs (and related practices) that serve this population. Data should be collected to comprehensively assess needs; determine the most effective allocation of resources; and develop effective and appropriate services, supports, and interventions. These data, when added to the existing knowledge base, will create a foundation for providers to adapt their practices to provide more culturally and linguistically competent care to LGBT youth. Research should also identify those supports, practices, policies, programs, and service delivery models that result in positive outcomes for LGBT youth, including increased connections to the community, increased levels of self-esteem, reductions in suicide attempts, decreased experiences of stigma, and increased family acceptance. Studies should also focus on positive aspects of lesbian or gay identity—belonging to a community, creating families of choice, forging strong connections with others, serving as positive role models, developing empathy and compassion, living authentically and honestly, gaining personal insight and sense of self, getting involved in social justice and activism, being able to self-define gender roles, and exploring relationships—all of which contribute to the healthy development of youth (Riggle, Whitman, Olson, Rostosky, & Strong, 2008). These psychosocial dimensions afford extensive opportunities for developing services and supports that are proactive in cultivating resilience in LGBT youth and their families. An assets-based research agenda is likely to have significant practice implications throughout service delivery systems and ultimately benefit LGBT youth and their families, as well as the communities in which they live and thrive.

STANDARDS FOR CARE

System of care values and principles specify that young people should have access to, and receive, a wide array of culturally and linguistically responsive services and supports tailored to meet their individualized needs. System of care principles should guide youth-serving agencies[1] to ensure they are knowledgeable, appropriately attentive to all forms of cultural diversity, and responsive to the specific needs of LGBT youth. Helfgott and Gonsoulin (Chapter 10) identify 10 key strategies for effectively serving LGBT youth and their families in systems of care:

1. Conduct agency self-assessment and ongoing continuous quality-improvement efforts.

2. Implement policy and practice guidelines to ensure a safe, supportive environment for LGBT youth.

3. Promote staff knowledge and development about LGBT youth and their families.

4. Incorporate culturally and linguistically appropriate intake processes, data collection, and information sharing.

5. Promote safe, supportive, and culturally and linguistically competent environments in youth-serving agencies.

---

[1]Although this book focuses on youth and youth-serving systems, many of the recommended strategies are applicable to children who are LGBT and the systems that work to support them.

6. Implement practices that respect LGBT youth and affirm their identity.
7. Promote healthy and supportive peer connections.
8. Strengthen family connections.
9. Promote access to affirming services and supports.
10. Facilitate community outreach and engagement.

Youth-serving agencies will need to collaborate to achieve these standards of care and ensure that LGBT youth experience dignity and affirmation and receive supports and services that foster their positive development. This collaboration may necessitate addressing individual and organizational resistance and bias. This can be challenging work, but systems of care can advance this work by framing these efforts in an inclusive vision, similar to the vision the Substance Abuse and Mental Health Services Administration's national work group adopted (discussed later in this chapter); being principled in their communication, decision making, policies, and practice; and using the data, research, and recommended strategies in this book and other related literature to build awareness and foster more inclusive, supportive environments. LGBT-inclusive social marketing, as Rubenstein et al. discuss (Chapter 15), can inform communities about the toxic effects of negative attitudes and behaviors toward LGBT youth, their families, and the youth of LGBT-headed families accessing youth-serving systems. Effective social marketing is a positive core strategy that can be mobilized within system of care communities to build awareness, change behavior, and improve outcomes for LGBT youth.

As a principle, youth-guided care asserts that young people should have a voice in matters related to disclosure about their sexual orientation or gender identity. Youth have a right to refuse discriminatory treatments or practices, should have access to supportive resources related to their sexual orientation or gender identity, and deserve to be protected by the systems designed to provide them with care, protection, and support. Accordingly, we encourage systems of care and providers to promote youth empowerment and create opportunities for LGBT youth to be involved in leadership opportunities that affect policy and practice. Family members of LGBT youth, as well as LGBT-headed families of non-LGBT youth, should be involved in implementing policies and practices to create safe, supportive environments for these youth and families.

Further, supportive adults in the lives of LGBT youth make a difference by helping these youth achieve positive outcomes (Ryan, 2010). LGBT youth who have supportive professionals and other adults in their lives feel empowered, validated, pride in who they are, safe, and protected, which has a positive impact on their social support connections, sense of autonomy, power over their own lives, and general well-being (Freundlich & Avery, 2004; Mallon, Aledort, & Ferrera, 2002; Ragg, Patrick, & Ziefert, 2006). Securing the involvement of supportive adults in the care of LGBT youth will promote the well-being of LGBT youth and enhance positive behavioral and emotional outcomes (Matarese, Chapter 12).

PRACTICES FOR PROVIDERS

When system of care principles drive the mission and practices of an agency (or system), an organization is more capable of meeting the needs of *all* children, youth, and their families receiving services and supports. Providing an environment that fosters healthy and supportive peer and family connections and ensures access to supportive services may be challenging. Therefore, ongoing review of policies, practices, training, and other program components will be essential to ensure that culturally and linguistically responsive services and supports are delivered and safe, supportive agency environments for LGBT youth are maintained consistently. Part of this review should involve continuous quality improvement efforts by communities, such as surveys of youth, families, and staff members to identify areas for improvement. As Poirier et al. discuss (Chapter 2), individual and organizational self-assessment are critical components of this continuous quality improvement process and can help communities advance efforts to enhance culturally and linguistically competent services and supports.

Throughout this book, clinical practices and guidelines are articulated so that providers can apply them to enhance the delivery of culturally and linguistically competent care for LGBT youth and their families. A significant theme is the provision of a welcoming, safe environment, ranging from the overt display of welcoming symbols (e.g., pink triangle, rainbow flag) to the adoption of welcoming approaches from front desk staff to clinical and service providers and language on forms youth and families are asked to complete when accessing services. These guidelines, such as demonstrating comfort with asking questions regarding sexual orientation (Choudhury et al., 2009; Washington & Murray, 2005), using gender-neutral pronouns, embracing terms and language that youth use to reference themselves (Lambda Legal, National Alliance to End Homelessness, National Center for Lesbian Rights, & National Network for Youth, 2009; National Youth Advocacy Coalition, 2009), and avoiding heteronormative language (e.g., asking a male youth if he has a girlfriend rather than whether he is dating someone) will build a climate conducive to promoting trust and the provision of welcoming care for LGBT youth and their families. Community members and other stakeholders building the foundation of a successful system of care are encouraged to

- Take a stand on behalf of LGBT youth and advocate for equality and culturally and linguistically responsive treatment and services and supports
- Enhance their own understanding and that of others around about LGBT youth and their experiences
- Connect with community-based provider organizations to provide training and information about community resources for LGBT youth—and in instances where these supports are limited, work with other communities, technical assistance providers, and LGBT-affirming organizations outside the local area to develop these resources

- Identify and connect with welcoming, affirming faith-based organizations to raise awareness around the need for ongoing support for LGBT youth and to provide related information to their youth and families
- Promote the display symbols of support (e.g., rainbow flags, pink triangles) throughout provider organizations and facilities that are, in practice, safe environments for LGBT youth and their families
- Work with local LGBT-affirming community organizations to secure greater support, including resources (e.g., LGBT youth groups) for LGBT youth as well as providers and organizations
- Advocate for antibullying policies as well as nondiscrimination and other protections for LGBT youth within schools, in addition to other LGBT-affirming policies throughout youth-serving organizations and the entire community

At the federal level, the Child, Adolescent and Family Branch (CAFB) in the Center for Mental Health Services of the Substance Abuse and Mental Health Services Administration (SAMHSA) at the U.S. Department of Health and Human Services has established a national work group[2] to address the needs of LGBT children and youth and their families who receive federally funded services and supports through the CAFB's programs. The national work group—composed of youth, family members, researchers, direct service and technical assistance providers, policy makers, program administrators, and others—collaborates to develop strategies, resources, materials, and technical assistance modules to meet the work group's vision for LGBT youth and their families: "All children, youth, and families in the populations of focus live, learn, work, play, thrive, and participate fully in safe, supportive communities where culturally and linguistically competent services and supports are available, accessible, and appropriate" (SAMHSA Center for Mental Health Services, Child, Adolescent, and Family Services Branch, 2010, p. 1).

System of care communities can affirm this vision by offering culturally and linguistically competent services and supports to LGBT youth as they navigate successfully into adulthood. Moreover, they can actively promote positive change within their communities. Systems of care that include families, schools, providers, the faith community, youth-serving sectors, and the larger community can promote safe and supportive environments, resilience, help-seeking behavior, and social inclusion by undertaking groundbreaking initiatives, programs, services, and supports. By engaging LGBT youth and their families, systems of care can collaborate effectively to play a vital role in the lives of LGBT youth to create positive change by improving behavioral and emotional outcomes for these youth.

---

[2]You can access more information about the national work group online (http://www.tapart nership.org/COP/CLC/lgbtqi2sWorkgroup.php).

References

Acevedo-Polakovich, I.D., Bell, B., Gamache, P.E., & Christian, A.S. (2011, June). Service accessibility for lesbian, gay, bisexual, transgender, and questioning youth. *Youth & Society*, 1–23. doi:10.1177/0044118X11409067

Achermann, J.C., & Hughes, I.A. (2007). Disorders of sex differentiation. In P.R. Larsen, H.M. Kronenbery, & S. Melmed (Eds.), *Williams textbook of endocrinology* (11th ed., pp. 743–848). Philadelphia, PA: Saunders.

AIDS Action. (2001). *What works in HIV prevention for youth*. Retrieved from http://www.aidsaction.org/legislation/pdf/ww4youth_final.pdf

Alexander, L.B., & Dore, M.M. (1999). Making the parents as partners principle a reality: The role of the alliance. *Journal of Child and Family Studies, 8*(3), 255–270. doi:10.1023/A:1022059127934

Alie, L. (2011). *Parental acceptance of transgender and gender nonconforming children* (Unpublished doctoral dissertation). John F. Kennedy University, Pleasant Hill, CA.

Allen, L. (2009). Disorders of sexual development. *Obstetrics and Gynecology Clinics of North America, 36*(1), 25–45.

Almeida, J., Johnson, R.M., Corliss, H.L., Molnar, B.E., & Azrael, D. (2009). Emotional distress among LBGT youth: The influence of perceived discrimination based on sexual orientation. *Journal of Youth & Adolescence, 38*(7), 1001–1014.

American Academy of Pediatrics, Committee on Bioethics. (1995). Informed consent, parental permission, and assent in pediatric practice. *Pediatrics, 95*(2), 314–317.

American Psychiatric Association. (1980). *Diagnostic and statistical manual of mental disorders* (3rd ed.). Washington, DC: Author.

American Psychiatric Association. (2000a). *Diagnostic and statistical manual of mental disorders* (4th ed., text rev.). Washington, DC: Author.

American Psychiatric Association. (2000b). *Therapies focused on attempts to change sexual orientation (reparative or conversion therapies): Position statement*. Retrieved from http://www.psych.org/Departments/EDU/Library/APAOfficialDocumentsandRelated/PositionStatements/200001.aspx

American Psychiatric Association. (2010). *Gender dysphoria*. Retrieved from http://www.dsm5.org/proposedrevision/Pages/GenderDysphoria.aspx

American Psychological Association. (1993). *Lesbian, gay, & bisexual youths in the schools*. Retrieved from http://www.apa.org/about/governance/council/policy/schools.aspx

American Psychological Association. (2000). Guidelines for psychotherapy with lesbian, gay, and bisexual clients. *American Psychologist, 55,* 1440–1451.

American Psychological Association. (2002). *Ethical principles of psychologists and code of conduct*. Retrieved from http://www.apa.org/ethics

American Psychological Association. (2008). *Sexual orientation and homosexuality*. Retrieved from http://www.apa.org/helpcenter/sexual-orientation.aspx

American Psychological Association Task Force on Appropriate Therapeutic Responses to Sexual Orientation. (2009). *Report of the task force on appropriate therapeutic responses to sexual orientation.* Washington, DC: Author. Retrieved from http://www.apa.org/pi/lgbt/resources/therapeutic-response.pdf

American School Counselor Association. (2007). *The professional school counselor and LGBTQ youth.* Alexandria, VA: Author. Retrieved from http://asca2.timberlake publishing.com/files/PS_LGBTQ.pdf

American School Health Association. (2009). *Sexual minority youth in schools.* Kent, OH: Author. Retrieved from http://www.ashaweb.org/files/public/Resolutions/Sexual _Minority_Youth_In_Schools_2009.pdf

Ammerman, S.D., Ensign, J., Kirzner, R., Meininger, E.T., Tornabene, M., Warf, C.W., ... Post, P. (2004). *Homeless young adults ages 18–24: Examining service delivery adaptations.* Nashville, TN: National Health Care for the Homeless Council, Inc.

Anderson, A.L. (1998). Strengths of gay male youth: An untold story. *Child and Adolescent Social Work Journal, 15*(1), 55–71.

Anderson, L.M., Scrimshaw, S.C., Fullilove, M.T., Fielding, J.E., Normand, J., & the Task Force on Community Preventive Services. (2002). Culturally competent healthcare systems: A systematic review. *American Journal of Preventive Medicine, 24*(3S), 68–79.

Anguksuar, L.R. (1997). A postcolonial perspective on Western [mis]conceptions of the cosmos and the restoration of indigenous taxonomies. In S.E. Jacobs, W. Thomas, & S. Lang (Eds.), *Two-spirit people: Native American gender identity, sexuality, and spirituality* (pp. 217–222). Chicago: University of Illinois Press.

Argenti, P.A., Howell, R.A., & Beck, K.A. (2005). The strategic communication imperative. *MIT Sloan Management Review, 46*(3), 83–89.

Arviso, V. (2008, March). *Honoring our children, tolerance within the Indian community.* Retrieved from http://nativecases.evergreen.edu/collection/cases/honoring-children. html

Avery, A.M., Hellman, R.E., & Sudderth, L.K. (2001). Satisfaction with mental health services among sexual minorities with major mental illness. *American Journal of Public Health, 91*(6), 990–991.

Bailey, J.M. (1995). Sexual orientation of adult sons of gay fathers. *Developmental Psychology, 31*(1), 124–129.

Bailey, J.M., & Zucker, K.J. (1995). Childhood sex-typed behavior and sexual orientation: A conceptual analysis and quantitative review. *Developmental Psychology, 31*(1), 43–55.

Bakker, L.J., & Cavender, A. (2003). Promoting culturally competent care for gay youth. *Journal of School Nursing, 19*(2), 65–72.

Balsam, K.F., Huang, B., Fieland, K.C., Simoni, J.M., & Walters, K.L. (2004). Culture, trauma, and wellness: A comparison of heterosexual and lesbian, gay, bisexual and two-spirit Native Americans. *Cultural Diversity and Ethnic Minority Psychology, 10*(3), 287–301.

Barkham, M., & Mellor-Clark, J. (2003). Bridging evidence-based practice and practice-based evidence: Developing a rigorous and relevant knowledge for the psychological therapies. *Clinical Psychology and Psychotherapy, 10,* 319–327.

Barr, K. (2009, November 6). Talk on LGBT tolerance, family support draws rapt attention in Kalamazoo. *Kalamazoo Gazette.* Retrieved from http://www.mlive.com/news/kalamazoo/index.ssf/2009/11/talk_on_lgbt_tolerance_draws_r.html

Barth, R.P. (1990). On their own: The experiences of youth after foster care. *Child and Adolescent Social Work, 7,* 419–440. doi:10.1007/BF00756380

Beam, C. (2008). *Transparent: Love, family, and living the T with transgender teenagers.* New York, NY: Mariner Books.

Bearse, M., Fieland, K., & Stately, A. (2007, April). *Welcoming our children back into the circle: Suicide & alienation among two-spirit youth and strengthening our communities through two-*

spirit inclusion. Presented at the meeting of the National Indian Child Welfare Association annual conference.

Beaty, L.A. (1999). Identity development of homosexual youth and parental and familial influences on the coming out process. *Adolescence, 34*(135), 597–601.

Beeson, J. (2009, September). Safe spaces training module [6 Series Video Training Module]. *National Youth Advocacy Coalition.* Retrieved from http://www.nyacyouth.org/pages.php?id=20

Berlan, E.D., Corliss, H.L., Field, A.E., Goodman, E., & Austin, S.B. (2010). Sexual orientation and bullying among adolescents in the Growing Up Today Study. *Journal of Adolescent Health, 46,* 366–371.

Bernard, B. (2004). *Resiliency: What we have learned.* San Francisco, CA: WestEd.

Biegel, S. (2010). *The right to be out: Sexual orientation and gender identity in America's public schools.* Minneapolis: University of Minnesota Press.

Biegel, S., & Kuehl, S.J. (2010, October). *Safe at school: Addressing the school environment and LGBT safety through policy and legislation.* Retrieved from http://nepc.colorado.edu/publication/safe-at-school

Bieschke, K., Perez, R., & DeBord, K. (2007). *Handbook of counseling and psychotherapy with lesbian, gay, bisexual, and transgender clients* (2nd ed.). Washington, DC: American Psychological Association. doi:10.1037/11482-000

Birkett, M., Espelage, D.L., & Koenig, B.W. (2009). LGB and questioning students in schools: The moderating effects of homophobic bullying and school climate on negative outcomes. *Journal of Youth and Adolescence, 38*(7), 989–1000.

Birkey, A. (2011, January 13). Minneapolis school board passes stringent anti-gay bullying, pro-LGBT curriculum. *The Minnesota Independent.* Retrieved from http://minnesota independent.com/76262/minneapolis-school-board-passes-stringent-anti-gay-bullying-pro-lgbt-curriculum

Blackwood, E., & Wiering, S. (1999). *Same-sex relations and female desires: Transgender practices across cultures.* New York, NY: Columbia University Press.

Blake, S.M., Ledsky, R., Lehman, T., Goodenow, C., Sawyer, R., & Hack, T. (2001). Preventing sexual risk behaviors among gay, lesbian, and bisexual adolescents: The benefits of gay sensitive HIV instruction in schools. *American Journal of Public Health, 91*(6), 940–946.

Block, R.G., & Matthews, J.D. (2006). Meeting the needs of GLB youth in residential care settings: A framework for assessing the unique needs of a vulnerable population. In Roy W. Rodenhiser (Ed.), *Assessment in residential care for children and youth* (pp. 181–199). Binghamton, NY: Haworth Press.

Blome, W.W. (1997). What happens to foster kids: Educational experiences of a random sample of foster care youth and matched group of non-foster care youth. *Child and Adolescent Social Work Journal, 14,* 41–53. doi:10.1023/A:1024592813809

Boehmer, U. (2002). Twenty years of public health research: Inclusion of lesbian, gay, bisexual, and transgender populations. *American Journal of Public Health, 92*(7), 1125–1130.

Bostwick, J.M., & Martin, K.A. (2008). Drs. Bostwick and Martin reply. *The American Journal of Psychiatry, 165*(2), 266.

Boxer, A.M., Cook, J.A., & Herdt, G. (1999). Experiences of coming out among gay and lesbian youth: Adolescents alone? In C. Levine & N. Dubler (Eds.), *The adolescent alone: Decision making in health care in the United States* (pp. 121–138). New York, NY: Cambridge University Press.

Brave Heart, M.Y.H., & DeBruyn, L. (1998). The American Indian holocaust: Healing historical unresolved grief. *The Journal of the National Center, 8,* 60–79.

Brill, S., & Pepper, R. (2008). *The transgender child: A handbook for families and professionals.* San Francisco, CA: Cleis Press.

Brinkley, E., & Hawley, L. (2012, February). *Working with issues of sexuality as a school counselor.* Presented at Sexual Orientation and Gender Identity Issues in Education, Rochester, MI.

Broberg, S. (1999, Summer). Gay/straight alliances and other controversial student groups: A new test for the Equal Access Act. *Brigham Young University Education and Law Journal, 87–*137.

Brotman, S., Ryan, B., Jalbert, Y., & Rowe, B. (2002a). Reclaiming space—regaining health: The health care experiences of two-spirited people in Canada. *Journal of Gay and Lesbian Social Services, 14*(1), 67–87.

Brotman, S., Ryan, B., Jalbert, Y., & Rowe, B. (2002b). The impact of coming out on health and health care access: The experiences of gay, lesbian, bisexual and two-spirited people. *Journal of Health & Social Policy, 15*(1), 1–29.

Brown, E.R., Ojeda, V.D., Wyn, R., & Levan, R. (2000). *Racial and ethnic disparities in access to health insurance and health care.* Los Angeles, CA: UCLA Center for Health Policy Research and Kaiser Family Foundation.

Browne, A.J., & Fiske, J. (2001). First nations' women's encounters with mainstream health care services. *Western Journal of Nursing Research, 23,* 126–147.

Bullough, B., & Bullough, V. (1993). *Crossdressing, sex, and gender.* Philadelphia: University of Pennsylvania Press.

Byard, E. (2010). *Reflections from the First Federal Bullying Summit.* Retrieved from http:// www.glsen.org/cgi-bin/iowa/all/news/record/2607.html

Calimach, A. (2000). *The world history of male love: Homosexual traditions: The two-spirit tradition.* Retrieved from http://www.gay-art-history.org/gay-history/gay-customs/native -american-homosexuality/two-spirit-native-american-gay.html

Canfield-Lenfest, M. (2008). *Kids of trans resource guide.* Retrieved from http://www .colage.org/programs/trans/kot-resource-guide.pdf

Carroll, L. (2010). *Counseling sexual and gender minorities.* Upper Saddle River, NJ: Pearson Education.

Carter, R.T. (1995). *The influence of race and racial identity in psychotherapy.* New York, NY: Wiley.

Cass, V. (1979). Homosexual identity formation: A theoretical model. *Journal of Homosexuality, 4*(3), 219–235. doi:10.1300/J082v04n03_01

Catalano, R.F., Berglund, M.L., Ryan, J.A.M., Lonczak, H.S., & Hawkins, J.D. (2004). Positive youth development in the United States: Research findings on evaluations of positive youth development programs. *Annals of the American Academy of Political and Social Science, 591,* 98–124.

Center for Mental Health in Schools at UCLA. (2011, April). *Embedding bullying interventions into a comprehensive system of student and learning supports.* Los Angeles, CA: Author. Retrieved from http://smhp.psych.ucla.edu/pdfdocs/embeddingbullying.pdf

Center for Social and Emotional Education. (2010, January). *School climate research summary.* New York, NY: Author. Retrieved from http://www.schoolclimate.org/climate/ documents/SCBrief_v1n1_Jan2010.pdf

Centers for Disease Control and Prevention. (1992). 1993 revised classification system for HIV infection and expanded surveillance case definition for AIDS among adolescents and adults. *Morbidity and Mortality Weekly Report (MMWR), 41(RR-17).* Retrieved from http://www.cdc.gov/mmwr/preview/mmwrhtml/00018871.htm

Centers for Disease Control and Prevention. (1997). *Principles of community engagement.* Atlanta, GA: Author. Retrieved from http://www.cdc.gov/phppo/pce

Centers for Disease Control and Prevention. (2008a). *HIV in the United States.* Retrieved from http://www.cdc.gov/hiv/topics/surveillance/united_states.htm

Centers for Disease Control and Prevention. (2008b). *HIV/AIDS among youth*. Retrieved from http://www.cdc.gov/hiv/resources/factsheets/youth.htm

Centers for Disease Control and Prevention. (2008c). *HIV among gay, bisexual, and other men who have sex with men*. Retrieved from http://www.cdc.gov/hiv/topics/msm/index.htm

Centers for Disease Control and Prevention. (2009). *Suicide: Facts at a glance*. Retrieved from http://www.cdc.gov/ViolencePrevention/pdf/Suicide-DataSheet-a.pdf

Chamberlain, P. (2002). Treatment foster care. In B.J. Burns & K. Hoagwood (Eds.), *Community treatment for youth: Evidence-based interventions for severe emotional and behavioral disorders* (pp. 117–138). New York, NY: Oxford University Press.

Chan, C. (1995). Issues of sexual identity in an ethnic minority: The case of Chinese American lesbians, gay men, and bisexual people. In A. D'Augelli & C. Patterson (Eds.), *Lesbian, gay, and bisexual identities over the life span: Psychological perspectives* (pp. 87–101). New York, NY: Oxford University Press.

Charles, C., Gafni, A., & Whelan, T. (1997). Shared decision-making in the medical encounter: What does it mean? (or it takes at least two to tango). *Social Science and Medicine, 44*(5), 681–692.

Chasnoff, D. (Director). (2003). *Let's get real* [Film]. San Francisco, CA: GroundSpark.

Chasnoff, D. (Director and Coproducer). (2009). *Straightlaced: How gender's got us all tied up* [Film]. San Francisco, CA: GroundSpark.

Chesir-Teran, D., & Hughes, D. (2009). Heterosexism in high school and victimization among lesbian, gay, bisexual, and questioning students. *Journal of Youth and Adolescence, 38*(7), 963–975.

Child Welfare League of America, & Lambda Legal. (2010). *Getting down to basics: Tools to support LGBTQ youth in care*. Retrieved from http://www.lambdalegal.org/publications/getting-down-to-basics

Cho, S., Laub, C., Wall, S., & Daley, C. (2004). *Beyond the binary: A tool kit for gender identity activism in schools*. Retrieved from http://transgenderlawcenter.org/pdf/beyond_the_binary.pdf

Choudhury, P.P., Badhan, N.S., Chand, J., Chhugani, S., Choksey, R., Husainy, S., & Wat, E.C. (2009). Community alienation and its impact on help-seeking behavior among LGBTIQ South Asians in Southern California. *Journal of Gay & Lesbian Social Services, 21,* 247–266.

Clarke, V., Ellis, S., Peel, E., & Riggs, D.W. (2010). *Lesbian gay bisexual trans & queer psychology: An introduction*. Cambridge, United Kingdom: Cambridge University Press.

Clements, J.A., & Rosenwald, M. (2007). Foster parents' perspectives on LGB youth in the child welfare system. *Journal of Gay & Lesbian Social Services: Issues in Practice, Policy & Research, 19*(1), 57–69.

Clements-Nolle, K., Marx, R., Guzman, R., & Katz, M. (2001). HIV prevalence, risk behaviors, health care use, and mental health status of transgender persons: Implications for public health intervention. *American Journal of Public Health, 91*(6), 915–921.

Coates, S.W. (2008). Intervention with preschool boys with gender identity issues. *Neuropsychiatrie de l'enfance et de l'adolescence, 56,* 392–397.

Cochran, B.N., Stewart, A.J., Ginzler, J.A., & Cauce, A.M. (2002). Challenges faced by homeless sexual minorities: Comparison of gay, lesbian, bisexual, and transgender homeless adolescents with their heterosexual counterparts. *American Journal of Public Health, 92*(5), 773–777.

Cochran, S.D., & Mays, V.M. (2000). Lifetime prevalence of suicide symptoms and affective disorders among men reporting same-sex sexual partners: Results from NHANES III. *American Journal of Public Health, 90*(4), 573–578.

Cohen, S., Underwood, L.G., & Gottlieb, B.H. (2000). *Social support measurement and intervention: A guide for health and social scientists.* London, United Kingdom: Oxford University Press.

Cohen, S., & Wills, T.A. (1985). Stress, social support, and the buffering hypothesis. *Psychological Bulletin, 98,* 310–357.

Cohen-Kettenis, P.T. (2010). Psychosocial and psychosexual aspects of disorders of sex development. *Best Practice and Research: Clinical Endocrinology and Metabolism, 24*(2), 325–334.

Cohen-Kettenis, P.T., & Pfäfflin, F. (2003). *Transgenderism and intersexuality in childhood and adolescence: Making choices.* Thousand Oaks, CA: Sage Publications.

COLAGE. (2010a, November 10). *Making GSAs inclusive of youth with LGBTQ parents.* Retrieved from http://www.colage.org/resources/making-gsas-inclusive-of-youth-with-lgbt-parents

COLAGE. (2010b, November 10). *Not so gay: Differences between KOTs and children with LGB/Q parents.* Retrieved from http://www.colage.org/resources/not-so-gay-differences-between-kots-and-children-with-lgbq-parents

COLAGE. (2010c, November 10). *Tips for medical professionals for making better/safer environments for children with LGBT parents.* Retrieved from http://www.colage.org/resources/tips-for-medical-professionals-for-making-bettersafer-environments-for-children-with-lgbtq-parents

Coleman, E. (1987). Assessment of sexual orientation. *Journal of Homosexuality, 14*(1-2), 9–14.

Collaborative for Academic, Social, and Emotional Learning. (2003). *Safe and sound: An educational leader's guide to evidence-based social and emotional learning programs.* Chicago, IL: Author.

Conger, J.J. (1975). Proceedings of the American Psychological Association, incorporated, for the year 1974: Minutes of the annual meeting of the council of representatives. *American Psychologist, 30*(6), 620–651.

Consortium on the Management of Disorders of Sex Development. (2006a). *Clinical guidelines for the management of disorders of sex development.* Rohnert Park, CA: Intersex Society of North America.

Consortium on the Management of Disorders of Sex Development. (2006b). *Handbook for parents.* Rohnert Park, CA: Intersex Society of North America.

Cook, R., Fleishman, E., & Grimes, V. (1991). *A national evaluation of Title IV-E foster care independent living programs for youth, Phase 2.* (Final Report for Contract No. 105-87-1608). Rockville, MD: Westat.

Cook, R.J. (1991). *A national evaluation of the Title IV-E foster care independent living programs for youth: Phase 2.* (Contract No. OHDS 105-87-1608). U.S. Department of Health and Human Services. Rockville, MD, Westat.

Corliss, H.L., Shankle, M.D., & Moyer, M.B. (2007). Research, curricula, and resources related to lesbian, gay, bisexual, and transgender health in US schools of public health. *American Journal of Public Health, 97*(6), 1023–1027.

Cox, K.F. (2006). Investigating the impact of strength-based assessment on youth with emotional or behavioral disorders. *Journal of Child and Family Studies, 15*(3), 287–301.

Cox, K., Baker, D., & Wong, M.A. (2010). Wraparound retrospective: Factors predicting positive outcomes. *Journal of Emotional and Behavioral Disorders, 18,* 3–13.

Crisp, C., & McCave, M.L. (2007). Gay affirmative practice: A model for social work practice with gay, lesbian, and bisexual youth. *Child and Adolescent Social Work Journal, 24*(4), 403–421.

Crockett, L.J., Iturbide, M.I., Torres-Stone, R.A., McGinley, M., Raffaelli, M., & Carlo, G. (2007). Acculturation stress, social support, and coping: Relations to psychological adjustment among Mexican American college students. *Culture, Diversity, Ethnicity, Minority Psychology, 13*(4), 347–355.

Cross, T. (1995). Cultural issues and responses: Defining cultural competence in child mental health. *Contemporary Group Care Practice Research and Evaluation, 5,* 4–6.

Cross, T., Bazron, B., Dennis, K., & Isaacs, M. (1989). *Towards a culturally competent system of care: A monograph on effective services for minority children who are severely emotionally disturbed: Volume 1.* Washington, DC: National Center for Cultural Competence, Georgetown University Center for Child and Human Development.

Cross, T., Earle, K., Solie, H.E-H., & Manness, K. (2000). Cultural strengths and challenges in implementing a system of care model in American Indian communities. In *Systems of care: Promising practices in children's mental health, 2000 Series* (Vol. 1, pp. 1–106). Washington, DC: Center for Effective Collaboration and Practice, American Institutes for Research.

Crutsinger-Perry, L. (2009, February 19). *Social Marketing 101* [Session 4 of the "Youth & HIV" webinar series]. National Youth Advocacy Coalition. Retrieved from http://www.nyacyouth.org/resources/best_practices.php

Crutsinger-Perry, L., & Webster, I. (2009, January). Creating safe spaces for LGBTQ youth [Session 3 of the "Youth & HIV" webinar series]. National Youth Advocacy Coalition. Retrieved from http://www.nyacyouth.org/resources/best_practices.php

Cummins, S.K., & Jackson, R.J. (2001). *The built environment and children's health.* Retrieved from http://www.cdc.gov/healthyplaces/articles/The%20Built%20Environment%20and%20Children%20Health.pdf

Curtain, M. (2002). Lesbian and bisexual girls in the juvenile justice system. *Child and Adolescent Social Work Journal, 19*(4), 285–301.

D'Augelli, A. (2002). Mental health problems among lesbian, gay, and bisexual youths ages 14 to 21. *Clinical Child Psychology and Psychiatry, 7*(3), 433–456. doi:10.1177/1359104502007003039

D'Augelli, A. (2006). Developmental and contextual factors and mental health among lesbian, gay, and bisexual youths. In A.M. Omoto & H.S. Kurtzman (Eds.), *Sexual orientation and mental health: Examining identity and development in lesbian, gay, and bisexual people* (pp. 37–53). Washington, DC: American Psychological Association. doi:10.1037/11261-002

D'Augelli, A.R. (2002). Mental health problems among lesbian, gay, and bisexual youth ages 14 to 21. *Clinical Child Psychology and Psychiatry, 7*(3), 439–462.

D'Augelli, A.R., Grossman, A.H., Salter, N.P., Vasey, J.J., Starks, M.T., & Sinclair, K.O. (2005). Predicting the suicide attempts of lesbian, gay, and bisexual youth. *Suicide and Life-Threatening Behavior, 35*(6), 646–660. doi:10.1521/suli.2005.35.6.646

D'Augelli, A.R., Grossman, A.H., & Starks, M.T. (2006). Childhood gender atypicality, victimization, and PTSD among lesbian, gay, and bisexual youth. *Journal of Interpersonal Violence, 21,* 1–21.

Davis, K.E., & Travis, D.J. (2010). Culture and leadership in systems of care. In G.M. Blau & P.R. Magrab (Eds.), *The leadership equation: Strategies for individuals who are champions for children, youth, & families the multicultural workforce* (pp. 199–226). Baltimore, MD: Paul H. Brookes Publishing Co.

Delemarre-Van de Waal, H.A., & Cohen-Kettenis, P.T. (2006). Clinical management of gender identity disorder in adolescents: A protocol on psychological and paediatric endocrinology aspects. *European Journal of Endocrinology, 155*(Suppl 1), S131–S137.

Denny, D. (2004). Changing models of transsexualism. In U. Leli & J. Drescher (Eds.), *Transgender subjectivities: A clinician's guide* (pp. 25–40). Binghamton, NY: Haworth Medical Press.

Denny, D. (2006). Transgender communities of the United States in the late twentieth century. In P. Currah, R.M. Juang, & S. Minter (Eds.), *Transgender rights: History, politics, and law* (pp. 171–191). Minneapolis, MN: University of Minnesota Press.

Dessens, A., Slijper, F., & Drop, S. (2005). Gender dysphoria and gender change in chromosomal females with congenital adrenal hyperplasia. *Archives of Sexual Behavior, 34*(4), 389–397.

De Vries, A.L.C., Cohen-Kettenis, P.T., & Delemarre-Van de Waal. H. (2006). Clinical management of gender dysphoria in adolescents. In *Caring for transgender adolescents in BC: Suggested guidelines* (pp. A1–A11). Vancouver, BC, Canada: Vancouver Coastal Health, Transcend Transgender Support & Education Society, and the Canadian Rainbow Health Coalition. Retrieved from http://transhealth.vch.ca/resources/library/tcpdocs/guidelines-adolescent.pdf

Diamond, L.M. (2006). What we got wrong about sexual identity development: Unexpected findings from a longitudinal study of young women. In A. Omoto & H. Kurtzman (Eds.), *Sexual orientation and mental health: Examining identity development in lesbian, gay, and bisexual people* (pp. 73–94). Washington, DC: American Psychological Association. doi:10.1037/11261-000

Diamond, M. (2004). Sex, gender, and identity over the years: A changing perspective. *Child and Adolescent Psychiatric Clinics of North America, 13*(3), 591–607.

Diaz, R.M., & Ayala, G. (2001). *Social discrimination and health: The case of Latino gay men and HIV risk.* New York, NY: Policy Institute, National Gay & Lesbian Task Force.

Draper, N. (2010, September 27). Anoka-Hennepin schools implored to protect GLBT students. *Minneapolis-St. Paul Star Tribune.* Retrieved from http://www.startribune.com/local/north/103902163.html

Draughn, T., Elkins, B., & Roy, R. (2002). Allies in the struggle: Eradicating homophobia and heterosexism on campus. *Journal of Lesbian Studies, 6*(3/4), 9.

Dreger, A. (1998). *Hermaphrodites and the medical invention of sex.* Boston, MA: Harvard University Press.

Dreger, A.D. (1998). "Ambiguous sex"—or ambivalent medicine? Ethical issues in the treatment of intersexuality. *The Hastings Center Report, 28*(3), 24–35.

Drescher, J. (2010). Queer diagnoses: Parallels and contrasts in the history of homosexuality, gender variance and the Diagnostic and Statistical Manual. *Archives of Sexual Behavior, 39,* 427–460.

Drummond, K.D., Bradley, S.J., Peterson-Badali, M., & Zucker, K.J. (2008). A follow-up study of girls with gender identity disorder. *Developmental Psychology, 44*(1), 34–45. doi:10.1037/0012-1649.44.1.34

Duggan, P. (2001, September 9). *Slain Navajo teenager a powerful symbol for gay activists.* Retrieved from http://www.sfgate.com/cgi-bin/article.cgi?f=/c/a/2001/09/09/MN110577.DTL

Dunbar, E. (2006). Race, gender, and sexual orientation in hate crime victimization: Identity politics or identity risk? *Violence and Victims, (21)*3, 323–327.

Dunn, D. (2010, November). *Some issues in teaching critical thinking.* Colloquium for the faculty of The George Washington University, Washington, DC.

Dunne, C., & Goode, T. (2004). *Using a book club to confront attitudinal barriers.* Retrieved from http://www11.georgetown.edu/research/gucchd/nccc/resources/practices.html

Duran, E. (2006). *Healing the soul wound: Counseling with American Indians and other Native peoples.* New York, NY: Teachers College Press.

Duran, E., & Duran, B. (1995). *Native American postcolonial psychology.* Albany: State University of New York Press.

Dwyer, K., & Osher, D. (2007). *Safeguarding our children: An action guide revised and expanded.* Longmont, CO: Sopris West Educational Services.

Egan, S., & Perry, G. (2001). Gender identity: A multidimensional analysis with implications for psychosocial adjustment. *Developmental Psychology, 37*(4), 451–463.

Ehrbar, R., Witty, M., Ehrbar, H., & Bockting, W. (2008). Clinical judgment in the diagnosis of gender identity disorder in children. *Journal of Sex and Marital Therapy, 34,* 385–412.

Ehrensaft, D. (2007). Raising girlyboys: A parent's perspective. *Studies in Gender and Sexuality, 8*(3), 269–302.

Ehrensaft, D. (2011). *Gender born, gender made.* New York, NY: The Experiment.

Eisenberg, M.E., Ackard, D.M., & Resnick, M.D. (2007). Protective factors and suicide risk in adolescents with a history of sexual abuse. *The Journal of Pediatrics, 151*(5), 482–487.

Ekins, R., & King, D. (2006). *The transgender phenomenon.* Thousand Oaks, CA: Sage Publications.

Elze, D., & McHaelen, R. (2009). Moving the Margins: Training Curriculum for Child Welfare Services with Lesbian, Gay, Bisexual, Transgender, and Questioning (LGBTQ) Youth in Out-of-Home Care. Retrieved from http://www.lambdalegal.org/publications/moving-the-margins

Elze, D.E. (2006). Working with gay, lesbian, bisexual, and transgender students. In C. Franklin, M.B. Harris, & P. Allen-Meares (Eds.), *The school services handbook: A guide for school-based professionals* (pp. 861–870). New York, NY: Oxford University Press.

Epple, C. (1998). Coming to terms with Navajo Nadleehi: A critique of berdache, gay, alternative gender and two-spirit. *American Ethnologist, 25*(2), 267–290.

The Equity Project. (n.d.). *The Equity Project.* Retrieved from http://www.equityproject.org/

Espinoza, R. (2008). *Lesbian, gay, bisexual, transgender, and queer grantmaking by U.S. foundations.* New York, NY: Funders for Lesbian and Gay Issues. Retrieved from http://www.lgbtfunders.org/files/FLGI%202006.report.final.pdf

Evans-Campbell, T., & Walters, K.L. (2004). Catching our breath: A decolonization framework for healing indigenous families. In R. Fong, R. McRoy, & C.O. Hendricks (Eds.), *Intersecting child welfare, substance abuse, and family violence: Culturally competent approaches* (pp. 266–292). Alexandria, VA: Council on Social Work Education.

Farmer, E.M.Z., Mustillo, S., Burns, B.J., & Holden, W.E. (2008). Use and predictors of out-of-home placements within systems of care. *Journal of Emotional and Behavioral Disorders, 16*(5). doi:10.1177/1063426607310845

Farr, R.H., Forssell, S.L., & Patterson, C.J. (2010). Parenting and child development in adoptive families: Does parental sexual orientation matter? *Applied Developmental Science, 14,* 164–178.

Fassinger, R.E. (1991). The hidden minority: Issues and challenges in working with lesbian women and gay men. *Counseling Psychologist, 19,* 157–176.

Feinberg, L. (1996). *Transgender warriors: Making history from Joan of Arc to Dennis Rodman.* Boston, MA: Beacon Press.

Fergusson, D.M., Horwood, L.J., & Beautrais, A.L. (1999). Is sexual orientation related to mental health problems and suicidality in young people? *Archives of General Psychiatry, 56,* 876–880.

Fieland, K.C., Walters, K.L., & Simoni, J.M. (2007). Determinants of health among two-spirit American Indians and Alaskan natives. In I. Meyer & M. Northridge (Eds.), *The health of sexual minorities: Public health perspectives on lesbian, gay, bisexual and transgender populations* (pp. 268–300). New York, NY: Springer.

Fisher, S.K., Easterly, S., & Lazear, K.J. (2008). Lesbian, gay, bisexual and transgender families and their children. In T. Gullotta & G. Blau (Eds.), *Family influences on childhood behavior and development* (pp. 187–208). New York, NY: Routledge.

Floyd, F.J., & Stein, T.S. (2002). Sexual orientation identity formation among gay, lesbian, and bisexual youths: Multiple patterns of milestone experiences. *Journal of Research on Adolescence, 12*(2), 167–191. doi:10.1111/1532-7795.00030

Forquera, R. (2001). *Urban Indian health.* Menlo Park, CA: The Henry J. Kaiser Family Foundation.

Frank, M.L., & Lester, D. (2002). Self destructive behaviors in American Indian and Alaska Native high school youth. *American Indian and Alaska Native Mental Health Research, 10*(3), 24–32.

Frazer, M.S., & Pruden, H. (2010). *Reclaiming our voice: Two-spirit health & human service needs in New York State.* Albany: New York State Department of Health AIDS Institute.

Friedman, M.S., Koeske, G.F., Silvestre, A.J., Korr, W.S., & Sites, E.W. (2006). The impact of gender-role nonconforming behavior, bullying, and social support on suicidality among gay male youth. *Journal of Adolescent Health, 38,* 621–623.

Freundlich, M., & Avery, R.J. (2004). Gay and lesbian youth in foster care: Meeting their placement and service needs. *Journal of Gay & Lesbian Social Services, 17*(4), 39–57. doi: 10.1300/J041v17n04_03

Gamache, P.E., & Lazear, K.J. (2009). *Asset-based approaches for lesbian, gay, bisexual, transgender, questioning, intersex, two-spirit (LGBTQI2-S) youth and their families in system of care.* (FMHI pub. no. 252). Tampa, FL: University of South Florida, College of Behavioral and Community Sciences, The Louis de la Parte Florida Mental Health Institute, Research and Training Center for Children's Mental Health.

Gangamma R., Slesnick, N., Toviessi, P., & Serovich, J. (2008). Comparison of HIV risks among gay, lesbian, bisexual and heterosexual homeless youth. *Journal of Youth and Adolescence, 37*(4), 456–464.

Garnets, L., Hancock, K.A., Cochran, S.D., Goodchilds, J., & Peplau, L.A. (1991). Issues in psychotherapy with lesbians and gay men: A survey of psychologists. *American Psychologist, 46*(9), 964–974.

Garofalo R., Deleon J., Osmer E., Doll, M., & Harper, G.W. (2006). Overlooked, misunderstood and at-risk: Exploring the lives and HIV risk of ethnic minority male-to-female transgender youth. *Journal of Adolescent Health, 38,* 230–236.

Garofalo, R., Wolf, R.C., Kessel, S., Palfrey, S.J., & DuRant, R.H. (1998). The association between health risk behaviors and sexual orientation among a school-based sample of adolescents. *Pediatrics, 101*(5), 895–902.

Garofalo, R., Wolf, R.C., Wissow, L.S., Woods, E.R., & Goodman, E. (1999). Sexual orientation and risk of suicide attempts among a representative sample of youth. *Archives of Pediatrics & Adolescent Medicine, 153*(5), 487–493.

Garrett, M.L., & Barrett, B. (2003). Two-Spirit: Counseling Native American gay, lesbian and bisexual people. *Journal of Multicultural Counseling and Development, 31*(2), 131–142.

Gastaud, F., Bouvattier, C., Duranteau, L., Brauner, R., Thibaud, E., Kutten, F., & Bougneres, P. (2007). Impaired sexual and reproductive outcomes in women with classical forms of congenital adrenal hyperplasia. *The Journal of Clinical Endocrinology & Metabolism, 92*(4), 1391.

Gates, G.J. (2006). *Same-sex couples and the gay, lesbian, bisexual population: New estimates from the American Community Survey.* Los Angeles, CA: The Williams Institute. Retrieved from http://williamsinstitute.law.ucla.edu/wp-content/uploads/Gates-Same-Sex-Couples-GLB-Pop-ACS-Oct-2006.pdf

Gay, Lesbian & Straight Education Network. (2007). *Gay-straight alliances: Creating safer schools for LGBT students and their allies.* (GLSEN Research Brief). New York, NY: Author. Retrieved from http://www.gsanetwork.org/files/resources/GLSEN-GSAbrief.pdf

Gay, Lesbian & Straight Education Network. (2008). *ThinkB4YouSpeak educator's guide for discussing and addressing anti-gay language among teens.* Retrieved from http://www.thinkb4youspeak.com/ForEducators/GLSEN-EducatorsGuide.pdf

Gay, Lesbian & Straight Education Network. (2009). *Day of Silence organizing manual.* Retrieved from http://www.dayofsilence.org/downloads/2009_Manual_FINAL.pdf

Gay, Lesbian & Straight Education Network. (2010). *2009 National School Climate Survey: Nearly 9 out of 10 LGBT students experience harassment in school.* Retrieved from http://www.glsen.org/cgi-bin/iowa/all/news/record/2624.html

Gay, Lesbian & Straight Education Network. (2011). *About gay-straight alliances (GSAs).* Retrieved from http://www.glsen.org/cgi-bin/iowa/all/library/record/2342.html?state=what

Gay, Lesbian & Straight Education Network. (n.d.a). *ThinkB4YouSpeak campaign web site.* Retrieved from www.thinkb4youspeak.com

Gay, Lesbian & Straight Education Network. (n.d.b). *Tools & tips: Educators.* Retrieved from http://www.glsen.org/cgi-bin/iowa/all/educator/index.html

Gay, Lesbian & Straight Education Network, & Harris Interactive. (2008). *The principal's perspective: School safety, bullying and harassment, a survey of public school principals.* New York, NY: Author. Retrieved from http://www.glsen.org/binary-data/GLSEN_ATTACHMENTS/file/000/001/1167-2.pdf

Gay, Lesbian & Straight Education Network, & Harris Interactive. (2012). *Playgrounds and prejudice: Elementary school climate in the United States: A survey of students and teachers.* Retrieved from http://www.glsen.org/binary-data/GLSEN_ATTACHMENTS/file/000/002/2027-1.pdf

Gay-Straight Alliance Network. (n.d.). *What is a GSA?* Retrieved from http://www.gsanetwork.org/what-we-do

Georgetown University Center for Child and Human Development, National Center for Cultural Competence. (2011). *Linguistic competence: Definition.* Retrieved from http://www11.georgetown.edu/research/gucchd/nccc/foundations/frameworks.html#lcdefinition

Germain, C.B., & Patterson, S.L. (1988). Teaching about rural natural helpers as environmental resources. *Journal of Teaching in Social Work, 2,* 73–90.

Gilley, B.J., (2006). *Becoming two-spirit: Gay identity and social acceptance in Indian country.* Lincoln: University of Nebraska Press.

Gilley, B.J., & Co-Cké, J.H. (2005). Cultural investment: Providing opportunities to reduce risky behavior among gay American Indian males. *Journal of Psychoactive Drugs, 37*(3), 293–298.

Glicken, M.D. (2006). Resilience in gay, lesbian, bisexual, and transgender (GLBT) individuals. In M.D. Glicken (Ed.), *Learning from resilient people: Lessons we can apply to counseling and psychotherapy* (pp. 157–169). Thousand Oaks, CA: Sage Publications.

Goldsmith, S.K., & Institute of Medicine Committee on Pathophysiology & Prevention of Adolescent & Adult Suicide. (2002). *Reducing suicide: A national imperative.* Washington, DC: National Academies Press.

Goode, T., Haywood, S., Wells, N., & Rhee, R. (2009). Family-centered, culturally and linguistically competent care: Essential components of the medical home. *Pediatric Annals, 38*(9), 505–512.

Goode, T., & Jackson, V. (2005). *Cultural and linguistic competency: What systems of care are telling us.* Unpublished report.

Goode, T., & Jones, W. (2009). *Linguistics definition.* Retrieved from http://www11.georgetown.edu/research/gucchd/nccc/documents/Definition%20of%20Linguistic%20Competence.pdf

Goode, T., Jones, W., Jackson, V., Bronheim, S., Dunne, C., & Lorenzo-Hubert, I. (2010). *Cultural and Linguistic Competence Family Organization Assessment Instrument.* Washington, DC: National Center for Cultural Competence, Georgetown University Center for Child and Human Development. Retrieved from http://www.gucchdgeorgetown .net/NCCC/CLCFOA/NCCC_CLCFOAAssessment.pdf

Goode, T., Jones, W., & Mason, J. (2002). *A guide to planning and implementing cultural competence organizational assessment.* Washington, DC: National Center for Cultural Competence, Georgetown University Center for Child and Human Development.

Goode, T., Trivedi, P., & Jones, W. (2010). *Cultural and linguistic competence assessment for disability organizations.* Washington, DC: National Center for Cultural Competence, Georgetown University Center for Child and Human Development. Retrieved from http://www.gucchdgeorgetown.net/NCCC/CLCADO

Goode, T.D. (2009). *Promoting Cultural Diversity and Cultural Competency: Self-Assessment Checklist for Personnel Providing Behavioral Health Services and Supports for Children, Youth and Their Families.* Washington, DC: National Center for Cultural Competence, Georgetown University Center for Child and Human Development.

Goode, T.D. (2010). *A guide for using the Cultural and Linguistic Competence Family Organizational Assessment Instrument.* Washington, DC: National Center for Cultural Competence, Georgetown University Center for Child and Human Development. Retrieved from http://www.gucchdgeorgetown.net/NCCC/CLCFOA/

Goode, T.D., Dunne, M.C., & Bronheim, S.M. (2006). *The evidence base for cultural and linguistic competency in health care.* The Commonwealth Fund (Pub. No. 962). Retrieved from http://www.medicalleadership.org/downloads/CP_Cultural_and_Linguistic _Competancy.pdf

Goodenow, C. (1993). Classroom belonging among early adolescent students: Relationships to motivation and achievement. *Journal of Early Adolescence, 13,* 21–43.

Goodenow, C. (2004). *2003 Youth Risk Behavior Survey results.* Malden: Massachusetts Department of Education.

Goodenow, C., Szalacha, L., & Westheimer, K. (2006). School support groups, other school factors, and the safety of sexual minority adolescents. *Psychology in the Schools, 43,* 573–589.

Gooren, L.J.G., & Delemarre-Van de Waal, H. (1996). The feasibility of endocrine interventions in juvenile transsexuals. *Journal of Psychology & Human Sexuality, 8*(4), 69–74.

Gottlieb, B.H. (1983). *Social support strategies* (Sage Studies in Community Mental Health). Thousand Oaks, CA: Sage Publications.

Gottlieb, B.H. (1988). *Marshalling social support.* Thousand Oaks, CA: Sage Publications.

Gough, B., Weyman, N., Alderson, J., Butler, G., & Stoner, M. (2008). "They did not have a word": The parental quest to locate a "true sex" for their intersex children. *Psychology and Health, 23*(4), 493–507.

Green, R. (1987). *The "sissy boy syndrome" and the development of homosexuality.* New Haven, CT: Yale University Press.

Greene, B. (1994). Lesbian and gay sexual orientations: Implications for clinical training, practice, and research. In B. Greene & G. Herek (Eds.), *Psychological perspectives on lesbian and gay issues: Vol. 1. Lesbian and gay psychology: Theory, research, and clinical applications* (pp. 1–24). Thousand Oaks, CA: Sage Publications.

Greene, J., Ennett, S., & Ringwalt, C. (1999). Prevalence and correlates of survival sex among runaway and homeless youth. *American Journal of Public Health, 89*(9), 1406–1409.

Greytak, E.A., & Kosciw, J.G. (2010). *Year one evaluation of the New York City Department of Education Respect for All training program.* New York, NY: GLSEN.

Griffin, C.W., Wirth, M.J., & Wirth, A.G. (1996). *Beyond acceptance: Parents of lesbians and gays talk about their experiences.* New York, NY: St. Martin's Press.

Griffin, D.W., & Bartholomew, K. (1994). Models of the self and other: Fundamental dimensions underlying measures of adult attachment. *Journal of Personality and Social Psychology, 67,* 430–445.

Griffin, P., Lee, C., Waugh, L., & Beyer, C. (2005). Describing roles that gay-straight alliances play in schools: From individual support to social change. In J.T. Sears (Ed.), *Gay, lesbian, and transgender issues in education: Programs, policies, and practices* (pp. 167–181). New York, NY: Harrington Park Press.

Griffin, P., & Ouellett, M.L. (2002). Going beyond gay-straight alliances to make schools safe for lesbian, gay, bisexual, and transgender students. *Angles, 6*(1), 1–8. Retrieved from http://idahossc.com/wp-content/uploads/2010/03/Going-Beyond-Gay-Straight -Alliances.pdf

Grim, J.A. (2000). Cultural identity, authenticity, and community survival: The politics of recognition in the study of native American religions. In L. Irwin (Ed.), *Native American spirituality: A critical reader* (pp. 37–60). Lincoln: University of Nebraska Press.

Grossman, A.H., & D'Augelli, A.R. (2006). Transgender youth: Invisible and vulnerable. *Journal of Homosexuality, 51,* 111–128. Retrieved from http://hayworthpress.com/web/JH

Grossman, A.H., & D'Augelli, A.R. (2007). Transgender youth and life-threatening behaviors. *Suicide and Life Threatening Behavior, 37*(5), 527–537.

Grossman, A.H., D'Augelli, A.R., Howell, T.J., & Hubbard, S. (2005). Parent's reactions to transgender youth's gender nonconforming expression and identity. *Journal of Gay and Lesbian Social Services, 18*(1), 3–16.

Gruskin, E.P., Hart, S., Gordon, N., & Ackerson, L. (2001). Patterns of cigarette smoking and alcohol use among lesbians and bisexual women enrolled in a large health maintenance organization. *American Journal of Public Health, 91*(6), 976–979.

Gupta, D.K., & Menon, P.S. (1997). Ambiguous genitalia—an Indian perspective. *Indian Journal of Pediatrics, 64*(2), 189–194.

Gurley, D., Novins, D.K., Jones, M.C., Beals, J., Shore, J.H., & Manson, S.M. (2001). Comparative use of biomedical services and traditional healing options by American Indian veterans. *Psychiatric Services, 52*(1), 68–74.

Haas, A.P., Eliason, M., Mays, V.M., Mathy, R.M., Cochran, S.D., D'Augelli, A.R., & Clayton, P.J. (2011). Suicide and suicide risk in lesbian, gay, bisexual, and transgender populations: Review and recommendations. *Journal of Homosexuality, 58*(1), 10–51.

Hall, H.I., Song, R., Rhodes, P., Prejean, J., An, Q., Lee, L.M., . . . Janssen, R.S. (2008). Estimation of HIV incidence in the United States. *Journal of the American Medical Association, 300*(5), 500–529. doi:10.1001/jama.300.5.520

Halperin, D.T., Steiner, M.J., Cassell, M.M., Green, E.C., Hearst, N., Kirby, D., . . . Cates, W. (2004). The time has come for common ground on preventing sexual transmission of HIV. *Lancet, 364*(9449), 1913–1914.

Hammer, H., Finkelhor, D., & Sedlak, A.J. (2002). *Runaway/thrownaway children: National estimates and characteristics.* Retrieved from http://digitalcommons.unl.edu/humtraff data/20

Hanson, T.L., Austin, G., & Lee-Bayha, J. (2003). *Student health risks, resilience, and academic performance: Year 1 report.* Los Alamitos, CA: WestEd. Retrieved from http://chks.wested .org/resources/APIreportY1.pdf

Hanssmann, C., Morrison, D., & Russian, E. (2008). Talking, gawking, or getting it done: Provider trainings to increase cultural and clinical competence for transgender and gender-nonconforming patients and clients. *Sexuality Research & Social Policy, 5*(1), 5–23.

Harper, C. (2007). *Intersex*. New York, NY: Berg.

Harper, G.W., & Schneider, M. (2003). Oppression and discrimination among lesbian, gay, bisexual, and transgendered people and communities: A challenge for community psychology. *American Journal of Community Psychology, 31*(3/4), 243–252.

Harris Interactive. (2010, July 13). *Gay and lesbian adults are more likely and more frequent blog readers* [Press release]. Retrieved from http://www.harrisinteractive.com/News Room/PressReleases/tabid/446/mid/1506/articleId/435/ctl/ReadCustom%20 Default/Default.aspx

Hatzenbuehler, M.L. (2011). The social environment and suicide attempts in lesbian, gay, and bisexual youth. *Pediatrics, 127*. Retrieved from http://pediatrics.aappublications .org/content/early/2011/04/18/peds.2010-3020.abstract

Hazel, K.L., & Mohatt, G.V. (2001). Cultural and spiritual coping in sobriety: Informing substance abuse prevention for Alaska Native communities. *Journal of Community Psychology, 29*(5), 541–562.

Hekma, G. (1994). A female soul in a male body: Sexual inversion as gender inversion in nineteenth-century sexology. In G. Herdt (Ed.), *Third sex, third gender: Beyond sexual dimorphism in culture and history* (pp. 213–240). New York, NY: Zone Books.

Helping Individual Prostitutes Survive. (n.d.). *Organization home page*. Retrieved from http://hips.org

Henning-Stout, M., James, S., & Macintosh, S. (2000). Reducing harassment of lesbian, gay, bisexual, transgender, and questioning youth in schools. *School Psychology Review, 29*(2), 180–191.

Herek, G.M. (2003). The psychology of sexual prejudice. In L. Garnets & D.C. Kimmel (Eds.), *Psychological perspectives on lesbian, gay, and bisexual experiences* (pp. 157–164). Irvington, NY: Columbia University Press.

Hernandez, M., & Nesman, T. (2006, February). *Conceptual model for accessibility of mental health services to culturally/linguistically diverse populations.* Presented during the grantee communities workshop "Operationalizing cultural competence for implementation in systems of care" at the 19th Annual Research Conference: A System of Care for Children's Mental Health: Expanding the Research Base, Tampa, FL.

Hernandez, M., Nesman, T., Mowery, D., & Gamache, P.E. (2006). *Examining the research base supporting culturally competent children's mental health services (Making children's mental health services successful series, pub. no. 240-1).* Tampa, FL: University of South Florida, Louis de la Parte Florida Mental Health Institute, Research & Training Center for Children's Mental Health. Retrieved from http://rtckids.fmhi.usf.edu/rtcpubs/Cultural Competence/services/default.cfm

Herrell, R., Goldberg, J., True, W.R., Ramakrishnan, V., Lyons, M., Eisen, S., & Tsuang, M.T. (1999). Sexual orientation and suicidality: A co-twin control study in adult men. *Archives of General Psychiatry, 56*(10), 867–874.

Hill, D.B., & Menvielle, E. (2009). You have to give them a place where they feel protected and safe and loved: The views of parents who have gender-variant children and adolescents. *Journal of LGBT Youth, 6,* 243–271.

Hill, D.B., Menvielle, E., Sica, K.M., & Johnson, A. (2010). An affirmative intervention for families with gender variant children: Parental ratings of child mental health and gender. *Journal of Sex & Marital Therapy, 36,* 6–23.

Hill, P.H., & Pargament, K.I. (2003). Advances in the conceptualization and measurement of religion and spirituality: Implications for physical and mental health research. *American Psychologist, 58*(1), 64–74.

Himmelstein, K.E.W., & Brückner, H. (2010). Criminal-justice and school sanctions against non-heterosexual youth: A national longitudinal study. *Pediatrics, 127*(1), 49–57. doi:10.1542/peds.2009-2306

Hines, M. (2004). Psychosexual development in individuals who have female pseudo-hermaphroditism. *Child and Adolescent Psychiatric Clinics of North America, 13*(3), 641–656.

Holman, C., & Goldberg, J.M. (2007). Ethical, legal, and psychosocial issues in care of transgender adolescents. *International Journal of Transgenderism, 9*(3-4), 95–110. doi:10.1300/J485v09n03_05

Holmes, S.E., & Cahill, S. (2005). School experiences of gay, lesbian, bisexual and transgender youth. In J.T. Sears (Ed.), *Gay, lesbian, and transgender issues in education: Programs, policies, and practices* (pp. 63–76). New York, NY: Harrington Park Press.

Homelessness Resource Center. (2010). *Learning from the field: Expert panel on youth who are LGBTQI2-S and homeless, summary of proceedings.* Retrieved from http://homeless.samhsa.gov/ResourceFiles/igkfngko.3.6.pdf

Homelessness Resource Center. (n.d.). *Trauma informed care.* Retrieved from https://admin.na6.acrobat.com/_a966410469/p86988983/?launcher=false&fcsContent=true&pbMode=normal

Hooks-Wayman, R., & Sicilliano, C. (2009, March 27). *The first step is an open mind: Best practices for working with LGBTQ youth* [Webcast]. Homelessness Resource Center. Retrieved from http://homeless.samhsa.gov/Resource/HRC-Webcast-Resources-The-First-Step-is-an-Open-Mind-Best-Practices-for-Working-with-LGBTQ-Youth-45610.aspx

Hooper, V. (2004). *Gay, lesbian, and bisexual youth: Facing challenges, building resilience.* New York: New York University Child Study Center.

Horvath, A.O., & Symonds, B.D. (1991). Relation between working alliance and outcome in psychotherapy: A meta-analysis. *Journal of Counseling Psychology, 38,* 139–149.

Hughes, T.L., & Eliason, M. (2002). Substance use and abuse in lesbian, gay, bisexual and transgender populations. *The Journal of Primary Prevention, 22*(3), 263–298.

Hunter, J., & Schaecher, R. (1987). Stresses on gay and lesbian adolescents in schools. *Social Work in Education, 9*(3), 180–189.

Hurwitz, R.S. (2010). Long-term outcomes in male patients with sex development disorders—How are we doing and how can we improve? *Journal of Urology, 184*(3), 831–832.

Hyde, J. (2005). From home to street: Understanding young people's transitions into homelessness. *Journal of Adolescence, 28*(2), 171–183.

Indian Health Service. (1997). *Trends in Indian health, 1996.* Rockville, MD: U.S. Department of Health and Human Services, Public Health Service, Indian Health Service, Office of Planning, Evaluation and Legislation, Division of Program Statistics.

Institute of Medicine. (2011). *The health of lesbian, gay, bisexual, and transgender people: Building a foundation for better understanding.* Washington, DC: National Academies Press.

Ireys, H.T., Sills, E.M., Kolodner, K.B., & Walsh, B.B. (1996). A social support intervention for parents of children with juvenile rheumatoid arthritis: Results of a randomized trial. *Journal of Pediatric Psychology, 21*(5), 633–641.

Irvine, A. (2010). We've had three of them: Addressing the invisibility of lesbian, gay bisexual, and gender nonconforming youths in the juvenile system. *Columbia Journal of Gender and Law, 19*(3), 675–702.

Isaacs, M. (1998). *Towards a culturally competent system of care volume III, the state of the states: Responses to cultural competence and diversity in child mental health.* Washington, DC: Georgetown University Child Development Center, Center for Child Health and Mental Health Policy.

Isaacs, M. (2010, May). *Meeting overview, goals and objectives.* Presented at Integrating Evidence and Practice: Developing an Inclusive Framework for Effective Mental Health Services for Children and Their Families. ICF Macro and National Alliance of Multiethnic Behavioral Health Associations, sponsored by Child, Adolescent and Family Branch, Center for Mental Health Services, Substance Abuse and Mental Health Services Administration, Washington, DC.

Isaacs, M., Jackson, V., Hicks, R., & Wang, E. (2008). Cultural and linguistic competence and eliminating disparities. In B. Stroul & G. Blau (Eds.), *The system of care handbook: Transforming mental health services for children, youth and families* (pp. 301–328). Baltimore, MD: Paul H. Brookes Publishing Co.

Israel, G., & Tarver, D. (1997). *Transgender care: Recommended guidelines, practical information, & personal accounts.* Philadelphia, PA: Temple University Press.

Jackson, R.A., McCloskey, K.A., & McHaelen, R.P. (2011). *A sexuality & gender diversity training program: Increasing the competency of mental health professionals.* Sarasota, FL: Professional Resource Press.

Jacobs, J., & Freundlich, M. (2006). Achieving permanency for LGBTQ youth. *Child Welfare: Journal of Policy, Practice, and Program (Special Issue: LGBQ Youth in Child Welfare), 85*(2), 299–316.

Jacobs, S.E., Thomas, W., & Lang, S. (Eds.). (1997). *Two-spirit people: Native American gender identity, sexuality and spirituality.* Urbana: University of Illinois Press.

Jamil, O.B., Harper, G.W., & Fernandez, M.I. (2009). Sexual and ethnic identity development among gay-bisexual-questioning (GBQ) male ethnic minority adolescents. *Cultural Diversity and Ethnic Minority Psychology, 15*(3), 203–214.

Jezewski, M.A., & Sotnik, P. (2001). *The rehabilitation service provider as culture broker: Providing culturally competent services to foreign born persons.* Buffalo, NY: Center for International Rehabilitation Research Information and Exchange.

Jiang, Y., Perry, D.K., & Hesser, J.E. (2010). Adolescent suicide and health risk behaviors: Rhode Island's 2007 Youth Risk Behavior Survey. *American Journal of Preventive Medicine, 38*(5), 551–555.

Johannsen, T.H., Ripa, C.P.L., Mortensen, E.L., & Main, K.M. (2006). Quality of life in 70 women with disorders of sex development. *European Journal of Endocrinology, 155*(6), 877.

Kaiser Family Foundation. (2002). *National Survey of Physicians Part I: Doctors on disparities in medical care.* Washington, DC: Author.

Kalamazoo Gay & Lesbian Resource Center. (2005). *2005 youth health and safety survey.* Contact: KGLRC, 629 Pioneer Street, Suite 102, Kalamazoo, Michigan, 49008.

Kamradt, B. (2001). Wraparound Milwaukee: Aiding youth with mental health needs. *Juvenile Justice, Journal of the Office of Juvenile Justice and Delinquency Prevention, 7*(1), 14–23.

Karkazis, K., Tamar-Mattis, A., & Kon, A.A. (2010). Genital surgery for disorders of sex development: Implementing a shared decision-making approach. *Journal of Pediatric Endocrinology and Metabolism, 23*(8), 789–805.

Karkazis, K.A. (2008). *Fixing sex: Intersex, medical authority, and lived experience.* Durham, NC: Duke University Press.

Kazak, A.E., Cant, M.C., Jensen, M.M., McSherry, M., Rourke, M.T., Hwang, W., . . . Lange, B.J. (2003). Identifying psychosocial risk indicative of subsequent resource use in families of newly diagnosed pediatric oncology patients. *Journal of Clinical Oncology, 21*(17), 3220.

Keyes, C.L.M. (2004). Risk and resilience in human development: An introduction. *Research in Human Development, 1*(4), 223–227.

Kim, R. (2009). *A report on the status of gay, lesbian, bisexual and transgender people in education: Stepping out of the closet, into the light.* Washington, DC: National Education Association. Retrieved from http://www.nea.org/assets/docs/glbtstatus09.pdf

King, M., Semlyen, J., Tai, S., Killaspy, H., Osborn, D., Popelyuk, D., & Nazareth, I. (2008). A systematic review of mental disorder, suicide, and deliberate self harm in lesbian, gay and bisexual people. *BMC Psychiatry, 8*(1), 70.

Kinsey, A.C., Pomeroy, W.B., & Martin, C.E. (1948). *Sexual behavior in the human male.* Philadelphia, PA: WB Saunders.

Kinsey, A.C., Pomeroy, W.B., Martin, C.E., & Gebbard, P.H. (1953). *Sexual behavior in the human female.* Philadelphia, PA: WB Saunders.

Kitts, R.L. (2005). Gay adolescents and suicide: Understanding the association. *Adolescence, 40,* 621–628.

Klein, K., Sepekoff, B., & Wolf, T.J. (1985). Sexual orientation: A multi-variable dynamic process. *Journal of Homosexuality, 11*(1/2), 35–49.

Knudson, G., De Cuypere, G., & Bockting, W. (2010). Recommendations for revision of the DSM diagnoses of gender identity disorders: Consensus statement of The World Professional Association for Transgender Health. *International Journal of Transgenderism, 12*(2), 115–118. doi:10.1080/15532739.2010.509215

Kohlberg, L. (1966). A cognitive-developmental analysis of children's sex role concepts and attitudes. In E.E. Maccoby (Ed.), *The development of sex differences* (pp. 82–173). Stanford, CA: Stanford University Press.

Kosciw, J.G., & Diaz, E.M. (2006). *The 2005 National School Climate Survey: The experiences of lesbian, gay, bisexual and transgender youth in our nation's schools.* New York, NY: GLSEN.

Kosciw, J.G., & Diaz, E.M. (2008). *Involved, invisible, ignored: The experiences of lesbian, gay, bisexual and transgender parents and their children in our nation's K–12 schools.* New York, NY: GLSEN. Retrieved from http://www.glsen.org/binary-data/GLSEN _ATTACHMENTS/file/000/001/1104-1.pdf

Kosciw, J.G., Diaz, E.M., & Greytak, E.A. (2008). *2007 National School Climate Survey: The experiences of lesbian, gay, bisexual, and transgender youth in our nation's schools.* New York, NY: GLSEN. Retrieved from http://www.glsen.org/binary-data/GLSEN _ATTACHMENTS/file/000/001/1290-1.pdf

Kreiss, J.L., & Patterson, D.L. (1997). Psychosocial issues in primary care of lesbian, gay, bisexual, and transgender youth. *Journal of Pediatric Health Care, 11*(6), 266–274.

Krieger, I. (2011). *Helping your transgender teen: A guide for parents.* New Haven, CT: Genderwise Press.

Kuhnle, U., Bullinger, M., & Schwarz, H.P. (1995). The quality of life in adult female patients with congenital adrenal hyperplasia: A comprehensive study of the impact of genital malformations and chronic disease on female patients' lives. *European Journal of Pediatrics, 154*(9), 708.

Kuhnle, U., Bullinger, M., Schwarz, H.P., & Knorr, D. (1993). Partnership and sexuality in adult female patients with congenital adrenal hyperplasia. *The Journal of Steroid Biochemistry and Molecular Biology, 45*(1-3), 1–3.

Laird, J. (1996). Invisible ties: Lesbians and their families of origin. In J. Laird & R. J. Green (Eds.), *Lesbians and gays in couples and families: A handbook for therapists* (pp. 89–122). San Francisco, CA: Jossey-Bass.

Lambda Legal. (n.d.). *Know your rights: LGBTQ youth and youth living with HIV in foster care and juvenile justice systems.* New York, NY: Author.

Lambda Legal, National Alliance to End Homelessness, National Center for Lesbian Rights, & National Network for Youth. (2009, April 10). *National recommended best practices for serving LGBT homeless youth.* Retrieved from http://www.endhomelessness .org/files/2239_file_Recommended_Best_Practices_for_LGBT_Homeless_Youth _4_9_09_.pdf

Lambda Legal, & National Youth Advocacy Coalition. (2008). *Bending the mold: An action kit for transgender students.* Retrieved from http://www.nyacyouth.org/docs/uploads/ LL_TransKit_FINAL_Lores.pdf

Larkin Street Youth Services. (2009). *Best practices for meeting the needs of lesbian, gay, bisexual, transgender and questioning homeless youth.* San Francisco, CA: Author.

LaSala, M. (2010). *Coming out, coming home: Helping families adjust to a gay or lesbian child.* New York, NY: Columbia University Press.

Laumann, E.O., Gagnon, J.H., Michael, R.T., & Michaels, S. (1994). *The social organization of sexuality: Sexual practices in the United States.* Chicago, IL: University of Chicago Press.

Lazear, K., Doan, J., & Roggenbaum, S. (2003). *Youth suicide prevention school-based guide— Issue brief 9: Culturally and linguistically diverse populations (FMHI Series Publication #218-9).* Tampa, FL: Department of Child and Family Studies, Division of State and Local Support, Louis de la Parte Florida Mental Health Institute, University of South Florida.

Lazear, K., & Gamache, P.E. (2008, February 26). *Summary report: The lesbian, gay, bisexual, transgender, questioning, intersex and two-spirit youth and families (LGBTQI2-S) research collaborative.* Tampa, FL: University of South Florida: Louis de la Parte Florida Mental Health Institute, Research & Training Center for Children's Mental Health.

Lazear, K.J., Pires, S.A., Isaacs, M.R., Chaulk, P., & Huang, L. (2008). Depression among low-income women of color: Qualitative findings from cross-cultural focus groups. *Journal of Immigrant Minority Health, 10*(2), 1557–1912.

Learning First Alliance. (2001, November). *Every child learning: Safe and supportive schools.* Alexandria, VA: Association for Supervision and Curriculum Development. Retrieved from http://www.learningfirst.org/publications/safeschools

Lease, S.H., Horne, S.G., & Noffsinger-Frazier, N. (2005). Affirming faith experiences and psychological health for Caucasian lesbian, gay, and bisexual individuals. *Journal of Counseling Psychology, 52*(3), 378–388.

Lee, C. (2002). The impact of belonging to a high school Gay/Straight Alliance. *The High School Journal,* (Feb/March), 13–26.

Lee, P.A., & Houk, C.P. (2010). The role of support groups, advocacy groups, and other interested parties in improving the care of patients with congenital adrenal hyperplasia: Pleas and warnings. *International Journal of Pediatric Endocrinology, 2010.* Article ID 563640, 4 pages. doi:10.1155/2010/563640

Lee, P.A., Houk, C.P., Ahmed, S.F., Hughes, I.A., & International Consensus Conference on Intersex organized by the Lawson Wilkins Pediatric Endocrine Society and the European Society for Paediatric Endocrinology. (2006). Consensus statement on management of intersex disorders. *Pediatrics, 118*(2), 488–500.

Leidolf, E.M., Curran, M., & Bradford, J. (2008). Intersex mental health and social support options in pediatric endocrinology training programs. *Journal of Homosexuality, 54*(3), 233–242.

Lemoire, S.J., & Chen, C.P. (2005). Applying person-centered counseling to sexual minority adolescents. *Journal of Counseling & Development, 83*(2), 146–154.

Lev, A.I. (2004). *Transgender emergence: Therapeutic guidelines for working with gender-variant people and their families.* New York, NY: Haworth Press.

Lev, A.I. (2005). Disordering gender identity: Gender identity disorder in the DSM-IV-TR. *The Journal of Psychology & Human Sexuality, 17*(3/4), 35–69.

Lev, A.I. (2006a). Intersexuality in the family: An unacknowledged trauma. *Journal of Gay and Lesbian Psychotherapy, 10*(2), 27–56.

Lev, A.I. (2006b). Transgender communities: Developing identity through connection. In K.J. Bieschke, R.M. Perez, K.A. DeBord, K.J. Bieschke, R.M. Perez, & K.A. DeBord (Eds.), *Handbook of counseling and psychotherapy with lesbian, gay, bisexual, and transgender clients* (2nd ed., pp. 147–175). Washington, DC: American Psychological Association. doi:10.1037/11482-006

Lev, A.I. (2009). The ten tasks of the mental health provider: Recommendations for revision of the World Professional Association for Transgender Health's Standards of Care. *International Journal of Transgenderism, 11*(2), 74–99.

Lev, A.I., & Sennott, S. (2012). Understanding gender nonconformity and transgender identity: A sex positive approach. In P.J. Kleinplatz (Ed.), *New directions in sex therapy: Innovations and alternatives* (2nd ed). New York, NY: Routledge.

Lev, A.I., Winters, K., Alie, L., Ansara, Y., Deutsch, M., Dickey, L., ... Susset, F. (2010). *Response to proposed DSM-5 diagnostic criteria.* Professionals Concerned With Gender Diagnoses in the DSM. Retrieved from http://professionals.gidreform.org

Livny, A., & Guarino, K. (2010, May 5). *Creating trauma-informed programs: Youth drop-in centers and beyond* [Webcast]. Homelessness Resource Center. Retrieved from http:// homeless.samhsa.gov/Resource/HRC-Webcast-Resources-Creating-Trauma -Informed-Programs-Youth-Drop-in-Centers-and-Beyond-48559.aspx

Lombardi, E. (2001). Enhancing transgender health care. *American Journal of Public Health, 91*(6), 869–872.

Lombardi, E., & van Servellen, G. (2000). Building culturally sensitive substance use prevention and treatment programs for transgendered populations. *Journal of Substance Abuse Treatment, 19*(3), 291–296.

Lourie, I.S., Katz-Leavy, J., & Stroul, B.A. (1996). Individualized services in a system of care. In B.A. Stroul & R.M. Friedman (Eds.), *Children's mental health: Creating systems of care in a changing society* (pp. 429–450). Baltimore, MD: Paul H. Brookes Publishing Co.

Low, B.P., & Andrews, S.F. (1990). Adolescent suicide. *Medical Clinics of North America, 74*(5), 1251–1264.

Macgillivray, I.K. (2007). *Gay-straight alliances: A handbook for students, educators, and parents.* New York, NY: Harrington Park Press.

Majd, K., Marksamer, J., & Reyes, C. (2009). *Hidden injustice: Lesbian, gay, bisexual, and transgender youth in juvenile courts.* San Francisco, CA: The Equity Project. Retrieved from http://www.equityproject.org/pdfs/hidden_injustice.pdf

Mallon, G. (1992). Gay and no place to go: Assessing the needs of gay and lesbian adolescents in out-of-home care settings. *Child Welfare, 71*(6), 547–556.

Mallon, G. (1997). Basic premises, guiding principles, and competent practices for a positive youth development approach to working with gay, lesbian, and bisexual youths in out-of-home-care. *Child Welfare, 76*(5), 591–609.

Mallon, G. (1998). *We don't exactly get the welcome wagon: The experiences of gay and lesbian adolescents in child welfare systems.* New York, NY: Columbia University Press.

Mallon, G. (2001). *LGBTQ youth issues.* Washington, DC: Child Welfare League of America.

Mallon, G. (2010). *LGBTQ Youth issues: A practical guide for youth workers serving lesbian, gay, bisexual, transgender, and questioning youth.* Washington, DC: Child Welfare League of America.

Mallon, G., & DeCrecenzo, T. (2006). Transgender children and youth: A child welfare practice perspective. Washington, DC: Child Welfare League of America.

Mallon, G.P., Aledort, N., & Ferrera, M. (2002). There's no place like home: Achieving safety, permanency, and well-being for lesbian and gay adolescents in out-of-home care settings. *Child Welfare, 81,* 407–439.

Malouf, M.A., Inman, A.G., Carr, A.G., Franco, J., & Brooks, L.M. (2010). Health-related quality of life, mental health and psychotherapeutic considerations for women diagnosed with a disorder of sexual development: Congenital adrenal hyperplasia. *International Journal of Pediatric Endocrinology.* doi:10.1155/2010/253465

Malouf, M.A., Wisniewski, A.B., & Migeon, C.J. (2003). Gender and reproduction in women with congenital adrenal hyperplasia. *Pediatric Research, 53,* 828.

Malpas, J. (2011). Between pink and blue: A multi-dimensional family approach to gender nonconforming children and their families. *Family Process, 50*(4), 453–470.

Manley, S. (2011, June 26). To: New York with love [Web log post]. Retrieved from http://nerdyapple.com/to-new-york

Marksamer, J. (2011). *A place of respect: A guide for group care facilities serving transgender and gender non-conforming youth.* Retrieved from http://www.nclrights.org/site/DocServer/A_Place_Of_Respect.pdf?docID=8301

Marmot, M. (2005). Social determinants of health inequalities. *Lancet, 365*(9464), 1099–1104.

Marshall, M.P., Friedman, M.S., Stall, R., King, K.M., Miles, J., Gold, M.A., & Morse, J.Q. (2008). Sexual orientation and adolescent substance use: A meta-analysis and methodological review. *Addiction, 103*, 546–556. doi:10.1111/j.1360-0443.2008.02149.x

Martinez, K., Francis, K., Poirier, J., Ornelas, B., Cayce, N., SooHoo, J., & Johnson, A. (2010). *A system of care team guide to implementing cultural and linguistic competence.* Technical Assistance Partnership for Child and Family Mental Health, Cultural and Linguistic Competence Community of Practice. Retrieved from http://www.tapartnership.org/docs/SOCTeamGuideToImplementingCLC.pdf

Masten, A.S., & Powell, J.L. (2003). A resilience framework for research, policy, and practice. In S.S. Luthar (Ed.), *Resilience and vulnerability: Adaptation in the context of childhood adversities* (pp. 1–28). New York, NY: Cambridge University Press.

Masten, A.S., & Reed, M.-G.J. (2002). Resilience in development. In C.R. Snyder & S.J. Lopez (Eds.), *Handbook of positive psychology* (pp. 74–88). New York, NY: Oxford University Press.

Mathis, D. (2010). GMHC launches 'I Love My Boo' campaign aimed at Black, Latino gays. *LGBTQNATION.* Retrieved from http://www.lgbtqnation.com/2010/10/gmhc-launches-i-love-my-boo-campaign-aimed-at-black-latino-gays

Matteson, D. (1996). Counseling and psychotherapy with bisexual and exploring clients. In B. Firestein (Ed.), *Bisexuality: The psychology and politics of an invisible minority* (pp. 185–213). Thousand Oaks, CA: Sage Publications.

McCarn, S.R., & Fassinger, R.E. (1996). Revisioning sexual minority identity formation: A new model of lesbian identity and its implications for counseling research. *The Counseling Psychologist, 24,* 508–534.

McDaniel, J.S., Purcell, D., & D'Augelli, A.R. (2001). The relationship between sexual orientation and risk for suicide: Research findings and future directions for research and prevention. *Suicide and Life-Threatening Behavior, 31,* 84–105.

McIlroy, C. (2009). *Transphobia in Ireland, research report.* Retrieved from http://lgbtdiversity.com/attachments/b2ed7003-602f-44db-8fbf-1839720adfe7.PDF

McIntosh, D., & Eschiti, V.S. (2009). Cultural aspects of American Indian HIV/AIDS prevention. *Journal of Cultural Diversity, 16*(2), 71–78.

McWayne, J., Green, J., Miller, B., Porter, M., Poston, C., Sanchez, K.T., & Rivers, J. (2010). Lesbian, gay, bisexual, and transgender health disparities, and President Obama's commitment for change in health care. *Race, Gender & Class, 17*(3-4), 273–287.

Media Awareness Network. (2009). *Media awareness network marks safer internet day with new tools to address cyber bullying in Canadian classrooms* [Press Release]. Retrieved from http://www.media-awareness.ca/english/resources/media_kit/news_releases/2009/021009.cfm

Mental Health America. (2012). *Bullying and gay youth.* Retrieved from http://www.nmha.org/go/information/get-info/children-s-mental-health/bullying-and-gay-youth

Menvielle, E.J., & Tuerk, C. (2002). A support group for parents of gender-nonconforming boys. *Journal of the American Academy of Child and Adolescent Psychiatry, 41,* 1010–1013.

MetLife Mature Market Institute, Lesbian and Gay Aging Issues Network of the American Society on Aging, & Zogby International. (2006, November). *Out and aging: The MetLife study of lesbian and gay baby boomers.* Westport, CT: MetLife Mature Market Institute.

Meyer, I. (2010). The right comparisons in testing the Minority Stress Hypothesis: Comment on Savin-Williams, Cohen, Joyner, and Rieger. *Archives of Sexual Behavior, 39*(6), 1217–1219.

Meyer, I.H. (2003). Prejudice, social stress, and mental health in lesbian, gay, and bisexual populations: Conceptual issues and research evidence. *Psychological Bulletin, 129*(5), 674–697.

Meyer-Bahlburg, F.L (2010). From mental disorder to iatrogenic hypogonadism: Dilemmas in conceptualizing gender identity variants as psychiatric conditions. *Archives of Sex Behavior, 39,* 461–476.

Meyer-Bahlburg, H., Dolezal, C., Baker, S., & New, M. (2008). Sexual orientation in women with classical or non-classical congenital adrenal hyperplasia as a function of degree of prenatal androgen excess. *Archives of Sexual Behavior, 37*(1), 85–99.

Meyer-Cook, F., & Labelle, D. (2004). Namaji: Two-spirit organizing in Montreal, Canada. *Journal of Gay and Lesbian Social Services, 16*(1), 29–51.

Miceli, M. (2002). Gay, lesbian and bisexual youth. In D. Richardson & S. Seidman (Eds.), *Handbook of lesbian and gay studies* (pp. 200–214). Thousand Oaks, CA: Sage Publications.

Miceli, M. (2005). *Standing out, standing together: The social and political impact of gay-straight alliances.* New York, NY: Routledge.

Migeon, C.J., Krishnan, S., & Wisniewski, A.B. (2007). *Ambiguous genitalia in the newborn.* Retrieved from http://www.endotext.org

Miles, P., Bruns, E.J., Osher, T.W., Walker, J.S., & National Wraparound Initiative Advisory Group. (2006). *The Wraparound process user's guide: A handbook for families.* Portland, OR: National Wraparound Initiative, Research and Training Center on Family Support and Children's Mental Health, Portland State University.

Mizocka, L., & Lewis, T.K. (2008). Trauma in transgender populations: Risk, resilience, and clinical care. *Journal of Emotional Abuse, 8*(3), 335–354.

Mohr, J.J., & Fassinger, R.E. (2003). Self-acceptance and self-disclosure of sexual orientation in lesbian, gay, and bisexual adults: An attachment perspective. *Journal of Counseling Psychology, 50*(4), 482–495.

Monette, L., Albert, D., & Waalen, J. (2001). *Voices of two-spirited men: A survey of aboriginal two-spirited men across Canada.* Toronto, ON, Canada: 2-Spirited People of the 1st Nations.

Moscicki, E.K. (1997). Identification of suicide risk factors using epidemiological studies. *Psychiatric Clinics of North America, 20,* 499–517.

Mottet, L., & Ohle, J. (2003). *Transitioning our shelters: A guide to making homeless shelters safe for transgender people.* New York, NY: The National Coalition for the Homeless and National Gay and Lesbian Task Force Policy Institute.

Muller, A. (1987). *Parents matter.* New York, NY: Naiad.

Mustanski, B.S., Garofalo, R., & Emerson, E.M. (2010). Mental health disorders, psychological distress, and suicidality in a diverse sample of lesbian, gay, bisexual, and transgender youths. *American Journal of Public Health, 100*(12), 2426–2432.

National Advisory Council on LGBTQ Homeless Youth. (2009). *National recommended best practices for serving LGBT homeless youth.* Retrieved from http://www.nyacyouth.org/docs/uploads/Recommended-Best-Practices-for-LGBT-Homeless-Youth-040909.pdf

National Association of School Nurses. (2003). *Sexual orientation and gender identity/expression* (Position Statement). Silver Spring, MD: Author. Retrieved from http://www

.nasn.org/PolicyAdvocacy/PositionPapersandReports/NASNPosition StatementsFull View/tabid/462/smid/824/ArticleID/47/Default.aspx

National Association of School Psychologists. (2006). *Position statement on gay, lesbian, bisexual, transgender, and questioning youth*. Bethesda, MD: Author. Retrieved from http://www.nasponline.org/about_nasp/pospaper_glb.aspx

National Association of Social Workers. (1996/1999). *Code of ethics of the National Association of Social Workers*. Retrieved from http://www.socialworkers.org/pubs/code/code.asp

National Association of Social Workers. (2001). *NASW standards for cultural competence in social work practice*. Washington, DC: Author. Retrieved from http://www.socialworkers.org/practice/standards/NASWCulturalStandards.pdf

National Cancer Institute. (1989). *Making health communication programs work: A planner's guide*. (NIH Publication 89-1493). Washington, DC: U.S. Government Printing Office. Retrieved from http://www.cancer.gov/cancertopics/cancerlibrary/pinkbook

National Center for Cultural Competence. (2002). *Cultural Competence Health Practitioner Assessment*. Washington, DC: Georgetown University Center for Child and Human Development. Retrieved from http://nccc.georgetown.edu/features/CCHPA.html

National Center for Cultural Competence. (2006). *A guide for using the Cultural and Linguistic Competence Policy Assessment Instrument*. Washington, DC: National Center for Cultural Competence, Georgetown University Center for Child and Human Development. Retrieved from http://www.clcpa.info/document.html

The National Child Traumatic Stress Network. (2006). Trauma among lesbian, gay, bisexual, transgender, or questioning youth. *Culture and Trauma Brief, 1*(2). Retrieved from http://www.nctsnet.org/nctsn_assests/pdf/culture_and trauma_brief_LGBT_youth.pdf

National Coalition for LGBT Health. (2011). *What we're working on*. Retrieved from http://lgbthealth.webolutionary.com/content/what-were-working

National Education Association. (2006). *Strengthening the learning environment: A school employee's guide to gay, lesbian, bisexual, & transgender issues* (2nd ed.). Washington, DC: Author. Retrieved from http://www.nea.org/assets/docs/mf_glbtguide.pdf

National Institutes of Health. (2007, July 19). *Health research with diverse populations (R01)*. Retrieved from http://grants.nih.gov/grants/guide/pa-files/PA-07-409.html

National Juvenile Defender Center. (2009). *Code of ethics*. Retrieved from http://www.npjs.org/docs/NJDA/NJDA_Code_of_Ethics.pdf

National Network for Youth. (2002). *Agency Readiness Index: A self assessment and planning guide to gauge agency readiness to work with lesbian, gay, bisexual and transgender youth*. Washington, DC: Author.

National Urban Indian Family Coalition. (2008). *Urban Indian America: The status of American Indian and Alaska Native children and families today*. Retrieved from http://www.aecf.org/~/media/Pubs/Topics/Special%20Interest%20Areas/SW%20border%20and%20American%20Indian%20Families/UrbanIndianAmericaTheStatusofAmericanIndianan/Urban%20Indian%20America.pdf

National Youth Advocacy Coalition. (2004). *FREE: Friends, for real, educating and empowering*. Retrieved from http://www.nyacyouth.org/docs/FREE_guide_print1.pdf

National Youth Advocacy Coalition. (2009). *Nationally recommended best practices for serving LGBT homeless youth*. Retrieved from http://www.nyacyouth.org/docs/uploads/Recommended-Best-Practices-for-LGBT-Homeless-Youth-040909.pdf

National Youth Advocacy Coalition. (2010, July 28). *Best practices in internet outreach*. Retrieved from http://nyacyouth.org/userfiles/files/Internet%20Outreach%20Best%20Practice.pdf

National Youth Advocacy Coalition. (n.d.a). *Executive summary of national youth HIV test-ing data.* Retrieved from http://www.nyacyouth.org/docs/ExecSummary.pdf

National Youth Advocacy Coalition. (n.d.b). *You Know Different social marketing campaign toolkit: Using social marketing as an outreach strategy to reach youth for HIV testing.* Retrieved from http://youknowdifferent.org/pdfs/YKD_toolkit.pdf

Nemoto, T., Operario, D., Keatley, J., Han, L., & Soma, T. (2004). HIV risk behaviors among male-to-female transgender persons of color in San Francisco. *American Journal of Public Health, 94*(7), 1193–1199.

Nemoto, T., Operario, D., Keatley, J., Nguyen, H., & Sugano, E. (2005). Promoting health for transgender women: Transgender resources and neighborhood space (TRANS) program in San Francisco. *American Journal of Public Health, 95*(3), 382–384.

Nestle, J., Wilchins, R., & Howell, C. (2002). *GenderQueer: Voices from beyond the sexual binary.* Los Angeles, CA: Alyson Publications.

New York State Office of Children and Family Services. (2009). *Promoting a safe and re-spectful environment for lesbian, gay, bisexual, transgender, and questioning children and youth in out-of-home placement.* Retrieved from http://www.ocfs.state.ny.us/main/policies/search/searchright.asp

Noh, S., Beiser, M., Kaspar, V., House, F., & Rummens, J. (1999). Perceived racial discrimi-nation, depression and coping: A study of Southeast Asian refugees in Canada. *Journal of Health and Social Behavior, 40,* 193–207.

Nuttbrock, L., Hwahng, S., Bockting, W., Rosenblum, A., Mason, M., Macri, M., & Becker, J. (2010). Psychiatric impact of gender-related abuse across the life course of male-to-female transgender persons. *Journal of Sex Research, 47*(1), 12–23.

O'Brien-Teegs, D. (2008). *Two spirit women* (2nd ed.). Retrieved from http://www.2spirits.com/Two%20Spirit%20Women.pdf

Ogunwole, S. (2002). *We the people, American Indians and Alaska Natives in the United States. Census 2000 Special Reports.* Washington, DC: U.S. Department of Commerce, Eco-nomics and Statistics Administration, U.S. Census Bureau.

Osher, D. (2011). *Making the case for the importance of school climate and measurement* [Webinar]. Retreived from http://safesupportiveschools.ed.gov/index.php?id=9&eid=1358

Osher, D., & Kendziora, K. (2010). Building conditions for learning and health adoles-cent development: A strategic approach. In B. Doll, W. Pfohl, & J. Yoon (Eds.), *Hand-book of youth prevention science* (pp. 121–140). New York, NY: Routledge.

Osher, D., Kendziora, K., & Chinen, M. (2008, March). *Student connection research: Final narrative report to the Spencer Foundation.* Washington, DC: American Institutes for Research.

Osher, D., Sprague, J., Weissberg, R.P., Axelrod, J., Keenan, S., Kendziora, K., & Zins, J. E. (2008). A comprehensive approach to promoting social, emotional, and academic growth in contemporary schools. In A. Thomas & J. Grimes (Eds.), *Best practices in school psychology V, Vol. 4* (pp. 1263–1278). Bethesda, MD: National Association of School Psychologists.

Oswald, R.F. (2002). Resilience within the family networks of lesbians and gay men: Intentionality and redefinition. *Journal of Marriage and Family, 64*(2), 374–383.

Otis, M.D. (2003). One community's path to greater social justice. *Journal of Gay & Les-bian Social Services, 16*(3), 17–33.

Pablo, C. (2008, April 10). *Acceptance is crucial for two-spirit people.* Retrieved from http://www.straight.com/article-140096/acceptance-crucial-twospirit-people

Pancoast, D.L. (1980). Finding and enlisting neighbors to support families. In J. Garbar-ino & S.H. Stocking (Eds.), *Protecting children from abuse and neglect* (pp. 109–132). San Francisco, CA: Jossey-Bass.

Parents, Families and Friends of Lesbians and Gays. (1995). *Our daughters & sons: Questions & answers for parents of gay, lesbian & bisexual people.* Retrieved from http://www.pflag.org/fileadmin/user_upload/Publications/Daughters_Sons.pdf

Parents, Families and Friends of Lesbians and Gays. (1997). *Faith in our families: Parents, families and friends talk about religion and homosexuality.* Retrieved from http://www.pflag.org/fileadmin/user_upload/Publications/Faith_Families.pdf

Parents, Families and Friends of Lesbian and Gays. (2008). *About PFLAG.* Retrieved from http://community.pflag.org/Page.aspx?pid=267

Parents, Families and Friends of Lesbians and Gays. (2009). *READ THIS...before you put our metatarsals between your maxilla and mandible: Straight for equality in healthcare.* Retrieved from http://community.pflag.org/Document.Doc?id=297

Parents, Families & Friends of Lesbians and Gays. (2010). *Straight for equality in health care: A PFLAG chapter field guide.* Retrieved from http://community.pflag.org/Document. Doc?id=347

Parents, Families & Friends of Lesbians and Gays. (n.d.). *PFLAG faith field guide: Chapter structure, program and activity ideas for outreach to faith communities.* Retrieved from http://pflag.dreamhosters.com/hosted-files/CIS/faith_field_guide_final.pdf

Paul, J.P., Catania, J., Pollack, L., Moskowitz, J., Canchola, J., Mills, T., ... Stall, R. (2002). Suicide attempts among gay and bisexual men: Lifetime prevalence and antecedents. *American Journal of Public Health, 92*(8), 1338–1345.

Perrin, E.C. (2002). *Sexual orientation in child and adolescent health care.* New York, NY: Springer. Kluwer Academic Plenum Publishers.

Pfäfflin, F., & Cohen-Kettenis, P.T. (2006). Clinical management of children and adolescents with intersex conditions. In S.E. Sytsma (Ed.), *Ethics and intersex* (pp. 215–223). Dordrecht, the Netherlands: Springer.

Phillips, S., McMillen C., Sparks J., & Ueberle, M. (1997). Concrete strategies for sensitizing youth-serving agencies to the needs of gay, lesbian, and other sexual minority youths. *Child Welfare, 76*(3), 393–409.

Pires, S.A. (2002). *Building systems of care: A primer.* Washington, DC: Technical Assistance Center for Children's Mental Health, Center for Child Health and Mental Health Policy, Georgetown University Child Development Center.

Pires, S.A. (2010). *Building systems of care: A primer* (2nd ed.). Washington, DC: National Technical Assistance Center for Children's Mental Health, Georgetown University Center for Child and Human Development.

Pittman, K., O'Brien, R., & Kimball, M. (1993, February). *Youth development and resiliency research: Making connections to substance abuse prevention.* Prepared for the Issue Forum on Successful Youth Development: Building Resiliency. Washington, DC: Academy for Educational Development, Center for Youth Development & Policy Research.

Planned Parenthood Mid-Hudson Valley, Inc., Mental Health Association in Ulster County, Inc., & University of Maryland Center for Mental Health Services Research, and the New York Association for Gender Rights Advocacy. (2007). *Enhancing cultural competence: Welcoming lesbian, gay, bisexual, transgender, queer people in mental health services* (2nd Ed.). Retrieved from http://www.rainbowheights.org/downloads/2ndEd%20 LGBT%20KIT%2010-23-07.pdf

Pleak, R. (2009). Formation of transgender identities in adolescence. Conference proceedings: Hormones, identities, and cultures: Clinical issues in transgender youth. *Journal of Gay and Lesbian Mental Health, 13,* 282–291.

Ploderl, M., & Fartacek, R. (2007). Childhood gender nonconformity and harassment as predictors of suicidality among gay, lesbian, bisexual, and heterosexual Austrians. *Archives of Sexual Behavior, 38*(3), 400–410.

Poirier, J.M., Francis, K.B., Fisher, S.K., Williams-Washington, K., Goode, T.D., & Jackson, V.H. (2008). *Practice brief 1: Providing services and supports for youth who are lesbian, gay, bisexual, transgender, questioning, intersex or two-spirit*. Washington, DC: National Center for Cultural Competence, Georgetown University Center for Child and Human Development. Retrieved from at http://nccc.georgetown.edu/documents/lgbtqi2s.pdf

Politz, B. (1996). *Making the case: Community foundations and youth development* (2nd ed.). Washington, DC: Center for Youth Development and Policy Research, Academy for Educational Development, Foundations for Change.

Prochaska, J.O., & Velicer, W.F. (1997). The transtheoretical model of health behavior change. *American Journal of Health Promotion, 12*(1), 38–48.

Quintana, N.S., Rosenthal, J., & Krehely, J. (2010). *On the streets: The federal response to gay and transgender homeless youth*. Washington, DC: Center for American Progress.

Rachlin, K., Dhejne, C., & Brown, G.R. (2010). The future of GID NOS in the DSM 5: Report of the GID NOS working group of a consensus process conducted by the World Professional Association for Transgender Health. *International Journal of Transgenderism, 12*(2), 86–93. doi:10.1080/15532739.2010.509209

Ragg, M., Patrick, D., & Ziefert, M. (2006). Slamming the closet door: Working with gay and lesbian youth in care. *Child Welfare, 85*(2), 243–265.

Rahimi, S. (2005, March 17). *Gay Native Americans rediscover "two-spirit" identity*. Retrieved from http://www.imdiversity.com/villages/native/dialogue_opinion_letters/pns_gay_twospirits_0305.asp

Rauso, M., Ly, T.M., Lee, M.H., & Jarosz, C.J. (2009). Improving outcomes for foster care youth with complex emotional and behavioral needs: A comparison of outcomes for wraparound vs. residential care in Los Angeles County. *Emotional & Behavioral Disorders in Youth, 9*, 63–68, 75.

Ray, N. (2006). *Lesbian, gay, bisexual and transgender youth: An epidemic of homelessness*. New York, NY: National Gay and Lesbian Task Force Policy Institute and the National Coalition for the Homeless. Retrieved from http://www.thetaskforce.org/downloads/HomelessYouth.pdf

Reback, C.J., & Lombardi, E.L. (2001). HIV risk behaviors of male-to-female transgenders in a community-based harm reduction program. In W. Bocking & S. Kirk (Eds.), *Transgender and HIV: Risks, prevention, and care* (pp. 59–68). New York, NY: Haworth Press.

Reilly, T. (2003). Transition from care: Status and outcomes of youth who age out of foster care. *Child Welfare, 82*(6), 727–746.

Remafedi, G. (1999a). Sexual orientation and youth suicide. *Journal of the American Medical Association, 282*(13), 1291–1292.

Remafedi, G. (1999b). Suicide and sexual orientation: Nearing the end of controversy? *Archives of General Psychiatry, 56*(10), 885–886.

Remafedi, G. (2002). Suicidality in a venue-based sample of young men who have sex with men. *Journal of Adolescent Health, 31*(4), 305–310.

Remafedi, G., Farrow, J.A., & Deisher, R.W. (1991). Risk factors for attempted suicide in gay and bisexual youth. *Pediatrics, 87*(6), 869–875.

Remafedi, G., French, S., Story, M., Resnick, M., & Blum, B. (1998). The relationship between suicide risk and sexual orientation: Results of a population-based study. *American Journal of Public Health, 88*(1), 57–60.

Resnick, M.D., Bearman, P.S., Blum, R.W., Bauman, K.E., Harris, K.M., Jones, J., ... Udry, J.R. (1997). Protecting adolescents from harm: Findings from the National Longitudinal Study on Adolescent Health. *Journal of the American Medical Association, 278*(10), 823–832.

Rew, L., Whittaker, T.A., Taylor-Seehafer, M.A., & Smith, L.R. (2005). Sexual health risks and protective resources in gay, lesbian, bisexual, and heterosexual homeless youth. *Journal for Specialists in Pediatric Nursing, 10*(1), 11–19.

Rich, A. (1994). *Blood, bread, and poetry: Selected prose 1979-1985.* New York, NY: W.W. Norton.

Rich, C.L., Fowler, R.C., Young D., & Blenkush, M. (1986). San Diego suicide study: Comparison of gay to straight males. *Suicide and Life Threatening Behavior, 16*(4), 448–457.

Richardson, G.E. (2002). The metatheory of resilience and resiliency. *Journal of Clinical Psychology, 58*(3), 307–321.

Riggle, E.D.B., Whitman, J.S., Olson, A., Rostosky, S.S., & Strong, S. (2008). The positive aspects of being a lesbian or gay man. *Professional Psychology: Research and Practice, 39*(2), 210–217.

Riley, E.A, Sitharthan, G., Clemson, L., & Diamond, M. (2011). The needs of gender-variant children and their parents according to health professionals. *International Journal of Transgenderism, 13*(2), 54–63.

Rivers, I., & Carragher, D.J. (2003). Social-developmental factors affecting lesbian and gay youth: A review of cross-national research findings. *Children & Society, 17*, 374–385. doi:10.1002/CHI.771

Robert Wood Johnson Foundation. (2009). *Studying state legislation of cultural and linguistic competence.* Retrieved from http://www.rwjf.org/reports/grr/059024.htm

Robertson, M.J., & Toro, P.A. (1998). *Homeless youth: Research, intervention, and policy.* Retrieved from http://aspe.hhs.gov/progsys/homeless/symposium/3-Youth.htm

Robinson, J.P., & Espelage, D.L. (2011). Inequities in educational and psychological outcomes between LGBTQ and straight students in middle and high school. *Educational Researcher, 40*(7), 315–330.

Rockefeller College. (2010). *Working with lesbian, gay, bisexual, transgender, and questioning youth in foster care settings: Training professional development program.* New York, NY: University of Albany.

Rodriguez, M.J., Rubenstein, L., & Huff, B. (2008). Social marketing. In B.A. Stroul & G.M. Blau (Eds.), *The system of care handbook: Transforming mental health services for children, youth, and families* (pp. 359–379). Baltimore, MD: Paul H. Brookes Publishing Co.

Rosario, M. (2009). African-American transgender youth. *Journal of Gay & Lesbian Mental Health, 13*, 298–308.

Rosario, M., Hunter, J., & Gwadz, M. (1997). Exploration of substance abuse among lesbian, gay, and bisexual youth: Prevalence and correlates. *Journal of Adolescent Research, 12*, 454–476.

Rosario, M., Hunter, J., Maguen, S., Gwadz, M., & Smith, R. (2001). The coming-out process and its adaptational and health-related associations among gay, lesbian, and bisexual youths: Stipulation and exploration of a model. *American Journal of Community Psychology, 29*(1), 133–160.

Rosario, M., Schrimshaw, E.W., & Hunter, J. (2004). Ethnic/racial differences in the coming-out process of lesbian, gay, and bisexual youths: A comparison of sexual identity development over time. *Cultural Diversity and Ethnic Minority Psychology, 10*(3), 215–228.

Rosario, M., Schrimshaw, E.W., & Hunter, J. (2005). Psychological distress following suicidality among gay, lesbian, and bisexual youths: Role of social relationships. *Journal of Youth and Adolescence, 34*(2), 149–161.

Roscoe, W. (1998). *Changing ones: Third and fourth genders in Native North America.* New York, NY: St. Martin's Press.

Rotheram-Borus, M.J., Rosario, M., Van Rossem, R., Reid, H., & Gillis, J. (1995). Prevalence, course, and predictors of multiple problem behaviors among gay and bisexual adolescent males. *Developmental Psychology, 31*(1), 75–81.

Rottnek, M. (Ed.). (1999). *Sissies and tomboys: Gender noncomfority and homosexual child-hoods.* New York: New York University Press.

Rudolph, S., & Epstein, M.H. (2000). Empowering children and families through strength-based assessment. *Reclaiming Children and Youth, 8*(4), 207–209.

Russell, G.M., & Richards, J.A. (2003). Stressor and resilience factors for lesbians, gay men, and bisexuals confronting antigay politics. *American Journal of Community Psychology, 31*(314), 313–328.

Russell, S.T. (2010a). Contradictions and complexities in the lives of lesbian, gay, bisexual, and transgender youth. *The Prevention Researcher, 17*(4), 3–6.

Russell, S.T. (2010b). Supportive social services for LGBT youth: Lessons from the safe schools movement. *The Prevention Researcher, 17*(4), 14–16.

Rutter, M. (2007). Commentary: Resilience, competence, and coping. *Child Abuse & Neglect, 31*(3), 205–209.

Rutter, M., & Rutter, M. (1993). *Developing minds: Challenge and continuity across the life span.* New York, NY: BasicBooks.

Ryan, C. (2003). LGBT youth: Health concerns, services and care. *Clinical Research and Regulatory Affairs, 20*(2), 137–158.

Ryan, C. (2009). *Helping families support their lesbian, gay, bisexual, and transgender (LGBT) children.* Washington, DC: National Center for Cultural Competence, Georgetown University Center for Child and Human Development.

Ryan, C. (2010). Engaging families to support lesbian, gay, bisexual and transgender (LGBT) youth: The Family Acceptance Project. *The Prevention Researcher, 17*(4), 11–13.

Ryan, C., & Futterman, D. (1998). *Lesbian and gay youth: Care and counseling.* New York, NY: Columbia University Press.

Ryan, C., Huebner, D., Diaz, R.M., & Sanchez, J. (2009). Family rejection as a predictor of negative health outcomes in white and Latino lesbian, gay, and bisexual young adults. *Pediatrics, 123*(1), 346–352.

Ryan, C., Russell, S.T., Huebner, D., Diaz, R., & Sanchez, J. (2010). Family acceptance in adolescence and the health of LGBT young adults. *Journal of Child and Adolescent Psychiatric Nursing, 23*(4), 205–213.

Saewyc, E.M., Skay, C.L., Bearinger, L.H., Blum, R.W., & Resnick, M.D. (1998). Sexual orientation, sexual behaviors, and pregnancy among American Indian adolescents. *Journal of Adolescent Health, 23*(4), 238–247.

Saewyc, E.M., Skay, C.L., Hynds, P., Pettingell, S., Bearinger, L.H., Resnick, M.D., & Reis, E. (2007). Suicidal ideation and attempts in North American school-based surveys: Are bisexual youth at increasing risk? *Journal of LGBT Health Research, 3*(2), 25–36.

Safran, M.A., Mays, R.A., Jr., Huang, L.N., McCuan, R., Pham, P.K., Fisher, S.K., … Trachtenberg, A. (2009). Mental health disparities. *American Journal of Public Health, 99*(11), 1962–1966.

Safren, S.A., & Heimberg, R.G. (1999). Depression, hopelessness, suicidality and related factors in sexual minority and heterosexual youth. *Journal of Consulting and Clinical Psychology, 67*(6), 859–866.

Salomonsen-Sautel, S., Van Leeuwen, J.M., Gilroy, C., Boyle, S., Malberg, D., & Hopfer, C. (2008). Correlates of substance use among homeless youths in eight cities. *American Journal of Addictions, 17*(3), 224–234.

Sanchez, N.F., Rabatin, J.P., Sanchez, J.P., Hubbard, S., & Kalet, A. (2006). Medical students' ability to care for lesbian, gay, bisexual, and trangendered patients. *Family Medicine, 38*(1), 21–27.

San Francisco Lesbian Gay Bisexual Transgender Community Center. (2011). *Youth program, supporting the future of the LGBT community.* Retrieved from www.sfcenter.org

Sausa, L.A. (2005). Translating research into practice: Trans youth recommendations for improving school systems. *Journal of Gay and Lesbian Issues in Education, 3,* 15–28.

Savin-Williams, R. (1989). Parental influences on the self-esteem of gay and lesbian youths: A reflected appraisals model. *Journal of Homosexuality, 17*(1-2), 93–109.

Savin-Williams, R., & Dube, E. (1998). Parental reactions to their child's disclosure of gay/lesbian identity. *Family Relations, 47,* 1–7.

Savin-Williams, R.C. (1994). Verbal and physical abuse as stressors in the lives of lesbian, gay male, and bisexual youths: Associations with school problems, running away, substance abuse, prostitution, suicide. *Journal of Consulting and Clinical Practice, 62,* 261–269.

Savin-Williams, R.C. (2001). A critique of research on sexual-minority youths. *Journal of Adolescence, 24*(1), 5–13.

Savin-Williams, R.C., & Diamond, L.M. (2000). Sexual identity trajectories among sexual-minority youths: Gender comparisons. *Archives of Sexual Behavior, 29*(6), 607–627.

Schaeffer, T., Tryggestad, J., Mallappa, A., Hanna, A., Krishnan, S., Chernausek, S., & Wisniewski, A. (2010). An evidence-based model of multidisciplinary care for patients and families affected by classical congenital adrenal hyperplasia due to 21-hydroxylase deficiency. *International Journal of Pediatric Endocrinology.* doi:10.1155/2010/692439

Schaffner, L. (1999). Violence and female delinquency: Gender transgressions, and gender invisibility. *Berkeley Women's Law Journal, 14,* 40–65.

Schober, J.M. (1999). Quality-of-life studies in patients with ambiguous genitalia. *World Journal of Urology, 17*(4), 249–252.

School Social Work Association of America. (2009). *Gay, lesbian, transgender, bisexual, and questioning youth* (Resolution Statement). Sumner, WA: Author.

Scout, J.B., Bradford, J., & Fields, C. (2001). Removing the barriers: Improving practitioners' skills in providing health care to lesbians and women who partner with women. *American Journal of Public Health, 91,* 989–990. Retrieved from http://ajph.aphapublications.org/cgi/reprint/91/6/989

Sears, J.T. (2005). *Gay, lesbian, and transgender issues in education: Programs, policies, and practices.* New York, NY: Harrington Park Press.

Sell, R.L. (1997). Defining and measuring sexual orientation: A review. *Archives of Sexual Behavior, 26*(6), 643–658.

Shaffer, D., Fisher, P., Hicks, P.H., Parides, M., & Gould, M. (1995). Sexual orientation in adolescents who commit suicide. *Suicide & Life Threatening Behavior, 25*(Suppl.), 64–71.

Shariff, S. (2005). Cyber-dilemmas in the new millennium: School obligations to provide student safety in a virtual school environment. *McGill Journal of Education, 40*(3), 457–477. Retrieved from http://mje.mcgill.ca/index.php/MJE/article/viewFile/586/468

Silenzio, V.M.B., Pena, J.B., Duberstein, P.R., Cerel, J., & Knox, K.L. (2007). Sexual orientation and risk factors for suicidal ideation and suicide attempts among adolescents and young adults. *American Journal of Public Health, 97*(11), 2017–2019.

Skinner, W.F. (1994). The prevalence and demographic predictors of illicit and licit drug use among lesbians and gay men. *American Journal of Public Health, 84*(8), 1307–1310.

Slijper, F.M.E., Drop, S.L.S., Molenaar, J.C., & De Muinck Keizer-Schrama, S.M.P.F. (1998). Long-term psychological evaluation of intersex children. *Archives of Sexual Behavior, 27*(2), 125–144.

Smith, A. (2005). *Conquest: Sexual violence and American Indian genocide.* Cambridge, MA: South End Press.

Smith, D.M., & Mathews, W.C. (2007). Physicians' attitudes toward homosexuality and HIV: Survey of a California medical society-revisited (PATHH-II). *Journal of Homosexuality, 52,* 1–9.

Spirito, A., & Esposito-Smythers, C. (2006). Attempted and completed suicide in adolescence. *Annual Review of Clinical Psychology, 2,* 237–266.

Steensma, T.D., & Cohen-Kettenis, P.T. (2011). Gender transitioning before puberty? *Archives of Sexual Behavior, 40*(4), 649–650. doi:10.1007/s10508-011-9752-2

Stern-Ellis, H., & Killen-Harvey, A. (2007). *Effectively working with gay, lesbian, bi-sexual and transgender youth.* Retrieved from http://www.nctsnet.org/nctsn_assets/pdfs/Culture_Trauma_Killen_Harvey_Stern_Ellis_3-22-07.pdf

Stone, J. (2006, June). *Post-Colonial stress, historical trauma, and mental health/substance abuse disorders.* Paper presented at the IHS/SAMHSA National Behavioral Health Conference, San Diego, CA.

Stone Fish, L., & Harvey, R.G. (2005). *Nurturing queer youth: Family therapy transformed.* New York, NY: W.W. Norton.

Straus, T., & Valentino, D. (2001). Retribalization in urban Indian communities. In S. Lobo & K. Peters (Eds.), *American Indians and the urban experience* (pp. 85–94). Walnut Creek, CA: AltaMira Press.

Strommen, E. (1993). "You're a what": Family member reactions to the disclosure of homosexuality. In L. Garnets & D. Kimmel (Eds.), *Psychological perspectives on lesbian and gay male experiences* (pp. 248–266). New York, NY: Columbia University Press.

Stroul, B., Blau, G., & Friedman, R. (2010). *Updating the system of care concept and philosophy.* Washington, DC: National Technical Assistance Center for Children's Mental Health.

Stroul, B., Blau, G., & Sondheimer, D. (2008). Systems of care: A strategy to transform children's mental healthcare. In B. Stroul & G. Blau (Eds.), *The system of care handbook: Transforming mental health services for children, youth and families* (pp. 3–24). Baltimore, MD: Paul H. Brookes Publishing Co.

Stroul, B., & Friedman, R. (1986). *A system of care for children and youth with severe emotional disturbances* (rev. ed.). Washington, DC: Georgetown University Child Development Center, National Technical Assistance Center for Children's Mental Health.

Stroul, B.A. (2002). *Systems of care: A framework for system reform in children's mental health* (Issue Brief). Washington, DC: National Technical Assistance Center for Children's Mental Health, Georgetown University Child Development Center, Georgetown University.

Stroul, B.A., & Friedman, R.M. (1996). The system of care concept and philosophy. In B.A. Stroul (Ed.), *Children's mental health: Creating systems of care in a changing society* (pp. 3–23). Baltimore, MD: Paul H. Brookes Publishing Co.

Substance Abuse and Mental Health Services Administration. (2011, Fall/Winter). *LGBTQI2-S workgroup update.* Retrieved from http://tapartnership.org/docs/LGBTQI2-S_NationalWorkgroup_update_December2011_Issue3.pdf

Substance Abuse and Mental Health Services Administration Center for Substance Abuse Treatment. (2001). *A provider's introduction to substance abuse treatment for lesbian, gay, bisexual, and transgender individuals.* Washington, DC: U.S. Department of Health and Human Services.

Substance Abuse and Mental Health Services Administration Center for Mental Health Services, Child, Adolescent, and Family Services Branch. (2008). *Cultural and linguistic competence implementation study: Summary report.* Washington, DC: U.S. Department of Health and Human Services.

Substance Abuse and Mental Health Services Administration Center for Mental Health Services, Child, Adolescent, and Family Services Branch. (2009a). *A blueprint for addressing suicide issues in systems of care.* Unpublished manuscript.

Substance Abuse and Mental Health Services Administration Center for Mental Health Services, Child, Adolescent, and Family Services Branch. (2009b). *A comprehensive vision: A logic model addressing suicide issues in system of care communities.* Unpublished manuscript.

Substance Abuse and Mental Health Services Administration Center for Mental Health Services, Child, Adolescent, and Family Services Branch. (2010, September 21). *National workgroup to address the needs of children and youth who are LGBTQI2-S and their families: Logic model vision.* Unpublished manuscript.

Sue, D.W., Bingham, R., Porche-Burke, L., & Vasquez, M. (1999). The diversification of psychology: A multicultural revolution. *American Psychologist, 54,* 1061–1069.

Sue, D.W., Capodilupo, C., Torino, G., Bucceri, J., Holder, A., Nadal, K., & Esquilin, M. (2007). Racial microaggressions in everyday life: Implications for clinical practice. *American Psychologist, 62*(4), 271–286.

Sue, D.W., & Torino, G.C. (2005). Racial-cultural competence: Awareness, knowledge, and skills. In R.T. Carter (Ed.), *Handbook of racial-cultural psychology and counseling: Training and practice* (pp. 3–18). New York, NY: Wiley.

Sullivan, T.R. (1994). Obstacles to effective child welfare service with gay and lesbian youths. *Child Welfare, 73*(4), 291–304.

Suter, J.C., & Bruns, E.J. (2009). Effectiveness of the wraparound process for children with emotional and behavioral disorders: A meta-analysis. *Clinical Child and Family Psychology Review, 12,* 336–351.

Swinomish Tribal Mental Health Project. (1991). *A gathering of wisdoms: Tribal mental health; a cultural perspective.* La Conner, WA: Swinomish Tribal Community.

Szalacha, L.A. (2003). Safer sexual diversity climates: Lessons learned from an evaluation of Massachusetts safe schools program for gay and lesbian students. *American Journal of Education, 110*(1), 58–88.

Szymanski, D.A., Kashubeck-West, S., & Meyer, J. (2008). Internalized heterosexism: Measurement, psychosocial correlates, and research directions. *The Counseling Psychologist, 36*(4), 525–574. doi:10.1177/0011000007309489

Toomey, R.B., Ryan, C., Diaz, R.M., Card, N.A., & Russell, S.T. (2010). Gender-nonconforming lesbian, gay, bisexual, and transgender youth: School victimization and young adult psychosocial adjustment. *Developmental Psychology, 46*(6), 1580–1589. doi:10.1037/a0020705

Toro, P.A., Dworsky, A., & Fowler, P.J. (2007). Homeless youth in the United States: Recent research findings and interventions. In D. Dennis, G. Locke, & J. Khadduri (Eds.), *Toward understanding homelessness: The 2007 National Symposium on Homelessness Research* (pp. 6-1–6-33). Washington, DC: Office of the Assistant Secretary for Planning and Evaluation.

Toro, P.A., & Goldstein, M.S. (2000). *Outcomes among homeless and matched adolescents: A longitudinal comparison.* Presented at the 108th Annual Convention of the American Psychological Association, Washington, DC.

Trevor Project. (2009). *"I'm glad I failed": Social marketing results.* West Hollywood, CA: Author.

Troiden, R. (1988). Homosexual identity development. *Journal of Adolescent Health, 9,* 105–113.

Troiden, R. (1989). The formation of homosexual identities. In G. Herdt (Ed.), *Gay and lesbian youth* (pp. 43–74). New York, NY: Harrington Park Press.

Tuckman, B.W. (1965, June). Developmental sequence in small groups. *Psychological Bulletin, 63*(6), 384–399. Retrieved from http://psycnet.apa.org/journals/bul/63/6/384. doi:10.1037/h0022100.

Turning Point Social Marketing National Excellence Collaborative. (n.d.). *The basics of social marketing: How to use marketing to change behavior from the social marketing national excellence collaborative.* Seattle, WA: Turning Point National Program Office. Retrieved from http://www.turningpointprogram.org/Pages/pdfs/social_market/smc_basics.pdf

U.C. Davis Center for Reducing Health Disparities. (2009). *Building partnerships: Conversations with LGBTQ youth about mental health needs and community strengths.* Retrieved from http://www.dmh.ca.gov/PEIStatewideProjects/docs/Reducing_Disparities/BP _LGBTQ.pdf

Ulrich, R. (2010). *American Indian nations from termination to restoration, 1953-2006*. Lincoln: University of Nebraska Press.

Urban Native Youth Association. (2004). *Two-spirit youth speak out!* Retrieved from http:// www.unya.bc.ca/downloads/glbtq-twospirit-final-report.pdf

U.S. Census Bureau. (2011). *State & county quickfacts*. Retrieved from http://quickfacts. census.gov/qfd/states/26/2642160.html

U.S. Commission on Civil Rights. (2004). *Native American health care disparities*. Washington, DC: Office of the General Counsel.

U.S. Department of Education, Office for Civil Rights. (2010a, October 26). *Dear colleague letter harassment and bullying (October 26, 2010) background, summary, and fast facts*. Retrieved from http://www2.ed.gov/about/offices/list/ocr/docs/dcl-factsheet -201010.pdf

U.S. Department of Education, Office for Civil Rights. (2010b, October 26). *Dear colleague letter: Harassment and bullying*. Retrieved from http://www2.ed.gov/about/ offices/list/ocr/letters/colleague-201010.html

U.S. Department of Education, Office of Elementary and Secondary Education. (2011, June 14). *Dear colleague letter*. Retrieved from http://www2.ed.gov/policy/elsec/ guid/secletter/110607.html

U.S. Department of Health and Human Services, The Office of Minority Health. (2001). *National standards for culturally and linguistically appropriate services in health care*. Washington, DC: Author. Retrieved from http://minorityhealth.hhs.gov/assets/pdf/checked/ finalreport.pdf

U.S. Department of Health and Human Services, The Office of Minority Health. (2008). *Organizational infrastructure*. Washington, DC: Author. Retrieved from http://minority health.hhs.gov/templates/browse.aspx?lvl=3&lvlID=466

U.S. Department of Justice. (2004). *Crime in the United States: 2004*. Retrieved from http://www.fbi.gov/ucr/cius_04/offenses_reported/hate_crime/index.html

U.S. Public Health Service. (2001). *National strategy for suicide prevention: Goals and objectives for action*. Rockville, MD: U.S. Deptartment of Health and Human Services, Public Health Service.

Vaccaro, A., August, G., & Kennedy, M.S. (2012). *Safe spaces: Making schools and communities welcoming to LGBT youth*. Santa Barbara, CA: Praeger.

Vance, S.R., Cohen-Kettenis, P.T., Drescher, J., Meyer-Bahlburgd, H.F.L., Pfäfflin, F., & Zucker, K.J. (2010). Opinions about the DSM gender identity disorder diagnosis: Results from an international survey administered to organizations concerned with the welfare of transgender people. *International Journal of Transgenderism, 12*(1), 1–14.

Vanderburgh, R. (2008). Appropriate therapeutic care for families with pre-pubescent transgender/gender-dissonant children. *Child and Adolescent Social Work Journal, 26*, 135–154.

Van Leeuwen, J.M., Boyle, S., Salomonsen-Sautel, S., Baker, D.N., Garcia, J.T., Hoffman, A., & Hopfer, C.J. (2006). Lesbian, gay, and bisexual homeless youth: An eight-city public health perspective. *Child Welfare, 85*(2), 151–170.

Visootsak, J., & Graham, J.M., Jr. (2006). Klinefelter syndrome and other sex chromosomal aneuploidies. *Orphanet Journal of Rare Diseases, 1*(42). doi:10.1186/1750-1172-1-42

Wald, M., & Martinez, T. (2003). *Connected by 25: Improving the life chances of the country's most vulnerable 14-24 year olds*. Menlo Park, CA: William and Flora Hewlett Foundation.

Waldram, J.B. (1990). The persistence of traditional medicine in urban areas: The case of Canada's Indians. *American Indian and Alaska Native Mental Health Research, 4*, 9–29.

Walker, B. (1989). The future of public health: The Institute of Medicine's 1988 report. *Journal of Public Health Policy, 10*(1), 19–31.

Walker, J., & Bruns, E. (2007). *Wraparound: Key information, evidence, and endorsements.* Retrieved from http://www.rtc.pdx.edu/PDF/pbWraparoundEvidenceRecognition.pdf

Wallace, R., & Russell, H.T. (2010). *Gender identity disorder in children: A critique of two dominant voices* (Unpublished article).

Wallien, M.S., & Cohen-Kettenis, P.T. (2008). Psychosexual outcome of gender-dysphoric children. *Journal of American Academy of Child Adolescent Psychiatry, 47*(12), 1413–23.

Walls, N., Potter, C., & Leeuwen, J. (2009). Where risks and protective factors operate differently: Homeless sexual minority youth and suicide attempts. *Child & Adolescent Social Work Journal, 26*(3), 235–257.

Walls, N.E., Kane, S.B., & Wisneski, H. (2010). Gay-straight alliances and school experiences of sexual minority youth. *Youth & Society, 41,* 307–332.

Walters, K.L., Simoni, J.M., & Horwath, P.F. (2001). Sexual orientation bias experiences and service needs of gay, lesbian, bisexual, transgendered, and two-spirited American Indians. *Journal of Gay and Lesbian Social Services, 13*(1/2), 133–149.

Wardenski, J.J. (2005). A minor exception? The impact of *Lawrence v. Texas* on LGBT youth. *Journal of Criminal Law and Criminal Justice, 95*(4), 1363–1410.

Ware, W. (2010). *Locked up and out: Lesbian, gay, bisexual, and transgender youth in Louisiana's juvenile justice system.* Retrieved from http://jjpl.org/new/wp-content/uploads/2010/06/Locked-Up-Out.pdf

Warne, G., Grover, S., Hutson, J., Sinclair, A., Metcalfe, S., Northam, E., & Murdoch Children's Research Institute Sex Study Group. (2005). A long-term outcome study of intersex conditions. *Journal of Pediatric Endocrinology & Metabolism, 18*(6), 555–567.

Warne G.L., & Raza, J. (2008). Disorders of sex development (DSDs), their presentation and management in different cultures. *Reviews in Endocrine and Metabolic Disorders, 9*(3), 227–236.

Washington, T., & Murray, J.P. (2005). Breast cancer prevention strategies for aged black lesbian women. *Journal of Gay & Lesbian Social Services, 18*(1), 89–96. doi:10.1300/J041v18n0107

Weinberg, M.S., Williams, J.S., & Pryor, D.W. (1994). *Dual attraction: Understanding bisexuality.* New York, NY: Oxford University Press.

Wentzel, K.R. (1997). Student motivation in middle school: The role of perceived psychological caring. *Journal of Educational Psychology, 89,* 411–419.

Wheeler, M.L. (2011). Capitalizing on diversity: Navigating the seas of the multicultural workforce and workplace. *Bloomberg Businessweek.* Retrieved from http://www.businessweek.com/adsections/diversity/diversehome.htm

Whitbeck, L., & Hoyt, D. (1999). *Nowhere to grow: Homeless and runaway adolescents and their families.* New York, NY: Aldine de Gruyter.

Whitbeck, L.B., Chen, X., Hoyt, D.R., Tyler, K.A., & Johnson, K.D. (2004). Mental disorder, subsistence strategies, and victimization among gay, lesbian, and bisexual homeless and runaway adolescents. *Journal of Sex Research, 41*(4), 329–342.

Whitbeck, L.B., McMorris, B.J., Hoyt, D.R., Stubben, J.D., & LaFromboise, T. (2002). Perceived discrimination, traditional practices, and depressive symptoms among American Indians in the upper Midwest. *Journal of Health and Social Behavior, 43*(4), 400–418.

Wichstrom, L., Hegna, K., Wichstrom, L., & Hegna, K. (2003). Sexual orientation and suicide attempt: A longitudinal study of the general Norwegian adolescent population. *Journal of Abnormal Psychology, 112*(1), 144–151.

Wilber, S., Ryan, C., & Marksamer, J. (2006). *Best practices guidelines: Serving LGBT youth in out-of-home care.* Washington, DC: Child Welfare League of America.

Willging, C.E., Salvador, M., & Kano, M. (2006). Unequal treatment: Mental health care for sexual and gender minority groups in a rural state. *Psychiatric Services, 57*(6), 867–870. doi:10.1176/appi.ps.57.6.867

Winters, K. (2009). *Gender madness in American psychiatry: Essays from the struggle for dignity.* Charleston, SC: BookSurge Publishing.

Wisniewski, A.B., Migeon, C.J., Malouf, M.A., & Gearhart, J.P. (2004). Psychosexual outcome in women affected by congenital adrenal hyperplasia due to 21-hydroxylase deficiency. *Journal of Urology, 171*(6), 2497–2501.

Wolitski, R.J., Stall, R., & Valdiserri, R.O. (2008). *Unequal opportunity: Health disparities affecting gay and bisexual men in the United States.* Oxford, United Kingdom: Oxford University Press.

Wooten, A. (2008). Schools, LGBT parents and the need to be involved. *Windy City Times.* Retrieved from http://www.windycitymediagroup.com/gay/lesbian/news/ARTICLE .php?AID=18158

The Workgroup on Adapting Latino Services. (2008). *Adaptation guidelines for serving Latino children and families affected by trauma* (1st ed.). San Diego, CA: Chadwick Center for Children and Families.

World Health Organization. (2003). *The world health report 2003: Shaping the future.* Retrieved from http://www.who.int/whr/2003/en/whr03_en.pdf

World Health Organization. (2007). *International classification of diseases and related health problems* (10th rev.). Geneva, Switzerland: Author.

The World Professional Association for Transgender Health. (2011). *Standards of care for the health of transsexual, transgender, and gender nonconforming people* (7th version). Retrieved from http://www.wpath.org/documents/Standards%20of%20Care%20V7%20 -%202011%20WPATH.pdf

Woronoff, R., Estrada, R., & Sommer, S. (2006). *OUT of the Margins: A report on regional listening forums highlighting the experiences of lesbian, gay, bisexual, transgender, and questioning youth in care.* Washington, DC: CWLA and Lambda Legal. Retrieved from http:// www.eric.ed.gov/ERICWebPortal/search/detailmini.jsp?_nfpb=true&_&ERIC ExtSearch_SearchValue_0=ED492067&ERICExtSearch_SearchType_0=no &accno=ED492067

YES Institute. (2008). *Communication solutions.* Retrieved from http://www.yesinstitute .org/education/courses/communication_solutions.php

Youth Migration Project of Toronto. (2010). *Two-spirit youth talk about coming to Toronto.* Retrieved from http://www.2spirits.com/youthmigration.pdf

Yunger, J., Carver, P., & Perry, D. (2004). Does gender identity influence children's psychological well-being? *Developmental Psychology, 40*(4), 572–582.

Zeiler, K., & Wickstrom, A. (2009). Why do "we" perform surgery on newborn intersexed children? The phenomenology of the parental experience of having a child with intersex anatomies. *Feminist Theory, 10*(3), 359–377.

Zickler, P. (2000). Nicotine craving and heavy smoking may contribute to increased use of cocaine and heroin. *NIDA NOTES.* Retrieved from http://archives.drugabuse.gov/ NIDA_notes/NNvol15N5/Craving.html

Zimmerman, M.A., & Arunkumar, R. (1994). Resiliency research: Implications for schools and policy. *Social Policy Report, 8*(4), 1–20.

Zucker, K., & Bradley, S. (1995). *Gender identity disorder and psychosexual problems in children and adolescents.* New York, NY: Guilford.

Zucker, K.J. (2006). Gender identity and intersexuality. In S.E. Sytsma (Ed.), *Ethics and intersex* (pp. 165–181). Dordrecht, the Netherlands: Springer.

Zucker, K.J. (2008). Children with gender identity disorder: Is there a best practice? *Neuropsychiatrie de l'Enfance et de l'Adolescence, 56*(6), 358–364.

Zuger, B. (1984). Early effeminate behaviors in boys: Outcome and significance for homosexuality. *Journal of Nervous and Mental Disease, 32,* 449–463.

Index

Tables, figures, boxes, and footnotes are indicated by *t, f, b,* and *n,* respectively.

AANNY, *see* AIDS and Adolescents Network of New York
Aayahkwew, 90
Abuse
  alcohol and drug abuse, 96, 114, 199
  emotional abuse, 209
  in out-of-home care settings, 178
  physical abuse, 209
  sexual abuse, 34, 81, 178, 198, 211
  sexual assaults, 97, 137, 212, 239
  tobacco abuse, 114
Academics, 160, 161, 161*f,* 198–199
Acceptance, 56–57, 78
Access to services and supports, 119, 120*f,* 155–156, 178–180
Accord Alliance, 83, 256*f*
Action, 225
Administrators, 220–221
Adolescents
  gender identity development in, 48–49
  supporting families and youth, 81–82
  transgender and gender nonconforming, 54–55
  see also Youth
Adult advocacy groups, 217–218
Advocacy, 57–59, 61–62
  self-advocacy, 76–77
Advocacy groups, 217–218
Advocacy organizations, 230–231
Advocacy Services for Kids, 20
Advocates for Informed Choice, 85
Advocates for Youth, 256*f*
Affirming services and supports, 155–156
African American youth, 39, 64–65, 112, 119, 163*n*
Age, 72
Age-appropriate discussions, 80
Agency policies, 148, 153
Agency self-assessment, 146–147
AI/AN youth, *see* American Indian and Alaska Native youth
AIDS, *see* HIV/AIDS
AIDS and Adolescents Network of New York (AANNY), 245
AIS/DSD Parents Group, 85

AIS/DSD Support Group, 83
Alaska Natives, 88, 163
  see also American Indian and Alaska Native (AI/AN) youth
Alcohol abuse, 96, 114
Alcohol dependence, 97
Ali Forney Center (New York City, New York), 209
ALSO Out Youth (ALSO), 19–20
Ambientejoven, 256*f*
Ambiguity, 78–79
Ambiguous genitalia, 68
American Academy of Pediatrics, 139
American Counseling Association, 139
American Indian, 88
American Indian and Alaska Native (AI/AN) youth, 87, 88, 163*n,* 234
  bias and lateral violence against, 94–95
  challenges to receiving culturally and linguistically competent health care, 93–94
  LGBT youth, 98–103, 235–236
  relationship with non-native LGBT society, 98–103
  social marketing to, 232, 235–236
  theories and practice strategies for working with, 103–104
  two-spirit youth, 98–103, 235–236
American Psychiatric Association, 40, 44, 113, 139
American Psychological Association (APA), 139, 169, 186
  The Healthy Lesbian, Gay, and Bisexual Students Project, 256*f*
  The Lesbian, Gay, Bisexual, and Transgender Concerns Office, 257*f*
  Task Force on Appropriate Therapeutic Responses to Sexual Orientation, 138–139
American School Counselor Association, 169
American School Health Association, 169
Androgen insensitivity syndrome [AIS], 72
Androgynes, 45
Anoka-Hennepin School District (Minnesota), 189

Anti-LGBT remarks, 163
Antibullying policies, 164, 165
Antidiscrimination policies, 164
APA, *see* American Psychological Association
Approachability, 166
Arab American youth, 163*n*
Asian or Pacific Islander youth, 163*n*
Assessment
  agency or organizational self-assessment, 25–32, 146–147
  comprehensive, of child and family, 60
  gender assessment, 62
Assets-based approaches, 116–118, 124–126
Assigned sex, 70
Association for Lesbian, Gay, Bisexual & Transgender Issues in Counseling, 257*f*
Association of Gay and Lesbian Psychiatrists, 257*f*
Attitudes, 30–32
Atypical gendered behavior, 70
Autopsy, psychological, 193
Availability, 119, 120*f*

Balance, 56, 59*b*
Bar culture, 114
Bardaj, 90
"The Basket and the Bow, A Gathering of Lesbian & Gay Native Americans" conference, 99
The Bears, 218
Behavior(s)
  ambiguity regarding, 78–79
  atypical gendered behavior, 70
  self-harming, 189–205
  suicidal, 196–197, 202*b*–204*b*
  suicide-related, 114–116, 202*b*
Behavior change, 225
  other audiences to engage, 239–249
  recommended practices for reducing suicide-related behavior, 199–201
  social marketing to promote help-seeking behavior, 223–250
  trans-theoretical model of health behavior change, 225
Berdache, 90
BIA, *see* Bureau of Indian Affairs
Big brothers, 156
Big sisters, 156
Bing, 251
Biological sex, 45, 69, 70
Black men, 3
Black Men Together, 218
"Blended" cultural styles, 100
Blogs, 238
A Blueprint for Addressing Suicide Issues in Systems of Care (SAMHSA), 201
Book clubs, 120–121

Books, youth-friendly, 151
"Bottom" surgery, 61
Bullying, 159*n,* 163
  antibullying policies, 164, 165
  cyberbullying, 245
Bureau of Indian Affairs (BIA), 89
Burlington County Family Support Organization (New Jersey), 19

Caregivers
  resources for, 248
  supporting, 38–39
Case study, 227
Cass's model, 35
Castro Housing, 210, 217
Caucasian youth, 39, 112, 119, 163
Causation, 255
CDC, *see* Centers for Disease Control and Prevention
Center for American Progress, 221
Center for Mental Health Services
  Child, Adolescent and Family Services Branch (CAFB), 13–14, 125, 201, 270, 272
  Lesbian, Gay, Bisexual, Transgender, Questioning, Intersex, or Two-Spirit (LGBTQI2-S) National Workgroup, 13–14, 270, 272
Center of Excellence for Transgender Health, 257*f*
Centers for Disease Control and Prevention (CDC), 192
CGSAEP, *see* Children's Gender and Sexuality Advocacy and Education Program
Change
  LGBT, questioning, intersex, or two-spirit (LGBTQI2-S) theory of, 123*f,* 123–124
  strategies for systemwide change, 169–171
  see also Behavior change
Changing sex, 51
Child assessment, comprehensive, 60
Child Welfare League of America, 17*n*
Child welfare system, 95–96, 128
Children
  gender-variant, 52
  LGBT, 269*n*
  transgender and gender nonconforming, 43–66
  see also Youth
Children of Lesbians and Gays Everywhere (COLAGE), 232, 257*f*
Children's Gender and Sexuality Advocacy and Education Program (CGSAEP), 56
Children's Mental Health Initiative (CMHI), 174, 201, 202*b*–204*b*
Children's National Medical Center, 56
Christianity, 101

Circles of Care grant program (SAMHSA), 101–102
"Claim your Rights" campaign, 237
CLC, *see* Cultural and linguistic competence
Clinical Guidelines for the Management of Disorders of Sex Development in Childhood (Consortium on the Management of Disorders of Sex Development), 77, 78
Clinical outcomes, 204*b*
Clubs, school-based, 165
CMHI, *see* Children's Mental Health Initiative
Code-switching, 100
COLAGE, *see* Children of Lesbians and Gays Everywhere
Coleman's model, 35
Collaboration, 230–231
Coming out, 5–7, 35, 37*t*, 37–39, 98, 112, 135
Commitment, 35
Communication
  age-appropriate discussions, 80
  with family, friends, schools, and other institutions, 79–80
  with Native peoples, 100–101
  Self-assessment Checklist for, 29–30
Community
  connections with, 217–218
  examples of, 19–24
  promoting, 229–230
  recommendations for members, 185*b*
  social marketing to, 240–242
Community engagement, 18, 156
Community-focused cultural and linguistic competency, 120–122
Community learning, 17–18
Community outreach, 156
Competence, 12
  see also Cultural and linguistic competence (CLC); Cultural competence
Comprehensive assessment
  of child and family, 60
  gender assessment, 62
A Comprehensive Vision—A Logic Model Addressing Suicide Issues in System of Care Communities (SAMHSA), 201
Conduct disorder, 4
Confidentiality, 150–151
Conflict resolution, 28
Confusion stage, 36
Congenital adrenal hyper-plasia, 69
Connection(s)
  with community, 217–218
  as condition for learning, 160, 161*f*
Consensus Statement on Management of Intersex Disorders, 73
Consortium on the Management of Disorders of Sex Development, 77, 78
Constituency building, 129–130

Consultation, 62, 64
Contemplation, 225
Continuous quality improvement (CQI), 146–147
Conversion therapies, 138–139
Correlation, 255
Couch surfing, 209
Counseling
  challenges common among LGBT youth, 137–139
  recommended practices, 134–136
Countertransference, 136
CQI, *see* Continuous quality improvement
Cree, 90
Cross-gender behavior, 44
Cross-gender identification, 49
Cultural and linguistic competence (CLC), 9, 10–12
  challenges to receiving, 93–94
  community-focused, 120–122
  development of, 14
  for disorders or differences of sex development, 71–73
  environmental, 151–152
  for fostering resiliency, 118–122
  in health care, 93–94
  inclusive plans for, 15–16
  increasing, 13–14
  for intake processes, data collection, and information sharing, 150–151
  rationale for, 12–13
  self-assessment, 25–32, 27*b*
  in services and supports, 9–24
  strategies to move forward, 14–19
  terms for, 88
  for transgender and gender nonconforming children and youth, 64–65
  see also Cultural competence
"Cultural and linguistic competence in focus" learning events (TA Partnership), 17–18
Cultural brokers, 86
Cultural competence, 10–11, 118, 119
  environmental, 151
  improving, 119, 120*f*
  Internet-based information and resources for, 251–266
  organizational, 119–120, 120*f*
  for transgender and gender nonconforming children and youth, 43–66
  ways to promote, 151
  see also Cultural and linguistic competence (CLC)
Cultural considerations, 28, 118, 144
  ethnic considerations, 39
  for providers, 100–101
  for social marketing campaigns, 235–236
  strategies to increase responsiveness, 23

Cultural mastery, 12
Culturally queer, 233
Curriculum, 168–169, 170
Cyberbullying, 245

Data analysis, 27*b*
Data collection, 27*b*, 150–151
Data dissemination, 27*b*
Day of Silence (DOS) Project, 258*f*
"Dear Abby," 118
Decision making, 28
  shared, 76
Depression, 95
Depressive symptomatology, 3
Detention facilities, 175–176
Development, 149
  of gender identity, 47–49
  of identity, 97–98
  psychosocial, 34–35
  of sexual identity, 33–41
  of two-spirit identity, 89–91
Diagnostic and Statistical Manual of Mental
    Disorders (3rd ed., *DSM-III*) (APA), 1, 49
Diagnostic and Statistical Manual of Mental
    Disorders (4th ed., text rev.; *DSM-IV-TR*)
    (APA), 44, 49–50, 53, 70, 71, 113
Diagnostic and Statistical Manual of Mental
    Disorders (5th ed., *DSM-V*) (APA), 49
Differences of sex development, *see* Disorders
    or differences of sex development (DSD)
Disclosure, 58*b*, 80
Discovery, 58*b*
Discrimination, 3
  nondiscrimination policies, 147–149, 165
Disorders, v
Disorders or differences of sex development
    (DSD), 67–86
  age-appropriate discussions of details, 80
  cultural and linguistic competence
    considerations for, 71–73
  individuals and families affected by, 68–71
  integrating into family life, 77–78
  key recommendations for, 85–86
  and sexual identities, 70–71
  terminology of, 71–72
  and transgender identities, 70
Don't Ask Don't Tell policy, 237
DOS Project, *see* Day of Silence Project
Drop-In Center (New Orleans, Louisiana),
    208*n*, 214, 217
Drug abuse, 96, 114, 199
DSD, *see* Disorders or differences of sex
    development
DSD Families, 83
DSM, *see* Diagnostic and Statistical Manual of
    Mental Disorders
Dubuds, 90

Early childhood, 47–48
Education
  elementary school, 163
  for homeless youth, 214–215
  see also School(s)
Elementary school, 163
Emotional abuse, 209
Employment, 214–215
Empowerment, youth, 108*b*
Environment(s), 63
  culturally competent, 151
  physical, 29
  policy recommendations for proactively
    improving, 165–166
  safe, supportive, and culturally and
    linguistically competent, 151–152
  safe, welcoming, 16–17
  school, 165–166
  Self-Assessment Checklist for, 29
The Equity Project, 175*n*
Ericson, Erik, 34–35
Eroticization, 99
Ethical considerations, 103
Ethnicity, 10, 39, 73
Evidence-based approaches, xiii, 124
Exemplary practice, 134
Exploration, 35

Facebook, 238
FACT, *see* Family Acceptance of Children and
    Teens
"Fairness Campaign," 240
Faith-based organizations, 24
Families
  affected by disorders or differences of sex
    development, 68–71
  building systems of care for, 127–140
  communication with, 79–80
  effective support for, 111–126
  with gender nonconforming children and
    youth, 55–59, 58*b*–59*b*
  integrating disorders or differences of sex
    development into, 77–78
  key strategies for serving, 269–270
  needs of, 1–8
  rejection by, 5–7
  as self-advocates, 76–77
  social marketing to, 247–249
  strengthening, 154–155
  supporting through puberty and adoles-
    cence, 48–49
  with transgender and gender nonconform-
    ing children and youth, 55–59
  ways to support, 154–155
Family acceptance, 5–7, 56
Family Acceptance of Children and Teens
    (FACT), 21–22

Family Acceptance Project (FAP), 21, 258*f*
Family assessment, comprehensive, 60
Family-centered approach, 144–145
Family cohesion, 199
Family emergence model, 56
Family Support Organization (Burlington
    County, New Jersey), 120–121
FAP, *see* Family Acceptance Project
Federal efforts, recent, 171
Federal Partners in Bullying Prevention
    Summit, 245
Female, 67
Female-to-male transsexuals (FTMs/transmen),
    45
Fetishism, 99
Foster care, 95–96, 209–210
Foster homes, 175
Friends, 79–80
Fuentes, Vanessa A., 207, 221
Full inclusion, 187*b*
Future directions, 65–66

"Gay," 163
Gay, Lesbian & Straight Education Network
    (GLSEN), 24, 162–163, 170, 230, 259*f*
    "ThinkB4YouSpeak" campaign, 245–246,
    247
Gay & Lesbian Medical Association, 258*f*
Gay & Lesbian Resource Center, 20
Gay and Lesbian March, 99
Gay and Lesbian Pride Month, 237
Gay Pride Day, 237
Gay pride events, 237
Gay–Straight Alliance (GSA) Network, 259*f*
Gay–straight alliances (GSAs), 4–5, 63, 164*n*,
    166–168, 200
Gender(s)
    comprehensive assessment of, 62
    Navajo genders, 92
    normative development of, 47–48
    and suicide risk, 198
    third-gender, 67
    two-spirit or alternate gender, 92
Gender-affirming policies, 63
Gender diversity, 63
Gender dysphoria, 46, 49–51
Gender Education & Advocacy, 259*f*
Gender exploration, 57, 63
Gender expression, 57
Gender identity, 45, 63
    ambiguity regarding, 78–79
    development of, 47–49
    transgender identity, 70, 113
Gender identity disorders (GID), 49, 70, 113
Gender nonconforming children and youth
    family emergence stages for, 58*b*–59*b*
    gender identity development in, 47–49
Gender-related risk, 198

Gender roles, 46, 48
Gender segregation, 63–64
Gender-specific competent clinical care, 60
Gender Spectrum, 260*f*
Gender variance, 52, 56
Gendered behavior, atypical, 70
Gendered terms, 67
Genderqueer, 45, 67
Genetic sex, 69
Genital ambiguity, 69
Genital reconstruction, 61
Genitoplasty, 76
"Gentle" sons, 48
Geography, 73
GID, *see* Gender identity disorders
Girls, 175
GLBT Host Home Program (Minneapolis,
    Minnesota), 210
GLBT National Youth Talkline, 260*f*
GLSEN, *see* Gay, Lesbian & Straight Education
    Network
Google, 252–253
Grades 3–6, 163
Grades 6–12, 163
Gramercy Residence of Green Chimneys
    (New York City, New York), 210
Great Lakes Center for Education Research
    and Practice, 165–166
GroundSpark, 170
Group foster care, 209–210
Group home programs, 210
Group processes, 28
GSAs, *see* Gay–straight alliances
Guide for Professionals, iii, iv, 29, 30, 31, 32
"Guidelines for Psychotherapy with Lesbian,
    Gay, and Bisexual Clients" (APA), 134
Gwa wa enuk First Nation (Canada), 103

Handbook for Parents, 78, 80
Handshakes, 101
Harassment
    federal prohibition of, 171
    physical and verbal, 4, 163
    student harassment, 161
Hawaii, 88
Healing
    holistic, 107*b*
    indigenous practices, 101–102
Health, 1–8, 57
Health behavior change, 225
Health care, 93–94, 214
Health disparities
    definition of, 192
    related to self-harming behaviors, 192–193
Health navigators, 213
Healthy and Supportive Peer Connections, 154
Healthy Lesbian, Gay, and Bisexual Students
    Project (APA), 256*f*

Help-seeking behavior, 223–250
Hermaphrodites, 67
Heterosexism, 138, 177, 194–196
High-risk sexual behaviors, 4
Hispanic men, 3
Hispanic or Latino youth, 163n
Historical trauma, 93, 97, 107b
HIV/AIDS, 64–65, 113–114, 230
HIV/AIDS clinics, 130
Holistic healing, 107b
Homeless LGBT youth, 175, 207–221
    data and research needs, 219–220
    housing for, 209–210
    identifying and engaging, 208–209
    needs of, 211–212
    policy and practice for, 220–221
    policy recommendations for, 221
    recommendations for administrators and
        supervisors, 220–221
    recommendations for employees serving, 220
    service needs of, 213–215
Homeless services
    assistance programs, 209
    recommendations for service providers,
        215–219
    safe spaces in, 216
Homelessness, 95–96, 128, 208–209
Homelessness Resource Center (HRC), 208,
    260f
Homophobia, 90, 95
Homosexuality, 34, 94, 113
Hope, 102–103
Host Home program, 208n, 210
Hotlines, 130
Housing, 209–210
HRC, see Homelessness Resource Center;
    Human Rights Campaign
Human Rights Campaign (HRC), 170, 261f
Humor, 101
Hunter College, 263f
Hwame, 92

"I Love My Boo" campaign, 230
Identity, 46
    practices that affirm, 152–154
    two-spirit experience and, 91
    see also Gender identity; Sexual identity
Identity acceptance, 35
Identity assumption, 35, 197
Identity comparison, 35
Identity confusion, 35
Identity development, 82, 97–98
Identity pride, 35
Identity synthesis, 35
Identity tolerance, 35
IHS, see Indian Health Service
"I'm Glad I Failed" campaign, 227, 232
Inclusion, full, 187b

Inclusive Organizational Culture, 144
Indian, 88
Indian Health Service (IHS), 94
Indigenous communities, 88n, 101–102
Information, 61, 63, 254
    evaluating sources, 253–254
    Internet-based, 251–266
    see also Resources
Information management, 80
Information sharing, 150–151
Informed support, 61
Institute of Medicine (IOM), 1, 195, 268
Institutionalized heterosexism, 177
Intake forms, 150
Intake processes, 150–151
Integration, 35
Inter/Act, 85
Interactional theory of homosexual identity
    development, 34
Interagency Working Group on Youth
    Programs, 171
Intergenerational trauma, 93
International Classification of Diseases (WHO), 49
International Two-Spirit Gathering, 91, 99
Internet-based resources, 99, 251–266
    recommended web sites, 255, 256f–266f
Intersectionality perspective, 125
Intersex, 46, 67, 72
Intersex disorders, 73
Invisibility, 238
IOM, see Institute of Medicine
Isolation, 152
It Gets Better Project, 261f

Joseph, Robert, 103
Juvenile justice system, 175

Kalamazoo Community Mental Health and
    Substance Abuse Services (Michigan), 20
Kalamazoo Family Acceptance collaborative, 21
Kalamazoo Gay & Lesbian Resource Center, 20
Kalamazoo Gazette, 21
Kalamazoo Public Schools (Michigan), 20
Kalamazoo Wraps (Kalamazoo, Michigan),
    20–22
Klinefelter syndrome, 68
Kwido, 90

Lakota, 92
Lakota Sioux, 90
Lambda Legal, 17n, 24, 261f
Language, 28, 71–72
    see also Cultural and linguistic competence
        (CLC)
Larkin Street Youth Services (San Francisco,
    California), 208n, 210, 211, 213, 215, 217,
    218
Latino youth, 39, 112, 119, 163n

Leadership, 129
Learning
  community learning, 17–18
  conditions for, 160–162, 161f
  "Cultural and Linguistic Competence in
    Focus" learning events (TA Partnership),
    17–18
  social-emotional, 160, 161f
Lecesne, James, 227
Lesbian, gay, and bisexual (LGB) youth
  APA guidelines for working with, 40
  in negative social environments, 164
  see also Lesbian, gay, bisexual, and transgender
    (LGBT) youth
Lesbian, gay, bisexual, and transgender (LGBT),
  43
Lesbian, gay, bisexual, and transgender (LGBT)
  children, 269n
Lesbian, Gay, Bisexual, and Transgender
  Concerns Office (APA), 257f
Lesbian, gay, bisexual, and transgender (LGBT)
  identity, 177, 190, 191f
Lesbian, gay, bisexual, and transgender (LGBT)
  youth, 13
  AI/AN and two-spirit youth, 98–103,
    235–236
  counseling for, 134–136, 137–139
  in detention facilities, 175–176
  with formal system involvement, 175–177
  homeless, 175, 207–221
  Internet-based information and resources
    for, 251–266
  key strategies for serving, 269–270
  with LGBT family members, 226
  Native American, 87–109
  in out-of-home care settings, 173–187, 183b,
    185b
  outreach to, 228–249
  populations, 111–112, 226
  practice-level recommendations for
    supporting, 184b
  protective factors for, 2–5
  relationship with LGBT society, 98–103
  risk factors for, 112–116
  risks for, 2–5
  school experiences of, 162–165
  school policies, programs, and practices that
    promote safety and well-being for, 165
  service needs, 7–8
  social marketing campaigns to, 235–236
  standards of care for, 141–157
  strategies to improve school conditions for,
    165–171
  suicide and self-harming behaviors among,
    189–205
  support for, 111–126
  systems of care for, 127–140
  ways to support, 154–155

Lesbian, gay, bisexual, transgender, queer, and
  questioning (LGBTQ), 43, 162
Lesbian, Gay, Bisexual, Transgender, Question-
  ing, Intersex, or Two-Spirit (LGBTQI2-S)
  National Workgroup (SAMHSA Center
  for Mental Health Services, Child,
  Adolescent and Family Branch), 13–14,
  270, 272
Let's Get Real, 170
LGB youth, see Lesbian, gay, and bisexual youth
LGBT, questioning, intersex, or two-spirit
  (LGBTQI2-S) theory of change, 123f,
  123–124
LGBT History Month, 237
LGBT Suicide Prevention Hotline (Trevor
  Project), 265f
LGBTQ Host Home program (Chicago,
  Illinois), 210
LGBTQ Issues and Child Welfare web page
  (NRCPFC), 263f
LGBTQI2-S Learning Community (TA
  Partnership), 265, 265f
LGTBQ, see Lesbian, gay, bisexual, transgender,
  queer, and questioning
Life course perspective, 125
Life-span models, 36–37
Linguistic competence, 9–24
  see also Cultural and linguistic competence
    (CLC)
Linguistic terms, 88
LinkedIn, 238
Local LGBT youth services, 130

Major depression, 4
Making Health Communication Programs Work,
  224–225
Male, 67
Male cross-dressers, 45
Male-to-female transsexuals (MTFs/transsexual
  women), 45
Maryland, 187b
Materials, 29, 254
Medical information, 62
Men who have sex with men (MSM), 3,
  197–199
Mental health, 96–97, 161, 199
Mental Health America, 169
Mental health disparities, 192
Mental health professionals, 74–75
Mental health services, 121f, 121–122
Menvielle, Edgardo, 56
Middle Eastern or Arab American youth, 163n
Minnesota, 22, 199
Minnesota Adolescent Health Survey, 163n
Minority stress, 125, 190, 191f
Mojave, 92
MSM, see Men who have sex with men
Multicultural campaigns, 234

Multiracial youth, 163n
Mutations, 69
MySpace, 238

NAC, see National Advisory Council on
  LGBTQ Homeless Youth
Nadleehi, 90, 92, 235
NALGAP, see National Association of Lesbian,
  Gay, Bisexual and Transgender Addiction
  Professionals
National Action Alliance for Suicide
  Prevention, 195
National Advisory Council on LGBTQ
  Homeless Youth (NAC), 220
National Association of Lesbian, Gay, Bisexual
  and Transgender Addiction Professionals
  (NALGAP), 262f
National Association of School Nurses, 169
National Association of School Psychologists,
  169
National Association of Social Workers, 17n
National Cancer Institute, 224–225
National Center for Cultural Competence,
  17n, 27, 27b, 28
National Center for Lesbian Rights, 17n, 262f
National Center for Transgender Equality, 262f
National Children's Mental Health Awareness
  Day, 237
National Coalition for LGBT Health, 263f
National Coming Out Day, 237
National Day of Silence, 245
National Education Association, 168, 169
National Education Policy Center, 165–166
National evaluation, 202b–204b, 204
National Evaluation of the Comprehensive
  Community Mental Health Services for
  Children and Their Families Program, 174
National Gay and Lesbian Task Force, 216
National Juvenile Defender Center, 186
National Resource Center for Permanency
  and Family Connections (NRCPFC),
  263f
National Standards for Culturally and
  Linguistically Appropriate Services in
  Health Care, 11
National Strategy for Suicide Prevention (NSSP),
  195
National Youth Suicide Prevention program,
  21–22
Native, 88
Native American, 87n, 88
Native American Church, 101
Native American youth, 87–109, 163n
Native Hawaiians, 88
Navajo, 90, 92, 235
Needs assessment, 15
Negative social environments, 164
Negotiation, 56, 58b–59b

Networking, social, 237–238
New York State Office of Children and Family
  Services (NYS OCFS), 147
Niizh manitoag, 91
"No tolerance" policy, 105
Nondiscriminatory policies, 147–149
Normative gender development, 47–48
Northern Algonquin (Ojibwe), 91
NRCPFC, see National Resource Center for
  Permanency and Family Connections
NSSP, see National Strategy for Suicide Prevention
NYAC, 230, 238, 246
NYS OCFS, see New York State Office of
  Children and Family Services

Objectification, 99
OCSI, see Our Children Succeed Initiative
Office for Civil Rights, 171
Office of Minority Health, 11
Ogokwe, 90
OHC settings, see Out-of-home care (OHC)
  settings
Ojibwa, 90
Ojibwe, 91
Organization-focused cultural competency,
  119–120, 120f
Organizational culture, inclusive, 144
Organizations, 13–14
Other, 99
Other-gendered, 67
Our Children Succeed Initiative (OCSI), 22–24
"Out. Proud. Sober.", 230
Out-of-Home Care Project, 261f
Out-of-home care (OHC) settings, 173–187
Outreach, 228–249
Outside In (Portland, Oregon), 208n, 215
Ownership, shared, 27b

Pacific Islander youth, 163
Parent Support Network of Rhode Island, 19
Parenting Strategies, 78–80
Parents
  as advocates, 57–59
  resources for, 248
  supporting, 38–39
Parents, Families and Friends of Lesbians and
  Gays (PFLAG), 20–21, 40, 56, 117–118,
  130, 263f
  "Claim your Rights" campaign, 237
  points to consider for social marketing to
    families, 247–248
  resources for parents and families, 249
Parents, Families and Friends of Lesbians and
  Gays (PFLAG) Detroit, 218
Partial androgen insensitivity syndrome, 69
Partnership for Children (Burlington County,
  New Jersey), 19
Pauite, 90

Pediatricians, 62
Peer connections, 154
Perceptions, 161–162
PFLAG, *see* Parents, Families and Friends of Lesbians and Gays
Physical abuse, 209
Physical environment, 29
Physical harassment and assault, 4, 97, 163
Physical transition, 61
Physician-moderated support groups, 73
Planning
  inclusive, 15–16
  service planning, 131–133
  team service planning, 122
  wraparound, 122, 131–132
Plaxo, 238
Policy
  agency policies, 148, 153
  next steps for, 267–272
  recommendations for homeless LGBT youth, 221
  recommendations for supporting LGBT youth in out-of-home care settings, 183*b*
Populations, 226
Positive symbols, 151
Positive youth development, 145
Practice-based evidence, 102
Practices
  improving, 220
  next steps for, 267–272
Pre-coming out, 35
Precontemplation, 225
Preferences
  name and pronoun, 63
  practices that support, 152–154
Preparation, 225
Prevention, xiii, xvi
Psychological autopsy, 193
Psychosocial development, 34–35
Psychosocial support, 82–84
Puberty, 81–82
Public awareness, expanded, 218–219
Public health, 1–8

Quality improvement, *see* Continuous quality improvement
Queer/questioning (Q), 162*n*, 231, 243–244

Race/ethnicity, 10, 39, 73
Rainbow Heights Club (Brooklyn, New York), 211
Rainbow symbols, 17
Rajski, Peggy, 227
Reading materials, youth-friendly, 151
Recommendations, vi, 215
  for addressing needs of two-spirit youth, 106*b*–108*b*

for administrators and supervisors, 220–221
assets-based, 124–126
for counseling, 134–136
for employees serving LGBT homeless youth, 220
for families, 55
for homeless service providers, 215–219
for pediatricians, 62
for professionals, 59–62
for schools and residential facilities, 63–64
for sexual identity development and expression, 40–41
for systems of care, 104–105
for systems of care community members and stakeholders, 185*b*
for youth in out-of-home care settings, 182–185
The Red Circle Project, 263*f*
Reducing Suicide: A National Imperative (IOM), 195
Referrals, 61, 62, 84
Reparative or conversion therapies, 50, 138–139
Reproductive sex, 69
Research
  assets-based, 124–126
  new directions for, 268–269
  next steps for, 267–271
  recommended areas for, 125, 183*b*, 249–250
  on resiliency, 122–126
  school experience findings, 162–165
  for supporting homeless LGBT youth, 219–220
Residential facilities, 63–64
Resilience, 111–126
  bolstering, 38
  definition of, 116
  fostering, 118–122
  key recommendations for building, 126
  promoting, 228–230
  research needs for, 122–126
Resilience theory, 116
Resource Center, 20
Resources, 61, 63, 168–169
  evaluating sources, 253–254
  Internet-based, 251–266
  for parents and families, 249
  for parents/caregivers, 248
  recommended web sites, 255, 256*f*–266*f*
  Self-Assessment Checklist for, 29
  on self-harming behavior, 193–194
  tips for locating information and resources online, 251
Responsibility, shared, 143–144
Retraditionalization, 102, 236
Rhode Island Positive Educational Partnership, 19
Risk factors, 112–116

Risks, 2–5
Runaways, 175, 207–208
Ruth Ellis Center (Detroit, Michigan), 208*n*, 213, 218–219
Ryan, Caitlin, 21

Safe Harbor, 119
Safe On Campus, 119
Safe Schools Coalition, 264*f*
Safe Space, 119
Safe Zones, 119, 167–168
Safety, 28
    as condition for learning, 160, 161*f*
    environmental, 151–152
    in homeless services, 216
    at school, 159–172
Same-sex relationships, 94
SAMHSA, *see* Substance Abuse and Mental Health Services Administration
Sarasota Partnership for Children's Mental Health (Florida), 19–20
Scenario, 131–132
School(s)
    climate and conditions for learning, 160–162
    communication with, 79–80
    nondiscrimination and antibullying policies, 165
    policies, programs, and practices that promote safety and well-being for LGBT youth, 165
    policy recommendations for proactively improving, 165–166
    recommendations for working with transgender and gender nonconforming children and youth, 63–64
    research findings, 162–165
    safe and supportive, 159–172
    social marketing to, 244–247
    strategies to improve conditions, 165–171
    supportive environments, 165
    unsafe environments at, 161
School absences, 203*b*
School-based support groups or clubs, 165
School connectedness, 198–199
School Psychology Review, 162
School Social Work Association of America, 169
Screening procedures, 150
Secondary sex characteristics, 69
Segmenting, 226
Segregation by gender, 63–64
Self-advocacy, 76–77
Self-assessment, 25–32
    agency self-assessment, 146–147
    four-step process, 27
    key recommendations for, 27*b*
    lessons learned, 28
Self-Assessment Checklist, 29–32

Self-harm, 189–190
Self-harming behavior, 3, 189–205
    definition of, 194
    health disparities related to, 192–193
    prevention of, 204–205
    sources of information about, 193–194
Self-identify, 67
Self-label, 67
Sensitization, 35
Sergeant, J. Danée, 211, 219
Service Array, 133
Service needs, 7–8
Service planning, 122, 131–133
Service providers
    cultural considerations for, 100–101
    practices for, 244*b*, 271–272
    social marketing to, 242–244
Services
    affirming, 155–156
    culturally and linguistically competent, 9–24
    family-centered approach for, 144–145
    guiding principles for delivery of, 142–145
    improving processes to enhance, 129–130
    integration with supports, 187*b*
    pathway to, 130–131
    structuring system of care functions to facilitate, 130–139
Sex
    ambiguity regarding, 75, 78–79
    changing, 51
    disorders or differences of sex development, 67–86
    of rearing, 70
    and suicide risk, 198
    survival sex, 212–213
Sex assignment, 70
Sex-related risk, 198
Sexual abuse, 34, 81, 178, 198, 211
Sexual assaults, 97, 137, 212, 239
Sexual identity
    definition of, 45, 194
    disorders or differences of sex development and, 70–71
    expression of, 33–41
    important considerations for, 33–34
Sexual identity development, 33–41
    life-span models of, 36–37
    milestones in, 36–37
    models of, 34–37
    recommended practices for, 40–41
    stage models of, 34–35
Sexual intercourse, unprotected, 199
Sexual objects, 99
Sexual orientation, 33–34, 46–47
    definition of, 33
    victimization based on, 163
Sexual orientation bias, 97

Sexuality Information and Education Council
  of the United States, 264f
Shaker Church, 101
Shared decision making, 76
Shared responsibility, 143–144
SickKids, 77
Skipping school, 4
SOC, see Standards of Care (WPATH)
Social ecology perspective, 125
Social-emotional learning, 160, 161f
Social environment, 164
Social inclusion, 223–250
Social isolation, 4
Social marketing
  to AI/AN LGBT and two-spirit youth,
    235–236
  audience identification, 226–227
  campaigns, 223n
  case study, 227
  to communities, 239–249
  cultural considerations for, 235–236
  definition of, 224–225
  to families, 247–249
  key concepts, 250
  lessons learned, 223–224, 228–249
  message delivery, 236–239
  messages for youth, 231–236
  other audiences, 239–249
  to promote social inclusion and help-seeking
    behavior, 223–250
  to providers, 242–244
  recommended areas for future research,
    249–250
  to schools, 244–247
Social networking, 237–238
Social transition, 61
Social vulnerability, 4
Socioeconomic status, 73
Soul wounds, 93
South Asian LGBT youth, 228
Spirit wounds, 93
Spiritual supports, 107b
Squatting, 209
Staff, 63, 216–217
Staff development, 149–150, 165
Stage models, 34–35
Stakeholders, 185b
Standards of care, 74, 141–157, 269–270
Standards of Care (SOC) (WPATH), 44, 52,
  59–60
STARS, 231, 241, 243–244, 246, 249
STARS for Children's Mental Health, 229
Stereotyping, 99
Stigma, 12, 39, 194–196
Stone, Joseph, 104
Stone, Randy, 227
"Straight allies," 5
Straight for Equality, 265f

Straightlaced: How Gender's Got Us All Tied Up,
  170
Street youth, 207–208
Strength, 15, 102–103
Stress, minority, 125, 190, 191f
"Structured home" model, 210
Student harassment, 161
Substance Abuse and Mental Health Services
  Administration (SAMHSA), 24, 201
  A Blueprint for Addressing Suicide Issues in
    Systems of Care, 201
  Center for Mental Health Services, 13–14,
    201, 270, 272
  Children's Mental Health Initiative (CMHI),
    201
  Circles of Care grant program, 101–102
  A Comprehensive Vision—A Logic Model
    Addressing Suicide Issues in System of Care
    Communities, 201
  Homelessness Resource Center (HRC), 208
  national work group, 125
  Systems of Care grant program, 101–102
Substance use, 199, 212–213
Suicide, 189–205
  prevention of, 200–201, 201–202
  protective factors for, 197–199
  recommended efforts to prevent, 200–201
  risk factors for, 203b
  among two-spirit youth, 96–97
Suicide attempts, 97, 164n, 196–197
  factors protective against, 199
  risk of, 203b
Suicide-related thoughts and behaviors,
  114–116, 202b–204b
  prevalence of, 202b
  recommended practices for reducing,
    199–201
Suicide risk, 97, 197–199
Supervisors, 220–221
Support(s), 56, 81
  affirming, 155–156
  as condition for learning, 160, 161f
  culturally and linguistically competent, 9–24
  family-centered approach for, 144–145
  improving processes to enhance, 129–130
  informed, 61
  integration with services, 187b
  pathway to, 130–131
  psychosocial, 82–84
  spiritual, 107b
  structuring system of care functions to
    facilitate, 130–139
  for two-spirit youth, 106b–107b
  for youth in out-of-home care settings,
    178–180
Support groups
  referrals to, 84
  school-based, 165